COSTUME DESIGN

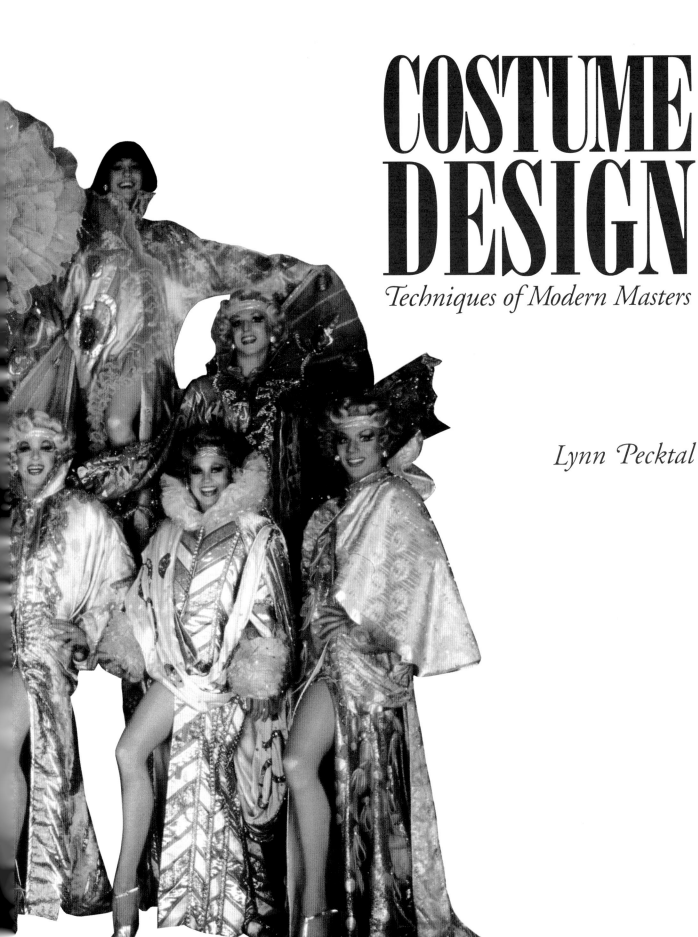

COSTUME DESIGN

Techniques of Modern Masters

Lynn Pecktal

BACK STAGE BOOKS
an imprint of Watson-Guptill Publications
New York

To my sister,
RITA P. PEW
With much love
and appreciation

Frontispiece:
Costume designs by Theoni V. Aldredge
for the Cast of La Cage aux Folles
Choreographed by Scott Salmon
Directed by Arthur Laurents
Palace Theatre, New York (1983)
(Photograph by Gregory Heisler,
originally published in Life *magazine)*

Page 6:
Costume design by Tony Walton for Patti LuPone as Reno Sweeney in Anything Goes
Choreographed by Michael Smuin
Directed by Jerry Zaks
Beaumont Theatre, New York (1987)

Page 8:
Costume designs by Bob Mackie for Baryshnikov in Hollywood
Produced and directed by Don Mischer
CBS television special (1982)

Copyright © 1993 by Lynn Pecktal

First published by Back Stage Books, an imprint of Watson-Guptill Publications, a division of BPI Communications, L.P., 1515 Broadway, New York, NY 10036

Library of Congress Cataloging-in-Publication Data
Pecktal, Lynn.
    Costume design : techniques of modern masters / Lynn Pecktal.
       p. cm.
    Includes index.
    ISBN 0-8230-8311-X
    1. Costume design. 2. Costume designers—Interviews. I. Title
    TT507.P363 1993
    792'.026'0922—dc20   92-41428
                                                           CIP

Manufactured in Hong Kong

First printing, 1993

1 2 3 4 5 6 7 8 9 / 99 98 97 96 95 94 93

Edited by Paul Lukas
Designed by Jay Anning
Graphic production by Hector Campbell
Text set in 10-point Adobe Garamond

Acknowledgments

Many people have been enormously helpful during the writing of this book. I am especially indebted to these costume designers for their interviews and for providing designs: Theoni V. Aldredge, Randy Barcelo, Zack Brown, Patton Campbell, Alvin Colt, Jane Greenwood, Desmond Heeley, Ann Hould-Ward, Willa Kim, William Ivey Long, Santo Loquasto, Bob Mackie, Carrie Robbins, Ann Roth, José Varona, Tony Walton, Miles White, and Patricia Zipprodt.

I should also like to thank these designers, both past and present, for designs and sketches: Boris Aronson, Lucinda Ballard, Gregg Barnes, John Lee Beatty, Lewis Brown, Jeanne Button, Franco Colavecchia, John Conklin, Lindsay W. Davis, Raoul Pène du Bois, William and Jean Eckart, Ben Edwards, Eldon Elder, Hal George, Peter J. Hall, Peter Harvey, Toni-Leslie James, Dorothy Jeakins, Robert Edmond Jones, Sam Kirkpatrick, Allen Charles Klein, Andrew B. Marlay, Charles E. McCarry, Oliver Messel, Tanya Moiseiwitsch, Motley, David Murin, Marcos Oksenhendler, Robert O'Hearn, Martin Pakledinaz, Robert Perdziola, Lester Polakov, John Scheffler, Irene Sharaff, Eduardo Sicangco, Tony Straiges, Rouben Ter-Arutunian, and Freddy Wittop.

I am most appreciative to these generous individuals for loaning works from their collections: Lisa Aronson, Mr. and Mrs. William G. Blessing, Lewis Brown, Peter Harvey, Leigh Rand, and Paul Stiga.

Others should be mentioned for their special assistance: Todd Kauchick, Mitchell Bloom, Frank Krenz, Cynthia Doty, Abby Okin, Barbara Matera, Parsons-Meares, the Costume Depot, the Lincoln Center Library, Duane Michals, Gregory Heisler, Jim Ryan, the staff at Bob Mackie's, and Pam Jordan of the Yale Drama School Library. And I owe a debt of gratitude to Tony Walton for suggesting initially to Watson-Guptill that I do a book with them.

I would like to thank Brian Pew, who did much of the photography, Kenneth Pew, and other photographers credited in the book. Rita P. Pew did a phenomenal job typing the manuscript and doing research.

I am greatly indebted to the staff at Watson-Guptill for their fine work. My sincere thanks to Mary Suffudy, Publisher; Jay Anning, designer of the book; Hector Campbell, the book's production manager; and Paul Lukas, my editor, who has made invaluable contributions to the project. I am most grateful for all.

Reno Sweeney
S.S.

Patti Lupone.

CONTENTS

INTRODUCTION

This is a book about some of the most successful and exciting costume designers in the entertainment world. For over a quarter-century, their work has proved to be nothing less than sensational. The designers in this volume do Broadway plays and musicals, as well as ballets and operas. Their talents also extend into other diversified venues of show business: They create costumes for films, television, nightclubs, revues, ice shows, pageants, music hall productions, award presentations, fashion shows, circuses, industrials, hotel extravaganzas, commercials, Off-Broadway, rock concerts, and regional theatres.

These costume designers work not only in New York, but in Hollywood, London, Canada, South America, Australia, Europe, and other international locales. Whatever they design for the characters and the performers, it is a sure bet that these artists will always be on target with the appropriate visual attire. I salute them all!

A few preliminary notes: First, readers will note that there are "intermission" spreads, featuring work by an assortment of designers, appearing in between the book's 18 interviews. The intent here was threefold—to provide a short break between the interviews, to display a greater variety of designs, and to present the work of as many talented designers as possible.

The dates shown in the captions usually refer to the year the production opened. However, in some instances these dates may vary—sometimes a designer will do a sketch a year or so in advance, and on occasion may even make a sketch after the show has opened.

Finally, in the production listings that accompany the start of each interview, the notations "S," "C," and "L" refer to settings, costumes, and lighting, respectively.

A Conversation with
THEONI V. ALDREDGE

Theoni V. Aldredge took time to chat in the design studio at Barbara Matera's, on lower Broadway. Aldredge, who now lives in Bedford Hills, New York, with her husband, the actor Tom Aldredge, is a native of Greece. She was educated at the Goodman Theatre of the Art Institute in Chicago, and her first Broadway assignment was designing the costumes for Geraldine Page in Tennessee Williams's *Sweet Bird of Youth* in 1959, at the Martin Beck Theatre. Since then she has become one of the most prolific designers of the New York stage, and has designed costumes for more than 150 Broadway shows and numerous Off-Broadway productions. For many years she was the principal designer for the New York Shakespeare Festival. She has designed for television specials, operas, ballets, and films; her film credits include *Harry and Walter Go to New York, Network, The Champ, The Rose, Moonstruck, Other People's Money, We're No Angels, Ghostbusters,* and *Annie.*

Aldredge's considerable talents have not gone unnoticed by her peers. For her work in *The Great Gatsby* in 1974, she won an Academy Award and the British Society of Films and Television Arts Award. She has received Tony Awards for *La Cage aux Folles, Annie,* and *Barnum,* and has won varied Drama Desk, Drama Critics, and Maharam awards for her designs in the theatre.

BREAK A LEG
Costume designs by Theoni V. Aldredge, for Rene Auberjonois and Julie Harris
Directed by Charles Nelson Reilly
Palace Theatre, New York (1979)

How did you become interested in designing costumes for the theatre?

I came from Greece—I was born and raised there. It was the war-torn years in Europe, and I just wanted to go to someplace where there hadn't been a war. It was difficult to explain to my father. He was surgeon general in Greece and a member of Parliament. And being the only girl in the family, he thought it would be crazy for me to come to America. All we knew about America at the time—I'm talking about the late '40s and '50s—was what we used to see in films. My father said, "If you go there, what do you want to do?" I really didn't have anything specific in mind at the time. I just wanted to get out for a year. And I thought, "Well, what about fashion design?" He said, "For fashion you have Rome next to you, and you have Paris next to you. Why would you want to go to America?"

That didn't take very well. Then I asked him about theatre. I said, "How about if I stick with theatre and see how it goes?" And my father thought it would last a year and then I would be back. So I came here and I went to the Goodman Theatre of the Art Institute in Chicago.

To study costume design?

To study theatre. I really just did not know what I wanted to do and I felt time would go by, and maybe time would tell. I went and I tried theatre and I fooled everyone, including myself, because I was good. And I was interested, and the school was great. I won my first scholarship and I said, "Well, maybe I am better than I thought. Maybe I can make it." I told my father what I had done and he was quite proud. I stayed my four years at Goodman and everything went well. In my last year I was married to Tom Aldredge, an acting student.

Then we asked ourselves, "Where do we go next?" The next thing was to go to New York. Everybody hears about New York—that's where the theatre is. We came that Christmas, just to see what New York was like, and went to see two plays that I loved. I said, "If this is theatre, then this is home. This is where I want to be." One play was *A Streetcar Named Desire,* and the other was *Death of a Salesman.* They were the greatest. And I felt possibly that someday I could work for these people and be part of a family like this. So we arrived in New York knowing literally nobody.

What happened after that?

I bumped into a lady I had met in Chicago. Her name was Geraldine Page. At the time she was doing a play called *Sweet Bird of Youth* at the Martin Beck Theatre. Elia Kazan was directing and Jo Mielziner was doing the scenery. She said, "I've seen your work and I'm going to tell Mr. Kazan. Maybe you can have an interview with him." So I went to see him. He took one look at me and asked, "Are you French?" I said, "No, sir. I'm Greek." He said, "Okay. Now do you want to do this?" He gave me the script. I had never read it before, but I did some sketches for him and he approved them, and it was fine. And that was my first show.

I still remember that opening night. I looked up and saw the names on the marquee. There was Paul Newman and Geraldine Page with Mr. Kazan directing, Tennessee Williams writing, and Jo Mielziner designing. And I thought, "Where do you go from here when you start with the very best at the very top?"

What better introduction could you have?

I had been in New York less than a year, and it was a strike year. I owe a lot to the

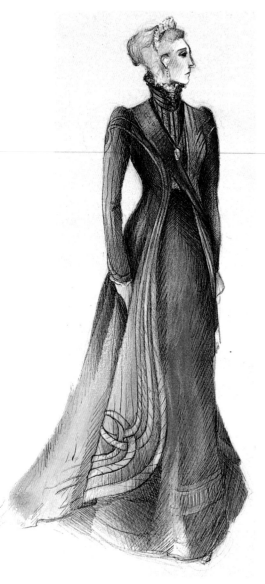

HAMLET
Costume designs by Theoni V. Aldredge,
for Kathleen Widdoes as Gertrude
and Bob Gunton as Claudius
Directed by Joseph Papp
New York Shakespeare Festival,
the Public Theatre, New York (1982)

"We're just starting a play here and we have no money. We have a $120 and we're putting on *Romeo and Juliet*." I did this play and scrounged fabrics from wherever I could, and the kids in the show brought fabrics from home, and it looked pretty darned good, it really did! And I went on and stayed with Joe Papp for over 20 years. I was his resident designer for a long time.

You've done shows for him downtown and uptown in the park.

For Joe I've done almost every Shakespearean play written. And in the end he gave me a wonderful home in the theatre. Any time he asked about anything, I'd be there, because he allowed you to grow. He allowed you to make mistakes, but he was always there to support you and to advise you when you made them. Joe never stifled you, he just let you go.

You have worked with a number of well-known scenic designers, including Robin Wagner.

Of course, Robin came into my life with a little play called *A Chorus Line*. And Joe Papp gave a young man named Michael Bennett, just 31, a play to rehearse and put together. When I first met Michael, Joe said, "This is our designer," and he said, "Well, I've never worked with Theoni, but I really would like to try and I would like to have her on one of my shows." It was the beginning of an amazing six to eight years with that man, because as young as he was, he taught me about collaboration! With him, you were part of a show; you weren't just the costume designer. He wanted your opinion about a number or a song or a scene. You were part of a family and he kept us all together, Robin and Tharon Musser and myself. And we did everything together after *A Chorus Line: Dreamgirls, Ballroom,* and *Chess* in London.

When you did the famous finale costumes for *A Chorus Line*, how did they come about?

Those came about because we talked and talked about them. Michael actually wanted red. His comment was, "The kids think they've made it, they are now in a show! So I want a big red number." I said, "No. Because they think they've made it,

late Miss Page, who took a chance on an unknown. She was from the same school. She was before me and she had seen something I had done there. How lucky can you get? But once you're given the chance, you've got to deliver something, because the opportunity will never knock twice. Then the plays started to come, and Jo Mielziner always recommended me for everything he did after that, and I just loved the man.

How did you start to work with Joe Papp?

Somebody mentioned that he was having a little theatre in the basement of a church way up at 100-and-something street. So I picked myself up and went, and I told him I would like to design whatever he was doing. And he said, it's still a fantasy, it is not reality. This is their fantasy. So to me, red is too definite a color! This champagne thing I want to do is just a fantasy. It's not a real color."

He kind of looked at me and said, "Well, I don't know. It better work out, because if it doesn't then it's coming out of your salary!" I said, "What salary? Do you know what we make here, Michael? We make five hundred to do a show, so if you want to take it, take it."

That particular year I took off three days before dress rehearsal. Paramount flew me to California. I was nominated for my Oscar for *The Great Gatsby* and, as God had it, I won. I came back, and a day later we were going to have a dress rehearsal. When I walked into that little Newman Theatre, which Michael adored, it was all done up with a sign saying, "Welcome Back!" and hundreds of white balloons.

Now it was dress rehearsal at the Public Theatre. The finale started and I thought, "Oh, what's he going to say about this finale with the champagne-colored clothes?" I was sitting there very quietly in my seat. And the first kid came on and there's dead silence. The second one came on and again dead silence. The third kid came on. Then suddenly I felt somebody tap me on the shoulder. I turned around and Michael was there, looking at me and saying, "You're right!" It takes a big man to say, "You're right."

And I fell in love with Michael and that was it. He was an incredible person. Actually, after he died I just didn't want to work anymore. This man was such a challenge. He was never satisfied until you gave him the very best that you could. He would never say, "This is fine." You always knew you could do a little bit better. And he made you want to do it.

All of you were part of a great collaborative team.

Yes, there is Tharon [Musser], who is a magician as far as lights—the woman tells a story with just a turn of a switch. And Robin [Wagner], who is loving and caring, and Bob Avian, who had been Michael's partner and co-choreographer. It was a family, and, of course, Michael was the force behind it all. If you have

ONWARD VICTORIA
Costume design by Theoni V. Aldredge
Directed by Julianne Boyd
Martin Beck Theatre, New York (1980)

not experienced this sort of thing in the theatre, I feel sorry for you. Because theatre itself is a hardcore thing and it is tough work. But if you have that once in life, you can cope with the rest.

You have designed the costumes for many different shows. Do you ever have a mental block about what to do for the next show? Does that come up?

It does and it doesn't. Sometimes when you hit a show that's the same period you say to yourself, "I'd better watch it." You tell yourself, "I did this in the '30s and this is the '30s, and where are you going now?" But every time with a new director, there's a new point of view. There's a new eye and that keeps you going. I think when it comes to the point where I either get bored or it's the same old idea,

I might as well quit. But it's never the same, because the faces are fresh, or the director or choreographer is new. But we work mainly for the actors. I mean, the people of the theatre are artists. We work for a specific person and a specific piece of work, and we try to help. And any ego problems, they don't belong in this family. If you have them, get out.

When you design big period shows, do you like to do lots of research yourself?

I used to do it all myself. My assistants help a lot, and at this point I have an assistant, Woody Lane, who is quite fabulous and who helps me tremendously. I don't do lots of research. I used to go through thousands of books, and I got so confused. I finally decided that if it's a period show, then it's seen through a

DREAMGIRLS
Costume designs by Theoni V. Aldredge
Directed and choreographed by Michael Bennett
Imperial Theatre, New York (1981)

contemporary audience. So you have to make it palatable for them to buy it. For instance, if you do the '30s, women wore no bras, women were built in a certain way, women sat a certain way, women walked a certain way. The modern body is not the same. So you kind of adjust to make it palatable to an audience of today, and yet you don't lose the line of the silhouette of a period.

If I'm doing research for Shakespeare, I like to go to tapestries and things like that, and not use books so much. When I did *Nick and Nora*, I liked to look at the lives of real people that lived in those days. I like to take, say, Garbo, and follow her through her life. I enjoy seeing what she wore when she went swimming or when she played tennis, and not really look at fashion magazines. I just try to make the clothes a bit more real. But then it also depends on the body of the particular person. And you know that you are really trying to service the actors, and in the end, if they're not comfortable, you're not going to look good.

When you did *La Cage aux Folles*, were there specific problems to deal with in making men look beautiful like women?

Well, number one, it is a fallacy that men do not like pretty things. If you notice, which bird has the finest plumage? It's the male bird, not the female. These kids in the show freaked out in the beginning. The first time we did makeup and put high heels on them, they looked in the mirror and said, "My God, I look like my mother! I look like my sister! I look

La Cage aux Folles
Costume designs by Theoni V. Aldredge
Choreographed by Scott Salmon
Directed by Arthur Laurents
Palace Theatre, New York (1983)

like my maiden aunt!" Well, by the time we opened, you couldn't keep them away from the lashes and all the things.

There were specific problems, because guys were not used to the padding. And I certainly had to do padding. They had to have bosoms and they had to have hips. So I built them out on the side to make the figure become more womanly. And I promised them I would not ask them to shave their chests or their legs—that would be cruel. I mean, they had to do the show every night. So we put a double pair of hose on them and nobody noticed anything. And after breaking about a couple of hundred pairs of high-heeled shoes, they learned how to walk properly.

It was a lot of fun to do, because we did it all in great humor, and I've never done pretty dresses on girls who got more enjoyment out of them than my

guys did. They thought it was something really theatre, let's pretend, "I am now a girl." And finally it was true theatre, because we were pretending. I had a great time backstage with them.

Comment on the production of *Hair*, when Joe Papp did it downtown.
I did the original one in 1967. We had just moved into the new complex. There were no budgets. We spent as little as we could. Joe never said, "You only have three dollars." The clothes then at the time were pretty much what the kids wore. It was the flower children, if you remember, and they gave me what they had of their own. We painted the blue jeans and did stuff like that. And I must tell you, when they did it on Broadway, they changed it a lot. I loved the way it was downtown.

I did not do it on Broadway, because I

had a fight with the producers. And my fight was about not taking all of us. I said, "Excuse me, where are the rest of us? Where is Ming Cho Lee? And where is Gerry Freedman, who directed originally?" And they said, "You're making a mistake. The show is going to make a lot of money." I said, "Fine, I wish you well, but I work with these people, and I just don't think so." When we first got the script of the original, we had two pages. And all of us together developed this show, and they owed Mr. Freedman and Mr. Papp a great deal. Of course, I know I missed a lot of money. But it's not all about money, is it? It didn't freak me out. We spent so much time on the show, and what I liked about it, it was done very simply, and it was about an era and its kids. They decided to put in on Broadway, and there's nudity and there's this and that. I said, "Why?" It really wasn't

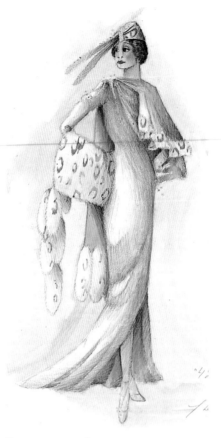

PRIVATE LIVES
Costume design by Theoni V. Aldredge,
for Elizabeth Taylor
Directed by Milton Katselas
Lunt-Fontanne Theatre, New York (1983)

FORTY-SECOND STREET
Costume design by Theoni V. Aldredge
Directed and choreographed by
Gower Champion
Winter Garden Theatre, New York (1980)

ANNIE
Costume design by Theoni V. Aldredge,
for Miss Hannigan
Choreographed by Peter Gennaro
Directed by Martin Charnin
Alvin Theatre, New York (1977)

necessary. And also, when I work with people we become a family. You just don't turn around and say, "They hired me, how about you?"

Of all the shows you've done, has there been one that was an especially big design challenge?

Believe it or not, as simple as it looks, *A Chorus Line* was a huge challenge for me. We had a long time. We watched the kids rehearse and tell stories. Most of them were their stories. I saw what they came in with, and what they felt comfortable in, and I took a lot of Polaroids of these kids. What was challenging about it was to make the show look real. It had to look real and yet theatrical enough for an audience to say, "Okay, I'm in the theatre now." And the most challenging thing of all was the color,

because Tharon went from cold lights to warm lights to show lights. So a green had to work with reality, which was just a bare light bulb, and it had to work with a pink light, and it had to work with show light. We worked so hard preparing that show. I spent more time on *A Chorus Line* than on any show I've ever done. Nobody understood it except those of us who did it. *Dreamgirls* was a tough show to do, too.

Why was it a difficult show?

Because so much happened. It was a travelogue, and these people traveled and changed periods and moved on. It's the story of these three singers, and it all had to be done in front of your eyes without a break, and nobody got offstage, and it was challenging as far as the fast changes were concerned. Every time they

appeared, it was 10 years later, and then 10 years later. It never stood still. It was totally like a movie. It was fade-ins, fade-outs, moving, carrying on—bingo! This is coming. It was an amazing show. And for Michael it was one of his finest-tuned shows. Technically, the scenery was a miracle.

I think *La Cage aux Folles* was another challenge. When I first read it, I said to Arthur [Laurents], "How is the show going to go? What are you thinking?" He said, "Theoni, it is a love story. It is a love story between two men." He promised me a love story and he gave me a love story. I never felt offended, because the way people choose to live is not for me to criticize or to make fun of. The show was treated like a love story and I thank him for it. And when George Hearn got up and sang, "I Am What I Am," it just took my breath away. Because it's for all of us. I am what I am and you are what you are. And if we don't like it, too bad!

When you worked on *Forty-second Street* with Robin and Tharon, did the costumes come first or did the scenery come first? Did you go back and forth?
The scenery always comes first technically, not color. The scenery has to go for bids first, and it has to be made before anything else. It takes the longest to make. We all come together and talk about it. We all sit and talk about color. It's such a close collaboration when I work with these people.

And we also had a wonderful time with another gentleman, Gower Champion. Unfortunately, it was his last show, and it was my first with him. I'd never worked with Gower before, and he was a joy. I'll never forget when we had done the last number. Originally, Gower wanted black and white. And when we went to Washington, I said, "Gower, I think we made a mistake, because the floor is black and you aren't going to see your dancers' feet if they're wearing black shoes." He said, "I think we made a mistake, too," and I said, "Why don't we call David [Merrick] and admit it, and maybe he will let us do it in color."

David had been very nice to me, and we found him on a great day. So I talked to him and he said, "I know, we need color in there, don't we?" I said, "Yes. I

didn't know how to say it, but I think you're right again." And he let us do it in color, and finally it was all oranges and reds and gold. And I remember we got down fast to see Barbara Matera, who makes all my clothes. She's an extension of me, and she's a wonderful lady.

Then we took it to Washington. I was still sitting there in the theatre and I said, "Please, God, let it be good, because the costumes cost over $100,000." There were 60 people in the show. And when the curtain went up and this bright red and gold came out, I said, "Okay." Afterwards I saw Gower around back, and he was pleased. He just said, "I love you and bless you."

Do you look back on plays with as much fondness as the musicals you have designed? They are a different ballgame, are they not?
Oh, yes. In dramatic shows you're much closer to your actor, and what he wears is very important. It's not all about pretty clothes. It's about everything an actor becomes, it's character time. The actors are much closer, too, because they depend a lot on each other. It's not "I'm not in this number, I don't care." It's a whole different atmosphere in a character play.

Do actors expect you to make them feel good in clothes, whether it's dramatic or musical?
Yes. My job is to make them become somebody else. I don't think it's fair for

an actor not to feel right in what he wears. When the curtain goes up, I can go across the street and have a cup of coffee, but the actors have to get on that stage and do it. So you work for them. You do it for yourself, too, because you selfishly want them to look right. On the other hand, you're working for somebody, and you shouldn't impose your taste on an actress just because you like, say, olive green. But you have to please actors. You have to make them happy. They are my bread and butter. Designing for them is what I love doing, and they make my life possible.

If you were putting a few of your favorite plays in a time capsule, what would they be?
The Threepenny Opera at Lincoln Center, after downtown. I thought it was a beautiful play. I liked the design end of it. And Mr. Foreman directed and left me pretty much alone. I did it mainly with black and white, and Doug Schmidt did the wonderful scenery. Of course, *Sweet Bird* was a landmark for me, because it was my beginning, and I also loved doing Tennessee Williams. I enjoyed a lot of things I did for Lincoln Center, and a lot of the Shakespearean plays I've done. I loved doing *Hamlet* with Julie Harris. I would see her backstage—you know, it's open there in the park—I went back one time and saw her sitting there, and she was weeping. I asked her what

FAR LEFT: CLOTHES FOR A SUMMER HOTEL
Costume design by Theoni V. Aldredge, for Geraldine Page
Directed by José Quintero
Cort Theatre, New York (1980)

LEFT: GYPSY
Costume design by Theoni V. Aldredge, for Tyne Daly
Original choreography by Jerome Robbins, reproduced by Bonnie Walker
Directed by Arthur Laurents
St. James Theatre, New York (1989)

was the matter, and she said, "I'm so tormented." I asked her why, and she said, "But there are 2,000 people out there." I said, "Yeah, they've all come to see you." And she just calmed down.

I loved doing *The Belle of Amherst*. It was a one-woman show with Julie Harris, and with Charles Nelson Reilly directing. I also enjoyed doing *A Delicate Balance*, with the Cronyns.

What are your feelings on opening night?

Just before the curtain on opening night, I go back to give the actors a hug. You know, in the end they're all just supersensitive children. They need that one little hug. On opening night, I'm never in the front of the house. I'm always backstage. Somehow when they come off, they like to see your face. And it's nice as they go by just to touch them and say, "Okay, it's zippers up and buttons buttoned."

When you did the original *Annie*, was designing for the children a particular problem?

No. The mothers were the problem. They wanted the children to look pretty. And when we arrived in Washington, and everyone was getting ready to go and do the show, I saw the mothers doing the lipstick and all that. I said, "Hey, everybody, these are orphans." They said, "Oh, we don't tell the children that." I said, "But how do you think they earn their weekly pay? By playing orphans! Somebody should tell them something, you know." Finally, I said, "Mothers out! Everybody, out of this room!" And I took some shoe polish, some brown stuff, and smudged their little faces. I wiped off the lipstick and I said, "Now you may go on." And it was fine. One mother said, "My kid looks better in curls," so I replied, "But she is not Shirley Temple."

I don't know what happened to the second *Annie*. Nobody talked to anybody. When you saw scripts that said CONFIDENTIAL, I said, "Excuse me, I don't talk confidential clothes." I mean, I have to show up and somebody's got to make them. So what's confidential? Just don't tell anybody the ending!

Of all the musicals you have done, are there two or three that are favorites?

It would be *A Chorus Line* and *Dreamgirls*. Believe it or not, my big chance in designing musicals was given to me by Arthur Laurents in 1962, and I had a great time doing it. It was called *I Can Get It for You Wholesale*, with Miss Streisand. I also loved doing *Ballroom* with Michael Bennett. *Gypsy* has to be

THE GRAND TOUR
*Costume design by Theoni V. Aldredge,
for the Stiltwalker
Choreographed by by Donald Saddler
Directed by Gerald Freedman
Palace Theatre, New York (1979)*

one of the musicals I will never forget. And I will forever thank Arthur Laurents for doing it again.

Comment briefly on designing for ballet and for film.

I do a lot of ballet. And number one, in ballet your costume is in continuous motion. It never stands still. So you think of it as in motion. You never think of it as standing still, because ballet costumes never stand still. Your fabrics are flowing, and you have to think of them in another way.

Film is another kettle of fish. You don't get to know all your actors as well.

The good thing about film is that if you make a mistake, you get to see that very night in the rushes, where they show what they shot that day. And if your director is understanding at all, you say, "Could we just reshoot this tomorrow?" So you get a chance to change something, even at the last minute.

In film, if you learn that the camera becomes a human eye, that's all you need to know. Otherwise, the color and the shape are the thing. As long as you remember that the camera is going to come up to this button here on my dress, then this button had better match the second one.

I did the film *Moonstruck* with Cher, and I loved the gentleness of it. I enjoyed working with Norman Jewison, who was my director for that. I also loved doing *Gatsby* because of my director, a British gentleman named Jack Clayton. He always made me feel he couldn't have done it without me. And boy, I would have done anything with him. I was hired two weeks before shooting.

How did you get everything ready to start?

He was so good to me. I kept saying, "Look, I thought this film was done." He said, "No, they changed the producers." He made the shooting schedule, and he promised me that he'd stick to it. I knew what came first and what needed a week. And then the next scene would take three weeks to shoot, and so on. So I did it like that—he never changed the schedule. And the big parties were going to be done two months into the film, so I had time. He was very cooperative, and I had beautiful people to dress. I had great help. Barbara Matera did marvelous clothes. And Woody Shelp did our hats—his hats weigh about half an ounce.

How many assistants do you have when you do a film?

I usually have one person with me.

Do you use the same people for film as you do for theatre?

Pretty much, because I think they should learn both, and you owe them that much. Most of my assistants have stayed with me for five to six years. They've all gone their ways. They've done well, and you'd like to leave something behind to bank on. Some of them weren't gracious enough to say thank you; others did, and those made up for the ones who didn't. It's that simple. I like to teach; I don't keep anything back. After all, where do designers come from finally? There's no such thing anymore as Off-Broadway. Off-Broadway has become so expensive. That's what we used to have, where we could do something for $200, and it does not exist anymore. So somebody's got to help.

Do you ever turn a show down because you're too busy?
You know, it hasn't happened yet. Films I have turned down, because I was doing a Broadway show. A film is sometimes done in California and on locations; a play is something I like to do one at a time. I always do. I try never to overlap them, because you have to do your best.

Have you ever known a director who was intimidated by your experience and talent and did not want to work with you because he didn't know how to approach the situation?
I don't think it went that far ever, but I've known people who I ended up working with who said, "Well, now, whatever you think." I said, "No, no. It's not like that. We take direction from your vision."

After doing so many shows, can you really get away from it all? Are you the type of person who can go to the beach or to a small town and walk and not think about the theatre?
When I'm at home, I don't think about the theatre. Both Tom and I live upstate in Bedford Hills, New York. We never talk about the theatre, or very little. Or if one of us has an opening night or something like that, then we say, "How is it going?" But we talk about the flowers we're planting or we talk about the walls we're painting, and that has kept us away from psychiatrists and from just going crazy. Most of our friends are non-theatre people. As for life itself, we never can plan on it, because sometimes I work and Tom doesn't; then he works and I don't. We've never taken a month off. We don't really have a life of our own. It's like being a doctor—you're on call.

BALLROOM
Costume design by Theoni V. Aldredge, for Dorothy Loudon
Directed and choreographed by Michael Bennett
Majestic Theatre, New York (1978)

If young students wanted to start designing costumes for the theatre, what would you tell them to do?
Most people will go to a drama school like NYU, or to Yale if they're lucky. Or they can go to any drama school they can, not only to learn, but to practice as they go. That's the way to do it. You just don't learn theatre from a book. You learn it from a book to a certain extent—you know how to read a script from a book—but if you don't do it, you'll never learn it. And in the theatre school I went to, we started building clothes from day one. So we knew how to construct something. And people that were involved in scenery started building their own sets. Besides that, it's a practical experience. I would go to a drama school and learn it.

And then I would discourage them from going on unless they really loved it.

MERLIN
Costume design by Theoni V. Aldredge
Choreographed by Christopher Chadman
Directed by Ivan Reitman
Mark Hellinger Theatre, New York (1983)

like *A Chorus Line* or *La Cage aux Folles.* But shows don't come along very often. So you do it because you love it. If you do it for any other reason, you're in the wrong business.

You would definitely advise practical experience.

Oh, absolutely. Get practical experience and apprentice with somebody and start from the bottom. Go into a costume shop and start shopping fabrics, so you know what the fabric is. You can understand how it drapes, how it molds, how it falls, what it does onstage. Learn from just shopping fabric. Watch drapers. A designer who doesn't know how to sew or how to correct a garment is no designer. Because you can be made a fool in a fitting room. You sit there and the draper says, "What do you want?" And you'd better know what you're talking about. It's all practical experience. We used to have summer stock—I don't know how much there is today. You see, that's the greatest school of all: You do a play every week and you do it yourself.

And you have to get it on.

Yes. You have to get it on for nothing. You have to learn it. You know, your brain just works overtime. I don't know where the kids go today.

Not too long ago you had several shows running at one time. Do you go back to visit and see how they're doing?

Yes. I had five of them running at one time. You think it's a visit; I call it policing. You go back to make sure that the kids are still okay. If you trust your wardrobe department, it's fine. But sometimes they're not so good.

Do they make changes sometimes without your knowing it?

They make changes without telling you. I see an actor with a shirt that should be white and it's slightly yellow. And that makes me ill. So you police your shows. You go backstage and do sort of little raids, where you're unannounced. You just walk in and say, "Oh, I just saw the first act. By the way, what kind of shoes were those?" You know, it's a fresh audience every night and the tickets are

This is a business where your ego goes right out the window. Forget it—it's nonexistent. You can't have it, except to help you do the best you can. You have to love it so much that you are willing to give up a lot of other things. And if you think you are going to get rich in this business, don't get into it, because you won't.

Even with a lot of companies running at once?

Well, if you are lucky enough to get a hit

expensive. Every audience has the right to see a show that's like an opening night.

When you do road companies of your shows, do you usually try to keep the costumes the same for the principals?
Yes, unless the body is so different that you've got to adjust to make it look right. Also, a director who would do a road company of his play to keep it fresh will also try and do something a little different every time, you know, because it makes it more interesting. For example, in *La Cage* Arthur Laurents said, "Change it a bit here and there." It was according to who the leading man was or who the leading woman was. We changed whatever he wanted changed, but we kept it as good as a Broadway show. We cannot underestimate an audience. They make it possible for us to build clothes. Without an audience, where are we?

What would you like to be doing 10 years from now?
If I'm able, I'd like to be doing what I'm doing. If I'm not, I would like to be growing flowers and probably be at some wonderful seashore in Greece. But knowing me and knowing Tom, I will die with a needle in my hand and Tom with a script. But then, that's what we love doing.

Also, I now work mainly for people I like. Thank God, my career has come to a point where I can say "no" to somebody I don't want to work for. And most of my things I really like and respect and have a good time doing.

What do you like most about working in the theatre?
What do I like most? The curtain going up. It's the immediacy of it. It's the live people, and it's exciting. There's the camaraderie of the kids getting together on opening night and just holding hands, and that little moment you really never forget. And an actor after a performance comes out and just puts his arms around you and says, "I love you" and "I thank you." I mean, you're paid, but this is the big pay. And it's Christmas backstage with the kids and their little gifts and flowers. We have a lot of Christmases, and it's love.

One last thing I want to say. I have had a very rich and rewarding life. I have had the guidance and support of Joe Papp for over 25 years, the amazing talent and love of Michael Bennett, the trust and care of Arthur Laurents, and the artistry and patience of Barbara Matera and so many, many more. I love them all, and dear Joe Papp, thank you for never forgetting my birthday. I hope for all they have contributed in my life, I was able to make this world a little prettier.

A ROUGH FOR THE GREAT GATSBY "MISS MIA FARROW" *Theoni V. Aldredge*

THE GREAT GATSBY, THE FILM
Costume design by Theoni V. Aldredge,
for Mia Farrow
Directed by Jack Clayton
Produced by David Merrick
Released by Paramount Pictures (1974)

PETER J. HALL
Costume designs for officers in Un Ballo in Maschera
Metropolitan Opera, New York (1980)
(Collection of Mr. and Mrs. William G. Blessing; photograph by D. James Dee)

FRANCO COLAVECCHIA
Costume designs for Rumpelstiltskin
Opera Company of Philadelphia (1978)

ROBERT O'HEARN
Costume design for Aida in Aida—*Act I*
Metropolitan Opera, New York (1962)
(Collection of Mr. and Mrs. William G. Blessing;
photograph by D. James Dee)

ROBERT O'HEARN
Costume design for Radames in Aida—*Act I*
Metropolitan Opera, New York (1962)
(Collection of Mr. and Mrs. William G. Blessing;
photograph by D. James Dee)

ROBERT O'HEARN
Costume design for Pharoah in Aida—*Act II*
Metropolitan Opera, New York (1962)
(Collection of Mr. and Mrs. William G. Blessing;
photograph by D. James Dee)

ROBERT O'HEARN
Costume design for the bodyguard in Aida—*Act I*
Metropolitan Opera, New York (1962)
(Collection of Mr. and Mrs. William G. Blessing;
photograph by D. James Dee)

RANDY BARCELO

I met with Randy Barcelo in his uptown Manhattan apartment, where he lives and maintains a studio. He was born in 1946 in Havana, Cuba. His first Broadway assignment was designing the costumes for *Lenny* in 1971, with direction by Tom O'Horgan. He has since designed sets and costumes for a wide range of works, including the Alvin Ailey Dance Theatre (*Opus McShann, For "Bird"—With Love*, and *Crossword*), the set for *The Magic of Katherine Dunham*, and costumes for *The Mooche*. For opera, Barcelo has designed the costumes for Leonard Bernstein's *Mass*, at the Kennedy Center, *Les Troyens*, at the Vienna State Opera, and *Salome* and *Lily*, for the New York City Opera, as well as the sets and costumes

for Stravinsky's *L'Histoire du Soldat*, at Carnegie Hall. In addition, he has designed for such organizations as the Syracuse Stage, the Folger Theatre Group, the Capital Repertory Company, the Milwaukee Repertory Theatre, the McCarter Theatre, INTAR, La Mama, and the American Music Theatre Festival.

Barcelo's skills also extend to other areas. He has designed the posters for many Off-Off-Broadway productions, and his paintings and other works of art have been exhibited in America and Europe. Barcelo, who has taught at Lester Polakov's Studio and Forum of Stage Design, has received a Maharam Award and a Tony nomination.

LES TROYENS
Costume designs by Randy Barcelo
Directed by Tom O'Horgan
Vienna State Opera (1976)

How did you first become involved in designing for the theatre?

My first ambition when I was a young guy was to be a performer. Actually, in design that is unusual; in other aspects of theatre it's not. I had always been involved in art and had gone to art school. And because I was born in Cuba and we had a revolution and exile to go into, I never really quite connected that there was a career in theatre design.

I come out of an architectural background. Both my parents are architects. So I grew up with what I call "permanent scenery" being done all around me. My main ambition when I was very young was to be a dancer. What I didn't quite understand at the time was that I was most impressed by the design of the ballets I had seen, rather than by the dancing itself.

I left Cuba and went to Florida, and then to Puerto Rico. Since Puerto Rico was a very small island, there definitely were no careers to be had there in the theatre or in the arts, so the obvious choice at the time was to move to New York to pursue a career in dancing.

And it was out of that that I met a lady who requested some costumes of me. She had seen some of the artwork I had done. It was at that point that I thought, "Oh, that's a profession!" So anyway, I did those costumes and it didn't seem so bad. I was still dancing and it seemed a pretty decent way of supplementing my work. And I thought that a lot of older ballet dancers either made tutus or some sort of stuff. So little by little I became fascinated by theatre design and costume design, and I went to Lester Polakov's.

Why did you go to study at Polakov's?

I went to Lester's because I was not interested in going back to college, and so Lester was exactly what I needed. It was a professional school that offered a hands-on kind of design approach, and it was nuts and bolts. And because I had dance experience, I was also interested in choreography, which became a very peculiar kind of combination.

But really wonderful in its own way.

Yes, absolutely. While I was going to Lester's I had a couple of summer stock jobs, and they involved my being a choreographer and a designer for the productions. It was unusual. You don't find that many people who say, "No, no, I won't dance, but I'll choreograph and design the costumes for you." So I got a lot of experience that way. I could make my mistakes and I could learn.

Did you start doing shows after being at Polakov's?

I was doing shows while I was at Lester's. Back then there was a very strong Off-Off-Broadway movement going on. It was the avant-garde time, and I was working like a lot of people do. I had been at the Shakespeare Festival, not designing shows but working in the shops. I had worked at a couple of shops, which again is not unusual. I took any kind of job that came my way, whether it was painting scenery, making or designing costumes, dancing, or whatever. I was between the ages of 18 and 20, so I was very young.

How did your first Broadway show come about?

That's one of those oddities of destiny. Tom O'Horgan had a major success with *Hair*. So he was a hot director at the time. And by then I had done two shows, *Gloria and Esperanza* and *The Moondreamers* at La Mama, both of which he had seen. He had a falling out with Ellen Stewart and had created a company that he called the "New Troupe." It was to be a touring company similar to what the La Mama troupe had been. So they were putting together three shows. And I had done a version of his *Tom Paine* for another producer in which there was a guy by the name of Jerry Cunliffe, who was in the New Troupe and had been in the La Mama Troupe. So when there was a need for costumes to be designed and made, Jerry suggested me, because Tom had seen the *Tom Paine* I had done and had liked the changes I had made. I was called on that, and so I went in and accepted it, and did three shows for him. And off of that I went into the blue yonder.

Then I bumped into Tom coming out of a movie on Third Avenue. He was in town from California. We chit-chatted and he gave me a ride over to the West Side. He was working on *Lenny,* the movie, and they were going to be shooting in New York. In the meantime, I had become a union member. So I said to him that I would be very interested in working on it when it came to New York, and asked him to let me know of any future projects.

And then I went off to Erie, Pennsylvania, to do a production of *The Unsinkable Molly Brown.* While there, I got this phone call from Tom saying that they had canceled the movie project and they were doing *Lenny* as a show. He said, "Would you be interested?" I said, "Of course, I would." So I came back to New York and met with him, and it turned out they had been thinking Off-Broadway, but all of a sudden it was Broadway and there it was! I thought, here is my first Broadway show—I'm going to go have it done in the shops. Well, that was not the case. It was like, "Can we create our shop, and can we do this the real

LENNY
Costume design by Randy Barcelo
Directed by Tom O'Horgan
Brooks Atkinson Theatre, New York (1971)

Off-Broadway way?" So I was very disappointed about that. I had to bow down and this little shop was created downtown.

We're talking about for costumes, right?

Yes, and we did all the costumes out of that space. It was strictly economics. I forget what the costumes ended up costing, because *Lenny* was a very elaborate project. Most of it was made. It had all kinds of fantasy sequences. They just didn't want to spend the money or didn't have the money. The project was real touch-and-go for quite a while until Michael Butler came in, so I don't know how much it cost at the time, but it wasn't that much compared to today's prices. After I realized that I wasn't going to go to Ray Diffen or anyone like that, I thought, "Well, alright, this is the way to do it and let's just be very enthusiastic about it."

Were Robin Wagner's sets done in a regular shop?

Yes. Robin also had a number of different craftsmen making different things at different places, certain things that would be too expensive at the shops. He would have things done at my space downtown, called the Electric Circus. He had drops made there, and puppets, and we had our little shop in the back. So all of this was done in a real kind of Off-Off-Broadway way, but with Broadway craftsmen, top-of-the-line craftsmen.

Did *Lenny* get you other shows?

Well, one could say it got me *Superstar,* but I don't know that that means truly anything. I got, for example, a lovely note from Joshua Logan, who thought my stuff was marvelous. And I thought, "Oh, brother, I'll do his next show." But I never heard from him again about anything. I got complimentary notes. And a herd of people called me and said they wanted to come and talk to us about working on a project, but that didn't happen.

It was a very auspicious debut, because I had wonderful reviews and it was a major hit, and with very reputable people. And at the time it was definitely rather avant-garde. One thing that has to

be remembered is that there was an avant-garde mood in the air, but that did not mean that Broadway was avant-garde by any means. So ultimately my next project after *Lenny* turned out to be *Superstar.*

Which Tom O'Horgan and Robin Wagner did.

Robin had been asked to design sets and costumes. So he passed it on and said, "Why don't you come and work with me, and you do the costumes?" I said, "Fine." At the time, Frank Corsaro was directing that show. We started working on it and then Frank Corsaro had an accident. That whole team of people was scrapped. Except Tom O'Horgan was then brought in, and since Tom had worked with Robin and Jules Fisher and me, we stayed together as a team. And instead of my collaborating with Robin, I ended up just moving on to the costume designer spot by myself. So in a way, I got that project by fate, I suppose. I've always felt that that's how things have happened in my life.

How would you describe the costumes that you designed for *Jesus Christ Superstar?*

Looking back on it now, I've always described them as sculptural, and now I would describe them as very minimalist. They were really just very simple shapes that clothed the people. At the time, the costumes were called "bizarre" and all sorts of nonsense, which I think really spoke very much to the lack of imagination, I think, of the people who were trying to describe them. And I really got fed up. I'd spent 10 years hearing about how bizarre I was. I longed to be considered for whatever projects were around. I thought, "If I only depend on the bizarre projects, I'm not going to have much work."

When you look back on a career 20 years later, you see the mistakes. You see what you did and you didn't. What I probably should have done was to try to get much more into rock and roll, but I was really more of a theatre person. Rock has never interested me. I missed a tremendous part of the business by not doing rock and roll. What I should have been doing was sets and production, rather than costumes. I never felt that rock and roll costumes were particularly interesting. There have been moments. But as a field I discovered they always wanted to go out to the racks and buy it, and rip it up or do whatever that mood was at the time. It certainly did not hold as much of an interest for me as opera or ballet did.

Since the original *Superstar,* how many times have you designed the costumes for it?

Curiously enough, not that many. I designed two at that time, in New York and Los Angeles, and now 20 years later I've done one for Frankfurt. In the interim, nobody had ever called me to design that production.

How did the production in Frankfurt vary from the original?

Oh, tremendously. It was totally redesigned, although the needs of the show are still the same. What I mean now is that it's a better show than I ever gave it credit to be. It's much more interesting, and rather than thinking of it as rock opera, it made me realize that it has nothing to do with rock. It's pop opera, and the rock in it is totally peripheral. I mean, it's just a sign of the times.

You did not do *Superstar* in London. They got someone totally different?

Yes. *Superstar* is one rare show that's been done totally different every single time. For whatever reason, those rights were never quite secure. At the time, I don't think O'Horgan knew what a detriment it would be to his pocketbook and career to not have it worked out that he had to do every production, because what happened was that we never established a look for that show. So every time they leased the rights to it, they did it a different way. Ultimately, a show looks a certain way because you do it the same way over and over.

How long did you spend designing *Superstar* for Germany?

Superstar always gets designed fast. I spent two weeks in Germany, but this show was already made here and we just shipped it out. Eaves did it because they

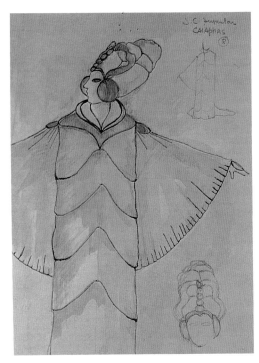

JESUS CHRIST SUPERSTAR
Costume designs by Randy Barcelo
Directed by Tom O'Horgan
Mark Hellinger Theatre, New York
(1971)

had a relationship with the producers. This last version has some stuff that I really like and has other stuff that, if I were designing it now, I would fight with the director and say no.

Like what, for instance?

Well, we did a little bit of historical quotations. The director wanted to mix Christianity in it. And we have some Christian symbols and Catholic symbols, which are a little too obvious, I think. Originally, his concept was to do sort of a history of Christianity, which the producers didn't want. But we still retain some of that idea. I've never done the show Biblically, which I've always wanted to do. Everybody goes, "No, no, no, we don't want to do it that way." I wish I had insisted—it's more interesting. I mean, I even did this as sort of neo-Biblical, but it's modern clothes for this kind of stuff.

Superstar was criticized a lot at the time. I just don't feel it was understood. And now, 20 years later, I think it was way ahead of its time. But it's not so much that the piece itself is so ahead of its time as the way it was conceived when it opened. I mean, you can conceive it as a concert with mikes and whatever, and the piece holds its own. But it was O'Horgan's staging that made it into a major pop opera.

When you designed costumes for *The Magic Show,* was that a different way of designing for you?

Whatever was involved with magic, yes. But it wasn't that much. There was some breakaway stuff and extra pockets, but that was about it. It was not like later on, when Doug Henning did *Merlin.* In that, he was involved in major tricks; all the tricks in *The Magic Show* were pretty simple-minded. What was truly involved was a very cartoon kind of show. So it had a rather different look from what I had been doing before.

Did you draw on anything in particular?

I think I drew on Giorgio Sant-Angelo. At the time I had seen a collection he had done and it had a lot of big polka dots. And that had stayed in my mind. I thought that seemed like a very playful approach to the show. Grover Dale, the director, wanted it to be playful and kind of childlike. So it really had very little to do with Doug Henning.

Doug really saw himself as Robin Hood, with these sort of masquerade costumes that he liked. I think he was disappointed that he didn't have many costumes in that show. I thought, "Do we really want him to pop out dressed as Robin Hood and Peter Pan and stuff like that?"

That was another case of a pretty slim show. It didn't get good reviews, but Doug did. Management was terrific on it. They took a look at the property and said, "Look, let's try to make a run of this." And they asked us to give up our royalties and everything to cut expenses to see if they could make a go of it. They mounted a good publicity campaign and pushed it, and it paid off. It ran four and a half years. I think it was the first show to do seven matinées and one evening performance. They were busing the kids in and later on it became the perfect production for saying, "Let's take the kids to a show that grandpa and grandma can enjoy too."

Of the productions you have done, would you say the costumes you designed for *Ain't Misbehavin'* are a lovely signature for you?
Of the Broadway productions, I would say *Ain't* is probably a signature piece. It's an ensemble piece, and I like very much how that whole puzzle fits together.

How did you go about all that?
The choreographer, Arthur Faria, was a major influence. He's the one that gave me the key of what they wanted. I never knew what Richard Maltby, Jr. wanted. Arthur always spoke for the two of them. And I felt this was probably the only time that anybody had truly approached me in a way that I liked. He said to me, "We want the costumes to be 'then,' not now, but we don't want any specific period." So I thought, "That's interesting. They can't be 1920s or 1930s or 1940s."

They had already done this at Manhattan Theatre Club, so they had a little experience in what their look was. He wanted a set of lace clothes, lace dresses. I said, "Why don't we try to get some vintage clothing and put it on the girls and look at what some of these vintage shapes do on them?" I thought that if I started drawing, we could go on for a long process, whereas if I put some stuff on them, that could inspire both of us, which is what I did. I rented a bunch of clothes from Early Halloween, an

antiques store. And we put them on the girls and arrived at ideas of necklines and things to have a departure point that we were both in agreement with.

Then I really collaged it. It was a skirt from this and a sleeve from that and a detail from that. And it just sort of evolved that way. The colors are what put it in and took it out of the period.

Describe the colors you used for the three women.
Well, a bright turquoise is not really a period color. It's a much more post-'50s color. Magenta is a couturier color, but it was not a 1930s or '40s color. Then there's a bright blue, a royal blue. So the shapes were period, they had a period flavor, yet the colors were not period. And everyone swore that their mother had dresses like that in their closet, which was fascinating to me.

The second act does have much more period colors. The first act's clothes are much brighter and much "glitzier" than the second act's. The show starts out very

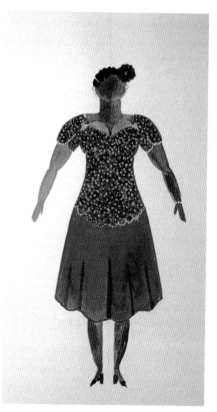  

AIN'T MISBEHAVIN'
Costume designs by Randy Barcelo
Musical numbers staged by Arthur Faria
Conceived and directed by Richard Maltby, Jr.
Longacre Theatre, New York (1978)

giddy and ends up being very serious. And so that was the whole point. The show ends with black and blue, and they do a coda. They are stripped of any kind of glitz, and this is interesting because it's a reverse of a show's usual visual progression. Some companies that have done the show without me have not understood why it was designed that way, and they like to glamorize the second act too much.

What about the men's costumes?
They were pretty straightforward. They were just good suits. The Andre De Shields character was a little more stylized. But it had to do with fit, and the lapels got a little wider. Originally, his suit was a pinstripe turquoise, which proceeded to go through all kinds of changes, because we found that fabric only once. And we couldn't just have 40 yards of it woven here, like they can in Europe—here you'd have to weave 40,000 yards. His blue suit kept on changing into myriad variations of turquoise-blue, and his other suit always remained the same green. So those are stylized versions. And he was sort of a dandy. The Fats Waller character is just a good suit with a period flair to accommodate large men. And the derbies were fun because of all the colors, but even on the last version of the show we couldn't get those colors anymore.

Did you keep the same designs on tour and in London?
Yes. Everywhere. The better summer stock companies call me when they do it. The poor ones just do it their own way. It's been done with my designs all over the world.

How did your association with the Alvin Ailey Dance Theatre come about?
I had sent them a letter and they called me, although not for a long time. I had just done *The Magic Show.* Jane Greenwood and I were both working at Brooks. They called her too, and I initially thought she had recommended me, but she had nothing to do with it.

And so I did this television program, and Alvin was a very difficult man. After that I thought I would never work with

him again. But then I did the costumes for *The Mooche* for his company, and that was a big success. I always called the work with Alvin mini-musicals. They were very theatrical pieces. They had sets, they had beginnings, middles, and ends, and a story of sorts. And they were always criticized because they didn't have as much pure dancing as his other pieces. They were truly lush, and they had a very special look about them. So that's how that started, and it lasted 15 years—not that it wasn't a bumpy ride.

After *The Mooche* I did a piece for him called *Black, Brown and Beige,* which was just awful. We didn't do anything for

THE MOOCHE
Costume designs by Randy Barcelo
Choreographed by Alvin Ailey
Alvin Ailey Dance Theatre, New York (1975)

years—I mean, he punished me after that. And then he came back to me and offered *For "Bird"—With Love,* a sort of dance-o-drama inspired by the life of sax player Charlie Parker, which Clive Barnes said afterwards was the greatest jazz ballet ever done. I did set and costumes for it.

What attracted me to the Ailey Company was that he was doing this kind of theatrical ethnicity that I loved, and that's what I liked about him. Alvin gave me the opportunity to do glamour, and I will always thank him for that. He would always say, "Our pieces are larger than life, Randy." So we'd always do "larger than life." I only did one sort of "tights" piece for him. That was in Italy. And I think those were the last two pieces he did. One was called *La Dea delle Acque,* which was for La Scala, and the *Opus McShann,* which was a beautiful piece for his company.

You designed both sets and costumes for *Opus McShann.* How would you describe it?

It was all like late-'20s and early-'30s. It took place in Kansas City and this was kind of a honky-tonk, but it was very glamorous. It was stunning. It was probably one of the most beautiful pieces I've ever done, because we talked about it for years. I was going to do a magenta and pink piece, and so finally—I don't know why I felt this was the one, and I didn't know he was dying—but I felt that was the time to do that. And the ballet was very entertaining. But there again, if the critics didn't say it was wonderful, the Ailey Company, including Alvin, would say, "Well, it didn't work," and they would get rid of it. I said to them, "Guys, you're not a Broadway show, you don't have to dump it. You can fix it."

You have designed the costumes for *Salome* and *Lily* at the New York City Opera.

Those were two kinds of flukish things. For *Salome* they called me. That was directed by Ian Strasfogel. I had wanted to do *Salome,* and somehow my name came up and *Salome* came up, and a friend of mine working at the Washing-ton Opera said, "Oh, he's always wanted to do that. Why don't you call him?" And that's how that happened. It was a very interesting-looking production, and controversial as well. It was my period of a lot of organic forms and things I was into at the time. The director originally had wanted a kind of Leon Bakst approach. I love Leon Bakst, but how am I going to improve on a master? All of a sudden, I thought I'd go my own way and see what happened. So that was the only project where I sculpted the costume designs.

Did you sculpt these figures for every major character?

Yes, it's a very small opera. The figures are about 14 inches high. And the reason I did that was because I wanted to see what they would look like from the front and back and sides. The designs were based on flowers and cobras and all sorts of stuff. I had no idea how to draw them, so that's why I started sculpting them. It seemed like a perfectly good way of doing them.

SALOME
Costume designs by Randy Barcelo
Directed by Ian Strasfogel
Opera Society of Washington, Washington, D.C. (1975)
New York City Opera (1975)

Then the other piece I did for the New York City Opera was *Lily,* which Tom O'Horgan directed. That was a new opera, and I loved those clothes. They were ethnic African clothes. The piece was not a success, but the clothes were beautiful, and they still remain among my favorites.

What do you like least about working in the theatre?

The meddling that goes on with what I'm doing. Everybody says, "Well, theatre is a collaborative effort." There is collaboration and I think it's wonderful. But I think collaboration can only be arrived at once you truly have a relationship with the people you are working with. I think it takes a long time. I think the collaboration I had with Alvin was that he used to say to me, "I mean larger than life" or "Kansas City" or "fabulous" or whatever. He would use a number of adjectives to give me a clue, and then he would let me go and create. I don't like to be bothered. I don't like to be meddled with.

What do you like most about working in the theatre?

When you have the freedom and the invention and the magic of it! I'm so happy when it all works and happens and looks terrific. When it works, it's like the most wonderful magic box! It just has magic to it. I almost become the kid and wonder how it all got there. It's lovely when people react and applaud, and one has given them joy. I think that's the biggest thrill of it all.

LILY
Costume designs by Randy Barcelo
Directed by Tom O'Horgan
New York City Opera (1977)

ANDREW B. MARLAY
Costume design for Oh Me!, Oh My!, Oh Youmans!
A project (1980)

DAVID MURIN
Costume design for The Royal Family
Williamstown, Massachusetts (1985)

ROUBEN TER-ARUTUNIAN
Costume designs for Katharine Hepburn as Viola in Twelfth Night
Stratford Connecticut (1960)
(Collection of Peter Harvey)

ANDREW B. MARLAY
Costume design for Oh Me!, Oh My!, Oh Youmans!
A project (1980)

DAVID MURIN
Costume design for The Royal Family
Williamstown, Massachusetts (1985)

JOSÉ VARONA
Costume design for Joan Sutherland in The Merry Widow—*Act III*
Vancouver Opera (1976)

SAM KIRKPATRICK
Costume design for Marsha Mason in Mary Stuart—*Act II*
Ahmanson Theatre, Los Angeles (1981)

ROBERT PERDZIOLA
Costume designs for Musetta in La Bohème
Santa Fe Opera (1990)

A Conversation with
ZACK BROWN

This conversation with Zack Brown took place at his Brooklyn townhouse. Born in Honolulu in 1949, Brown was educated at the University of Notre Dame and the Yale School of Drama. His Broadway debut came as set designer for *The Importance of Being Earnest*, at the Circle in the Square Theatre in 1977.

Since then, Brown has gone on to design sets, costumes, or both for an extraordinarily large number of productions. He made his debut at the Metropolitan Opera in New York in 1989, when he designed the sets and costumes for Verdi's *Rigoletto*. He has designed sets and/or costumes for the Arena Stage, the Guthrie Theatre, the Hartman Theatre, the McCarter Theatre Company, the Williamstown Theatre Festival, the Spoleto Festivals in Charleston, Spoleto, and Melbourne, the Edinburgh Festival, the American Repertory Theatre, the Arts Festival at Purchase, New York, Wolf Trap, the Manhattan Theatre Club, Harvard's Loeb Drama Center, Juilliard, and the Yale Repertory

Theatre. He won two Emmy Awards for his work on the televised broadcast of the San Francisco Opera's *La Gioconda*, and an Emmy nomination for the costumes for WNET's "Great Performances" production of *Tartuffe*. He won a Tony nomination for the sets for *The Importance of Being Earnest*, and Drama Desk Award nominations for *On Your Toes*, *Saint Joan*, and *Tartuffe*.

Brown's television design credits include the sets for WNET's "Dance in America" (*Jardin aux Lilas* and *La Sonnambula*). He has had numerous exhibitions of his work, including shows at the Gibbs Museum of Art (Theatre in Charleston), the Gimpel & Weitzenhoffer Gallery (Broadway Design, 1978–1988), the Prague Quadrennial (American Design Group), the Milwaukee Art Museum (Contemporary Stage Design), the Festival Club Gallery in Charleston, South Carolina, and The Calvert Collection, in Washington, D.C. (Paintings for the Stage).

LE NOZZE DI FIGARO
Costume designs by Zack Brown
Directed by Sonja Frisell
San Francisco Opera (1982)

How did you first become involved in designing for the theatre?

When I was leaving for college I thought I'd probably study something like industrial design, but I wanted a full liberal-arts education, not just art school. So I went to Notre Dame. Industrial design seemed practical—you know, cars, cereal boxes, and things like that. But as I was on the way out the door, almost literally, my father said he thought I should consider stage design. Now this was coming from someone who was a 20-year Navy veteran and graduate of Harvard Business School, with little background in theatre, so I was somewhat surprised. But he had turned down a full scholarship to the Chicago Art Institute in favor of Annapolis—it was wartime. I found out later he had been invited to go to New York, from his home in Kentucky, as the assistant to a well-known stage designer. And no, I really don't remember the name. I wish I did. Anyway, because I was always drawing costumes, or illustrations for Tolstoy novels, or historical scenes, I guess he could see that that was where I was headed.

You designed both sets and costumes at Notre Dame?

Yes. I started right away in the first year. In fact, the first thing I did was design costumes for Pirandello's *Enrico IV.*

Did they have a good theatre department when you were there?

Yes, actually, it was a very good department, because it was a combined effort between Notre Dame and St. Mary's, the women's college across the road, and because they provided me with the opportunity to design and to work in the shops. That's really the best way to learn, to get practical experience. Most of my earliest designing was costumes. I didn't do a set until my final year.

Was that by choice?

No, the technical director usually did the sets himself. But they didn't have anyone interested in costumes, so that fell to me.

Did you take courses and get credit for them?

There were no design courses.

How did you learn about fabrics, textures, color and style?

By trial and error. Some of it is a natural feel or instinct. I don't think you can be taught those things. You learn by doing. You can stand in front of a class and say this fabric will do this or that, but ultimately you have to try it out yourself and see what it does. Of course, you can narrow it down. There are certain fabric categories. You know you aren't going to make a little ballet dress out of wool melton, but whether you prefer rayon tissue faille to real silk must be the result of working with the fabrics and deciding which is most suited not only to the job but to the budget as well.

What happened after you got out of Notre Dame?

I applied to Yale and was accepted. Ariel Baliff was there at the time. But right after applying I decided I wanted to take a year off to do some woodcuts and painting, free from the pressures of school. So I did that in Boston, and the next year I went to Yale.

And you studied three years there and graduated?

Right. I stuck it out.

Were you both a set and costume design major at the drama school?

Yes. They make you do all three disciplines—lighting, too.

But sometimes one leans more to one than the other.

Yes. But I didn't.

What about the summers? Did you work in theatre?

The first summer I was at the Loeb Drama Center at Harvard, doing *The Threepenny Opera* and *Misalliance*, and I went back to the Loeb for a second summer because this was a semi-professional company then, and you could do quite good work.

Did you come to New York after you finished at the drama school?

Yes. I was lucky enough to have a position at Juilliard as the resident costume designer for the drama division. It was a year, but I began working on my own

Zack Brown's set and costume design credits include the following:

BROADWAY SETTINGS AND COSTUMES

Salome (1992)

Chinese Coffee (1992)

The Devil's Disciple (1988)

The Night of the Iguana (1988), S only; also presented at the Maly Theatre, Moscow

On Your Toes (1983)

Major Barbara (1980)

The Man Who Came to Dinner (1980)

Man and Superman (1978)

13 Rue de l'Amour (1978)

Saint Joan (1977), C only

Tartuffe (1977)

OPERA COMPANIES

Hamburg Staatsoper

Metropolitan Opera

Washington Opera

Dallas Opera

San Francisco Opera

Houston Grand Opera

Opera Company of Boston

Santa Fe Opera

New York City Opera

DANCE COMPANIES

American Ballet Theatre

Atlanta Ballet

Ballet West

Cincinnati Ballet

WITCHES
MACBETH
VERDI
Washington Opera '81

MACBETH
Costume design by Zack Brown
Directed by David Alden
Washington Opera, Opera House, the Kennedy
Center, Washington, D.C. (1981)

also, which started through Williamstown Theatre Festival and Arena Stage.

What was your first big show?
I think that would probably be Busoni's *Doktor Faustus* at Wolf Trap. And that was actually through a mutual friend from Yale, another designer, Donald Eastman, who had talked to Ronald Chase and Frank Corsaro. So they gave me the chance to do that.

You designed both sets and costumes?
Yes. There wasn't a lot of scenery, because Ronald is into film. There was a front scrim and a rear-projection screen and there were props or set pieces in between.

The reason this was the big break, if you want to call it that, was that Frank Rizzo was involved with Wolf Trap at that time, and he has been responsible for my relationship with the Washington Opera. It has gone on for 11 years now, and some 36 productions. So that's been a huge chunk of my career right there.

Do you prefer designing operas as opposed to plays?
I don't prefer it. In fact, at this point, I'm getting a little tired of opera and would prefer doing more ballet or more theatre, because I've been doing opera almost steadily. And you're solving the same problems over and over again, especially because at Washington Opera I'm expected to approach a production conservatively, or, that meaningless word, traditionally. They don't get very daring, and I'm anxious to do other things and to be a little more experimental.

How did your productions at Circle in the Square come about?
That germinated through Nikos Psacharopoulos. He talked to many regional theaters after my first summer at Williamstown, the first of which was the McCarter at Princeton. They had me do the scenery and costumes for *Design for Living.* That was originally for Michael Kahn, but he dropped out and Stephen Porter came in to the picture as director. So when Stephen was asked to do things at Circle in the Square, I began doing those.

Do you find that space interesting to work in?
I did. I didn't like it when they configured it into an arena space, because I thought the proportions were completely inhospitable. It was just too much of a "hot dog," just too long and narrow. But when you can put scenery at one end of the thrust you can make the space work, and I think I proved that several times.

Do you go about your design there in a different way? In terms of details, does it vary or do you design the same way?
You can design the costumes with more detail. In fact, the *Tartuffe* that I did there might as well have been real seventeenth-century clothing. And you wouldn't try to do that on the opera stage, because it would just be lost. Plus there's no reason to use fabrics that rich or that fine—you can't see them up close. You go for different effects on an opera stage, larger and broader.

When you are designing the sets and costumes for an opera, how do you like to go about working on them? How much time do you have?
You don't have enough time—that's almost always true. For instance, I usually find out what opera I'm going to be doing for Washington Opera about nine to eleven months prior, and that's not really enough time. The Met was very nice—I knew way ahead of time, three years ahead, that I would be doing *Rigoletto* and I was able to spend more time on it.

The first thing you do is study the piece itself as much as you can through composer's or librettist's correspondence, musical analyses, original source materials, and accounts or photos of previous productions. And you listen and follow the libretto, or score, if you read music, and make notes and a list of questions. You begin discussions with the director that decide the style or period, or answer questions like the number of supers, or necessity of changes for the chorus, and basically how you want to present the piece and what you want it to mean to the audience.

After these discussions you can begin more specific research.

Do you make sketches for every singer or performer?
It depends on what kind of time and budget you have. I've done two *Rigolettos*. The first time I did a set of costumes for the men's chorus that probably had 10 different designs, and then we did four of each in different fabrics. I refuse to do cookie-cutter choruses with whole groups of the same costumes unless it is a group of monks or something like that. When I did *Rigoletto* at the Met, they were kind of dismayed, because I came in with a different sketch for almost every chorus member.

How many sketches are we talking about?
Forty. When I did *La Gioconda* in San Francisco, that was a chorus of 80 with two costumes apiece, and there was a different design for every single one. I didn't draw them all. I used historic research. There was no time to draw everyone. But I almost always draw all the principals.

Do you go to every single fitting?
No. I'm very fortunate to have someone who has worked for me for over the last 12 years on most of these projects. Her name is Cynthia Doty and she usually takes care of the chorus fittings for me, among many other things. If it's a different period than we've done before, what I'll do is a few prototype chorus fittings, so that everyone knows exactly what I'm after. But because I'm usually involved with the scenery, I can't be in two places at once. I have to have someone else do those fittings, but I always do every principal.

CHRISTOPHER COLUMBUS
Costume design by Zack Brown
Directed by Roman Terleckyj
Washington Opera, Terrace Theatre, the Kennedy Center, Washington, D.C. (1985)

How many fittings do you have for principals?
You're lucky to get two. It's usually only one.

Do you do the first one in muslin?
Oh, rarely. No, the singers don't arrive soon enough to do that.

Do you have their measurements and work on a mannequin?
You work on a form and you have their terrible measurement sheets from their managements, which are almost never right. Then you see them two weeks before it's onstage. So you can't do muslin, it's almost impossible.

What is the average cost of an extravagant costume for a lady principal?
If I have things done in New York and if I want a ball gown beaded or something like that, I can spend up to $5,000 or $6,000 for a dress. But I can't do that in a

shop like Washington Opera's shop—there's no time or money for that. It just depends on how I want to split up the budget. If I've got a principal like the lead in *Fledermaus* or *The Merry Widow*—real leading-lady costumes—I'll have it done at Barbara Matera's, because I do want beading and a certain amount of whatever. So I apportion the budget to deal with that. When we sit down to budget a production in Washington, we don't even think of making an opera costume for less than $1,000 or $1,200. There are instances where you can, but they are very specific, like 12 priests in *Magic Flute*—multiples. So that's sort of the rule of thumb. And that's in a regional shop.

RUDDIGORE
Costume designs by Zack Brown
Directed by Peter Schifter
Washington Opera, Eisenhower Theatre, the
Kennedy Center, Washington, D.C. (1987)

Does management give you a lump sum budget, as opposed to an individual breakdown?
Yes, one of several advantages I have in Washington is that I'm given some control over how the money is spent. Most managements won't allow you to do that. I also have stock of my own 36 productions to pull from. What I do with Cynthia is figure out how much is to go for labor, fabrics, chorus, principals, millinery, and crafts, and how much can we pull? We split all that up and do the budget ourselves. And then we present it to Washington Opera for approval. But this is a unique situation.

What about wigs? Is that included in your part of the deal?
No, that's another whole thing.

Have you ever made sketches for a star performer in opera only to have the star performer not like them?

Not really. The only unpleasant situations I've come across in that category are when something has been redesigned. For instance, when I did the dresses for Renata Scotto in *La Gioconda*, she saw the sketches well ahead of time. We had preliminary fittings and she was happy as could be, and she ended up great. But then they had to be redone and adapted for Monserrat Caballé and subsequently for Ghena Dimitrova. I don't know about Caballé, because I wasn't there, but I went to Chicago and had to deal with Dimitrova. It was a nightmare. She had no concept of what they were supposed to be, how they fit into the overall scheme, or her own figure problems. She removed anything creating a silhouette, and succeeded in making herself look bad. And there's really nothing you could do about it.

But I don't work with superstars very often. Washington Opera can rarely afford them and they've built their reputation on doing opera more as theatre, and so they often use young American singers. They're much more flexible, and usually are suited to their roles. I also know most of them, so I haven't had very many bad experiences.

Do you also design for understudies at the same time?
No.

In other words, you just build one costume for a star performer and if an understudy has to go on you just hope the costume is okay?
There isn't money to do two. The Met often does two. For example, they made their second tenor in *Rigoletto* wear what Pavarotti wore, which I didn't really approve of. I'd done an alternate design, but they didn't seem to be willing to do anything else. But if they have someone singing Gilda who is tiny, and they've got a larger woman, then they're going to have to make two. Sometimes you have to make adjustments to the designs themselves.

Does the Met contact you about changes, or does the shop just go ahead and do them?
No. They just go ahead and do them, unfortunately.

How did this particular production of *Rigoletto* come about for you?
I'd heard that I'd been on their "list of designers to use" for some time. I'm sure Christine Hunter of the Gramma Fisher

Foundation had something to do with it, because she's on our board in Washington, and the Met's, and she paid for the production of *Rigoletto*. I suppose that's one reason. But they had to find a director willing to work with an American. It was directed by Otto Schenk. I was very happy *Rigoletto* was the opera I made my debut with.

Did it differ from the other production you did?
Yes. Drastically.

Was that because of the Met stage or the concept?
Because of the concept of the director.

And is it still in repertory there?
Yes, it has been for the past two years, and I know it's scheduled for the next year, so it's something they do a lot.

Do you go back to check on the openings?
No. I would invariably be upset. I think that's true of any production once it's up. The more you see it afterwards, the more you witness its disintegration because of cast changes and exigencies of repertory. Things wear out.

What happens to costumes at the Metropolitan Opera when the production has finished and it is no longer in repertory?
They're put in storage, and sometimes they are used. We had a few supers added that were not budgeted for and we went to the old production and took things, and adapted them.

When you designed costumes for the ballet, was there a particular place where you did research or got experience to know how toe shoes work and what tutus are made of and things like that?
I've only had experience with *Swan Lake* in Atlanta, and for Natalia Makarova in *On Your Toes*. In both cases I relied on the expertise of Barbara Matera. She's the best person doing dance clothes in the U.S. I believe Makarova has Barbara written into all her contracts. Through those experiences I learned a lot about dance things.
    Dancers have a whole agenda of

things they are concerned about. Their bodies are their instruments, and where you cut the different parts of the body with the line of the costume is very important to them. It's apples and oranges to compare dancers to opera singers. Dancers are athletes; opera singers are just regular people who happen to be able to make those notes. They are, as often as not, physically unsuited to the roles they are singing. Dancers are trained to do a particular thing. With

LA GIOCONDA
*Costume design by Zack Brown,
for Renata Scotto
Directed by Lotfi Mansouri
San Francisco Opera (1979)*

singers, it's a sort of natural ability to do something—not that they're not trained, but their major concerns are completely different. An opera singer wants to keep his costume away from his throat and to look thinner than he is. So you learn all those little tricks right away.

Do you find that choreographers know as much about what is involved in costumes for dancers as designers?
Oh, yes, and they know exactly what they want.

Because most of them have been dancers themselves?
Yes, and they know what shoes they want, what color tights they want, whether they want you to put powder on

the toe shoes because they're too shiny, and all of these very specific things.

When you do sketches for costumes, what materials do you work with?
Generally Bristol board, pencil, and watercolor, or just plain drawing paper. That's all, usually. There have been times when I have done whole collage sketches, but that requires a great deal more time.

Does your costume assistant do the swatching?
Sometimes she does. We usually get someone else to do that and the shopping. She's so busy with the organizational things, measurements, and all that bookkeeping.

What about research?
Sometimes she does research, or I hire an assistant specially for a project.

What about alternating with theatre and plays and musicals at the same time?
I would much prefer alternating. I'm doing a musical right now: *On the Town*, for the Hamburg Staatsoper.

How did this one come about?
I met John Neumeier—the director and choreographer—through Natalia Makarova during *On Your Toes*. A few years later he asked me to do a ballet treatment of *A Streetcar Named Desire* that he was going to do in Hamburg, but I wasn't available. Then last summer he called and asked me to do *On the Town*. And it's huge! The funny thing was that I had just done it the year before in Washington at the Arena Stage, but he had no idea.

And in a much simpler way, I'd think.
Yes, because there's no background—it's a lot of elaborate props. And costumes-wise, you don't have the resources at Arena Stage to do the things that the Hamburg Staatsoper can do. Plus it has John's own ballet company. He's got 40 dancers and they will all be in this. But I must add that the show at Arena was a career highlight. It was an excellent show and I had excellent collaborators, with director Doug Wager and choreographer Marcia Milgrom Dodge. It's not all in numbers.

THE MERRY WIDOW
Washington Opera '84

THE MERRY WIDOW
Costume designs by Zack Brown
Directed by Peter Schifter
Washington Opera, Opera House, the Kennedy
Center, Washington, D.C. (1984)

How are you coping with getting dimensions for the scenery and all the measurements for the performers?

I don't have to worry about that. I just do the sketches, hopefully. I've seen the performers. The scenery is a problem only in the difference between meters and feet, but we have an almost equivalent scale. So once you have the ground plan, you can start cooking.

How many assistants are you using for sets and costumes?

So far, on costumes, almost nobody, but Warren Karp has assisted me on the scenery. We started this *On the Town* many months ago, but it's not really done yet. This is a full-scale production

and I'm just starting on the costumes. There are over 200 of them.

Are you doing sketches for all 200?

No. All of the boys are sailors in the first scene and ballet, and many of them stay that way. I almost never draw men's suits if I can get a clear picture from an advertisement, a tailoring diagram, or some other source material. Then the tailors don't copy my mistakes or misinterpretations. Suit lines are very precise; this holds true for the uniforms, too. There is too much information available for me to take the time to draw them. But any special number becomes removed from reality, and these costumes I must sketch. So even with repeats, and the use of

source material, I will still end up doing over 100 drawings. For a situation like this I do two kinds of sketches, from simple diagrams or outlines used to convey information—no real figure—to real character sketches used to sell the idea of the character and their clothing to the director or performer.

And of course you don't do sketches for clothes that you might sometimes shop for.

No. You do. Sometimes you have to show the director what you are headed for. Maybe he'll be a sporty-type character and he'll have an argyle sweater. The director may not know what an argyle sweater is.

How did *On Your Toes* with director George Abbott come about?

That came about because John Mauceri was head of producing musical theatre at Kennedy Center and we had worked together on many operas for Washington Opera. He called and asked if I would like to design a musical called *On Your Toes*, with an Act I finale takeoff on Bakst's *Schéhérazade* and the Act II finale an Art Deco fantasy. I didn't hem and haw a lot. This was just before Balanchine died, so he was somewhat involved in the very early stages, and they hired the original director from 1936, George Abbott, Mr. Broadway. It was quite an experience, and a lot of fun for me. They restored all the orchestrations, and the show was hyped as being very true to the original. In spirit it was, but in point of fact, Mr. Abbott worked on the book extensively. The role for Makarova was given more focus, and musical material was extrapolated for a dance in her first scene. The "On Your Toes" ballet that Donald Saddler choreographed did not exist in the original. Peter Martins came in and did some new things for the "Princess Zenobia" and "Slaughter on Tenth Avenue" ballets.

I enjoyed that production, because I hadn't done many musicals at that point. I love musicals, and it wasn't like a revival—it was being created anew. I had a very nice relationship with Natasha and Donald Saddler, and it was a designer's dream in a way: You got to do Leon Bakst, Art Deco, and '30s high fashion, and all the realistic kids in the music classroom. It was just a whole mix of things. I got to try out some things with dance clothes, and I learned a lot on that show. It was a very pleasant learning experience.

How did you get along with George Abbott?

It was a funny collaboration. George Abbott is of the old school. He turned 97 while we were working on it! It wasn't a collaboration where you could get much out of him. It was a matter of "Well, Mr. Abbott, what do you think of 'Slaughter on Tenth Avenue'? What do you want that to look like?" He'd say, "Who cares, it's just a dive." Or you'd say, "What about the stage door scene?" And he'd say, "What about it?" And that's all I had to work with, from George, anyway.

That gave you a lot of freedom, didn't it?

Well, he was working very closely with Donald Saddler and John Mauceri, too. So there was input from other places. They certainly knew what they wanted or needed.

ON THE TOWN
Costume designs by Zack Brown
Directed and choreographed by John Neumeier
Hamburg Staatsoper (1991)

How many companies of that did you do?

Too many. Again, you watch a show disintegrate. You can improve costumes, but the scenery invariably got worse, because the touring producers didn't want to spend the money. Or it was going to theatres where it wasn't going to fit, so they'd leave half of it on the truck. It was that kind of thing.

What about the costumes?

They usually did new clothing, except for what we could save. But they always did new principals. They had to do the Dina Merrill role and Natasha over again, and I could make improvements on those each time.

What do you like least about working in the theatre?

That's a difficult question. Often I find the work unsatisfying artistically. You do get typecast, and can be asked to do the same kind of thing over and over again. Many times you have fulfilled everything asked of you to everyone's satisfaction and very real delight, but you haven't been able to grow, stretch, or experiment. Theatre is also a difficult thing because it is such a collaborative art. The success of a production really depends on whether there is a collaboration. The productions that I'm most proud of and that have looked the best are the ones where I have really tuned in with the director, choreographer, or whoever to come up with the product. The shows themselves were the best. And it doesn't happen that often. I can count the special productions that I've done on my hands.

Would you have any real favorite productions?

On the Town at Arena Stage was a happy experience, and so was *A Midsummer Night's Dream* at the Yale Repertory Theatre, directed by Alvin Epstein. It really was incredible—the cast included Carmen de Lavallade as Titania, Christopher Lloyd as Oberon, Meryl Streep as Helena, Joe Grifasi, Jerry Dempsey, and so on. I did the costumes and Tony Straiges did the set.

In many ways, the *La Gioconda* in San Francisco was a favorite. There is nothing artistically Earth-shattering about this opera, and I was given an "all-stops-out" budget because it was the first telecast from San Francisco Opera, and everyone was happy with the production—Luciano, Renata, and Mr. Adler. It was important for me, and it won me two Emmys. I'm afraid it also sealed my fate as a designer who only does big, grand, and opulent productions.

Artistically, the production I did of

RIGOLETTO
*Costume designs by Zack Brown,
for Luciano Pavarotti
Directed by Otto Schenk
Metropolitan Opera, New York (1989)*

The Saint of Bleecker Street with Menotti for the Spoleto Festival in Charleston was a highlight, and also the *La Bohème* he directed for Washington Opera. Both these productions were very fine in every category, and I did some of my best work.

If I'm a producer at a well-known opera company and I want to rent your costumes, do I call you? Or does management just go ahead and say, "Yes, it will be fine," and no one contacts you? Do you have any control over that?

I have some control. The Washington Opera has so many of my productions now they generally run the computer through about possible rentals that are confirmed, and I always see that schedule. For instance, we just opened *The Magic Flute* last December, and it was rented before it was designed, which I guess is a compliment. But I had all these companies calling me about aspects of production before I'd even thought about them! So we knew immediately that we'd better find out who was cast in these two companies. We found that Tamino was going to be too big and we saw that Pamina was probably going to be too small. We got all that information ahead of time and tried to make things work. So you do have to anticipate some of that.

Do you get a royalty at places like Washington and San Francisco for your costumes and sets when they play in repertory?

No, not when they play in their own venue. Only when they're rented to another company.

You design sets and costumes for a company and they remain there and play 100 years, and you don't get any royalties?

Right, none at all.

What about the Metropolitan Opera?

I receive royalties for the *Rigoletto*.

Comment on what you feel a set and costume designer should chat about with the lighting designer.

Color and directionality. I'm fortunate that I work very often with Joan Sullivan.

She is the resident lighting designer for Washington Opera, and our communication by now is so good that we don't have to have long talks unless we are going to try something completely new. We are probably going to try some projections for the first time this season, so we'll most likely have more contact. Also, I know she's not going to spring any horrible colors on me. She has excellent instincts.

So often if it's somebody new you are working with, a lot of your time and energy is spent just learning their language, and what they like and don't like. Sometimes you can achieve more if it's someone you know. That's why there are production teams. People are comfortable with certain people and they don't have to explain things ad nauseam.

Has a particular stage designer influenced you in your work?

Oh, yes, a lot have, and I should say a large part of my training is not so much Yale, but the fact that I went every summer to Stratford, Ontario, to watch almost their whole season of productions. I'd go up for a week and see everything they were presenting. In that situation they were dealing primarily with costumes and a lot of beautiful props. I saw the work of designers like Leslie Hurry, Desmond Heeley, Diedra Clancy, and Michael Annals. And Desmond always inspired me. He's one of the only designers I know who achieves effects on stage, and as much as I know, I can't figure out how he does it. I think that's a real art.

Do you think there's too much stress put on concepts in academics?

No. I just think there should be a balance. I think that you really must be able to conceptualize and come up with an idea and follow it through. But in order to do that, you have to have the practical also.

If there was anything that you could change in the course of your career, what would it have been?

The problem with this question is the supposition that one has any control over a career—that you can do certain things to shape and mold it. I could say I wished I had done more musicals, or

whatever, but I really just take what comes and do the best work I possibly can.

I could say I want to work with certain directors, that I would like to do certain projects, but short of having your agent make some calls, I don't really know any other way to make it happen than to do consistently fine work, and hope.

What would you like to be doing in 10 years?

I would like to be painting and perhaps teaching. I would like to be doing films, hopefully making a decent living. Wondering about where and when the next payment is is one aspect of this business that is pretty wearing.

If you hadn't taken the course your father suggested, what would you have done?

I thought about architecture, but not for long, because I can't add two and two and get four. So I thought that was out of the question. I don't think I would have stuck with industrial design, really. I don't know. I feel like I'm doing what I'm supposed to be doing, and that's a very happy thing.

I applied for a grant to take a year off to paint, to refuel and not be under deadline pressure all the time, but I no sooner applied than the Met called. I didn't ever think it would happen. It's a call I wasn't expecting. They don't use that many Americans. So it was out of the blue.

What do you enjoy most about working in the theatre?

Well, it's never really the same. There's always something different to sink your teeth into. For me, it's putting another whole world on stage, or turning a drawing for a set or a costume into the real thing, and interpreting a great play or opera in visual terms. I like to make beautiful things. It's that simple, too. And I like giving people pleasure, because that really comes back to me, especially in my situation in Washington—I've done so many productions there. The audiences there know me and share their enthusiasm, and that is very gratifying.

ELDON ELDER
Costume design for Foigard in The Beaux' Stratagem
Center Stage, Baltimore (1972)

PETER HARVEY
Costume design for Orpheus Descending
Coconut Grove Playhouse, Miami (1958)
(Photograph by Linda Alaniz)

JOSÉ VARONA
Costume design for Coppélia
Pennsylvania Ballet, Philadelphia (1978)

MARCOS OKSENHENDLER
Costume designs for contemporary 1990s cocktail dresses
The Daily News, New York (1991)

FRANCO COLAVECCHIA
Costume designs for (clockwise from top left) horses, birds, fish, and dragons in Rinaldo
Houston Opera (1975)

FRANCO COLAVECCHIA
Costume designs for the cat in Starbird
Texas Opera Theatre, Houston (1981)

FRANCO COLAVECCHIA
Costume designs for voodoo men in Treemonisha
Houston Opera (1975)

A Conversation with
PATTON CAMPBELL

Patton Campbell lives and works in a lovely apartment just off Central Park West on Manhattan's Upper West Side, where I discussed costume design and teaching with him. Born in 1926 in Omaha, Nebraska, Campbell was educated at Yale College and the Yale Drama School. He made his Broadway debut in 1955, designing the costumes for *Trouble in Tahiti* and *27 Wagons Full of Cotton*. He has designed costumes for operas, musicals, and plays, and for certain productions he has also created the scenery. His costume designs (with Howard Bay) for *Man of La Mancha* have been seen in numerous companies around the world since the show's premiere at the ANTA Washington Square Theatre in 1965. They were nominated for the Tony Award that season.

Campbell has designed scenery, costumes, and lighting for many Santa Fe Opera productions, including *Madame Butterfly* (which opened the theatre in 1967), *The Barber of Seville*, *The Abduction from the Seraglio*, *Anne Boleyn*, *Fledermaus*, *Falstaff*, *Capriccio*, *Cinderella*, *La Bohème*, *Ariadne auf Naxos*, and *The Rake's Progress*. He also did costumes for *Cosi Fan Tutte*, *Tosca*, and *Der Rosenkavalier*.

In addition, Campbell created the costumes for the first London stage production of *Gone With the Wind*, in 1972 at the Theatre Royal Drury Lane, and also did costumes for *Gone With the Wind* at Tokyo's Imperial Theatre in 1966. Other companies he has worked with are the Kansas City Lyric Theatre, the Houston Grand Opera, the Opera Company of Boston, SMU Opera Theatre, the Glimmer Glass Opera, the Empire State Institute of the Performing Arts, and the Omaha Community Playhouse. He has also designed for the films *Foul Play* and *The American Revolution*, and for the national companies of *Oliver!*, *After the Fall*, and *On a Clear Day You Can See Forever*. Campbell has also taught design at Columbia University, SUNY-Purchase, the New School of Social Research, SUNY-Stony Brook, Southern Methodist University, Pratt Institute, Brandeis University, Brooklyn College, New York University, and Barnard College.

WINGS OF THE DOVE
Costume design by
Patton Campbell
Directed by Christopher West
New York City Opera (1961)

How did you first become interested in designing costumes for the theatre?

It started with marionettes. My mother did marionettes for the Junior League in Omaha, where I was born. For my third birthday, my father built me a marionette stage and I was given a set of Goldilocks and the Three Bears. Then for my fifth birthday, I got a better stage and better marionettes. Somebody's mother had made the costumes for them. So it was theatre, and that's how it all started.

And then at that same time, I was seeing live productions, children's plays, by the Junior League, and also at the Omaha Community Playhouse, where I saw my first live theatre. My mother acted in some of those, too. Actually, my parents had their first kiss playing the romantic leads in the senior play at Omaha Central High School, where I would go later.

Were you involved with theatre in high school?

Yes. I acted in grade school and I also acted in high school. I didn't have much interest in design as a child, but in the eighth grade I recall we were asked to make a scrapbook of what we wanted to be when we grew up, and my choice was a theatrical costume designer. So I knew that far back. I was good in drawing and painting classes in high school, and at the same time I was acting in high school plays.

You went to the Yale Drama School. How did that come about?

Well, it came about because I had gone to Chicago during a between-semesters break. I was a sophomore and I went alone to see Gertrude Lawrence in *Lady in the Dark*. I absolutely fell in love with her. I began going to the Omaha Public Library to look at old *Theatre Arts* magazines and to find everything I could about this glamorous lady, whom I would ultimately know at the Cape Playhouse. And going through these back issues, I came upon the plans and elevations for the new Yale Drama School. So I set my goal to go there as soon as I could. Then, after two years in the Navy during the war, I went to Yale College, where I was able to overlap a year at the drama school, which would normally have been three years.

What did you major in?

Drama.

You could do that at Yale College?

Yes, you could do it over great protest, but finally they agreed that I could, because I convinced them that I was serious about a career in the theatre. We were the first G.I. class, so four boys were crammed into a room meant for two. I was the only one of the four who knew what he wanted to do. So I guess the powers at Yale College respected that.

The powers at Yale College?

Yes, at Yale College, which I did not enjoy. But I enjoyed the weekends in New York and I enjoyed the Yale Dramat and working in the basement on costumes. By then I was starting to design costumes and, actually, the first ones I did were for the Yale Dramat.

How did you get your first show in New York?

Well, it emanated from Yale. Donald Oenslager had been my professor there, and I took a major in stage design, meaning everything—scenery, costumes, and lighting. Don was helpful in getting me started. The first show was really a shopped, modern-dress one, and it never came into town. It was *Dear Charles*.

Did Oenslager ask you to do the costumes?

Yes. It was all off the rack. We might have made a few things at places that had workrooms then.

Patton Campbell's costume credits include the following:

BROADWAY

Man of La Mancha (1992)

Loot (1968)

The Natural Look (1967)

Come Live with Me (1967)

Agatha Sue, I Love You (1966)

The Glass Menagerie (1965)

All American (1962)

The Conquering Hero (1961)

There Was a Little Girl (1960)

Howie (1958)

A Hole in the Head (1957)

Fallen Angels (1956)

The Grand Prize (1955),
S and L only

NEW YORK CITY OPERA

La Traviata (1981)

The Student Prince (1980)

The Pirates of Penzance (1977)

La Belle Helene (1976)

The Ballad of Baby Doe (1976)

H.M.S. Pinafore (1975), and S

The Mikado (1974)

Susannah (1971)

The Makropoulos Affair (1970), and S

Carry Nation (1969)

Miss Julie (1965)

Capriccio (1965)

Lizzie Borden (1965)

Natalia Petrovna (1964)

Wings of the Dove (1961)

The Inspector General (1961)

JUILLIARD OPERA

Katya Kabanova (1964)

Gianni Schicchi (1964)

Il Tabarro (1964)

CENTRAL CITY OPERA

The Lady from Colorado (1964)

Madame Butterfly (1964)

OFF-BROADWAY

Great Scot! (1965)

A Month in the Country (1963)

The Makropoulos Secret (1957)

ON A CLEAR DAY YOU CAN SEE FOREVER
Costume designs by Patton Campbell
Dances staged by Leo Kharibian
Directed by Peter Coe
Hanna Theatre, Cleveland (1966)

Was it customary to make modern costumes back then?

A place like Bergdorf's had a custom-made department, and Hattie Carnegie did. And there was another place called Rosette Pennington, which would make things for ingénues. You would choose a model and they'd make it in your colors for the actress. So yes, there was a possibility then to have modern clothes made to order.

What happened next?

The next thing, which was actually my Broadway debut, was scenery. It was for a charming comedy called *The Grand Prize.* But I don't even keep it on my résumé, because I've become more successful in costume. That was a one-set modern interior of a working girl's apartment in a Murray Hill brownstone. As far as I'm concerned, my real debut was the triple bill called *All in One,* which was Bernstein's *Trouble in Tahiti* with Alice Ghost-

ley singing "Island Magic," and that was enchanting. It was on the bill with Tennessee Williams's *27 Wagons Full of Cotton,* in which Maureen Stapleton played Baby Doll. Paul Draper, the tap dancer, was the third, making it three in one.

How did that come about?

Through Eldon Elder, who had been a year ahead of me at Yale, and whom I had assisted as a scenic draftsman. And the chance came along to do these modern dress costumes, and I was delighted. That was the real beginning for me!

The next show was for the same management, Bowden and Barr, and that was Noël Coward's *Fallen Angels,* with Nancy Walker as a Noël Coward leading lady. Already it's intriguing, right? First of all, we changed the time to 1932, which was about the most beautiful modern period for women ever. So I went out to the Brooklyn Museum, where I had already learned to do research, working from actual costumes, and I drew endlessly and worked from fashion magazines of the period. I sketched with pencil in a spiral notebook. And then we took Nancy and Maggie Phillips—the other lady—out to the museum, and they literally played "dress up" in real 1932 clothes. We took a lot of photographs of what were called "down-in-back hats" and "profile hats," and beautiful bias-cut floral-chiffon evening dresses, that sort of thing. So it was drawing and working from the actual dresses. And for me, this was going to be my first show that wasn't contemporary.

Wasn't this kind of an unusual amount of research to do in this way? And also a terrific way?

Well, yes, it was terrific, and a bit unusual, but I knew no other way. Before that, I'd assisted Oenslager on *The Ballad of Baby Doe* on the costumes, so I had worked in period designs. That was a big show. He hired me to work with him on the costumes. I arrived at his office and he'd marked quite a few books with ideas he'd like to use. He had already gotten some samples while shopping for scenery fabrics. Then I began doing line drawings of the characters in *The Ballad of Baby Doe* and there were about 50 sketches for new costumes. A lot more would be taken from stock. We shopped the major fabrics at Gladstone's, which was above a Spanish restaurant—if you lost the tag, you could always identify a Gladstone's swatch by the stench of olive oil.

After I had done the line drawings, I assumed I would render them in watercolor. But Don was paying me by the hour, and because the drawings and fabric swatches were specific enough, I was able to put them to work at Brooks, where I'd done *Fallen Angels*. I felt secure at Brooks Costume, and the management at that time didn't even question putting them out to bids.

Then came the time in the shop, and Don wanted no part of that. He said, "Pat, I don't want to deal with their tessituras." He didn't even know what that meant. Actually, it's where the voice lies. He just plain didn't want to deal with the singers and, of course, I loved it. We had Walter Cassel, Martha Lipton, and

Delores Wilson in Central City and, of course, Beverly Sills came into it at the City Opera. That was her first great success with the company.

The Ballad of Baby Doe is an incredible challenge for a designer, because it starts in 1879 and it goes up to about 1895, the "Year of the Sleeve"; in fact, it goes a little beyond that. The billing for the production read, "Scenery, costumes, and lighting by Donald Oenslager." I was paid and I was happy and thrilled to have this amount of work to do. When the City Opera moved from City Center to New York State Theatre, Beverly Sills came back to the production, and we virtually remade it at Brooks.

One day in the shop I got a call from one of the secretaries in the office, and she said, "Pat, a terrible thing has happened and you should know about it now rather than opening night. The program's gone to press and it reads, 'Scenery and lighting by Donald Oenslager, Costumes by Patton Campbell.'" And she said, "I'm so sorry about it, but you know, you're the one who calls for fittings." Joan was new to the company and she hadn't realized my position. I was just very concerned about it. I called Don immediately, and I told him what had happened, and do you know what he said? "That's alright, Pat, you really did them, you know." I mean, that's a mentor. You see, Don and Kay Brown, the play agents, were the people who were most helpful to me, and through Don came Eldon. There's this kind of wonderful thing of passing the torch that I'm finding with my own students. I've seen it happening ever since I've taught at Columbia.

What about research? Do you enjoy doing it?

I'm just fascinated by research, and often when I start a show I have to make myself stop going to the library, the museums, or wherever, because I love that and I love teaching that. My students see a carousel of 80 slides in every session, which usually lasts between 12 and 14 weeks. I've collected slides from most of the great museums all over the world where I've been able to travel. I think travel is just the greatest thing that

can happen for anyone in the theatre. I don't mean just looking at the costume museums, but also architecture, paintings, sculpture, tapestries, and so forth.

When you travel, do you make lots of sketches?

Well, I do sometimes. If there are slides available, then you don't have to. I use little thumbnails that I've sketched in Siracusa in Sicily, for instance. I have a notebook that I carry with 3-by-5-inch pages, and I do a quick rough of something that I might not be able to buy as a slide or postcard.

Do you like to do several sketches before you settle on the final drawing?

We talked about the notebook stage, the research stage, and getting the stuff together. After that, what I like to do with directors whom I trust is to show them little color roughs the size of playing cards, and literally shuffle them onto the table. These may be several ideas, for a given dress, say. I like to do those tiny sketches very quickly with Nupastels. There are 96 colors in a box and you can do just color roughs, no details. I shop many of my own fabrics, because I don't want to show a director a print or a stripe or plaid that I can't acquire. When I'm working in patterns, I will invariably shop first.

Where do you go besides Gladstone's?

Well, Gladstone's has moved from the Spanish restaurant now. There's Orchard Street, which is fast diminishing, but Beckenstein's is still one of our principal sources, both for women and men. And they also have drapery fabrics. The scale of decorator prints will usually read better than a dress fabric, which is designed to be seen closer. So Beckenstein's has materials for women, men, and drapery fabrics, all on Orchard Street across from each other. The next place is Thirty-ninth and Fortieth Streets, where there are a lot of outlet places. They change over the years. The most reliable and most elegant and most accommodating is B. & J. Fabrics. Along Fifty-seventh Street there are some reasonably priced ones, and then there's Jerry Brown, which is astronomical, so one seldom goes there anymore. So there are three areas in the city. And then if you're working in patterns or plaids or stripes, invariably you go to Schumacher, and Stroheim and Romann. If you have a good budget, you would go to Scalamandre for really glorious silks.

Do you attend every fitting?
Oh, yes. I'm always there for the measurements. Not that I care about what they're writing down, but it's a chance for me to meet the performer and to get to know him or her. And obviously, as the measurements are being taken, you look at the body. A lot can get covered up. If a man is going to be in tights or hose, you've got to know what his legs are like. If a woman has physical problems, you've got to find it out right then. So it's measurements and then the muslin pattern, which is the first fitting. The muslin is a mock-up of what the finished costume will be, and it can be pretty detailed. Pencil marks are made on the muslin, indicating where embroidery might go or where a finish would be.

Do the muslin fittings go back a great number of years, and do they still exist in the same way today?
Oh, absolutely, because it would be stupid for a shop to cut into the actual fabric. Sometimes they can do it. I mean, a shop like Grace Costumes can. Grace was Karinska's head cutter and fitter during the great years. She can cut a bodice right into the fabric and you don't worry. But in general, certainly in *Man of La Mancha*, every costume is different, so you need individual muslins. For instance, the muleteers are in rough leather and tweed, all different. They're seventeenth-century, Velasquez-inspired work clothes.

How many productions have you done of *La Mancha?*
I'm now doing my sixth.

Do you have a good budget?
This was not bid. I simply said I wanted it done at Eaves Costume, who had done the 1977 revival, and the management respected my wishes. They had suggested alternatives, one of which I'm sure would have been more expensive, and the other one I don't even want to think about.

This management was initially extremely difficult for me, but once we had settled on the shop, all's been wonderful. We have virtually every rag that's worn in the prison made from scratch. There are about 50 changes, which is not a lot for a musical.

You have done many operas for New York City Opera. What would be one of your favorites?
I've done 20 in all. That's a lot. It's like saying, "What's your favorite child?" I guess I was proudest of *The Makropoulos Affair*, because I did the scenery for that too, and because I tended to do comic pieces—three of the Gilbert and Sullivans, for instance. So I felt with *The Makropoulos Affair* that Pagliacci got to play Hamlet. It's a very strong, dramatic piece, and doing it as the multimedia production, a photo milieu as we did, was very exciting. Ours was the first for the City Opera to use live action onstage with film from the bridge and two slide projectors upstage in the blacks.

Upstage in the theatre house?
Yes, up in the backdrop, and there were just two tiny slits, way upstage, which you could never see when they were on, because they would be projecting something onto the screens.

Were the slits off left and right?
No. They were center, left and right. And then both the film and the projections went on to nine different translucent screens, which were distorted rectangles

hung parallel to the foots on five different pipes to achieve a variety of changing patterns. And the scenery per se, the furniture and props, were photo blowups. We were working in a whole photographic medium. We would take a photograph of a real chair in the studio, then mount a blowup to actual size, and cut it apart and put it back together as a chair, but distorted like a photograph. So in the show, when the potion for everlasting life that the woman has taken is beginning to wear off, you see that in the furniture and in the props that are onstage, a distortion of life, black and white, like photographs of the period.

How would you describe what you did for the costumes for *Makropoulos*?

I was really dealing with the wardrobe of a prima donna, and it's specifically 1913, which is the "hobble skirt" period, an absolutely glorious period for women. It's the period of the great Parisian couturier Paul Poiret. He's the one who said, "I freed women's waists and I shackled their ankles." And so the woman is a prima donna in Prague at that time. Her first entrance into the lawyer's office seeking the lost potion is all in gray, in black, in monkey fur, and with jets and veiling, and it's very dramatic. She is wearing the same costume that she had worn in the film sequences when she's seen fleeing to the office.

We shot the exterior on a street in the East 80s in New York. John Lindsay was our mayor then, and was wonderful in promoting the film industry here in town, so we were able to use a whole block and shoot into the night. There are houses over there in that particular block that have a very European look, and that's exactly what we spotted and where we shot. And then, of course, the film runs all through.

The second time we see her she's sung a role in the opera house and she comes offstage exhausted. What role had she sung that night? It's not specified in the libretto or in the play by Karel Capek on which the opera is based. We are told that Rudolph II, Holy Roman Emperor in Prague in the year 1571, ordered his court physician, Dr. Makropoulos, to concoct a potion for everlasting life. But first it must be tested on the doctor's

THE MAKROPOULOS AFFAIR
Costume design by Patton Campbell
Directed by Frank Corsaro
New York City Opera (1970)

names in the libretto. Ekaterina Myshkin had a Russian sound, so Maralin Niska could wear her own costume from *Prince Igor*. Suppose Elsa Mueller was Mozart's first prima donna? Again, Maralin would be seen in her own blue velvet "Countess" dress from *Marriage of Figaro,* a role she was singing that season.

For Eugenia Montez, why not a prima donna of another sort: a street singer in a put-together "Carmen" costume. As for Ellian MacGregor, whose story is told in some detail in the libretto, we would now be in the early nineteenth century. For Ellian, John Crosby was kind enough to loan us the Tosca costume I had designed for Maralin in 1969—white satin crepe embroidered in gold with a saffron yellow Lyons velvet overtunic.

Having pretty well run the gamut from 1571 to 1913, I decided the role Emilia Marty had sung in 1913 was "La Mort de Cleopatre" as it might have been interpreted by Ida Rubenstein in a Leon Bakst–inspired theatrical costume. And the gold tiara on the Egyptian braids, gold lamé sheath, and turquoise, peacock-eye organza cape with a long train worked wonderfully as Emilia Marty dragged herself offstage to her dressing room. You see, she was now 342 years old!

Comment on designing the costumes for *La Belle Helene* at New York City Opera.

La Belle Helene was a delight to do. It was Offenbach's version of Paris and Helen. It was directed by Jack Eddleman, whom I've always loved working with, and the late Lloyd Evans designed the scenery. We decided to do it as an entertainment as it might have been presented to the Empress Eugenia in the Deuxième Empire. Lloyd's scenery was a very decorative, theatrical version of Sparta. And I was able to research theatrical costumes worn at the time, which were Grecian in origin but full of delightful anachronisms. I went to the Bibliothèque Nationale in Paris and found a lot of 1860s prints of actors in costumes, in classic tragedies or in comedies. I'd started here in New York at Lincoln Center and I didn't find much, but I found vast

16-year-old daughter, Elina. To everyone's horror, she falls into a coma. Left for dead in a crypt, Elina revives and escapes from Prague to start a new life as Ekaterina Myshkin. In all, four different names are mentioned, each with the initials "E. M." and all fatally beautiful. But who are they? Where did they live? That was up to the costume designer to decide—with the director's approval, of course.

Since Elina and the other ladies would now be shown in film sequences, there had to be a logical progression of time from 1571 to 1913. And since the scenes would all be one-shots, new costumes obviously could not be made. So stock was the answer, trying to match costumes with the places hinted at by the amounts in Paris, and then more at the Victoria and Albert in London, theatrical costumes of the 1860s.

When designing costumes, what have you found to be the most challenging production?

Well, obviously *Gone With the Wind*. And that turned out to be kind of an annuity over many, many years, because we first did a dramatic version in Tokyo produced by Toho, the great entertainment conglomerate. It was then like David Merrick, MGM, Radio City Music Hall, and the Latin Quarter combined, with film.

How did this come about for you?

That was through Kay Brown, the agent for the Margaret Mitchell estate. Kay had convinced Selznick to buy the novel for $50,000. She represented the Mitchell estate and Arthur Miller, Robert Anderson, Lillian Hellman, and a lot of playwrights of the time. The Mitchells wanted the production to not look ridiculous if it was to be done in Japan. Let's say, more positively, that they wanted it to look correct, to have the uniforms authentic, for instance. My contract read, "Mr. Campbell will design orthodox costumes of the 1860s in Southern America, indoors and out." Well, that sort of covered it. I didn't realize there were that many orthodox in the south at that time, but I got the idea, "indoors and out." I liked that.

How many costumes are we talking about?

Well, the first one, the dramatic version, was done in two parts, the first of which just went up to the movie intermission. There were certainly 500 costumes. I only did the principals for that one. They had in mind, of course, a musical version, because they'd grown tired of *Hello, Dolly!* and *Fiddler on the Roof* and our own *La Mancha*, and they wanted to do something of their own. So it seemed a curious choice at first. Then we discovered that the novel was the biggest best-seller, except for the Bible, in all of Japan. It's very popular. The movie is always playing somewhere off Ginza. I mean, in a revival house. And then, if you remember *Shōgun*, and how that tiny island was split

La Belle Helene
Costume designs by Patton Campbell
Directed by Jack Eddleman
New York City Opera (1976)

up into several principalities, they were always at war, civil war with father against son, brother against brother, exactly like ours. So they have a real feeling for that. And also, Scarlett as a strong woman— you see, women's liberation in Japan was just starting then, in 1966. It's certainly not there yet, but it's getting better. They're still in awe of a strong woman.

Ultimately they got their musical and commissioned Harold Rome to do the score, Joe Layton to direct and choreograph, and David Hays and me to design the scenery and costumes. We had a success in Tokyo and then it was completely remade, the costumes and scenery in London. Harold Fielding produced it and we ran a year at the Theatre Royal Drury Lane, all thanks to Harold's promotion of the coach party ladies.

Was it the same production in London?

Yes, it was virtually the same. But when Noël Coward came, he said, "There's nothing wrong with the show that couldn't be saved by cutting the second act and the child's throat."

Was this still going up to the first intermission?

No, it was the legitimate version. When we did the musical, it played right through. They love long theatre in Tokyo. You come to the theatre at six o'clock from your office and you book your table in one of 20 restaurants that are within the National Theatre, and then intermission becomes a big social event in the basement. You can have all variations of Japanese food, Chinese food, and even Steak House Scot.

At one point I asked for a costume count, and Harold Fielding got quite nervous, because he thought I was going to ask for more money. All those bodies that come in on the stretchers are in costumes, even if they are dummies. So we were well over 300, which, as I knew, was our union cutoff. But I was just curious.

Who was in the cast?

We had Harve Presnell and June Richie, who was in several movies with Alan Bates. She is a very, very pretty little lady with a lovely figure. She was a marvelous Scarlett. Then, of course, we did it again in California, and there was hope it would go beyond there, but it didn't.

How many total actors and actresses did you have to costume?

Let's say there were 20 principals and usually 16 dancers—eight boys and eight girls and a swing boy and a swing girl. Then there were 12 singers—six singing men and six singing women—who doubled into small roles. So there was a total of probably 50 in the cast.

It sounds like an interesting experience for you.

Oh, yes, it was. First of all, living and working in Tokyo was extraordinary.

How long were you there?

I had to commute, because of my teaching. The last time I was there was for two months. I know I was there all of December, because we opened on New Year's Day. In November I came home while things were being made, so I was there in October and December. In London the costumes were made at Bermans. And you just can't do better than that—they are the best costumiers in the world.

GONE WITH THE WIND, DRAMATIC VERSION
Costume designs by Patton Campbell, for Rhett (right), Scarlett (far right), and Belle (below)
Directed by Kazuo Kikuta
Imperial Theatre, Tokyo (1966)

How long did it take when you were in London?

For that one I was there the whole spring. I had to get someone to teach for me at Columbia. I had a flat, so I was a living and working Londoner.

Besides designers, who do you have in your classes at Columbia?

Playwrights, directors, managers, and dramaturgs.

When you teach costume design, how long does it take you to get through the program?

What I used to do when I started at Columbia was an ideal situation. In the first year I would go from the Greeks through the eighteenth century, but I would intersperse the so-called "learning sessions" with the critique of a project. And then in the second year we'd take the nineteenth century almost decade by decade, because the silhouette changes very fast then, both for men and for

women. Also, you have such a wealth of plays and operas and musicals and operettas that are done in the nineteenth century, so that the choice of projects is just glorious. Then in the third year, we'd concentrate on a thesis, possibly working in an apprentice situation or designing the shows in your own school.

When I first taught at Columbia, the regional theatres were just starting. It's great to be a part of a theatre, like at Minneapolis, where you become a family, like the New York City Opera is for me, or to be in Seattle, or to be in Dallas, and really be part of one of the marvelous theatres that are all over the country now. So as a young designer, your goal isn't necessarily that 10-block area around Times Square as the "be-all and the end-all."

I want to say that I've had as good workmanship in the shops of the regional theatres as I've had in New York. I had great trepidation when I first went to the Empire State Center of Performing Arts in Albany to do *Threepenny Opera*, but I found the work there to be skilled and sensitive—highly professional. And the same was true at SMU for *The Merry Wives* and when I returned to Omaha for *Teddy and Alice*.

What do you like least about working in the theatre?

The insecurity. I sometimes say, "If I'd known what it would be like, I wouldn't have made that scrapbook in the eighth grade." It's feast or famine. And I've been very fortunate in my career to have what's called a "full card" in our union, so that I have been able to go in and paint scenery as a subsidy. That's bread and butter; doing a show is dessert.

What do you like most in the theatre?

Teaching. If I could teach full-time, I'd be a very happy man. But at the time, I started at Columbia as an adjunct—that means part-time—and so it's been. And I just love being able to pass the torch, and I've passed it to directors as well as designers.

Do you find you learn as much from students as they learn from you?

Oh, all the time. When I show slides in my classes, students see things that I've

"The Merry Wives of Windsor" 1.
Sir John Falstaff

never looked at. They'll see an emblem on a costume or a banner or something like that, and they ask what that is, and I'll say, "I don't know, let's look it up." The questions are great, and they're not only from the master's-degree students at Columbia, who are hand-picked, but also from the "babes," as I call them, at Purchase, who are just one year out of high school and often don't have very good background. In fact some of them have *no* background. So their innocence is a joy to me. And their response is quite wonderful.

LEFT: THE MERRY WIVES OF WINDSOR
Costume design by Patton Campbell
Directed by Richard Poppino
Southern Methodist University Opera Theatre,
Dallas (1986)

BELOW: THE THREEPENNY OPERA
Costume designs by Patton Campbell
Directed by Bill Francisco
Empire State Institute of Performing Arts,
Albany, New York (1984)

LEWIS BROWN
Costume design for An Italian Straw Hat
Stratford Festival, Stratford, Ontario (1971)

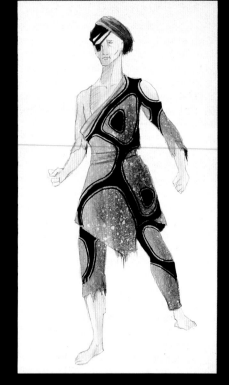

ROBERT O'HEARN
Costume design for Die Frau ohne Schatten
Metropolitan Opera, New York (1966)

GREGG BARNES
Costume design for Nibs in Peter Pan
Empire State Theatre, Albany (1987)

EDUARDO SICANGCO
Costume design for Walt Disney's Magic Kingdom on Ice
touring show (1985)

EDUARDO SICANGCO
Costume design for The Tooth of Crime
Hartford Stage Company, Hartford, Connecticut (1986)

GREGG BARNES
Costume design for Honeysuckle in The Snow Queen
Empire State Theatre, Albany (1989)

GREGG BARNES
Costume design for Kiss Me Quick
Before the Lava Reaches the Village
North Shore Music Theatre, Beverly, Massachusetts (1990)

EDUARDO SICANGCO
Costume design for The Tooth of Crime
Hartford Stage Company, Hartford, Connecticut (1986)

A Conversation with
ALVIN COLT

I visited with Alvin Colt in his spacious apartment on Riverside Drive in Manhattan. Born in Louisville, Kentucky, Colt studied stage design with Donald Oenslager at the Yale Drama School. His first Broadway show was designing the costumes for *On the Town* in 1944. His costume designs have been an important and distinguished asset to many memorable shows from coast to coast, and his versatile talents have encompassed every form of theatrical presentation, including Broadway, television, ballet, opera, nightclubs, films, and industrials.

Colt has been associated with more than 275 productions spanning over four decades. As a charter member of the Phoenix Theatre, he designed the costumes for 16 classics plus 15 for the National Repertory Theatre. For television, Colt has produced costume designs for all the major networks and has created the raiment for over 100 television programs, ranging from over 2,000 costumes for the 13-episode historical drama *The Adams Chronicles* to numerous spectacular musical production numbers seen on some of television's most memorable all-star specials. His costumes have been seen in four major operas, 10 ballets, two World's Fair extravaganzas, three feature films, three City Center revival-musicals, and a 26-week soap opera. His industrial shows include work for Buick, Oldsmobile, Ford, Chrysler, the General Motors Motorama, and the Milliken Breakfast shows. Colt is also the winner of the coveted Tony Award, for which he has been nominated four times, and is a four-time nominee for television's Emmy Award.

KING LEAR
Costume designs by Alvin Colt, for Cordelia (above) and Gloucester (right)
A project for Orson Welles (1946)

Did you have an interest in designing costumes before you went to Yale Drama School?

I thought I was going to be a set designer, but oddly enough that didn't happen. That was my major at the Yale Drama School, although I took the costume design courses. In those days summer theatre was very important. And I worked in several summer theatres, because I believe you learn more by doing than you do by going to school.

One summer I was at Ogunquit, Maine, and I was painting scenery and doing the lighting. I wasn't designing there, but it was a good summer job. And the last week of the summer season they had a small company of dancers called the Ballet Caravan. I'd never seen anything quite like that before. That company was run by a man named Lincoln Kirstein. I got to know the dancers and the man who was their production manager. And I was fascinated, especially with the costumes.

When I came to New York I contacted Lincoln to see if he could in some way advise me what to do with my career. I had introductions to Irene Sharaff, Aline Bernstein, Robert Edmond Jones, and Lee Simonson, and other designers of that era. I would see them and their advice would be, "Go back home, the theatre's a terrible place to work." They weren't very encouraging.

What happened to you next?

I got a job with a fabric company selling theatrical fabrics here in New York. It was called Maharam. And I went to Lincoln to tell him what I was doing and that I was making 15 dollars a week, plus commissions.

Anyway, I started selling Lincoln fabric for his little ballet company. And there came a point when he asked me if I would like to design one of the ballets. Of course, that was fantastic! And those were my first designs, for the Ballet Caravan company. It was a ballet called *Charade*. It was choreographed by Lew Christensen.

Did that lead to something else?

Well, it led to my doing 10 ballets for different companies. What a thrill to

design costumes for Leonide Massine's *Saratoga* for the Ballet Russe de Monte Carlo at the old Metropolitan Opera House with Oliver Smith's scenery. It was Oliver's first set.

Something else happened that eventually meant a great deal to me. One day, delivering fabrics to Lincoln's costume shop in the same building as the school of American Ballet, he said, "I want to take you somewhere to meet somebody." And he took me down another floor and we went into this empty room where there were three card tables with three ladies, and none of them spoke English—they were all speaking Russian. And one of the ladies was Barbara Karinska. She was making her first costumes in this country. They were for Jack Cole and his dancers, who were going to open at the Rainbow Room. So I started selling Karinska fabrics. We became close friends and, little did I know then, she one day would be making costumes from my designs for some of the most important Broadway shows.

Oh, she was fantastic. She absolutely revolutionized the making of costumes in this country. The way she handled fabric, created trimming, perfect-fitting

---

Among Alvin Colt's costume design credits are:

BROADWAY

Jerome Robbins' Broadway: On the Town (1989)

Lorelei (1974)

Sugar (1972)

Golden Rainbow (1968)

Here's Love (1963)

The Beauty Part (1962)

Wildcat (1960)

Greenwillow (1960)

Destry Rides Again (1959)

Li'l Abner (1956)

Pipe Dream (1955)

The Lark (1955)

Fanny (1954)

The Golden Apple (1954)

Top Banana (1951)

Around the World (1946)

On the Town (1944)

PHOENIX THEATRE

The Infernal Machine (1958)

Mary Stuart (1957)

The Diary of a Scoundrel (1956)

A Month in the Country (1956)

The Stronger (1956)

Miss Julie (1956)

The Carefree Tree (1955)

The Master Builder (1955)

The Doctor's Dilemma (1955)

Sing Me No Lullabye (1954)

The Sea Gull (1954)

Coriolanus (1954)

Madam, Will You Walk (1953)

NATIONAL REPERTORY THEATRE

John Brown's Body (1968)

Ring Round the Moon (1968)

She Stoops to Conquer (1968)

A Touch of the Poet (1967)

The Imaginary Invalid (1967)

TELEVISION

Night of 100 Stars III (1990), also I and II

Disney-MGM Theme Park Opening (1989)

Happy Birthday, Hollywood (1987)

NBC's 60th Anniversary Celebration (1986)

The Tony Award Shows (1971–1986)

Parade of Stars at the Palace (1983)

CBS's 50th Anniversary Celebration (1978)

The Adams Chronicles (1975)

The Prince of Homburg (1971)

GUYS AND DOLLS
Costume designs by Alvin Colt, for Vivian Blaine as Miss Adelaide
Left to right: "Sue Me"; "Take Back Your Mink"; street scene, Times Square; finale
Dances and musical numbers staged by Michael Kidd
Staged by George S. Kaufman
Forty-sixth Street Theatre, New York (1950)

and costumes that moved, it was just unbelievable. I worked in her shop at one time, kept my eyes wide open, and I learned a lot from her. She was extraordinary. Her interpretation of the designer's sketch was remarkable. Some time later, I started working with Ballet Theatre when it was first organized.

Was Oliver Smith a producer then?

That was before Oliver produced. Oliver was designing for them, but he was not one of the producers. No, I think the man's name was Richard Pleasant, and behind it all was Lucia Chase. And that's when I worked for Lucinda Ballard. She did *Giselle* and a lot of their first ballets. From there I started designing ballets for Ballet Theatre. Michael Kidd was then with Ballet Theatre and he was also with the Ballet Caravan. So Michael asked me to do his ballet, *On Stage*. It was Michael's first choreography. Oliver did the set. I designed another, *Slavonika*, and Balanchine's *Waltz Academy*. Anyway, they did *Fancy Free*, which I did not do. And as you know, out of *Fancy Free* evolved *On the Town*. And when *On the Town* came along, because I knew Oliver and Jerry Robbins, I was asked to do *On*

the Town. And that was my first Broadway show. That was in 1944. And that started me off on a Broadway career. Then I went from one show to another, and I've done 38 Broadway musicals and 37 Broadway plays, so far.

On the Town was an unusual musical at that time. It was the first musical done in a kind of realistic way. Musicals then were always 18 girls dressed alike. This was the first time a show had ever had that kind of choreography, or that kind of scenery. No other show had ever had a score like Lenny Bernstein wrote. Musicals in those days were not like that. This was the big innovative one. So the clothes were not spectacular. They were not the sort of costumes where you "oohed and ahhed." They were New York people—this was a show about New York. What there was was appropriate, but it wasn't absolutely what you called "eye-filling." *On the Town* was directed by George Abbott.

George Abbott, who's over 100 years old?

He really made that show into what it was. He was wonderful. We were only out of town 10 days and everyone was so

nervous. It was Betty Comden's and Adolph Green's first show. It was everybody's first show. George Abbott really brought it through. It's true. Everyone was scared to death, including me.

George Abbott had a show called *Barefoot Boy with Cheek*, which was a very cute show. Nancy Walker and Red Buttons were in it. It was a show about college kids. Jo Mielziner [with whom I would later do nine shows] designed the scenery. I went to see him and we got along very well. Since this was a college musical, Jo's idea was to do a lot of trees and branches, because it was autumn, the time kids go back to school. I said, "Well, if you're taking all the leaves off of the trees, I'll just put the leaves on the people." So I dressed them in autumnal colors. And it looked terrific.

Then something quite unusual happened. Through Lincoln I met a very famous Russian painter named Pavel Tchelitchew, and he became my mentor. He used to call me the sorcerer's apprentice. He was the sorcerer and I was the apprentice. He taught me a lot about the theatre, and in particular about costumes. He was very "theatre-minded,"

and was a great success with the ballet world and the theatre in Europe.

He was known equally well as a painter and as a theatre designer?
Absolutely. His sets for *Ondine* in Paris were extraordinary. He did many sets with Balanchine. He and Balanchine were great friends. And he was a big help in guiding my career in the right direction.

Orson Welles asked him to do a Broadway show called *Around the World in 80 Days*, with a score by Cole Porter, and he turned it down. But he said, "I have someone who I think will do a wonderful job, and I highly recommend him." And that's how I came to do it. It was a huge show. It took five different shops to turn out hundreds of costumes.

Did you design both sets and costumes?
No, I didn't do the sets—Bob Davison did. As I said, "I kept going into costumes."

What kind of budget did you have back then?
Well, it didn't take that much money to do shows. I don't know the budget. And

with Cole Porter and Orson Welles involved, it was a very important work, and spectacular! But the critics killed Orson. It only ran four or five weeks.

At Yale you studied sets with Oenslager and you must have studied costume design with Frank Poole Bevan.
Absolutely. Frank didn't like me because he was very short and I'm so tall. He told me to go home, that I didn't belong in the theatre.

Years later he must have eaten his words.
As a matter of fact, he did, and he was very nice about it. He congratulated me and he said, "I'm happy you're such a success."

When did you do *Guys and Dolls*? That was 1950, wasn't it?
Yes, 1950. I'll tell you the reason I got *Guys and Dolls*. They had signed another costume designer to do it. And something happened and they didn't approve the designs. Abe Burrows, who did the book, was the one who said, "These don't look like Runyon New York people. You've got to get whoever did *On the*

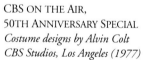

CBS ON THE AIR,
50TH ANNIVERSARY SPECIAL
Costume designs by Alvin Colt
CBS Studios, Los Angeles (1977)

Town, because they looked like people in New York." I'd never worked with Feuer and Martin, the producers. Of course, I had worked with Michael Kidd, who did the choreography—I'd done Michael's ballet. So that all latched together. I came in rather late on that particular show. But it was a big success, and it also established a kind of look for the show and a kind of character for all those Runyon people, which lived with it for a long time. Of course, it was such a big hit, and you know how the business is, "Get whoever did the last hit."

You did all the national companies?
Oh yes. I've done it in Sweden, in Vegas, in Iceland, in L.A., and at the City Center in New York, all using the original designs.

If you were asked to do it again today, would you do it in the very same way?
Well, I'd probably like to. It would depend on the director. I've got the whole show in a portfolio in such great detail you would not believe it. It's all there. It is one of my favorites and I love it.

Did you have anything in particular in mind when you did the "Take Back Your Mink" costumes? What would your comments be about those costumes?
What happened with "Take Back Your Mink"? The show was in Philadelphia a long time. It even moved to a different theatre in Philadelphia, which was unusual. Another show was coming in. Cole Porter's *Out of This World* was coming into the Shubert, so we moved to the

Erlanger which had not been occupied for years. But during the last week of the run they called me and said, "Come over on Sunday and bring your paints." And I thought, what in the hell are they talking about? Bring my paints and brushes?!

I went over Saturday night. Sunday we had a meeting in Frank Loesser's hotel room. And they said, "We're putting in a new number," because the second act had opened with the reprise of "A Bushel and a Peck." Frank played the new number, and of course we all fell on the floor. We loved it so. And they said, "How should they look?"

I said, "Well, as the lyrics say, it's 'Miss Adelaide and her debutantes.' It's going to be Miss Adelaide and Runyon's idea of a debutante. I think they should all look like Rita Hayworth types." I did some rough little drawings there in the hotel room and said, "Let's put them in gold lamé because there's nothing like that in the show." And we needed that kind of a lift, especially to open the second act.

And I came back to New York on Sunday night, went to Brooks Costume Company and put the lamé into work. I went back to Philadelphia on Friday with the costumes completed, and someone to fit them. They went on in the Saturday matinée. And it was a smash! The number was just so right, and so were the costumes!

Did the costume shops work the same way as they do today?
Well, they do and they don't. You see, when Karinska came in, the whole technique of making clothes changed. She had a whole new way of doing it and everybody wanted to go there.

What was different with her?
As I said earlier, it was the way she would do appliqué and her crocheted details and the way she saw things and colors. Of course, things didn't cost as much then. We did a musical called *First Impressions*, based on *Pride and Prejudice*, with Farley Granger and Polly Bergen. Abe Burrows directed and Peter Larkin did the scenery. Karinska made the costumes and they were absolutely beautiful.

NBC's 60TH ANNIVERSARY CELEBRATION
Costume design by Alvin Colt
NBC Studios, Burbank, California (1986)

I remember one of the reviews said, "Not since *My Fair Lady* have we seen such costumes." That was nice.

You asked about the shops. The shops have changed. There are new ones and some have gone. Today there is a whole technique in the craft area that was not so important then. There are shops that do wonderful things with stretch fabric, which didn't exist then, and painting on stretch, which is great! And you've got to be aware of all that if you are going to work in the theatre today. It is just like computers and everything new that has happened in offices. It's a whole different technique. And I think a lot of that has changed the look of costumes. I don't think *Cats* could have been done without stretch fabric and the painting on them.

The fundamentals, I think, are all more or less the same. There are certain shops that do certain things better than other shops. But that has always been that way. And there are some shops you like working in more than others.

Then there are also some managements that like to have competitive prices from the different shops. Some designers say, "I will only work in that shop!" That happens a lot. If you're not happy and you're not comfortable, your show is not going to look good. So you've got to really keep all that in mind.

How do you go about doing sketches? What do you do your work in?

Just watercolors. Some people do absolutely beautiful sketches, and I do sketches that I always say are working drawings for the workroom. Because it's what's onstage that counts. It's what you're seeing from out front. The audience doesn't know how you've arrived at it.

They don't care as long as it works.

As long as it works. They don't know how you started it or what has changed or who wanted this or who wanted that. Or what was thrown out or how many times it was done over. Or what it costs or any of that. All they know is what they see, what's in front of them. So a lot of times the costumes don't really walk off the paper because of the way they're drawn. Other times they might. They can just look at the sketches and say, "Well, there it is."

And sometimes designers do go back and revamp.

Some designers' sketches may be rather vague. And they have something in their head and they'll do it as they work along. Others will draw almost photographically and you can't go wrong.

MARY STUART
Costume design by Alvin Colt, for Eva Le Gallienne as Queen Elizabeth
Costume executed by Barbara Karinska
Directed by Tyrone Guthrie
Phoenix Theatre, New York (1957)

Do you do sketches for absolutely every figure in the show?

Oh yes. Unless it's something that has to be found. And even then sometimes you will do a drawing of something that's going to be purchased or rented to show your director and your producer what you're looking for, and you'll say, "This is what I'd like to have, but we may not end up with this because it might not be available." But it sets a visual tone of what you're looking for.

There again, some directors will leave it all up to you, and they won't say a word. Others will want to know every little detail. They might even come to the fitting. It depends on who they are and how they feel about it. A lot of them will look at sketches and won't know what you're talking about.

What would be two of your very favorite costume shows?

One of them would be *The Golden Apple*. That is sort of my very favorite. It had style and it was very new at the time, and it was with this wonderful group of people. Bill and Jean Eckart had the scenery almost designed when I came in, so I could see what the costumes were going to be against. And they had a very

ABIGAIL
EPISODE V
Sc. 1-2-3-5
JUNE - 1788
TRAVEL TO QUINCEY

Blue Raw silk
Pale Blue Fishu
Straw Hat.

LOUISA DANA

EPISODE IV - PARIS - AUTEUIL   "THE ADAMS CHRONICLES"
ABIGAIL - 1785
Sc. 18 h (NO HAT)
Sc. 30
Scene with Jefferson

Hat to back

KATHRYN WALKER

THE ADAMS CHRONICLES
Costume designs by Alvin Colt
Televised by PBS (1975)

definite style to the sets. Again, it was a very contemporary kind of look, even though it was a definite period piece with a certain look that they had designed and that I could relate to.

I took the characters and put them in the same color schemes throughout all the various periods. So there was a relation each time they came on. For instance, the character Penelope would always be in blue and white. The styles changed and the periods changed. They looked wonderful.

There was a number that Ulysses did, called "In My Store-Bought Suit." And Bill and Jean had a traveler that was striped black satin on black velour with a lot of tassels and fringe, and it looked beautiful! And I said, "Let's put all these men in black suits and pipe each suit in a different color with matching spats and gloves and hatbands." Well, everyone thought I was crazy with black suits against a black background. But it was a knockout! It just looked marvelous. It had style!

I guess *Guys and Dolls* was a favorite. But I'll tell you, I did some wonderful work with Eva Le Gallienne. I did *Mary Stuart* with her and Irene Worth, also

Elizabeth the Queen with Miss Le Gallienne as Elizabeth. She was inspiring to work with, a great artist, and there's no one like her today. What a joy to do *The Sea Gull, A Doll's House,* and *The Trojan Women* with Miss Le Gallienne!

Being a charter member of the Phoenix Theatre was very important. For one thing, Off-Broadway didn't exist then. That really was the beginning of it. And I was able to work with a lot of top talent people. I did 16 shows for the Phoenix, and they were all productions that you long to do but don't get to do very often, if at all. You don't get to design *Coriolanus, The Sea Gull, The Master Builder, The Infernal Machine, The Doctor's Dilemma, Six Characters in Search of an Author,* and plays of that caliber. Among the Phoenix directors were Tyrone Guthrie, John Houseman, Michael Redgrave and Herbert Berghof. I've been very lucky. I've worked with some very distinguished people.

You have worked with the top people.
And the kind of talent that does not exist today. I mean, you don't get to do a play with Tallulah Bankhead very often. I did a play called *Crazy October* that never

came to New York. That was a wild experience. She was a great star—she played the part of a slovenly woman who ran a roadside gas station/café. Oh, it was just an awful run-down place. Ben Edwards did a terrific set. I went to see Miss Bankhead at her Murray Hill townhouse, awash in ecru slipcovers with curtains drawn and quite dark. She sat far across the room and she asked, "What did you say your name was?" I said, "Alvin." She said, "Don't be ridiculous, darling, no one can be named Alvin." I said, "Miss Bankhead, I'm sorry, but that's my name."

So I did a "wrap-around" for her. Remember house aprons over sweaters and wedgie shoes? She loved all that. I said, "I think the wrap-arounds should be red." And she said, "Oh, put me in red. They won't be looking at anybody else onstage if you put me in red." And I put her in red. But her sweaters had to be cashmere lined with silk chiffon.

In your career, didn't you do as many plays as you did musicals?

You're quite right, almost exactly the same number. If you're a good designer, you have to be versatile. You've got to be able to do everything. It must never be said, "Well, he can't do this, he can only do feathers and sequins." I've never had that problem. A lot of designers today don't marry to the script. I always say, "If it's in the script, it'll be on their backs."

You've got to go to what the play is about and the essence of it. And you don't just put them in pink because it's a pretty color. You do it for some reason. I go time and time again to see shows, and what they're wearing is inappropriate. It might be beautiful, it might be expensive, and there may be a lot of work in it, but it doesn't belong in that particular play on that particular character. And it happens over and over. You've got to ask yourself, "*Why* does she look like that? What are they supposed to be?" I mean, it's in the script. I blame it on the directors and the producers just as much, because they should know better.

But they aren't trained as well.

No, but even the playwright should say, "That doesn't look like so and so..." When I did *The Beauty Part*—another of my favorites—with Bert Lahr, Charlotte Rae, Alice Ghostley, and Larry Hagman,

Noel Willman directed it and S. J. Perelman was the author. It was a real pleasure to work with Perelman. He was absolutely pure gold. We were out of town and after he saw all the costumes, I said, "Tell me, do you feel these are your people? Are these your characters, your friends?"

Well, he just couldn't get over it. He was thrilled! And that was all character costume, very tongue-in-cheek. Bert Lahr was just a charm to work with. He lived on Park or Fifth Avenue in one of those big, old buildings. The first time I went to see him, he opened the door and greeted me wearing an Indian blanket bathrobe, with a cord and tassel, and some comfy scuffs, and he had that wonderful face. He took me into the living room. It was very traditionally furnished, kind of Chippendale and elegant. Then I turned around and there on one wall, in a large, gilt antique frame, was a full-length, life-size portrait of him as the lion in *The Wizard of Oz*. And I looked at that and I almost wept. It just hit me so.

When they're professional like that and when they're real stars, they're so easy to work with. Lucille Ball was an angel.

What did you do with her?

Wildcat. She was absolutely marvelous. Of course, her character didn't require a

glamorous wardrobe. She wore blue jeans and a number of colorful shirts, but she was a delight. I worked with her other times in television, and did some really fabulous things for her.

Did you design differently for television than you would for the theatre?

No, but you have to be aware of certain colors, because the camera does tricks with colors, and you have to be aware of certain patterns, because the camera does funny things with those. But in conception and in working, I don't find it any different at all. Scheduling and time-wise, it is quite different—you don't work like in the theatre, where you have four or five weeks, a dress rehearsal, and several techs, and then you get the show on.

On *The Adams Chronicles*, I sometimes marvel at how it all got done. We did enormous things—13 episodes of historical drama, over 2,000 costumes, and a very tight shooting schedule. It was filmed in a large Manhattan studio and at various locations in New England, Philadelphia, Washington, and South Carolina. Sometimes two places at the same time.

Did you have a good budget for that?

HAPPY BIRTHDAY,
HOLLYWOOD
*Costume designs
by Alvin Colt, for
Silent Screen Vamps
ABC Television,
Shrine Auditorium,
Los Angeles (1987)*

At the time, I thought it was alright, but money is always a problem.

But you didn't build costumes?
Oh, yes, we built all the principals' clothes. Background people and extras were assembled from all over the world. And they'd arrive and you'd most always have to redo them. It was 150 years of fashion to cover.

I needed Empire dresses for a big ballroom scene. It was supposed to be in St. Petersburg, Russia, and they didn't have enough gowns here, so I called Western Costume Company in California and was told, "Oh, yes, we have just the right thing for you." The costumes arrived and they were all cut on the bias à la 1930s dresses, like some movie for Merle Oberon.

Empire obviously didn't cut on the bias.
No, of course not. And these dresses had wired bras, and all that Hollywood '30s style.

When you're doing a historical work, do you like to do a great deal of research?
Oh, you have to. In my library I have extraordinary books, some of the best, but you have to! You have a certain knowledge of it, naturally, in your background and from other sources, but you must look, see, and study the modes and manners of the era, the paintings. How did these people move, live, walk in a hoop skirt, sit down in a bustle, carry a gun, a fan? There are endless details.

In the many shows you've done, has one been more challenging than another?
I don't know. I think each one is a challenge. You've got to approach it and run with what it is. I guess some are more difficult than others, like *The Trojan Women*, with Margaret Webster directing. There have been those that have been bigger, larger, but that doesn't mean they're more difficult. It just depends. It's a combination of the creative collaboration. Sometimes it just breezes along, and at other times you have to rethink and do the sketches over until you hit it.

When you design costumes for Broadway plays or musicals, do you have plenty of time to do them? Is it a year? Or six months?
Oh, no, not a year. You usually have six or eight weeks to do the drawings and then another four or five weeks in the shop, or it could be a little longer.

You designed the costumes for *Top Banana*.
Top Banana was a big, razzle-dazzle, Winter Garden show, and there were a lot of comics in it—Phil Silvers, Frank Albertson, Rose Marie. Jo Mielziner did the witty sets.

Did you go out of town with it?
For the first opening. You always have to.

Did you know it would be a success out of town?
Well, Phil Silvers was a big star. And it was very funny. It was also about television, television stars, productions, and so forth. It was fun, and it was a big hit. Then, for the movie, they filmed it in the Winter Garden Theatre. It was taken right off the stage.

Comment on *Fanny*.
Josh Logan directed *Fanny*. It was a fascinating job with a lot of character costumes. It was my first time to work with Josh, and it was a show we all loved and loved doing. I think Josh was responsible for that, and for its being such a huge hit. And Jo Mielziner did his usual wonderful scenery. *Fanny* was also the first big show I did with David Merrick. David is a true Broadway producer. Later on I did two of his other big hits, *Destry*

HAPPY BIRTHDAY, HOLLYWOOD
Costume designs by Alvin Colt, for Mack Sennett Bathing Beauties ABC Television, Shrine Auditorium, Los Angeles (1987)

AROUND THE WORLD IN 80 DAYS
Costume designs by Alvin Colt, for Orson
Welles in the Magic Act (top left and right)
and for the Oka Saka Circus, Act I finale
(bottom left and right)
Choreography by Nelson Barclift
Staged by Orson Welles
Adelphi Theatre, New York (1946)

Rides Again, with Andy Griffith and Dolores Gray, directed by Michael Kidd, and *Sugar*, directed by the talented Gower Champion.

There's *Pipe Dream*. That was the only time I worked with Richard Rodgers and Oscar Hammerstein. And Helen Traubel was another experience. She was a famous opera star and she'd never appeared on Broadway. She was unique!

Was she nervous?
No. She was a wonderful, good-natured woman and she had a grandiose laugh. But she was a very big lady! Karinska made her dresses and tried to get her a waistline, and it wasn't easy. She was great in the show, very endearing and very effective. It was directed by Harold Clurman and Jo Mielziner did the sets. And what a treat to work with John Steinbeck, on whose book *Pipe Dream* won me a Tony Award.

When you have fittings in the costume shop, do you always attend every fitting?
Some designers don't. I do.

For principals as well as background people?
Everyone. I want to see every detail. Sometimes it makes the shop mad, but I want to see it all. Even in a big television production like *The Adams Chronicles*, I wanted to see every single extra before they went on camera. And I would put necklaces on, and I would put the earrings on, and I would do this and that. I would talk to the hair people. These people who didn't have any lines said, "We never had so much attention." They couldn't get over this. And it shows. It always shows.

How did *Li'l Abner* come about?
Michael Kidd. I did a lot of shows with him. Also, *Li'l Abner* needed someone who had a sense of humor—it was bringing Al Capp's cartoon to life. I found a way to do it and it's been copied ever since. Every single piece of costume was outlined in black. The buttons were outlined in black. Everything. It was all done with appliquéd tape. Karinska made that show. Everyone said she could

never do anything like that. I said, "Believe me, she'll do it beautifully," and she did.

The girls had to be very sexy, very busty, and the figures had to look cute, and she did all that to perfection. She had all the patches and details outlined in black and it paid off. The show was a major hit. It had an unusual style.

Did you also outline the shoes in black?
Depending on what they were. And they used my designs for the film. I did the film, but I didn't go to Hollywood. They bought the designs.

Were you pleased?
Yes. Except there was a big scene when the Dogpatch people go to Washington and disrupt an elegant diplomatic party. I had the Washington Society people very done up. They were all in grays, in contrast to the colorful, outrageous Dogpatchers, and looked beautiful, chic, and expensive. In the movie version they didn't use my high-society designs—they just bought dresses and it looked like it. Not the right way at all.

Some years ago you did *Wonder World* at the World's Fair.
That was quite an experience. Once again, that was with Michael Kidd. Leon Leonidoff was the producer; he was at Radio City Music Hall at the time. He was a dear, sweet man, but he was a little eccentric. He had the whole show designed before he hired Michael Kidd. Erté designed it in Paris. Then all the designs arrived. Michael said, "I can't use these. They can't dance in these. For instance, I'm doing a sports number and Erté's idea about a girl playing tennis was to put a headdress on her with tennis balls and rackets." And Michael wanted cute, active sport clothes, and he said, "We've got to get this show done, time is running out."

So they called me in and I looked at the designs. At the time, we laughed at them and thought they were a little old-fashioned. Today we look upon Erté designs as very special. There were stacks of sketches. I don't know what happened to them. Who knows where they are? Now they could be worth a fortune.

So I changed this and I changed that, and did new numbers and took this out and did all this sort of thing. And we got the show together. Then Mr. Leonidoff invited Erté over from Paris to see the dress rehearsal. And I said, "What have you done? These are not his costumes anymore. He's going to be very upset and unhappy." And Mr. Leonidoff said, "No, no." Well, Monsieur Erté arrived. He wasn't very tall; we made a great team! He was impeccably dressed and groomed, a perfect gentleman, and very French, so gentle and so polite, and he looked at everything. But there wasn't anything he could do—it was too late! I don't know what went on in his head. He didn't make the fuss I thought he was going to make. But I felt it was a terrible thing for him to experience.

The *Wonder World* was full of crazy things, some quite unbelievable: a water ballet with costumes full of electric lights; people arriving in elegant evening dress and sitting at tables in the water, half-submerged; a rocket-ship; a man flying in space; a water curtain that drenched the first audience; hundreds of dancers, swimmers, singers, clowns, and so forth, and scores of costumes.

When you work with actresses, do they have input on what they like and what they don't like?
Many actresses and actors—and directors—will have a preconceived idea of the look of the character, and if they are right and secure, their instincts can be a great value. When characters are well-defined in a script, the chances are you will be on the same wavelength. You can always tell at a fitting if rehearsals are going well by the attitude and mood of the actor. Even if nothing is said, it is always evident if there has been a rift of some sort, a favorite song or scene cut, or even something gone wrong in their personal life. An actress might have had an unfortunate costume catastrophe at the fitting of her last show and will arrive hostile, ready for battle. These are situations not handled on paper with paint and brush, but with tact, diplomacy, and plain common sense. One thing is certain: A good costume designer is just as much a star in his way as the actress is in

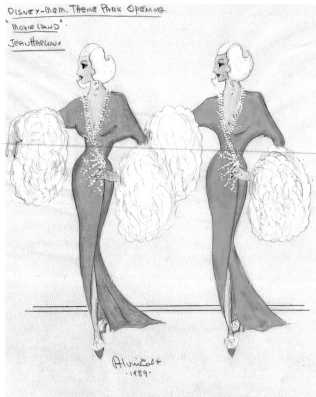

DISNEY-MGM THEME PARK
OPENING SPECIAL
*Costume designs by Alvin Colt, for
(left to right) 1920s Flappers; Jean Harlow
Dancers; Mae West character; Marie Antoinette
character*
NBC Television, Orlando, Florida (1989)

hers. Mutual respect is an unwritten the-atre law, and when this is followed, the end results will glow with satisfaction. A costume must aid an actor with his char-acterization. No costume, no matter how great, will remedy a miscast actor.

You did *Say, Darling,* with Vivian Blaine and David Wayne.
And Abe Burrows again, and Oliver Smith did the sets. I remember when we were in New Haven and Vivian came on for her first entrance and she looked so great. Abe Burrows said, "My God, Alvin, you saved me nine pages of dia-logue."

That's a big compliment.
Yes, it was. The character said that. That's why if it's in the script, it should be on their backs.

Tell me about *Greenwillow.*
Greenwillow was wonderful to do. That was with Tony Perkins. It had a beautiful score by Frank Loesser and it was won-derful to look at. I liked working with Joe Layton. I would say that was another of my favorite shows. It was very pretty and very inventive, with those people that lived in sort of a mythical village,

not at all like *Brigadoon.* I loved the show. Peter Larkin did fantastic sets.

You won a Tony Award for your cos-tume designs.
That was for *Pipe Dream* and *The Lark.* *The Lark* was quite a success. Playwright Lillian Hellman with Joe Anthony directing. And the cast was Julie Harris, Boris Karloff, and Christopher Plummer. Jo Mielziner's sets were outstanding. It was a very distinguished production, done in a selected realism style of the Joan of Arc era.

Do you prefer doing plays to ballets to musicals?
No, not at all. Each demands its own attention and its own way of thinking and its own style. I really haven't any choice. I love to do them all.

If you were offered theatre, television, or film, would you say you enjoy them all equally or would you stick to the-atre?
Well, film is another thing. Film is very time-consuming. And it's different from television. Television is produced with a much shorter schedule. I like doing tele-vision a lot, especially the very big spe-

DISNEY-MGM THEME PARK
MOVIELAND OPENING
MAE WEST

"DISNEY-MGM THEME PARK OPENING
MOVIELAND OPENING
MARIE ANTOINETTE

cials, like *Night of 100 Stars* and the Tony Awards shows. I haven't really done that many films. I know I would get used to it, if the property was interesting and the costumes were something I really wanted and loved to do. It's not easy—films are very difficult to do. They're hard.

For films, do you have to be on the set when they make changes?

You want to be there until your costumes are camera-okayed, and you can leave once they are established. Then you have to be sure the next day is ready. Schedule-wise, it's hard. There are times when they don't cast until the last minute. Like a film that was done in New York recently—they couldn't make up their minds between two actresses, different types and sizes, and decide who was going to play the part. So the designer provided wardrobe for both women, and had to have it on the set until the right woman was selected. That type of indecision would drive me crazy.

But that happens in films. It doesn't happen so much in television, because the scheduling is different. You get it done somehow and you also prepare. I did Liza Minnelli's triple play, a very

interesting project. There were three plays written by three different playwrights, with only one clue. It was called *Sam Found Out.* And each playwright wrote his version. Liza was in all three plays and in each one she was a different character. But we had scripts ahead of time, and could talk about it, and plan all of it at the same time. It wasn't piecemeal—we made it work. She knew exactly what she was going to look like. That was fine. And the same with the rest of the cast, which included Ryan O'Neal, Lou Gossett, Jr., and John Rubinstein. I liked that.

If you had to start all over again and prepare yourself for designing costumes for the theatre, would you change anything?

I don't think so. I was fortunate, having my three years at the Yale Drama School and my apprenticeship with the finest designers and painters. I've collaborated with some of the most important, successful, and distinguished fellow artists, on many major hits and some major flops. My work has been seen in every form of the entertainment industry and I always have kept learning by doing.

What do you like least about working in the theatre?

Least? The money. You never get enough! You're never paid enough for the amount of time and creative talent you bring to the production. Designers do a lot other than just designing. During meetings with the director and the producer, the designer will contribute ideas, with unlimited input, suggesting methods of interpretation, budget control, even casting, and no one ever knows this. It becomes a creative team, a collaboration. That's not in your contract. The job is not just turning out the required number of costumes or sets.

What do you like most about designing for the theatre?

It is an irreplaceable, rich, and rewarding experience. The success and joy of working with so many theatre artists, all creative people from vast and varied environments, all coming together to produce that every-night magic for an audience. A myriad of marvelous stories, anecdotes—some funny, many fascinating, a few sad, but all heartfelt—brings a life and career that lives in one's mind forever. In other words, the show never closes.

"Coppelia". Acto III

"Coppelia". Acto III

"Coppelia". Actos I, II y III

"Coppelia". y III

JOSÉ VARONA
Costume designs for Coppélia
Pennsylvania Ballet, Philadelphia (1978)

"The Nanny" - Rio de Janeiro

Rio

JOSÉ VARONA
Costume designs for (clockwise from top left) the Nanny, Infantry Soldier,
Mother Ginger, and Mother Commedia in The Nutcracker
Top left and right: Teatro Municipal, Rio de Janeiro (1985)
Bottom left: Miami City Ballet (1990)
Bottom right: San Francisco Ballet (1986)

A Conversation with
JANE GREENWOOD

I spoke with Jane Greenwood at her townhouse on Manhattan's Lower West Side. Greenwood, a native of Liverpool, England, was born in 1934. She studied first at the Liverpool Art School, then at the Central School of Arts and Crafts in England. Her first Broadway show was designing the costumes for *The Ballad of the Sad Café* in 1963, with Alan Schneider directing.

In addition to her Broadway work, Greenwood has designed costumes for a multitude of well-known companies: the Guthrie Theatre, the New York Shakespeare Festival, the Metropolitan Opera, the San Francisco Opera, the Houston Opera, the Robert Joffrey Ballet Company, the Alvin Ailey Dance Company, the Long Wharf Theatre, the McCarter Theatre Company, the American Shakespeare Festival, the Philadelphia Drama Guild, the Studio Arena Theatre, the American Repertory The-

atre, Playwrights Horizons, and Manhattan Theatre Company.

Among Greenwood's movies are *The Four Seasons, Arthur, Can't Stop the Music, Wetherby, 84 Charing Cross Road, Sweet Liberty*, and *Glengarry Glen Ross*. Her television projects include *The House Without a Christmas Tree* (and its sequels), *Kennedy* (a mini-series), *Heartbreak House*, the American Playhouse productions of *Shady Hill Kidnapping* and *Three Hotels*, and *Liberace*. She is on the faculty at the Yale School of Drama and has taught at Juilliard and Lester Polakov's Studio and Forum of Stage Design.

Greenwood won a Maharam Award for her costumes for *Tartuffe* at the Repertory Theatre at Lincoln Center and is an eight-time Tony nominee. She is married to scenic designer Ben Edwards. They have two daughters who are involved with costumes, Sarah in design and Kate in wardrobe.

ANDREA CHÉNIER
Costume designs by Jane Greenwood
Directed by Dino Yannopoulos
Metropolitan Opera, New York (1977)

How did you first become involved in designing for the theatre?

That's a complicated question, because there's not really one answer. I was in Liverpool at the beginning of the war in 1939. This was one of the first major cities in England to be heavily bombed. I was evacuated with my grandmother to Church Stretton in Shropshire. We had a running game, which I loved, that I named "Doll's Hospital." All the dolls had beds and were dressed in nightgowns and pajamas, and were tucked into their beds, and this went on endlessly. My grandmother used to make all the doll's clothes. Soon I became fascinated making them myself. That was perhaps the beginning.

When the war was over we went back to Liverpool. The theatre in England was very vital during this period, and many shows toured the provinces before they opened in London. My aunt Kate, who had returned from the Women's Air Force, took me on many theatre jaunts. I particularly remember *The Mask of Lomus*. It was danced by Margot Fonteyn and I thought it most beautiful.

After finishing school, I was unsure of what I wanted to be—an actress? A dancer? A painter? All considered unsuitable by my mother. I was finally allowed to continue studying at the Liverpool Art School, where I had classes in anatomy, plant drawing, life drawing, and dress design. Lucky for me, Arthur Ballard, a wonderful teacher, told me my work was too theatrical, and why didn't I apply to the Central School of Arts and Crafts in their theatre design program. I did, and they accepted me, and off I went to London.

Did you study dress design there?

Not dress design. In the three-year theatre program we studied period costume, the style and cut of clothes, and set and costume design. We were fortunate in having Jeanetta Cochrane running the department with Margaret Woodward, Pegarette Anthony, and Norah Waugh teaching. Norah wrote *Corsets and Crinolines* and *The Cut of Men's Clothes*. She also began *The Cut of Women's Clothes*, but she died before it was finished, and Margaret Woodward took on the task. Ironically, she was in a car crash before it was published, and Anthony Powell, who was also at the Central during the time I

OTHELLO
Costume design by Jane Greenwood,
for Raul Julia
Directed by Joe Dowling
Delacorte Theatre, Central Park,
New York (1991)

Among Jane Greenwood's costume credits are:

BROADWAY

A Streetcar Named Desire (1992)

I Hate Hamlet (1991)

Park You Car in Harvard Yard (1991)

Two Shakespearean Actors (1991)

The Circle (1989)

The Secret Rapture (1989)

Ah, Wilderness! (1988)

Long Day's Journey into Night (1988)

Lillian (1986)

The Iceman Cometh (1985)

Heartbreak House (1983)

Plenty (1983)

Medea (1982)

The Queen and the Rebels (1982)

Duet for One (1981)

The West Side Waltz (1981)

Romantic Comedy (1979)

The Kingfisher (1978)

Otherwise Engaged (1977)

A Touch of the Poet (1977)

California Suite (1976)

A Matter of Gravity (1976)

A Texas Trilogy (1976)

Who's Afraid of Virginia Woolf? (1976)

Same Time, Next Year (1975)

Cat on a Hot Tin Roof (1974)

A Moon for the Misbegotten (1973)

Finishing Touches (1973)

70, Girls, 70 (1971)

Hay Fever (1970)

Les Blancs (1970)

The Prime of Miss Jean Brodie (1968)

The Seven Descents of Myrtle (1968)

More Stately Mansions (1967)

Richard Burton's Hamlet (1964)

LINCOLN CENTER THEATRE

Oh, Hell (1989)

The Tenth Man (1989)

Our Town (1988)

OFF-BROADWAY

Absent Friends (1991)

Lips Together, Teeth Apart (1991)

The Lisbon Traviata (1989)

The Garden of Earthly Delights (1984)

Happy Days (1979)

The Umbrellas of Cherbourg (1979)

The House of Blue Leaves (1971)

LONG DAY'S JOURNEY INTO NIGHT
Costume design by Jane Greenwood, for Jason Robards
Directed by José Quintero
Neil Simon Theatre, New York (1988)

THE PRIME OF MISS JEAN BRODIE
Costume design by Jane Greenwood, for Zöe Caldwell
Directed by Michael Langham
Halen Hayes Theatre, New York (1968)

was, actually helped organize the publishing.

I was always sad that I did not return to England soon enough to be able to tell Norah just how important her books had become in the costume world in America. I think there is a copy in every costume shop, and this book was greatly responsible for the correct cutting of clothes, and for removing the bust darts from eighteenth-century bodices. Desmond Heeley taught a class in prop-making while I was at the Central. We loved his classes, and we would all go out afterwards and have spaghetti and red wine at a local Italian restaurant, and he told us stories of shows he was working on. *Prince of the Pagodas* was one he designed for Covent Garden. I am happy Anthony and Desmond are still good friends after all these years.

During my time at the Central

School I worked part-time in the evenings as many of the students did. One of my favorite people to work for was a milliner named Frank Winter. He made the headdresses for an elaborate production of *Aladdin on Ice*, designed by Loudon Sainthill. I sat in a corner and sewed 15 bells onto each headdress, 44 of them. When the skaters came onstage, the noise was deafening and the director told Loudon the bells had to go. I guess right then, that should have warned me about the theatre! After finishing at the Central School, I was offered a job running the wardrobe department at Oxford Playhouse. I was a "one-man band" at designing and making the costumes. It was tremendous training. I kept remembering Norah's words, "You can make a dress out of anything, even muslin, and if it is on the right silhouette, it will look wonderful." I notice time and time again

that it doesn't matter how much decoration is put on a garment—if it isn't the basic correct shape to start with, it never really looks right. Desmond Heeley came to design at Oxford and he introduced me to Tanya Moiseiwitsch.

Where did you go next?
To Stratford, Ontario, for two seasons. I worked as a draper in the costume shop and learned from Tanya, and a brilliant cutter named Ivan Alderman. He introduced me to Ray Diffen, who was to change the course of my life. Ray asked me to work in his costume shop in New York, and I started working as a draper. Some of the first costumes I worked on was for the opening season of the Guthrie, *The Miser*, with Hume Cronyn and Zoë Caldwell.

What was the first show you designed in New York?

The Importance of Being Earnest. Ray and I designed it together. It made me realize that I enjoyed designing and that I was missing it. Around that time I met Ben [Edwards]. This was on the night his house on Twentieth Street burned down! I had become friends with Ann Roth, who was also a good friend of Ben's. I called Ann and said, "Your friend's house is on fire," and she came rushing over. During the course of the evening, Ben arrived at my apartment. When the fire was over, after his first trip to the house, he presented me with an electric polisher for the floor, and a slab of bacon! We then went back to get the first-edition books and put them on my floor to dry.

When I came back from the Guthrie's first season, Ben was planning a production of *The Ballad of the Sad Café,* and he asked me if I would design the clothes. I was delighted! He encouraged me to take the union exam. I remember Robin Wagner was working with Ben at the time, and they were both very helpful in looking over my work.

So your first show was *The Ballad of the Sad Café,* with Ben designing the scenery and you designing the costumes?
Yes, *Ballad* with Ben was my first Broadway show. I can recall saying to him, "How on Earth am I going to design this play? I don't know anything about the South." He said, "Well, you'll look at the research." It's been an amazing education living with Ben, beginning right there when I was looking at the research.

You've collaborated on many shows with Ben.
Yes, we've done quite a lot together. After *Ballad,* we designed the Richard Burton *Hamlet,* which John Gielgud directed. He was an old friend of Ben's. He came to see *The Ballad of the Sad Café* and said, "Oh, I want you all to design the *Hamlet* I'm going to do with Richard Burton." And that included Jeannie Rosenthal for the lighting. Then we did *More Stately Mansions,* with José Quintero directing, and so on.

Do you find working with Ben on a show is different than working with other scenic designers?

Well, yes, in that we come home and talk about it more. There have been some very good collaborations: *The Iceman Cometh, A Moon for the Misbegotten, Medea,* the two Hepburn plays, *Finishing Touches, Texas Trilogy, Park Your Car in Harvard Yard,* and *A Streetcar Named Desire.*

RICHARD BURTON'S HAMLET
Costume design by Jane Greenwood
Directed by John Gielgud
Lunt-Fontanne Theatre, New York (1964)

Was it difficult raising a family while you both were working in the theatre?
Yes, it was very difficult. At the time I didn't realize it was so difficult. I used to wonder once in a while why I was so tired all the time! The good part was that we had this house and it became the base for all of us. We had housekeepers to take care of Kate and Sarah, and it seemed to work out very well, and either Ben would be going off and doing something or I would. We didn't seem to go away for a very long time together, so that the girls had security. But it was hectic. It's interesting, a lot of my students at Yale have said to me, "How did you manage to have a private life and a family?" It takes a lot of energy.

You've done several productions with David Hare. How did that come about?
I was asked to design a production of *Plenty* in Chicago at the Goodman. Gregory Mosher brought David here, and

we had a very pleasant afternoon talking about the production. It turned out I couldn't do it, and as it turned out neither could David. However, when David came to New York to direct the play at the Public Theatre, he asked me if I would design it. I did. That's when we became firm friends. Then after that I designed *Map of the World,* and I went to England and designed the movie of *Wetherby.*

Did he write and direct it?
Yes. Then I designed the clothes for *The Knife,* which he wrote. I went to the Guthrie to design costumes for *Pravda,* which Robert Falls directed, then *The Secret Rapture.*

Did you enjoy working in regional theatre as well as on Broadway?
Yes, you go to a complete theatre situation, not running to many different places, and there is usually a permanent staff. It's more of a family. In the commercial theatre, each production has a different set of requirements, but wherever the clothes are made, there's something about the nature of people who make clothes, which is fascinating. They are very skillful people indeed. The great thing is the collaboration between the artist putting something down on paper, and the people who turn it into the third dimension. But what we end up seeing onstage, or on film, or whatever, you know that the collaboration is incredibly important. If you don't have that, the design doesn't really come to life. You look at a brilliant artist like Picasso, and his costume sketches, the people who make the clothes pick up the sketches and run with them. I mean, a costume sketch has to excite the people who are going to make the clothes. Also, it has to excite the people who are going to wear them. They're going to bring the character to life, and you visually give them the blocks to start the race with.

How do you work? Do you make sketches for every costume when you do a show?
It all depends on the production. If I am designing a modern play, very often it's more expedient to give a collage of pictures from magazines, books, newspapers

Handwritten annotations on sketch:
43. ACT 2 · 1.
(WITHOUT SLEEVE
HANGINGS) ·
CORONET)

ADD -
SLEEVES ·
CORONET
CLOAK.

LEONORA
SHIRLEY

LA FAVORITA
*Costume design by Jane Greenwood,
for Shirley Verrett
Directed by Paul Emile-Deiber
San Francisco Opera (1973)*

give you about the character. But I remember what Boris Aronson said to me when we did the play *Incident at Vichy*. There was a row of men sitting on the stage waiting to be interrogated, and Boris said, "What are you putting them all in?" And I said, "I have these various sketches." And he said, "You need a collage, we need to see what those men are going to look like when they're sitting down, because the audience is going to look at them sitting down for a very long time." He was very insistent that we look at that row of colors together. And I did a little collage rather than individual drawings.

Who directed that production?
Harold Clurman.

What medium do you like to work in?
Mainly I use thin tracing paper and watercolor. It's not very durable, but I like it.

You've taught at the Yale School of Drama for many years. What do you find students want to know most about costume design?
What they're most interested in is doing it themselves. And they absorb what information you have to give them in varying size sponges. In their first year, they get a rigorous pounding by Ming Cho Lee and myself. They also are taught by Jennifer Tipton, Bill Warfel, Michael Yeargan, and Jess Goldstein. After the first year, they begin to design themselves for main stage productions, or "101" as we call it [in Room 101], which are with student writers and student directors. So they have a "hands-on" experience that goes on for the next two years. It's amazing to see the different approaches to design when they start designing for the main stage. In the third year, they design a production at the Rep.

Are they still involved as much in the concept on a production?
Oh, yes, I think that the concept and the discussion with the director and the writer, if the writer is there, are very important. And I think at Yale we do encourage an intellectual approach to design. I mean, we are not of the school

and say, "Something that has this feeling." And so often with modern plays, you are shopping. So to design something that you can't go and find is backtracking. It's a bit difficult for people to envision this perfect thing and then, if you don't find it, you've disappointed them somewhat. So I feel perhaps you don't always draw the modern version. But I think if you are designing something that's very stylized or in a very specific period, that you have to research and develop the costumes together with the information the author and director that says the designer should be seen and not heard. I think it's very important that designers contribute thoughts that they have about a production. And I do think that the relationship between directors and designers in some ways has changed since I first started.

Has it become a more collaborative effort?

I feel that it has. I think that probably had to do with the age and experience to a certain extent. And there are times when I do question why a director wants such and such a thing.

That's important, is it not?

It's very important, but when I was younger I was more reticent to ask this, and I feel that this is harder for young designers. But at Yale we encourage that. I think that it is wonderful to be nurtured in a relationship where you are constantly talking with directors and the writers, and the designers are all coming together. And so they go out after their three years at Yale and they have a peer group, and they can go off and work somewhere, and they grow, which is terrific.

How much emphasis do you put on pattern-making when you teach?

Students can take a course in pattern-making from Robin Hirsch, the assistant who runs the costume shop. She teaches a very good pattern-making course.

Do you attend all of your own fittings, or do you have assistants to help you?

No, I attend the fittings. That's when you have to be there and look. Very often the design process continues on during the fittings. Changes can be made to improve the costume for that particular actor playing that role. However, it is important for assistants to be part of the process, and very often it is another learning area for young designers.

Comment on how a young designer goes about dealing with designs in a costume shop for a Broadway show.

If you're doing a production now for Broadway, what usually happens is that you take the costume sketches for bids to the houses that you would like to make the clothes. Different shops do things differently, and they quite often become

THE CIRCLE
Costume design by Jane Greenwood
Directed by Brian Murray
Ambassador Theatre, New York (1989)

THE CIRCLE
Costume design by Jane Greenwood, for Glynis Johns
Directed by Brian Murray
Ambassador Theatre, New York (1989)

A CONVERSATION WITH JANE GREENWOOD 79

HINESE
NAITERS
AND
DRAGON
LEGS.

HOME AGAIN, HOME AGAIN
Costume designs by Jane Greenwood
Directed by Gene Saks
American Shakespeare Theatre, Stratford,
Connecticut (1979)

well known for certain kinds of clothes. You make that kind of selection because you become familiar and comfortable going to specific shops.

When you go with your set of sketches, the first thing the shops do is an estimate of what the costumes are going to cost. Next the shops call the producer and say, "Your show will cost such and such for the costumes." This estimate does not include wigs or shoes or jewelry. Then the producer will say, "This is so much money, can't you cut it down somehow? We don't have that much money." And you go back and ask, "Is there any way we can do this differently? Or what are we going to do?" And maybe they'll make some suggestions about doing things differently. But perhaps—hopefully—you've got enough money and you can have it all done the way you want to.

When it's settled where the clothes will be made, then they have the actors go into the shop to be measured. They very often take photographs of the actors and do both front and side views. It's very helpful to tailors to see how men stand so that they can see how a suit will drape on the body. I was quite impressed at Parsons-Meares when I was doing *I Hate Hamlet*. They took photographs of the fittings and the draper who was making the clothes could look at the fitting. One picture is worth a thousand words!

How many fittings do you feel are necessary?
I think you want one or two fittings to be comfortable. You'd probably want one with a muslin. And hopefully, if you do a good muslin fitting, then the next fitting in the fabric should be all that's required. But if you have something that is very complicated, you may have to have him—or her—back again, just to check one more time.

And hope that they haven't gained or lost weight.
Oh, yes. You know what actors always say when they start rehearsing: "And by the way, I'm going to lose five pounds or 10 pounds." Of course, if you had a nickel for every time an actor said that to you, you'd be very rich. It doesn't matter, you know—five pounds here or there doesn't really show onstage.

Do you find that it is the costume designer's role to encourage actors and actresses about how they look and how they wear a costume?
Yes, I do. But I think you also have to do that in collaboration with the choreographer or the director. I feel one always has to be tactful. I'll say to the director, "You know, it would be nice if she picked up her skirt with her upstage hand, rather than her downstage hand." They often say, "Oh, you tell her." It's also wonderful if the directors and actors and designer can all sit and discuss the concept of the designs together. That way, everyone knows what to aim for. I think everyone needs to be kind to each other, because this is a very difficult profession. People go onstage and put themselves in front of an audience or camera. And they need to feel as confident and as well supported as they can. If actors feel secure, then they will go out and give very confident performances; if they don't feel secure visually, they're not going to be as terrific.

Do you sometimes do research on how an actress should move in a costume or how to turn with a train? I mean even with your experience, do you ever feel on a production that you have to learn more?
Well, I think you are always learning more. That is the really great thing about this profession—you never stop learning, because everything you do is a new subject. And even when you go over old subjects, when you do Shakespeare once, when you do it twice, it's just as thrilling, because you see something new and you hear something new. You do another production, you do it another way. There are different people in it. And I just love that you always have this chance to learn. I say to students, "You know, you not only have to be an artist and a designer, but you have to be a historian. You have to be a really well-read person. You have to understand, you have to be a psychologist!"

What is the average cost of a period costume for man or woman?
You don't really put a price on it. Everything varies. A period costume depends on which period and where it is being made. The overheads for a New York shop, as compared to a regional theatre shop, are very different. You can spend an enormous amount of money, say, if you have an Elizabethan dress and you want to have a corset and a farthingale. And then you have the dress, and you have the ruff, and the ruffs around the sleeves, and the jewelry has to be made to go on the dress. It is astronomically expensive.

If you're doing a show in a regional production and it's a completely new production and you're building all the clothes there, do they give you a lump-sum budget, or do they give you an individual budget per costume?
They usually have a lump sum that is allocated for the clothes for that production. In most regional theatres they have a wardrobe supervisor or costume shop supervisor who actually is responsible for going over the sketches with the designer

and talking about the fabrics and the work required and whether the clothes have to be painted or appliquéd, or whatever various techniques are required for the clothes.

And in that way the costume manager really controls the budget, and may say to you, "Now look, we have these fabrics and you can pick something from these three." But you may have already brought a sample of something that you'd like, and you say, "I'd rather have this." Then they will say, "You know, that's really too expensive for our budget. Would you look at these and consider these other choices?" And you have to know where to say yes. Sometimes the fabric that you want is really very important for the look of the production, and it is better to economize in other areas and splurge on that. It all has to be balanced out—ultimately, you're responsible for the overall look.

I'm saying that to a certain extent you are responsible for the budget, because you can say, "No, I have to have that for the look, it's going to look like this." And in some instances, productions go over budget because of requirements, and the director will say, "Oh, no, we have to have that." And the designer will say, "We have to have that," and somehow, everybody goes back and scrambles around and finds a little bit more money.

In a regional theatre, when you are doing a period play, how much time do you like to have to make the costumes?
As much time as they have. If the production rehearses for six weeks, then you have six weeks to go ahead and handle the clothes. But if a very big production is being done, sometimes it can be started as much as six months ahead of time. That means the production will have to have been designed in advance. But I think that by and large, things happen in a period of six weeks to two months.

If you have designed the costumes for a long-running show and you have understudies, do you do separate clothes for understudies? Or does that happen after a show is declared a hit and runs?

After it's declared a hit. If a show is not going to run, we don't need any understudy costumes. I ran into Suzy Benzinger, and she was saying, "Now I have to start doing all the understudy clothes for *Miss Saigon*." Cameron Mackintosh has four understudies for every leading character. Suzy Benzinger co-designed the costumes for *Miss Saigon*. She came from Buffalo and worked with me as a young girl. I was very proud to see her name in the credits. So now she's dealing with all the understudies, and it's a big job—understudies are not always the same size. It helps if you have really good wardrobe supervisors, because sometimes they can duplicate a costume.

Do you make extras for stars in a show, in case one gets damaged, rather than fixing it during intermission?
Not so much for the theatre. When you are doing movies, you always have to have doubles and triples of things, in case, God forbid, something happens, because you can't keep 150 people on the sound stage waiting while you mend a frock. You've got to have backups. But that seems to exist more in the movies than it does in the theatre.

What about in opera?
At the Met, it's hard enough for them to get one frock finished in time if they have people flying in and singing a role that they're not expecting.

Are costumes made for everyone at the Met? They don't rent at the Met?
No. Well, you say they don't rent, but sometimes they'll rent a whole production from another opera house.

Like Houston, or Miami or San Francisco?
Yes. The opera world has realized that it is more economical for three opera houses to share an opera and to send it around than it is for each one to have its own production. And that is happening more and more.

Do you have a preference working in the theatre versus working in films or television?
Oh, I like them all. I think that when I go through a period of working in the theatre, I say, "Oh, wouldn't it be great to

CAN'T STOP THE MUSIC, THE FILM
Costume design by Jane Greenwood
Directed by Nancy Walker
Produced by Allan Carr (1980)

be working on a movie?" Because, you know, the minute the camera starts, that's it. You can't change the costume once the camera starts rolling! And then, when we're up at 5:00 every morning and having nervous convulsions about whether or not we have the right clothes for the day's shooting, I say, "Oh, wouldn't it be terrific to be doing something in the theatre." You know, if we didn't have the hemline correct for that night, we can say, "Oh, we'll get it right for tomorrow and it's not the end of the world." You know what I mean? The grass is always greener on the other side. But I like all the mediums.

Because each is different?
Each is different unto itself. But ultimately the designer has to fill the same

HAMLET
Costume design by Jane Greenwood
Directed by John Dexter
American Shakespeare Theatre, Stratford,
Connecticut (1969)

spaces. We have to give those characters that look, whether you're doing a film or an opera or a ballet. Ultimately you are creating that visual image for the audience to look at that tells you, in that heartbeat before they move or sing or dance or speak, just who that person is.

What would two or three of your favorite productions in the theatre be?
It's hard to say. I think we all find it difficult to pick one over another. I enjoyed *Our Town*, which we did at the Lyceum.

Who directed that production of *Our Town*?
Gregory Mosher. And it was a lovely experience. It's a wonderful play. Everything just seemed to come into focus and be right.

Did you do anything special that you enjoyed?
Less, simple. I'm beginning to feel less is better.

Do you have another production you especially liked?
I loved working on *The Prime of Miss Jean Brodie*. It was a long time ago [1968], and it was marvelous. I loved the relationship with Zoë Caldwell, and today we're still great friends. And we've done a lot of productions together, with Zoë as both an actress and a director, and it's a good collaboration. I enjoyed working with Tracey Ullman when she did *The Big Love* on Broadway. I was sorry her play was not well received—she's a very interesting actress, very special.

Martha Clarke, how much I admire her work, and how I loved our collaboration on *The Garden of Earthly Delights!* And perhaps best of all, darling José, José Quintero. I have worked with him so many times, starting with *Susannah and the Elders* for the Met's national company, and most recently the revival of *The Iceman Cometh*. I learned so much about O'Neill from José—what a gentleman he is, and what a superb director, and he has so much heart to give.

What do you like least about working in the theatre?
What I like least is designing modern shows, because everybody knows better than you do. That's coming from a very recent experience. And I go through waves of working on a play that requires modern clothes and I say to myself, "I'll never do this again." And I'm in one of those phases now. It's fascinating, you know, if you do a play based on the Middle Ages or the eighteenth century or the nineteenth century, people will collaborate with you. They talk about it, they'll look at it, and they will accept what is required of the character. But when it comes to a modern play, everybody thinks they know as much as you do, because everybody can pick up a magazine. Everybody can walk down the street and look in a shop window and say, "I saw it at so and so. They had it in the window. It was green."

But you don't want green, you want blue. They'll say, "But maybe they've got blue ones inside." There are endless stories I could tell about modern shows. And I find that they are difficult, because you're not always wanting to put something on an actress that she might think she looks perfectly wonderful in. You may be trying to do something a little different for the character.

This could be a whole dissertation on its own. And I would be very interested for you to ask other designers about this, because I think it is very difficult.

And the producer's wife has something at home that she would be perfect in.
The producer's wife, the writer's wife, the choreographer, the ushers. Try the ushers. I've been in a theatre doing a modern show and the director turned around and asked the usher what she thought!

What happens to clothes of well-known productions after the production closes?
Some of the important clothes go to the Museum of the City of New York. Productions are bought by costume houses. Eaves-Brooks has bought many costumes. Some productions are sent to universities and college theatres, and they take a tax deduction.

Sometimes, though, costumes don't look as wonderful when you see them close as they do when they're onstage, on the person. Sometimes it's just hard to look at them separated from the lighting and the scenery and the actor and the space and the moment. There is something so glorious about that moment that you can never quite recapture when you just see something on a dress stand in a museum or an exhibition.

Do you have the same assistants over a long period of time, or do you use different people on a show?

Well, I have had one assistant, David Charles, who has worked with me for 15 or 16 years. We are a bit like a terrible old married couple, you know, and we bicker and carry on. And people who don't know us very well think we are very strange, but we've been working together so long. I mean he's an associate, he's no longer an assistant.

Does he also help you with research and swatches?
Yes.

Then he knows the houses to go to for for fabrics?
Yes. And we'll start off together looking for things because sometimes if you go out and look at fabric in fabric shops you see things that put you on another track. I think you've always got to keep looking a little bit yourself. And if you find the right track, then you can send shoppers and people who swatch fabrics out again. But I think you've always got to keep your ear to the ground to see what's going on. There's always something new.

And I always feel when I go into a fabric store that it's like going into a candy store, and I get sort of a high from being so turned on by all these beautiful fabrics. I get very excited. And it's fascinating how when you're working on a particular production and you want only "muted tapestry-looking fabrics," you can go into a store with 10,000 pieces of fabric and find them. You know it's amazing how your antenna gets turned on to different things. You can go into a store and you can look around and your eye can find the three things you need out of a whole department.

If I wanted to start out to study costume design and go into legitimate theatre, what would I need for a background? What do I need to study?
I think you need to like looking at other people. You have to have a good sense of reading plays, and of stories. You have to have an imagination that you like to use. You need to look at pictures and art. You have to enjoy putting colors together. You have to enjoy looking, because that sense has to be highly developed. You have to have that mental filing cabinet, so that you look at things and store them

away. And 20 years later you go back and say, "Where is it? Where is it? Come out."

What do you like most about working in the theatre?
The collaboration with everybody and the charge it gives you when you see something onstage that you've had in your mind. And there it is. There is that moment when it's really very exciting. It's only a moment and then it goes away, and all the problems start again. But that moment is very exciting.

It's fascinating, because when you design a production and the clothes are made, and you can look at them in the costume shop, and you can put them on a dress form, and you can look at the spacing between the bows or you can look at the proportion of the beading or whatever, they're still *yours*. And then when the costumes go to the theatre,

they're there. And there's a very sad moment when you realize that you've done all you can do. And then you have to let somebody else take over. That's when the actors have to take them and make them theirs. And you go to the next project.

What would you like to be doing in the costume world 10 years from now? I would think you would still want to be teaching.
Another 10 years at Yale! My goodness. I've been there for 15—why not? They'll probably get tired of listening to me say, "Look at the silhouette." She keeps on saying that. She's been saying that for 15 years.

I don't know. I'd just like to be around designing, because I love it with a passion. It is my real joy of life. It supports you and it nurtures you, it gives you a reason to go on and to keep learning.

TARTUFFE
Costume designs by Jane Greenwood
Directed by Brian Bedford
Kennedy Center, Washington, D.C. (1982)

FRANCO COLAVECCHIA
Costume designs for Hansel and Gretel
Houston Opera (1977)

ROBERT O'HEARN
Costume designs for Sophia (left) and Octavian (right) in Der Rosenkavelier—*Act II*
Metropolitan Opera, New York (1969)

TANYA MOISEIWITSCH
Costume designs for Alfredo (left) and Flora (right)in La Traviata—*Act II*
Metropolitan Opera, New York (1980)
(Collection of Mr. and Mrs. William G. Blessing; photographs by D. James Dee)

FRANCO COLAVECCHIA
Costume designs for Hansel and Gretel
Houston Opera (1977)

A Conversation with
DESMOND HEELEY

Desmond Heeley resides on New York City's East Side. He was born in 1931 in Staffordshire, England, and was educated at the Ryland Art School near Birmingham. His first Broadway show was in 1967, designing the sets and costumes for *Rosencrantz and Guildenstern Are Dead*, by Tom Stoppard. Heeley has received two Tony awards, but his range extends well beyond Broadway—he has designed sets and costumes for opera, ballet, and classical theatrical productions around the world.

Heeley's first major commission was *Titus Andronicus* for Laurence Olivier and Vivien Leigh at Stratford-upon-Avon in 1955. Later, Sir Laurence invited him to design *Hamlet* as the opening production of the National Theatre. His long association with Michael Langham began at Canada's Stratford Festival Theatre, where he has designed numerous productions, including sets and costumes for *A Midsummer Night's Dream, The Country Wife, As You Like It, Arms and the Man, The Tempest, Coriolanus, The Misanthrope, Titus Andronicus, She Stoops to Conquer, The Duchess of Malfi, The Merchant of Venice, The Three Musketeers, Cosi Fan Tutte, Richard III, Henry IV, Henry V*, and *Much Ado About Nothing*. Among Heeley's set and/or costume designs for the Guthrie Theatre are *The Glass Menagerie, Arms and the Man, The Winter's Tale, The Matchmaker, Measure for Measure, King Lear, Cyrano de Bergerac, Oedipus the King*, and *Diary of a Scoundrel*, while his work for Stratford-upon-Avon has featured sets and/or costumes for *Romeo and Juliet, Much Ado About Nothing, The Merchant of Venice, Hamlet*, and *Toad of Toad Hall*.

THE MERCHANT OF VENICE
Costume designs by Desmond Heeley
Directed by Michael Langham
Stratford, Ontario (1989)

SWAN LAKE
Costume design by Desmond Heeley,
for Erik Bruhn
Choreographed by Erik Bruhn
National Ballet of Canada (1967)

Desmond Heeley's set and costume design credits include:

BROADWAY

The Circle (1989), S only

Camelot (1980)

Teibele and Her Demon (1979)

Rosencrantz and Guildenstern Are Dead (1967)

WEST END

Carving a Statue (1964), S only

Gentle Jack (1963), S only

Oh, Dad, Poor Dad (1961), C only

Farewell, Farewell Eugene (1959), C only

Titus Andronicus (1957), Co-designed

The Lark (1955), C only

METROPOLITAN OPERA

Manon Lescaut (1980)

Don Pasquale (1978)

Pelleas and Melisande (1972)

Norma (1970)

NEW YORK CITY OPERA

The Barber of Seville (1988)

South Pacific (1987)

Brigadoon (1986)

OTHER OPERA COMPANIES

English National Opera

Covent Garden

Glyndebourne Opera

Vienna State Opera

Royal Opera

BALLET COMPANIES

Houston Ballet

American Ballet Theatre

London Festival Ballet

National Ballet of Canada

Royal Ballet

Stuttgart Ballet

Sadler's Wells Ballet

Royal Swedish Ballet

English National Ballet

Deutsche Oper Berlin

Royal Winnipeg Ballet

Australian Ballet

NATIONAL THEATRE

The Way of the World (1967)

Hamlet (1963), C only

OLD VIC

The Double Dealer (1959)

Macbeth (1958)

Twelfth Night (1955)

How did you first become interested in designing costumes for the theatre?

I think it began in earnest when I discovered a book about Oliver Messel when I was 14 years old. I used to spend my Saturdays at a wonderful old-fashioned library in England. It was all Gothic cast iron and 1890s tiles. One filled out cards for the books you wanted, often guessing, and they would magically appear on solid wooden trolleys. You could spend as much time as you wanted. There were leather-topped tables and large colored-glass windows that opened onto a courtyard of apple trees in the spring. It was a good setting, don't you think, to discover one's hero?

The book on Messel, printed in 1933, contained pictures and drawings of two productions, *La Belle Helene*, called *Helen*, and *The Miracle*, a sort of mime play cum ballet with Diana Cooper as a nun, seen first as a statue and then as the living nun. Opposite the drawings was a photograph of the finished costume. Brave, don't you think? Then, wonder of wonders, there were photographs of the models, among which was the famous white bedroom with its swans and danc-ing figure and floating gauze. Let me tell you, it made a huge impression on this 14-year-old, an impression that has lasted some 40-odd years. The picture still thrills me.

There's a coda to this youthful discovery of mine: A while back I was designing *The Barber of Seville* for the New York City Opera. I had been to a meeting that was canceled just as I arrived that steaming July evening. Leaving the stage door in search of a cool drink, I passed the Ballet Shop, and like a bird dog, I spotted two Messel sketches in the shop window.

I gulped a little at the price and was told that they had a book on Messel. I said, "I know the one! Many thanks, but I have it," and hinted to the salesman that it contained more than a few mistakes. "No, this is an old one," he said. There was the book I had seen as a boy, a book that pointed me in a certain direction, and its cellophane cover with Oliver's sketch still intact was like new! It was like Christmas in July. I couldn't wait to get home with it!

I began keeping a scrapbook on Oliver from that day on. He seemed to be everywhere in print, from *Vogue* to *Picture Post*. I still have it and add to it whenever a scrap or clipping comes my way. David Reppa at the Met gave the best description of Messel's work. He said, "When the curtain goes up, it's as if someone had just arranged the most marvelous bowl of flowers."

What about schooling?

My schooling was, to quote Noël Coward, "to bring home the bacon," along with looking at reproductions of shows by Cecil Beaton, Tanya Moiseiwitsch, and the illustrations of Rex Whistler. And then later, I came across a magician named Lila de Nobili, a wonderful painter-designer who sadly has given up. The Motleys, Leslie Hurry—all of these people seemed to be able to produce a kind of magic and poetry on the stage. Believe me, I desperately wanted to be one of the brethren! After all this time, I do feel part of a way of life in this kind theatre.

You designed *Rosencrantz and Guildenstern Are Dead* in 1967. How did that come about?

Originally, the production was done at

THE BARBER OF SEVILLE
Costume designs by Desmond Heeley
Directed of Lotfi Mansouri
New York City Opera (1988)

the National in London, and then it came to Broadway and proved to be quite a success. The whole thing was like an adventure. It was my debut on Broadway, and to say that I was scared would be the understatement of all time. Of course, I didn't belong to the union and I had to have a covering designer. The scenery was fairly simple: a permanent set with rags for a surround and five pieces that flew in and out. Even so, I thought I would do 1-inch-to-the-foot drawings. I naïvely thought the larger the drawing, the more it would explain. Oh, the things we find out!

Ray Diffen was and is an old friend, and he and his shop built the costumes— and wonderfully, I might add. I think I was among the forefront of what are called "patchwork clothes." It all came about simply because Ray's shop was a treasure trove of fabrics. Nothing was thrown away. It was an Aladdin's cave of scraps, but for me it was a chance to use the scraps much as one might use paint.

On the setting end of things, it was somewhat alarming. Despite the huge drawings, everything was put together in a week and arrived in Washington, I swear, *damp*. So for the next four weeks there, I did my darndest to improve what we had. Each day I dragged ladders and my box of goodies and went to work. I was told I mustn't, but then no one stopped me. I was determined, and after

all, it was my debut, and with Ray and Tanya looking over my shoulder!

You mean because of the unions?
Yes. But by the time our stay was up, the stage crew and I had become good friends and I had all kinds of help from them, and they were pleasant to boot. The set looked closer to the model than when it had first arrived! We opened on Broadway and I received two Tony Awards, one for the set and one for the costumes. Looking back, that night was much more nerve-wracking than all the shenanigans it took to put the whole thing together. I must say it was a thrilling evening, even though I did speak when the orchestra was still playing, and also I walked off the wrong side. It was nerves, all nerves!

Did you get other work after that?
I did. I was asked to do *Norma* at the Met with Joan Sutherland, with a plea to use the revolve that had just been repaired. I never have been keen on revolves. *Norma* was different, and the whole world of the Met was fairly awe-inspiring. Thank heaven, it was a warm place to visit then.

The French director said that things should look like stone. Personally, I was much happier a few years later when we did sort of a spring cleaning on it and got rid of the revolve. It was much better, and the darling singers came right down as near to the audience as possible without knocking down the conductor.

When you start to work on both sets and costumes for a production, how does that go?

With costumes I sort of do a shopping list to get as much information as I can, so that time isn't wasted. The list goes like this: "Pericles wet, Pericles dry, where to put a pocket for the poison? Hamlet is black…" I take care of all the stuff folks need. And you're lucky if you know who is playing what. The jolly "C-word"— the *concept*—can and frequently does come later.

I do lots of research and then put it away. I try not to be tempted to use the Xerox in lieu of a sketch pad. If I can, I prefer to draw everything. For me, it's important that one's own signature should follow through on everything, props as well.

Getting the figure to stand away from the page is hard sometimes. On a good day I do have a knack for making the character move in my head, and that helps. Other than that, the mirror in the studio is used, you know, like a Disney animation, but it's such an instinctive thing.

As far as the whole picture goes, I make the characters to scale—half an inch to a foot—and I begin to sketch the set around them on a rough ground plan. All this is done in the model box, usually, with stiff paper and a pair of hair-cutting scissors and balsa cement— speed, you see. This way, I can't fool myself into thinking that I have acres of space to play with. One of the advantages of beginning this way is that I can start thinking about light from the start. I refine these rough models and the drafting comes last of all—ask any poor soul who has drafted for me!

Talk to me about working with Erik Bruhn on *Giselle*.

Working with Erik Bruhn on *Giselle* in Stockholm and Copenhagen was terrific. The first *Giselle* I did was in Stockholm. I'd seen the ballet, but I'd never designed it before, and I'd always wondered about the Wilis. They always seemed vacuous and characterless to me.

But Erik was very trusting. I found the Gautier story and learned that there were brides, and all of them died for love and were buried in unconsecrated ground! And that "the hems of their dresses were always damp." I thought this was wonderful.

I said to Erik in Stockholm, "Would you mind if we made the corps look like classical Miss Havishams—the dresses splashed down with yellow and gray, dying flowers, spangles, and the feel of mold—and for the opening of the ballet to have the veils from crown to hem to look like shattered cobwebs covered in dew? Erik, never one to waste words, said with the deep accent, "I like it; do it." His reaction was like a catapult for all of us to realize the idea. And then he added, "Those girls will wear wet white," an effect that has, sadly, left that particular ballet.

How did working in Stratford, Ontario, come about?

Michael Langham asked me to design *Hamlet* for the 1957 season in Stratford. When I arrived the theatre was under construction and [the designer] Tanya Moiseiwitsch was already there. It was a welcome of welcomes—there were no rules when I went there, and Tanya was my mentor throughout. Very gently and very quietly, she pointed out what we did and didn't do. In a very benign way, Tanya still looks over my shoulder. She has great faith in me. Tanya has an expression: "Will it serve?" And once you've managed that, then you can do it either expensively or cheaply. That first season changed my life. It is now 30 productions later.

When you do costumes at Stratford, do you like to make sketches and leave the work to them, or do you enjoy getting involved?

Oh, talk to some of the cutters and see what *they* say! In Stratford we have the luxury of having the costumes, props, wigs, shoes, and everything under one roof. I think all of this allows you to take your art a bit further. Incidentally, their footwear department rivals anything I have seen in Europe.

One of the most exciting things about

TITUS ANDRONICUS
Costume design by Desmond Heeley, for Vivien Leigh as Lavinia
Directed by Peter Brook
Stratford-upon-Avon, England (1955)

THE DUCHESS OF MALFI
Costume design by Desmond Heeley
Directed by Jean Gascon
Stratford, Ontario (1971)

AS YOU LIKE IT
Costume design by Desmond Heeley
Directed by John Hirsch
Stratford, Ontario (1983)

THE LILAC GARDEN
Costume design by Desmond Heeley
Choreographed by Antony Tudor
Royal Winnepeg Ballet (1990)

building clothes is seeing something appear in the round. When making a mock-up or muslin, or even when beginning to "sketch" on to the dressmaker's dummy itself—that's where working with a draper is extremely important. The "stranger" your costumes are—like for *Titus* or *Malfi,* say—the greater one relies on drapers and the dozens of craftspeople to help realize the picture.

You mentioned wigs and shoes. When you do costumes at Stratford, do you also like to get involved with these, and with makeup?
Absolutely. They are all part of the picture. It's up to one to make sure the wig department and millinery department come together at a fitting with a performer, knowing the needs of each other. This is when a mock-up of hair and headgear can save time and money, as

excessive as it seems. But best of all, working this way means that one doesn't have to solve technical problems on the performer, and by and by there are fewer feathers to be smoothed.

What about drawings for these?
I do drawings for all these: shoes, appliqués, decorations, the list could go on.

Do you like doing real clothes?
I'm not very good at doing real clothes. I greatly admire realism in movies and in some theatres, but it's the illusion of reality that intrigues me in the theatre; the heightening, the simplifying, enlarging, it's sculpture. It's engineering of a kind, I guess, and trying to conduct events to provide, when all is done, the atmosphere.

Do you ever construct an actual costume on a performer?

A little while back I designed *Phaedra* at Stratford with Patricia Conolly, an old friend, and we constructed the costume on her. It's always grand to design for Trish. She gives so much and the results have always been satisfying. As for Phaedra, there is movement to think about first of all—no set—and the height of the wig and headdress, and how to make the jewelry not upstage somehow. Then there is elusive painting and gilding by me on the several yards of very fine lisse that Trish used fantastically. Secretly, the doing and the fittings are what I love best!

Trish's appearance onstage was breathtaking. She was able to transform herself. She and the costume were one! It always makes me a little sad to see the costume on a hanger after the performance, and the veil as well, with very little of what some folks call "hanger appeal." But again, the magic happened with paint and light doing their job.

Lighting is another wildly important aspect. I like to leave a little leeway on a garment to see what else one can do after the likes of Duane Schuler and Michael Whitfield have completed their work—poets and artists, both of them.

Comment on how you went about using materials on *Love's Labour's Lost* at the Guthrie.

I do get a kick from using odd fabrics and things to achieve a feeling onstage. For *Love's Labour's Lost* at the Guthrie Theatre some years ago, dollars were in short supply, and the girls had to have three changes. This was where experience with the ballet—movement again—came in handy. The period was mid-eighteenth century. We did net petticoats. We used all sorts of white nylon organzas, gold and silver net, and florist's fake lace for the sleeve falls, stuff that's usually frowned upon. A few eyebrows were raised, as it did look a bit like a carnival when we started. But the shapes that Annette Garceau made were superb, and the bodices were beautifully cut. And we had lovely, tiny eighteenth-century wigs.

When the costumes were finished, I put all four on separate judys, and with pale blue and pale brown dye, I gently stained each one, so that all the harsh whites, silvers, and golds became softer. I used a little gold leaf and some good flowers. Next, some movement—thanks to Annette's cutting—and the air about them was different somehow. Four super actresses understood how to use them, the net skirts moved with them for fast movements, sitting, lolling, and when scrunched together. They had more than the illusion of the eighteenth century about them, and they were better than they would have been if we had spent a ransom at Scalamandre.

I'm not interested in "close to" costumes. I want to know how they move, the way they sit down. Costumes aren't

THE MERCHANT OF VENICE
Costume designs by Desmond Heeley
Directed by Michael Langham
Stratford, Ontario (1989)

meant to stand in one place. They should look wonderful standing still, but even more terrific when they are moving. The way they look from out front is what I'm really geared for. I'm using my scene-painter's eye when I'm designing clothes. So I always have half-closed eyes. And the cut, the shape, and the weight of the costumes are important. I love fittings.

Do you have muslins made at Stratford?

Yes. Sometimes, though, when drapers are so experienced, I feel it can be a waste of time. It depends on the fabric, if the fabric is, God forbid, $100 a yard. I think one can kill a costume with kindness too much love and too many tidges and pressings, and oddly enough it shows up onstage. I always think design is like cooking. You know, the better the ingredients, and the swifter you do it, the nicer it tastes. And if you love costumes to death, they will die on you.

When you hand in a set of designs at Stratford, what is the first thing that happens?

Say you've got 60 costumes in an average Shakespearean play. These are allocated to three or four different cutters and there is a discussion. Then it's a case of choosing fabrics. This can happen at different speeds. I always make separate drawings for wigs or any accessories that may be needed.

For a mask or jewelry?

Very much separate drawings. It begins to spread out, so the number of people you have to deal with gets larger and larger. It can be a bit exhausting sometimes, because I'm very much on a one-to-one basis. There are talks with the people who dye and paint, there are talks with hairdressers, and about jewelry, millinery, and shoes—it's endless!

You are known to use unusual materials. Tell me about some.

Well, masking tape of all kinds. Messel used to call it "God's blessing." The nice, thin, brown-paper one called Gum Strip is hard to find now. It is easy to cope with at the last minute when stuck in a hotel bedroom. And there's cooking foil, acetate, air-conditioner foam, Airex—oh,

lots of things! I am a good scrounger, though. I was once even called an Autolycus [from *The Winter's Tale*]— "the picker-up of unconsidered trifles."

I tend to think of fabrics in terms of paint and what stage light does to them. Velvets, in painting terms, are matte; harder surfaces, taffetas and silks, begin to reflect light. Damasks break up that surface. Going further, golds and silvers in some circumstances can give highlights. Also, varying transparent materials behave like glazes. Nets and organzas, those kinds of things, enhance dark on light—opposite colors, for instance.

But again, I tend to treat costumes like paintings. To me, fabric is like paint, whether it be glazes or organzas, or chiffon behaving like a watercolor. Each time I'm trying to do something that I haven't done before. I believe "fantasy" is a poor word—wow, it's been ironed out of all existence—but I do like the unusual, the odd, the strange, the slightly off-center things that you can do with clothes, especially period clothes.

How long would you have a costume in the shop at Stratford?

That's hard to tell. The shop handles as many as five or six productions at once with as many designers. Most crews, however, do love sewing on beautiful fabric for days. Jewels are fun, too. But grungy clothes don't come to life until they are onstage with an actor inside them. It is a little harder to bring forth.

Do they ever restrict your budget?

I don't *think* I've been restricted! On *The Merchant of Venice*, with Langham, just two or three years ago, we used a huge amount of stock. I don't mind doing that if it's suitable. It's very sensible. It only gets a little bizarre when the stock stuff has to be taken apart, refitted, and put back together again. Then you spend the money twice over on the labor. Sometimes the labor bill gives the moneybag people the odd heart attack.

Comment on doing drawings.

I do try very hard to draw and paint designs to look as much as possible like they will appear onstage. One always does tons of diagrams anyway, usually on the backs of the rendering.

We are talking here about doing sketches?

Yes. So many people have to read your intentions—producers, directors, drapers, propmakers, wigmakers—and they also can aid stage management.

Do you do overlay line drawings?

Not overlays, just more and more explaining on the sketches.

Are these just plain pencil and pen drawings?

Anything I can lay my hands on. Quite often they are one-to-one—depending if the clock is with me or against me.

Do you have a preference for designing classical productions, as opposed to interesting plays?

A challenge is always fun and definitely not a period piece. I did the set and costumes for the first production of Joe Orton's *Loot* in England. We still had the censor then. I guess one could say that comes under the heading of an interesting play—a dead body was heaved about the stage and eyeballs were rolling under sofas. Great fun!

Talk about Michael Langham and working as collaborators.

Before the war, Michael was going to be an attorney, and it shows—his mind sifts through plays and makes them lucid like no other director I know. He more than does his homework and works harder than anyone I know, and is always two jumps ahead. In the days of the Guthrie and at Stratford, and at Stratford in England too, he's very careful about the play and he goes to great lengths to make one understand it without gimmicks. The text is all. It is searched and it is gone over carefully.

I'll give an example of what he did as director on *Love's Labour's Lost*. In that play there are dozens of letters to and from various characters. It's a propmaker's nightmare. But Michael produced a paper for me as the designer, which was called "Postal Congestion in Navarre," where the play is set. In separate columns he told how each letter should look— small, tear-stained, large, folded many times, or what have you—the text of the letter, who it was from and to whom it was going, and a witty précis to boot. Also, it was grand for the actors, it got a sigh of relief from props, and a silent "thank you" from stage management. Oh, and it was a lovely souvenir to keep.

No one uses the thrust like Michael. He doesn't have to do Shakespeare Chinese or underwater to make the plays available to people. He's a hard taskmaster, and I do love him.

What would you say is the best feeling about designing costumes and sets?
The best feeling of all is when, God willing, they're successful, and when the actors and situations all work—one has no burden. Once they're on the stage, they don't belong to you any more. They belong to the performers. After they've been launched, it's goodbye and off to others.

Do you find actors like to ask you how their makeup and hair looks?
Yes. They're all different. It's a tricky area. Most actors know their own face. One hopes to help. With hair, I find actors and singers seem to have a fondness for red hair: "You know, darling, sort of auburn..."

What about designing for the thrust stage?
I've found that when I'm designing costumes and scenery for the thrust, I can't think of one without the other. In the thrust you can only give the audience the essentials. The whole joy of a thrust stage is to see with how little you can do it.

Again, it's like making a list of what you actually need. What the actors stand on is of supreme importance. Next comes the furniture and the props, and then things that are needed to tell the story. And if you take that as a sort of simplistic Bible, it's difficult to go wrong.

In the proscenium arch you're forever coping with masking and tons of stuff you don't see, and in some cases you may have to hide the lights, or maybe not. But I find I can do plays on the thrust more economically than in the proscenium. For plays, I prefer it to the proscenium, and sculpturally I think it is more exciting than staring at a picture in a box.

The Guthrie Theatre—Tanya's stage—can be the most thrilling space in the world to work on. And the pleasure of designing on it is that one has a chance of doing something for every seat in the house. Given a good director, I find one can say so much with so little. Ralph Funicello's *Dr. Faustus* some years ago at the Guthrie was a case in point. It was stunning.

You designed and constructed some small figures for the windows at Tiffany's in New York. How did that come about?
Through Gene Moore and Sam Kirkpatrick. "Carte blanche," they said, "do what you want." It was wonderful to sit down again and make things that didn't have to explain this or that and that didn't have to be scale. But how I wished they could have moved! It was all of the things I loved best, a mixture of painting, sculpture, and a collage of things that looked even more enticing, given the fact that they were behind glass and you couldn't touch them. Still a form of theatre, don't you think? With an audience peering in from the sidewalk. Also, in a funny way it was like making costumes to scale.

COPPÉLIA
Costume design by Desmond Heeley
Choreographed by Ben Stevenson
Houston Ballet (1991)

DON PASQUALE
Costume designs by Desmond Heeley
Directed by John Dexter
Metropolitan Opera, New York (1978)
(Collection of Mr. and Mrs. William G.
Blessing; photographs by D. James Dee)

Of your many productions, are there a couple you'd like to put in a time capsule?

I don't know about a time capsule—perhaps not a good idea unless we could pack in the performers, sound, light, music, and an audience. Sadly, it's all written on water, but then that's a good thing too, I think. Tony Guthrie's famous "On! On!" rings in my head often, about resting on what one has done. Memory lane is a dangerous path to wander down. If pressed, I guess I'd choose the ballet of *The Merry Widow*, first done in Melbourne with the incredible Bobby Helpmann, against all odds. What an adventure and, oh my, what rewards and excitement! Perhaps a little musical called *The Duenna* in Baltimore with Lance Mulcahy—a love affair with crew and company, one member of which was Mary Elizabeth Mastrantonio, who has a singing voice to take your breath away. It's hard. I've been lucky and I hate to play favorites.

You've worked with numerous directors. Who would be one of your most memorable directors?

Sir Lawrence [Olivier]. "Sir" is simply the most inspiring person I have ever met in the theatre, both in his personal loyalties and in his work—he dealt with you one-to-one. He, not a minion, would call and say, "We are doing so-and-so on such a date, are you free, and would you be interested?" For *Rosencrantz and Guildenstern*, for instance, I was in Canada at the time, when the golden voice of Olivier caused quite a stir at the switchboard. "Are you coming home for Christmas, dear boy? Perfect. We are in a little bind and would like to do this play. We have a very young director, dear boy, and I think we need one of those no-time/no-place ground plans you're so good at, dear boy! And we could perhaps use your lovely clothes from *Hamlet* [that opened the National Theatre]."

It was charm and passion, plus! Incredible! The whole thing was done in three weeks—models, designs, shopping—and we did Christmas, too. What I loved about the man was it was *he* who checked the ground plans and sight lines. "Half-hour changeover, dear boy? Don't think we can use your beautiful ground cloth!"

He seemed to be everywhere at once. His belief in people—the new director, myself, the costume shop—was great. He simply made every single person feel needed and cared for from start to finish. Oh, and so funny, too, but always with a whiff of the tiger about him. Do you wonder why we adored him?

At one time weren't the scenery and costumes executed in the theatre?
When I was young, I went to work at the Old Vic in London. The wardrobe was in the theatre where you rehearsed the plays, built the scenery, made the costumes and props, and opened. That was wonderful! Covent Garden used to be like that. The National Theatre used to be like that.

What do you hate most about the theatre?
Oh, negative people. People without humor. The word "concept." Bad manners—people who forget to say, "Thank you for a job well done." In the workroom, it's fluorescent light, no matter how bloody well it's been "color-corrected." It's like having to work with no eyelids.

When you did the costumes for *Giselle* in Berlin, would you attack them design-wise and material-wise, as you would anywhere else?
Oh, surely. But it's a different company and a different country. Different things might be available, or *un*available. Or, as was the case when doing that *Giselle,* I think it's just good manners to feel out their way of working first. It's interesting and it sure keeps you on your toes.

What do you like most about working in the theatre?
The first few hours when you begin to have a vision and everything seems possible, the pursuit of that vision, achieving it, and hopefully sharing it with the whole army of people who work with you to realize the picture, be it a play, an opera, or a ballet. The doing is all! And if a project goes really well, the satisfaction is for *all* concerned. Perhaps it's attempting new ways of doing things—the magic words, "What if…?"—and certainly working with friends. That's a grand part, or at least for me it is.

Part of me is astonished that here's a more-than-middle-aged man earning his keep by dressing grown people as mice, toy soldiers, and Spanish dolls—and girls as flowers—making pictures seem more nostalgic than they were when I began to design. I am still amazed that people pay you to do something that you enjoy doing.

In Houston, at the end of one of our *Nutcracker* performances, the Sugar Plum Fairy, a couple of toy soldiers, and some mice came onstage to meet a bunch of young people who had just seen the ballet. The Sugar Plum Fairy stayed in character as she spoke, en pointe. The boys, especially the small ones, were intrigued by the toy soldiers, who moved in spasms, and the mice, the whole thing. It gave an ache at the back of my throat to see such wonder on their faces. Now that does sound a little sentimental, I know, but it was *your* question about working in the theatre!

Now *Hedda Gabler* I might have to save for another day. I am not sure where a wonderful hobby starts and work ends. I can't believe my luck so far. So I eat my Wheaties and pray for everlasting energy!

MOTLEY
Costume designs for South Pacific
Majestic Theatre, New York (1949)
(Collection of Peter Harvey; photograph by Linda Alaniz)

CHARLES E. MCCARRY
Costume design for Dick Johnson in The Girl of the Golden West
Yale Drama School (1986)

ANDREW B. MARLAY
Costume design for Koko as the Lord High Executioner in The Mikado
Opera Theatre of St. Louis (1984)

MARTIN PAKLEDINAZ
Costume design for Penelope in The Cocoanuts
Arena Stage, Washington, D.C. (1988)

PETER HARVEY
Costume design for Firebird 2006
Colorado Ballet, Denver (1981)

ALLEN CHARLES KLEIN
Costume design for Calaf in Turandot
Miami, Dallas, Houston, and San Francisco Operas (1980)

PATTON CAMPBELL
Costume design for Mr. Page in The Merry Wives of Windsor
Southern Methodist University Opera Theatre, Dallas (1986)

JOHN LEE BEATTY
Costume design for Celia in As You Like It
Actors Theatre of Louisville, Louisville, Kentucky (1990)

A Conversation with
ANN HOULD-WARD

Ann Hould-Ward lives in Manhattan's Washington Heights. A native of Montana, she was educated at Mills College, the University of Virginia, and the Art Students League. Her first Broadway show was the Stephen Sondheim and James Lapine production of *Sunday in the Park with George* in 1984.

Hould-Ward has designed costumes for a wide range of productions at the Arena Stage, the Goodspeed Opera House, the Guthrie Theatre, La Jolla Playhouse, Playwrights Horizons, the New York Shakespeare Festival, the Manhattan Theatre Club, the Acting Company, the Denver Theatre Center, the Folger Theatre, the Pennsylvania Stage, the Santa Fe Opera, the Hartford Stage, the Seattle Repertory Theatre, and the Stratford Festival. During her career she has collaborated with directors

Michael Langham, Garland Wright, Vivian Matalon, Lou Galterio, Gerald Gutierrez, Michael Kahn, Zelda Fichandler, Martin Charnin, Paul Lazarus, Joe Layton, Gary Pearle, Julianne Boyd, Edward Stone, Dan Sullivan, Doug Wager, James Lapine, and JoAnne Akalaitis, and with choreographers Graciela Daniele and Lar Lubovitch. Her television and video credits include *Into the Woods* (for Public Television's "Great Performances" series), *Sunday in the Park with George* (for "Great Performances" and Lorimar Home Video), and *Hyde in Hollywood* (for "American Playhouse").

Hould-Ward has received the Maharam Award, the Los Angeles Drama Critics Circle Award, and the Denver Critics Circle Award, and has been nominated for the Tony, Drama Desk, Outer Critics Circle, and Helen Hayes awards.

INTO THE WOODS
*Costume designs by Ann Hould-Ward, for the Steward
(above) and Bernadette Peters as the Witch (right)
Directed by James Lapine
Martin Beck Theatre, New York (1987)*

How did you first become interested in designing costumes for the theatre?

When I was in undergraduate school I went to Mills College, in Oakland, California. I had wanted to be an actress, but I was a terrible actress, or so they thought. The department there was really against my continuing. I was 19 years old and married, and they felt that was a sign that I wasn't dedicated enough. However, at Mills I had to take a costume design class. I had a wonderful teacher, Rhoda-Gale Pollack. At the end of the first semester she took me aside and said, "You know, I think you have a talent in this, and maybe you should think about pursuing it." And that's how it began.

I was born and raised in rural Montana, and I had sewn clothing since I was a little girl in 4-H. I had always drawn—I would lay in bed at night and sketch things that I'd like to make. I used to create my own paper dolls, and I would not only design their clothes, but I'd make the shape of the doll, and I always say I'm still just making bigger paper dolls. I remember that even as a kid some of the things that fascinated me most in drawing were tactile things. I loved to put layers of construction paper together, and I still like to do that. I like to gob stuff onto things. By the time I was five or six I was doing that in my artwork, and I was trying to make it have more dimension than everybody else's in the class.

You started as an actress in college and then you went into costume design. Did you take a lot of design courses where you were?

Yes, at Mills I studied with Rhoda-Gale Pollack for a year, and then Richard Battle came in and taught costume design for my last two years. I also had a work-study program in the costume shop, so I was working, building the clothes for the shows there, and studying design. They were reasonably bright about knowing what courses I needed and I had a lot of art history and art studio classes at Mills. I think that was very important.

What happened after you were at Mills?

The year after I graduated from college, my son was born and we moved to Richland, Washington. My husband went to work there and I got involved with the junior college and designed the sets, lights, and costumes for all their productions for about a year. It was really the only theatre around. But they had a wonderful small thrust stage.

That was a terrific experience, wasn't it?

It was very good, and it was a point in

Among Ann Hould-Ward's costume design credits are the following:

BROADWAY

Falsettos (1992)

Into the Woods (1987)

Harrigan 'n Hart (1985)

Sunday in the Park with George (1984)

GUTHRIE THEATRE

Henry IV, Parts 1 and 2 (1990)

Henry V (1990)

Richard II (1990)

The Glass Menagerie (1988)

Hamlet (1988)

Richard III (1988)

Summer Vacation Madness (1982)

DENVER THEATRE CENTER

The Cherry Orchard (1986)

Don Juan (1985)

ARENA STAGE

Merrily We Roll Along (1990)

The Philadelphia Story (1986)

The Three Sisters (1984)

The Imaginary Invalid (1983)

FOLGER THEATRE

Othello (1986)

Romeo and Juliet (1986)

King Lear (1985)

PENNSYLVANIA STAGE

Just So (1985)

I Do, I Do (1984)

SEATTLE REPERTORY THEATRE

The Cherry Orchard (1990)

Truffles in the Soup (1989)

Tartuffe (1988)

GOODSPEED OPERA

Fiorello (1986)

The Jokers (1986)

OFF-BROADWAY

Hyde in Hollywood (1990)

1, 2, 3, 4, 5 (1990)

Cymbeline (1989)

Emily (1988)

On the Verge (1988)

Romeo and Juliet (1988)

Little Footsteps (1987)

Personals (1987)

Miami (1986)

DANCE COMPANIES

Ballet Hispanico

Pacific Northwest Ballet

NUEVO MUNDO
Costume designs by Ann Hould-Ward
Choreographed by Graciela Daniele
Ballet Hispanico, New York (1991)

time when I recognized somewhere inside my soul how exciting this was to do. And I continued to find a way to do it, even in a place where it was not easy.

You had planned to pursue this, with your family coming first?
I don't know. No, I don't think I was smart enough to actually figure that out. I remember from the time I was small that I had long-range goals. When I was 12 years old I sent for my first catalog from Mills, knowing that was where I wanted to go college, and I did. I always was a person who set these goals of what I wanted to do. I guess I thought everybody did that. I wanted to have a child, but I also knew that I wanted to continue to pursue a career.

Then we moved to Charlottesville, Virginia. My husband taught nuclear engineering at the University of Virginia, and for a year I worked in a studio situation that they had there. A number of artists had taken over an old school and had studio space. I was very interested in silk-screening on fabric and different textural ways of using fibers and stuff. After that year I went on and applied to graduate school at the University of Virginia and did my graduate work in theatre.

How long did that take?
It was a three-year program, but I did it in a year and a half. I studied with Lois Garren, and she was very instrumental in getting me to recognize how important it is to have a sense of humor in the theatre. Lois was dedicated to her students and what we did. She was very influential in my life in the sense that she spent many summers coming to New York and working at Betty Williams, working in the small shops, so that she brought that knowledge back to us as graduate students. It's very essential to have somebody who knows people who are actually doing this professionally. She was a tremendous influence on me—not just about the career of a designer, but the life of a designer.

What happened to you next?
My husband was asked by the French government to go to France. We went there and I was totally despondent. I

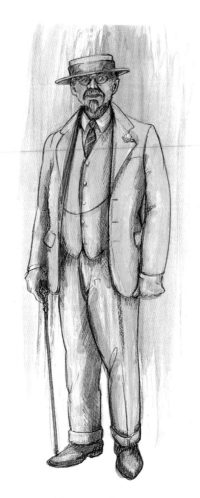

TIMON OF ATHENS
Costume design by Ann Hould-Ward
Directed by Michael Langham
Stratford Festival, Stratford, Canada (1991)

really wanted to come to New York and work in the theatre, because I'd had all this training to do that. I didn't like France and I couldn't figure out what to do with myself. I did not speak French, and so after a while I came back and brought my son; my husband stayed in France.

I had earlier written a number of letters to noted designers like Theoni Aldredge and Tony Walton and Pat Zipprodt. I said that I would really love to work with them. I'm sure they still get millions of letters to this day. And Pat was kind enough to have answered my letter. She wrote a lovely note saying, "Gee, I don't need anybody, thanks a lot, but maybe someday we'll meet." So when I came back to Montana from France, in 1977 or '78, since she had

written that letter, I tried to call her and ask if I could come and work with her. She had a message on her machine saying she was at the Colonial Theatre in Boston with a show, *King of Hearts.* I tried to call the theatre to get her and I made about 40 phone calls. They finally did get me through to Pat. I said, "Could I possibly come and work for you?" And she said, "Well, I really don't need anybody right now. Wait until I get home and see how things are." She was very nice about it. Then she asked, "Where are you?" I told her I was in Montana, and she said, "Oh my God, what are you doing in Montana?" So we had a conversation about where I was. Later, I went to Conrad, this little town in Montana where my folks are from, and I bought this big cowboy hat. I took a piece of rawhide and wrote this letter: "Dear Pat, please let me come. I really want to come to New York." And I shoved a big arrow through the hat and sent it in a big box to Pat. It was such a wild story. And it was so long ago, too.

Pat was delayed in Boston because the show was in trouble. She came back to New York, where the box with the hat had been sitting at the post office, and the day before the box was suppose to be sent back she actually picked it up. One more day and it would have just been sent back to Montana. Then she wrote me a six-page letter that I still have somewhere. It started out: "Dear Ann, alright, alright, you win, you can come." She was going to do something at the Met. I can't remember what it was. *Manon Lescaut,* I think.

So you finally came to New York?
Yes. Then I got here and we started to work on it and it turned out that this whole thing fell apart. So she had nothing she could do with me. But in the process I had never told her that I had a husband or a child, because I was afraid she wouldn't let me come. And over the period of months that I was with her, she found out these things. She said, "My God, you have this child. How could you do this?" I did it because that was the only way I could do it. I needed to do it. And so then when the thing at the Met didn't happen, she called her friend

Ben Benson, the head of Karinska's shop for City Ballet. And he happened to be looking for an assistant, because he had Rouben Ter-Arutunian in there to design *Dido and Aeneas* and *Le Bourgeois Gentil-homme*. And I came and started to work as Ben's assistant and was there for a year and a half. That was really my first job here, at City Ballet.

Did you then assist Patricia Zipprodt for some length of time?
After I went to work for Ben, I came back and I did assist Pat for at least two years. During that time I really began to realize that I had to go out and get some design credits, or else I was just going to continue being an assistant forever. And of course I was 28 or 29 when I arrived here, instead of your typical 23-year-old.

Where did you go to get design credits?
I took a year and did off-off-off-off-off-Broadway. I did not earn any money for a year. I went to all these little theatres in the Bowery, at the Apple Corps. I did tons of these tiny little theatres.

You just called up and got the job?
Yes. I started taking a portfolio around. It really had nothing in it that had ever been constructed since graduate school. And I started to work at these little companies and pull stuff from the Costume Collection and put things together that way.

And then, somehow at the end of that, I had met and gotten to know Garland Wright, the director. And Garland called me to do a show. Santo Loquasto was supposed to design a big show for Garland at the Guthrie—the phone rang one night and it turned out that Santo had bowed out of doing the show, and I was asked to do it. So I had three weeks to do *The Goldoni Trilogy*, which is a huge play, three plays together. It was like 190 costumes or something. And so that was the first major show I got to do. I think a lot of people build up through those regional theatres, the small regional theatres, and then a this and then a that, whereas my first regional credit was the Guthrie.

And I was young enough and excited enough that I didn't sleep. I designed it

DON JUAN
Costume design by Ann Hould-Ward
Directed by Garland Wright
Denver Theatre Center (1985)

in three weeks with no sleep. I just stayed awake. I had been out there as an assistant before and I was very wonderfully received. The people at the Guthrie were really my family.

You made sketches for all those 190 costumes?
Oh, I did. I have them.

Did you have any idea about whether or not you would succeed?
I'm not one of those people who knows how to be cautious. I'm not a person who knows how to contain and to look at it. So I was given this opportunity and I just did it.

Was that a nice collaboration with Garland Wright?
Yes, it was wonderful. I collaborated with him for many years.

How long were you at the Guthrie?
For that show I believe it was almost three months. It was a big show. I needed that.

What about the period of time until the next job comes about?
You know, sometimes when I'm lecturing to kids I say that you get "X" opportunity and you can figure that it's going to be a full year until you get another opportunity like that. So I always think that it's probably going to be a full year before you get a paying Off-Broadway show again. And when you get that first regional credit, it's going to be a full year until you get something else because of establishment. No one ever explained to me that it wasn't like an average working situation. No one ever explained to me that with freelance artists it is the choice of a life, not the choice of a career.

POSTHUMUS 1-1

CORDUROY JACKET - THIS WHOLE OUTFIT SHOULD LOOK NOT BRAND NEW - HE IS "POOR BUT HONEST"

CLOTEN WILL ALSO NEED A COPY OF THIS COSTUME TO WEAR FROM CHANGE IN 3-5.

Did you came back to New York after working out there?

Yes. I lived in Connecticut then, so I started sending out résumés. And surprise-surprise, no one paid any attention for a year. Then, six months later, Garland called and asked if I would do another show with him. We did *The Imaginary Invalid* at Arena Stage and it was well received. The next year Zelda Fichandler asked me to do *The Three Sisters* with her.

How did you get the show *Into the Woods?*

Basically it was a show from relationships with James Lapine and Stephen Sondheim from *Sunday in the Park with George.* Pat Zipprodt really brought me into *Sunday.* She called and said, "I have this new script, maybe we could do it together." And she was extremely gracious. She is my guiding light. I think she is so brilliant and is such an amazing artist.

So that's how you came to work originally on *Sunday in the Park with George?*

Yes. She suggested that we co-design, because basically I think they wanted to workshop it at Playwrights Horizons— she recognized she needed a collaborator to make that happen at a small theatre and was generous enough to let it be me.

How would you describe the costumes for *Into the Woods?*

It would be easier for me to describe it to someone who's blind. I would describe it as the feeling of a pussy willow, or the feeling of velvet. It was something that was so rich and wonderful to touch, and that's how I like to think of it to the eye. That's where I wanted it to journey for people's eyes. I feel that my eyes get this great joy out of seeing things that are like

the feeling of touch to me. Those fairy tales are rich to us—they are our inner structures from when we were very small, and they do contain that magic richness.

You have worked in dance. What has been one of your favorite productions?

Well, dance is my favorite. I shouldn't say that, I guess. I've been very fortunate in that I've done a lot of work with my friend Lar Lubovitch and with his company of dancers.

How did that come about?

Through *Into the Woods.* Lar was the choreographer for that show, and I remember one night during the heat of dress rehearsals I said to him, "I'd really like to design some dance things." He had never had a designer before. He had always kind of just put it together himself, or he had a designer who worked within his company. And so later on he

called me up and he said, "I'm doing a piece—would you design it?" To me, dance is so incredible and powerful, with strong strokes, and that's how I like to draw. I always say Lar dances like I like to draw. And that's exciting to me, to be able to develop that with another artist, with a choreographer and dancers. I can't do that with my body, but I can do it with my pencil. And I love the fact that they can really take it then soar with it. To design clothing for someone who sings beautifully is also wonderful, but I guess dance is special to me in that way. I've also done a lot of work with Graciela Daniele, who is another very powerful, strong choreographer. It is such an honor to be able to put clothing on their work.

When did you first become involved with Graciela Daniele?

A few years ago I wrote Graciela a letter

IMOGEN 1-3

and said that I really loved her work and would she look at my designs. She did, and we collaborated on a piece for Ballet Hispanico. We've done a number of dance pieces together, and I'm working on a new musical of *Captains Courageous* with her, which she is directing and choreographing.

What do you like least about working in the theatre?

I wish that I had time to develop more as a thinking artist. Unfortunately, because of our economy and because of the state the theatre has been in, designers must take so much work that it is hard to continue to develop yourself artistically and emotionally as a thinking designer. When we talk about people like Miles White, he is a thinking designer, with his head and his heart. I would love to have the time to do that. It would be great to have the

time to take part of my life and devote it to other kinds of painting and work.

Do you enjoy doing quite a bit of research on a production?

I'm a total, complete fiend about research. I think it is the result of being educated by two very good institutions. And I find that in assistants who've had very good educations. They know how to research well because they know how to research for a paper, and it's no different for a show. Good, thorough pictorial research, I guess to me that's the best. If you ask me what's the best thing about what I do, it's the treat for my eyes to do that, to see it onstage, and let my eyes have it, and then just the opportunity to learn about all the different kinds of people. I have been so fabulously blessed to experience and learn about the different things from the shows that I've done.

On this project with Graciela, for instance, I'm learning about New England fishermen. Many people have jobs where they push pencils all day and they don't learn; but at every turn someone is asking me and paying me to find out something new, and that's fantastic! The greatest thing is the continuing education of the freelance artist.

Was the kind of success you've had so far in the theatre what you imagined and wanted it to be?

I always wanted to be a success. And it was terrifying to come to New York and realize that that was not going to be easy. I guess I always had said to myself that it was important to me to be good, but now it's very important to me to do good work. That takes a certain amount of achievement to be able to do. In other words, you spend so many years trying to kind of claw your way up so that then you can finally say, "Wait a minute. I want to do good work. I want to accept it myself and say that was good work." I try to do that. I try to bring from my heart what I feel is good work. That's also a very Western ethic. I'm a very Western girl.

When you make sketches, do you lots of thumbnails? Do you hit it the first time? How do you work?

When I sit at the drawing table, I'm really doing the sketches that are going to be the actual sketches. Now usually what happens is that I start a sketch, and I sometimes do a thumbnail version of it. Then I go back to the director and see how that seems to be operating for him. I do this differently depending on who that person is. When I talk about wishing I had more time as an artist to be painting and drawing, I say that because that is a very free world where I do my own work. In theatre, or particularly in dance, I am part of a collaboration that is based in someone else's mind. And I must be able to make these hands work for that person's mind, not just for my mind. When I work with Lar, we often draw together. I come with little bodies drawn and we start doodling and I bring my paints, and we paint together. And he is across the table and he says, "Annie, maybe if the legs had gold stuff running up them." And then we do legs with gold stuff.

Whatever you put on the body of a human being who is going to come out on the stage and communicate orally, you will be able to forgive what's on his body once he starts to move his mouth. An actor can verbally get over clothes that are not communicating what they need to communicate. It doesn't make his job any easier, but he can do it. On the other hand, I feel that it is very important how you help the dancer to present himself, because he doesn't have the words to help him overcome a bad costume.

Do you find your collaborations with directors vary?
Every director is different. I often equate the relationships with marriages: Every marriage is different. What Vivian Matalon needs from me is totally different from James Lapine or Michael Langham or JoAnne Akalaitis. They all need support, they all need support with their vision. But with each director I must begin to find a way to operate that allows my hand to be a part of what is inside their brain.

Is there any kind of preparation that you feel you didn't get before you started out as a costume designer?
Yes. I went to a very tiny school in rural Montana. I graduated with a class of 15 from a high school of 69 students, and I never had any formal art training until I went to college. And I find that very sad. I wish I had the chance to be drawing and painting with a teacher before I got that opportunity—someone helping me to look at the world. I think that would have been very helpful. But there are a lot of small schools and kids in small places where the arts are just sorely overlooked because there is not money or effort to pursue it.

DON GIOVANNI
Costume designs by Ann Hould-Ward
Directed by Lou Galterio
Santa Fe Opera (1992)

Comment on collaborating with JoAnne Akalaitis on *Cymbeline* at the Public Theatre.

We did incredibly detailed research on *Cymbeline*. I believe we took almost six months to research it, and for a production at the Public Theatre, that is a long time. She had certain things in mind. She was interested in setting it in a Victorian situation, in tartan plaid, in India and paisleys. Basically, we did a lot of going around to museums together and we visited exhibits. I did reams of research for her and we began to put together the world of what this was.

How did you come to set it in the Victorian period?

JoAnne really felt that there were emotional ties to Victorian novels. She could find that place for Cymbeline to be, in kind of macabre Victorian novels, which I think is a justifiable idea. So that's the world we began to work from.

I tend to bring a great amount of research to directors, no matter who they are, because I feel that that is part of allowing them to seek themselves in the period. And I pretty much have developed a method with all these research boards that I carry everywhere.

What do you mean by "research boards"?

We take a piece of foam core board and we cover it from top to bottom with pieces of research. I sometimes call it the "Sears Catalog Method of Design," because directors can just kind of look at it and say, "I like that, I don't like that."

You're talking about an average size of about 30 inches by 3 feet?

Yes. Sometimes they're smaller. And with every show it varies with how you are going to work with the boards. Here is one for a musical about Hoagy Carmichael that I've been working on for about two years.

Where did you do the research?

This research was done for *Hoagy and Bix*. We went to Indiana University, where Hoagy went to school. We scoured research sources that were around there. There are a number of jazz libraries, historical collections of jazz memorabilia,

RICHARD III
*Costume design by Ann Hould-Ward,
for Catesby
Directed by Garland Wright
Guthrie Theatre, Minneapolis (1988)*

that kind of thing. I have a number of assistants who are really good at research. I tend to attract them, because they know if they work for me they're going to have to do an awful lot of it.

When did you learn this method of mounting on the board?

I started it and now everyone copies it. Years ago, when I assisted Pat, she used to do something like this on bought shows. She collages things together with little sketches.

What do you mean by "bought shows"?

Bought shows are where you're going to buy the clothes instead of making them.

Then I kind of began to take it a few steps further. I can walk into a room and very easily surround the director with a show. And some of the directors that I work with do not have real high concentration levels, and some of them have a lot of other things on their mind. To be able to walk in and put those boards up and surround them with the world that they are going to be creating is very helpful. It helps you get a lot of answers. We call them collage boards, but they're really research boards.

If I'm a director I might say, "I like photographs four and six but I don't like 14."

Right. Or, "I don't like this way," or "This would be a great way to think about the scene." Even on a huge board, if there's one key that I get into a scene, if there's one photograph that seems to get a director excited, then I can go on to do more research based on that one idea. Or begin to draw, based on that particular idea. It's a way that I can get responses. And it's a way that lets them into the design process.

How did your association with Michael Langham come about?

I'm very fortunate to work with people like Michael. I met him through my friend Doug Stein, the scenic designer. Doug had done a lot of work with Michael through the years, and he said, "I think you guys would really get along and enjoy each other." He has great technical knowledge of how to work with the actors and how to make their bodies respond and do what reads well from the stage. His knowledge of the theatre and of life in general makes him so exciting to be around and to work with. I enjoyed the *Timon of Athens*, which I did with him up at Stratford, Canada. He's a director who really loves to do the back and forth of "Oh, if we set it in the 1930s, how would this work? What would this be?"

Did you put the show in the 1930s?

Yes, we set it in 1930s Europe, and it was marvelously successful. Michael had directed that play at Stratford in the 1960s, when he was there. He had inherited a production that Peter Coe was

STAGES
Costume designs by Ann Hould-Ward
Choreographed by Graciela Daniele
Ballet Hispanico, New York (1991)

going to direct, and it was already set in the 1940s. Duke Ellington came up to do the music. So there was this strong, jazzy score, which they wanted to use again. As we began to talk, we realized that there were interesting relationships to Josephine Baker's going to Europe, and the African influences in wealthy Europe of the 1930s. And I became very interested in a German painter, Otto Dix. He had relationships to very wealthy people, but he had this strange way of dealing with them, even with the colors of their flesh. Many of these things just began to make this world with Michael. Michael is willing to inhabit that world with you, and he's such an incredibly strong director that the sense of the world is emanated throughout the production, and it makes the fruition of working with him tremendous, because you've built something together.

What kinds of materials do you like to use for sketches?
One of my assistants and I were laughing here in the studio the other day, because

I'm terrible—I use everything, and my sketches are so tactile. I draw and draw into the paper. I really work with anything that is handy. I swear I would use anything if it were nearby. But I use watercolor, a lot of pencil, inks, magic marker, and Crayola sometimes. And I use them all together.

You designed the costumes for *Falsettos* at the Golden.
Basically, *Falsettos* is a production that, when you're done, should look like the designer wasn't there. It needed to look like real New York people, like you and I sitting here. It was a very deep, meaningful collaboration with James Lapine, in the sense that we went on to investigate the piece and made changes through the whole process. We tried different shirts, different pants, and so on, and we moved them around in the play in order to see what worked for us.

But to me, *Falsettos* needed no clothes. *Falsettos* was so powerful in the rehearsal room—it is such a meaningful statement about our lives and about our people, the people of the theatre, the people that we love and the people that we've lost. And I guess to me that was the reason to do *Falsettos*. It was to have a chance to say to other people that this is all of our lives. We needed to do the design work so we could help communicate that to people, but I never looked at it as this huge, creative high.

What do you like most about working in the theatre?

I like the people. I like the fact that it's a gamble. For some people that's a hard thing, that you never know—will it run or won't it run. I've had assistants and other people I've known who really couldn't survive that life in the theatre, of not knowing where that next meal or next check would come from. You know, I'm a farmer's daughter—you planted your seeds in the spring, and if you were lucky it rained and they grew and you harvested them. But there were a lot of years where you just got hailed out or else there was no rain and you didn't get a crop. And I really think a Broadway show is exactly the same. Some years it hails and some years you have a great crop.

I love the humanity of the theatre. I love the fact that it is an expression of something from one person to another, and that it can be done without clothes, without sets, and without lights. To me, what's exciting is to be part of that process. It is my way into being part of that process that I happen to put clothes on them. Well, I do hope those clothes help someone to understand the idea. But the most important thing is the one-on-one communication. And I think the marvelous thing that we can do in the theatre is to let people know and understand they're in the theatre and yet communicate an idea to them that this is another person, sharing it on many levels. No one else can do that; only the theatre can do that. A movie can give you a very real version of this or that, but only the theatre can attack that point of fantasy within a human being sitting in a place, with another human being right there taking that journey too. That is my favorite thing about the theatre.

HAMLET
Costume design by Ann Hould-Ward
Directed by Garland Wright
Guthrie Theatre, Minneapolis (1988)

EDUARDO SICANGCO
Costume designs for the principals in Pagliacci
New York City Opera (1991)

EDUARDO SICANGCO
Costume designs for the chorus in Pagliacci
New York City Opera (1991)

EDUARDO SICANGCO
Costume designs for the principals in Pagliacci
New York City Opera (1991)

EDUARDO SICANGCO
Costume designs for the chorus in Cavalleria Rusticana
New York City Opera (1991)

A Conversation with
WILLA KIM

Willa Kim lives in a beautiful apartment on Manhattan's Upper West Side. I chatted with her about design for the theatre and dance. Kim studied fashion illustration at the Chouinard Institute of Art in Los Angeles, her hometown. Her first Broadway show was Edward Albee's *Malcolm*, in 1966 at the Shubert Theatre. Since then, she has designed sets and costumes for Glen Tetley's *Daphnis et Chlöe* and *Birds of Sorrow*, Eliot Feld's *Papillon* and *Scenes for the Theatre*, Smuin's *A Song for Dead Warriors* and *Shinju*, Margo Sappington's *Rodin* and Jiri Kylian's *Dream Dances*. Her opera credits include *The Magic Flute*, the American premiere of Menotti's *Help, Help, the Globolinks!*, and Henze's *The Stag King*, and sets and costumes for *Le Rossignol*

for the Santa Fe Opera and N.E.T., and San Francisco's *Tosca*.

Kim's career is brimming with professional honors: She has received Tony nominations for Peter Allen's *Legs Diamond*, Andrew Lloyd Webber's *Song and Dance*, Bob Fosse's *Dancin'*, and Joel Grey's *Goodtime Charley*. She has also won Tony Awards for Duke Ellington's *Sophisticated Ladies* and *The Will Rogers Follies;* an Emmy for *The Tempest* (choreographed by Michael Smuin); Drama Desk Awards for Maria Irene Fornes's *Promenade*, Sam Shepard's *Operation Sidewinder*, and Jean Genet's *The Screens* (for which she also won a Maharam Award and the Variety New York Drama Critics' Poll Award); and an Obie Award for Robert Lowell's *The Old Glory*.

THE WILL ROGERS FOLLIES
Costume designs by Willa Kim, for Showgirls
Directed and choreographed by Tommy Tune
Palace Theatre, New York (1991)
(Photograph by Duane Michals)

How did you first become involved in designing for the theatre?

I came to New York to assist Raoul Pène du Bois on costumes because we had worked together in Hollywood. I just fell into working with Raoul. I never studied design or theatre. I was a scholarship art major at school. One of my art instructors insisted that I take my portfolio to a studio in Hollywood. She set up an appointment for me. I was lugging this great big portfolio around to art studios and department stores. I was just delighted when Western Costume asked me to leave it. It was as big as I was and it was so heavy to carry around. The next thing I knew, I was working in the studios, and that's where I met Raoul.

When you assisted Raoul on costumes in Hollywood, did he do sketches, and did you find swatches and do research?

I didn't do anything. The director saw my portfolio, hired me, and had this perverse idea that he wanted me to be on the picture. I was hanging around the sound stages and was literally trying to get out of Paramount when Karinska saw me sitting around and asked me to do some work for her.

Karinska was out there?

Yes. And when she asked me, I said, "Oh sure." Then she immediately grabbed me as one of her assistants.

How long did you work for her?

Just for the movie out there. She was executing the clothes for it, and she had me scaling up Raoul's drawings to life-size for her so that all the details would be in proportion, and then doing color samples for dyeing and so on. She kept me busy both at work and afterwards, driving her around. It was a dizzying time for me—so much information through a heavy Russian accent. I was dreaming in Technicolor. I was totally unprepared, because I had not thought of designing as a career. I was interested in being an artist. I just happened to be handy to both Karinska and Raoul and ended up in New York. If I had wanted to be a designer, it couldn't have been a better preparation, because they were the two most inspiring artists working in theatre. Of course, I knew nothing about either one of them then. Los Angeles didn't have much theatre.

But when you came to New York did you continue to work for Raoul?

I did, yes.

How did your first show of your own come about?

Raoul was in Paris and his mother had died. So he decided he wanted to live away, and being such a Francophile and being a Pène du Bois, it was natural that he took this opportunity to live in Paris. I had gone away for about a year and I came back and decided that now was the time for me to finally make a decisive move. And that was to go back to what I felt was my true calling, if there is such a thing, and back to drawing and painting. About this time, a friend of mine, Arnold Weinstein, called and offered me this Off-Broadway show, and I said, "Oh, alright." And that was the beginning and the end of any thoughts of being a graphic artist.

Did he know of your work?

Well, I suppose. Off-Broadway isn't exactly the most lucrative area for a designer. One has to be willing to work for nothing, but it's a great training ground. So that's where I met John Wulp, Julia Miles, Sam Cohn, and a

---

Willa Kim's costume design credits include the following:

BROADWAY

Four Baboons Adoring the Sun (1992), Beaumont Theatre

The Will Rogers Follies (1991)

Legs Diamond (1988)

The Front Page (1986), Beaumont Theatre

Long Day's Journey into Night (1986)

Song and Dance (1985)

Sophisticated Ladies (1981)

Bosoms and Neglect (1979)

Dancin' (1978)

Goodtime Charley (1975)

Jumpers (1974)

Operation Sidewinder (1970)

The Office (1966)

Hail Scrawdyke! (1966)

AMERICAN PLACE THEATRE

Lydie Breeze (1982)

The Chicken Coop Chinaman (1972)

Sunday Dinner (1970)

Ceremony of Innocence (1968)

OFF-BROADWAY

The Screens (1971)

Promenade (1969)

Scuba Duba (1967)

Dynamite Tonight (1964)

Funnyhouse of a Negro (1964)

Helen (1964)

The Saving Grace (1963)

Fortuna (1962)

Red Eye of Love (1961)

DANCE COMPANIES

Joffrey Ballet

Glen Tetley Company

Royal Swedish Ballet

American Ballet Theatre

San Francisco Ballet

The Feld Ballets—NY

Alvin Ailey Company

Houston Ballet

Nederlands Dans Theatre

Harkness Ballet

Stuttgart Ballet

London Festival Ballet

Ater Balleto

National Ballet of Canada

Dance Theatre of Harlem

DAPHNIS ET CHLÖE
Costume designs by Willa Kim
Choreographed by Glen Tetley
Stuttgart Ballet (1975)

whole slew of people. That was really my first opportunity to work on my own. I found that it was exciting to be making my own decisions. I was seduced.

How do you like to work on a show as far as preparation is concerned? Do you like to do a great deal of research?
It all depends on the amount of time, and if there is time, of course, you wallow around in research. You put off the day of actually drawing. But if there isn't time, you jump right in and do it. I find that I do a lot of research.

What kind of paints do you use?
I use watercolors.

Do you do sketches for every character in the show, whether it's a musical, a ballet or an opera?
Oh, absolutely, I may do 20 sketches and then pick out of the group. I usually will do as many sketches as I can until I'm faced with a deadline and I have to stop. Otherwise, I'd probably just go on cranking out variations on an idea, obsessively.

It's a wonderful learning process, isn't it?
Doing sketches? Well, being trained as an artist rather than as a designer, it kind of satisfies this suppressed area where I really want to draw and paint. And for me

it's as important to do a good sketch as a good design. Very often, when I am really pressed for time, and especially on anything as large as a musical, I end up doing sketches in pencil on anything lying around and indicate color, and they turn out just as well. It's not that essential to do beautiful sketches, but that's always a kind of temptation that I fall into as I want to do good sketches.

Once I'm settled on a design and a sketch, I use that as a blueprint for what's going to happen. I don't deviate at all, because if I have to compromise and change, I find I have to change not only on that one particular thing, but the whole costume has to be rethought.

What about swatching? Do you have assistants?
When I was working Off-Broadway, I did my own. I didn't have assistants. And now, of course, the costume houses supply shoppers, and I do have assistants.

How did your first Broadway show come about?
That happened through working on an Off-Broadway show. Richard Barr, Edward Albee, and Clinton Wilder, who had produced the Off-Broadway show *Funnyhouse of a Negro*, then asked me if I would do *Malcolm*, which was their next

Broadway show. That's how that happened.

Did you approach that any differently than when you had been designing shows Off-Broadway?
I think it was less improvised, in the sense that I wasn't really limited to such a small budget. I could have costumes made in a costume shop instead of scrounging around trying to do things in a makeshift situation. It's very difficult in that sense, yes. But I was used to working in Broadway houses. I had spent so much time assisting Raoul that going into a Broadway house wasn't a new experience for me. In fact, I came into Off-Broadway overqualified—I had already been working on musicals and large shows on Broadway.

And you knew what to expect?
Yes, I knew. I wasn't a novice or an inexperienced designer moving into an area that can be intimidating.

After working on plays with Raoul Pène du Bois, doing plays of your own, how did designing for the ballet evolve?
Glen Tetley, who was a young choreographer at the time, had come in to direct something that I was working on. He was preparing an evening of ballets that he was choreographing, and he asked me to design one of the ballets. It turned out very successfully. It was called *Birds of Sorrow*, and it got wonderful reviews, and a lot of choreographers saw that evening of dance and started calling me. Once again, it was something I hadn't

thought about doing any more than I had thought about designing. It seems events kind of occurred, and the next thing I knew I was a ballet designer.

You've done many ballets.
Yes, but they all came out of this one experience working with Glen Tetley, and since then I've done a lot of Glen's ballets, too.

How does designing for the ballet differ from working on plays or musicals?
I think that you are involved, firstly, with movement, and, secondly, with synthesizing or getting at the essence of an idea, and you're released from any sense of realism. I feel that's the important thing. And you can suggest a period or an idea or an emotion without having to do it realistically, which is both liberating and also confining.

I learned the restrictions very quickly. I mean, it's such a physical medium that you have to take into consideration a lot of technical problems before you design.

Like what?
Lifts [how the person is going to be lifted], particular movements, what they need, the kind of shoes they're going to wear, or whether they're doing a lot of floor work. Also, you must not obstruct movement and line, which are essential to a dancer. And dance clothes have to be cleaned—washed, ideally—almost every time they're worn. So these are practical considerations.

Do you need to go to rehearsals?
I go to rehearsals before I design, yes.

What about fittings for dancers? Do you attend all of those?
Oh, yes, but I do that with everything I design, usually.

How many fittings would you have for a major dance piece with six principals?

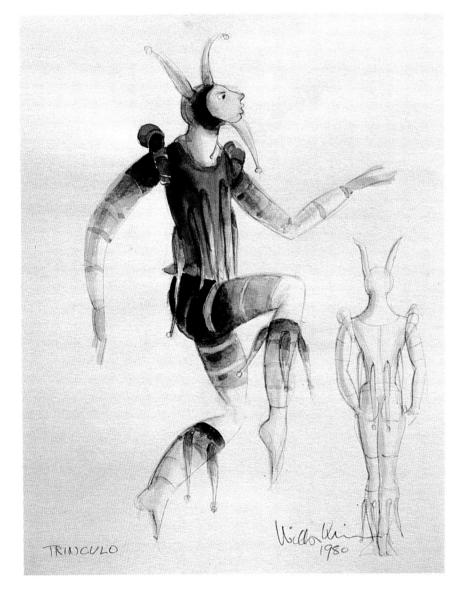

TRINCULO

THE TEMPEST, THE BALLET
Costume design by Willa Kim, for Trinculo
Choreographed by Michael Smuin
San Francisco Ballet (1980)

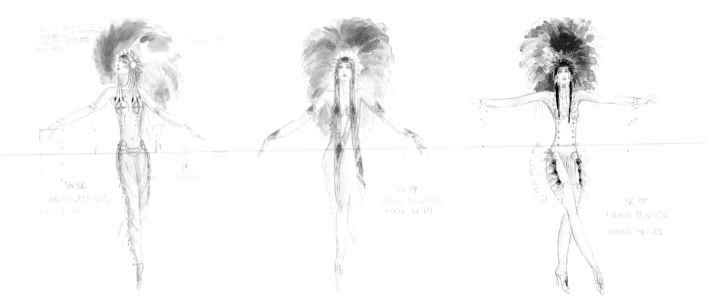

Usually you have what's called a muslin or pattern fitting, and then a fitting in the final fabrics, and finally, during tech rehearsal or dress rehearsal, which is what it comes down to nowadays, you have about three chances to alter your ideas or to elaborate. And if it's a painted costume, there would almost always be another fitting.

How do you go about a painted costume? Is that done on a form?
Yes.

Is it on a form that has the exact measurements of the dancers?
No, we're not privileged to have forms that really look like dancers for painting. What we have to do is use store dummies [mannequins]. But we do mark on the dancer the essential body parts, so we know where these things are. It's rather complicated. The fittings are painstaking and almost all the complications of the costume are fit right on the dancer rather than on the dummy.

If you really wanted to design a specific ballet, would you take it no matter what the fee or the budget?
I think so.

When you work on a production with other design collaborators, do you sometimes find that the costume ideas come first, then the scenery?
No, usually the scenery comes first, and of course the lighting designer tries to

THE WILL ROGERS FOLLIES
Costume designs by Willa Kim, for the Indian Princesses (page 114, top row), Marla Maples as Ziegfeld's Favorite (page 114, bottom), and Keith Carradine as Will Rogers (above, clockwise from top left: Opening Scene; Traveling Scene; Vaudeville Scene)
Directed and choreographed by Tommy Tune
Palace Theatre, New York (1991)

work with both scenery and costumes. You try to work within the color scheme that the scenic designer has laid out so that you're not really working at odds with each other. And if it's a very neutral background, then you can pretty much do what you want to do, using that to your advantage. When we did *The Will Rogers Follies*, some of the costumes were designed before the scenery, and before the color elevations.

In that case, Tony Walton was tied up with a movie. Doing *Will Rogers* was totally unexpected. We were told three weeks earlier that it wasn't going to happen that year, and then three weeks later we were told that it was. We all said, "It can't be done. We don't have the time to do it." Since Tony was working on a movie, we went to Hollywood to have our first production meeting with him. That was Jules Fisher, Tommy Tune, Jeff Calhoun, and myself. Fortunately, Tommy had his show almost completely outlined in his mind, as well as on paper. So it made it possible, because I don't think we could have done it otherwise. From this one production meeting we had to jump in and I had to start the costumes immediately in order to get them done on time. When Tony was finally through with this movie and was working on the scenery, he asked for my colors. So it worked the other way around in this instance. That happens, but not often.

You have worked on various productions with Tommy Tune. Does he always know what he wants the show to be?
Tommy comes to a production with a great deal of preparation. He has a strong visual sense, which he incorporates into a production. He really sets the parameters of how he wants to work, and what he wants the show to look like. So it's wonderful, because you're not floundering around. He also gives you a lot of research. And he keeps feeding you research on the direction he wants you to go. I think he does this with all departments. In fact, I'm sure of this.

Did he also know what he wanted in terms of scenery?
Yes, absolutely. Everything.

VARIATIONS ON AMERICA
Costume design by Willa Kim,
for Mikhail Baryshnikov
Choreographed by Eliot Field
City Center 55th Street Theatre, New York
(1977)

How many costumes did you do for *The Will Rogers Follies?*

Designs or actual costumes that were made? About 300 designs—we ended up with 200.

How long did you have to design all of those?

Not long. That was the problem. We started designing almost as we went into workshop, which preceded the actual rehearsal period. So that's no time at all.

You're saying just a matter of three or four weeks?

Yes. About three weeks. Actually, when they were in workshop, I was starting to design. It was that close. I mean, up until then it was thrashing around.

How many shops executed the clothes?

About five or six shops. The bulk of the show was done by Parsons-Meares. And I had expected Vincent Costumes to do the men's things, and when they backed out at the last minute I then had to throw some of the men's things into Parsons-Meares, which meant that some of the costumes that they were originally going to do had to be farmed out to the other places.

The costumes were executed in several shops because of the time element?

The time element, yes. Also, there aren't shops that are big enough to handle large musicals, especially if there is a time pressure, which always seems to be the case. If we had the luxury of being four months in a shop, we could have made the costumes all in one place.

You had three or four weeks to design the costumes, but how many weeks were they actually in the shops?

We were in the shops for over two months.

Did you have a good costume budget?

Yes. I think I had a million dollars.

How many assistants did you have?

I had two: Frank Krenz and Mitch Bloom.

You must be pleased with the reviews for the costumes, because they've been simply wonderful.

Yes. I'm very pleased. I'm sorry that a couple of the numbers, due to the time element, were eventually cut, but other than that, I was very pleased.

When you designed costumes for Tommy Tune in his concert appearance and for Baryshnikov in the ballet *Variations on America*, did they know specifically what they wanted?

I don't think so. What they want you to do is make them comfortable and attrac-

tive. Each project has different requirements. And if you help them with their role, you're fulfilling a very important part of the performance. You usually don't find much argument.

As a costume designer do you find it is part of your job to tell performers that they look good in their costumes and that they're going to look terrific?

I don't do that much coddling of a performer. No, I don't feel that's necessary. Some designers have a naturally gracious and flattering manner. It's just not a part of my style. I guess I don't feel that I have to. I want them to feel secure and I want them to feel the costume is right for what they are doing, but I think that's something I try to solve in the design rather than by giving them a snow job.

You designed the costumes for *Long Day's Journey into Night* **in 1986. Can you comment on how you approached that production?**

You are dealing not only with the emotional arc of the play, but also with realistic details, like the physical condition of the people that populate the play and the physical transformation that takes place during the play. And somehow, you have to take all of these elements, as well as what the performers look like, and try to convince the audience that this family situation is actually taking place.

We were concerned with the various emotional strains within the family—the deterioration of the mother, the father's insecurities and regrets, one son, an actor, who was on his way to becoming an alcoholic, and the other son's illness. In some way you have to try and make the costume not only help the actors in their portrayal, but let the audience understand that these are real people in this state. You help to set up the emotional tension in the play with your costuming.

Did you find that play as challenging as you would any other type of production, like dance?

Oh, yes. It's a totally different thing and it's nice to change gears and go down a different road and be preoccupied with different problems, and that's what a play like that does.

If I asked you to name three favorite productions for which you've designed the costumes, what would they be?

The Will Rogers Follies would be one of them, and probably *The Magic Flute* and *Le Rossignol*, which I did for Santa Fe.

Why was *The Magic Flute* **one of your favorite productions?**

Because for a designer, there's the possibility of using fantasy, of dealing with metaphysical ideas and subject matter, and it seems to me there are no limits to what a designer can do with that opera. You're only limited by your own talent or your ability to translate a drawing into a reality.

When I did that production on Santa Fe's open stage, we were sitting at dress rehearsal and it was so strange, because I wasn't thinking, and from the distance I saw what looked like the full moon coming up. And I thought, "Oh, my God, if that would only happen when we opened." And it was actually my costume coming up and I didn't even realize that. I had put a moon on the Queen of the Night's head, and these horse-hair clouds were all around it, and I sat there saying, "Oh, isn't that a lovely effect?"

When you designed the costumes for *Dancin'*, **was that a different type of musical for you?**

Not really, because it came right out of my doing dance clothes for ballet to a Broadway show. And that was applying the things that I knew, and I had developed in dance. A lot of the techniques and things that I had developed for dance I used in *Dancin'*. And things I did for Margo Sappington for the Calder ballet, a lot of the things that I worked out on her ballets, I've used in other ballets, and I think those techniques that I've developed for Margo have become part of the dance vocabulary.

What, for instance?

The painting technique, which is something I developed on dance costumes.

On what kind of fabrics?

On fabrics that have to be washed. These are paints that permanently impregnate the fabric and do not wash out. They're paints that I talked a factory in Brooklyn into letting me buy. They said they didn't want to be bothered, because they were a factory and they didn't want to fool around with any quibbling orders. I said, "You've got to let me buy some of this stuff. I want to use it for my dance costumes." It turned out that one of the men had a daughter that was taking dance lessons. I offered him tickets to the Joffrey Ballet and I said, "I will see that she gets a scholarship if you will sell me these paints." Robert Joffrey said, "Okay." And that's how we got those paints to begin with.

It's a very strange thing: 30 years later, the costume shops are all using the same paint that I talked this man into selling me. They still order their paints from him, and it has become a kind of cottage industry for him. None of them has ever gone out and tried to find a substitute

paint. They're silk-screen paints that also happen to work on nylon. And they were painting nylon fabrics when I first found them.

Did you just find the paints by searching and searching?

Yes. We really looked for them. I wanted a dress I had designed for a Sam Shepard play to be silk-screened instead of trying to do it with oil paints or acrylics, which stiffen and eventually crack, and have to be constantly redone. I got tired of going to the theatre and repainting everything that I had painted. I said to Eaves Costumes at the time, "I want this silk-screened and made as pliable as silk fabric that you find in stores to make these costumes." So they finally found this man and the paint dyes. After that, I was able to persuade him to sell me the paints to use on my dance costumes, which I did for Margo's ballet, *Weewis*. Also, we used nylon Lycra for the first time. This is the stretch fabric they make leotards out of.

For *Weewis* I did the clothes out of this new fabric, Lycra spandex, which is what bathing suits are made of today. But this is before bathing suits, before there was a single leotard at Capezio's. Capezio saw these things and wanted to know, and everyone wanted to know, what fabric it was that I used on these dancers, because they hadn't seen anything like these tight-fitting stretch garments before. One of the women who makes dance clothes came backstage and sought me out and said, "How do they get into these costumes?" She said, "I didn't see a zipper, I didn't see a single hook or eye or snap. I can't figure how they got into these." So I showed her the fabric, and she hadn't seen it before. Well, of course, now that fabric is used constantly in dance.

That's an exciting idea all the way around.

When I did *Rodin* for Margo we used the nylon Lycra made into unitards. We got the dancers into these unitards and on the dancers we marked the rib cage, the waistline, the hips, and the knees, and I had them paint those costumes to look like they were nude. I said, "We're going

UNDER THE SUN
Costume designs by Willa Kim
Choreographed by Margo Sappington
Shubert Theatre, Philadelphia (1976)

to appliqué with this other stretch fabric I found." All of these fabrics were being developed for underwear, like corsets. I said, "They'll have these strange shimmers on them in different places." The people that saw them couldn't figure out what they were looking at. They thought they were nude, but they knew they weren't, and yet they couldn't understand how these shimmers were happening on them in different places.

What was the name of the Calder ballet with Margo Sappington?
It was called *Under the Sun*. A lot of things that I did that were very playful for that ballet I've used in *Dancin'* for Bob Fosse, such as those balls that were swinging in the calypso number. I did that originally for Margo, so these ideas came out of designs for dance costumes.

Did you have to have dupes for *Dancin'*, in case one got torn?
They wait until they are totally worn out before they order another costume, unfortunately.

If a costume gets damaged during a number, who takes care of it?

The wardrobe mistress and her staff. There is an army of people backstage on a musical who do nothing but maintenance on costumes because of wear and tear.

You have had costumes executed in the shop in Canada. Comment on that.
The National Ballet of Canada has a wonderful workshop. I haven't done any original work for them. It's usually redoing something that I've already done. In the case of *Sphinx*, the painting was done in New York. We made the prototypes here. They then duplicated them for their alternate casts. For *Daphnis et Chlöe*, we borrowed the costumes that were done in New York for the Houston Ballet and had them sent to Canada, and they duplicated them there. It's so delightful working up there, because it seems to me that they are only driven by the desire to please you. And that's pretty good. They will say, "Oh, you don't like that? That isn't right? Well, we'll do it over again." How often do you get to hear that? And the scenery was also done wonderfully there.

So I was pleased, and they also did

Dream Dances beautifully. Here I think we borrowed the production from Joffrey, which was also done here. I was concerned about the fact that they didn't have the proper painters and the technique that I had developed in this country, and they said, "Oh, don't worry about it, we have it all now." And they showed me, and sure enough, the same painters that I had trained here had gone up there to do *Cats*, and so they had used the same paints that I had originally ordered, and the same techniques. I didn't do *Cats*, but the shop used the same paints that I had developed for *Cats*, and for every other painted show they've done. They had the same setup, the color charts, everything that I had originally done here for my ballets. They ordered the same paints from this little factory in Brooklyn. It has spread all over the world.

Can you comment on a particular Feld Ballet production that you designed costumes for?
It's hard. I can't do that. They're all so different because Eliot is such a prolific choreographer. He's also extremely articulate and brilliant, which isn't usually the case with most choreographers, who, like dancers, are often inarticulate. His ballets always spring from an idea. And they're fun to do.

Would he say, "I want this set of costumes to look like collages"?
No, that he doesn't do.

Do you say that to him, maybe?
Yes. I usually say, "This is what I think it should look like." And then he'll say, "Well, I don't think it should look like that." I'll say, "But this is what I like." So we argue.

And usually you win?
Sometimes. For *The Jig is Up*, he said, "We don't have the money for it."

What did you design for that ballet?
He said, "We're just going to have to buy things for it." And I said, "Okay." So I ran around and we bought a lot of stuff. But then I ended up cutting everything up and putting it back together like a collage. And it really ended up as one of the most unusual-looking ballets I've done. It was a work that just grew. I didn't start with a sketch or with an idea or anything. I just took things and got those dancers together and I said, "You put on this and you put on that." Then I would take scissors and cut this and that away and then put something else there instead and mixed everything up.

It was spontaneous.
It was a totally spontaneous, improvised thing. When I got through with that, we started dyeing and tying it this way and that way. So that it ended up a totally designed look.

Did you use the stretch fabric as a basic?
Well, of course I only used fabrics that I knew would move, like sweaters.

That you cut up?
Yes.

When you say "moved," did they hang down?
No. It's not that they moved in themselves, but that they would stretch and move with the body.

If you were shopping for clothes for a work, would you make sketches to show to a director?
No. I think if you want to go shopping, I don't think you can do sketches. What's the point of it? You're never going to find it. The minute you confine yourself to something on a piece of paper, it's not going to exist. You can set out to look for a summer bag in September and you won't find it. You can ask someone to go out and find a black dress and they'll suddenly have totally disappeared from the city. It's as if this giant vacuum came along and sucked away all the black dresses. It is like that when you go shopping. You can't find anything that even looks like what you've set out for, so you have to leave yourself free. You have to say, "Look, I'm going to try and find this thing. And if I find something else that I think is going to work, why not?" The director may hate it and you have to start all over again, but you do have to allow yourself the freedom. It's harder to shop than it is to make clothes.

Because you're searching so much, aren't you?
Yes. Because you wander around forever looking for something that specific. And I hate that kind of shopping. These off-the-rack clothes look like that. They all look alike. They all look as if they're stamped and cut out by the thousands with a saw.

How much time do you have to do a ballet, say for the Feld Ballet?
Usually it's not bad. Because he always shows me the work in progress, or very often when it's pretty much done.

Are we talking about six weeks?
Often six weeks, four weeks, three weeks.

How large would an average size ballet be?
Well, sometimes it is just three or six. But at the most it's 17 costumes, if he uses the full company. He's also restricted financially. Very often he'll do a big company work in leotards and tights, with maybe a belt, or something like a piping on the sleeve. It's just so minimal, because dance companies today are all literally broke.

When you teamed with choreographer Michael Smuin and designed the costumes for *The Tempest* for the San Francisco Ballet, how did you work on that production?
Well, I read the book, and saw the movements, and tried to create a feeling of the period, the slightest suggestion of the period, because it's a cumbersome period, and there's no way that any choreographer is going to want heavy costumes. Actually, that's not true—perhaps there are choreographers who would want to put their dancers into very heavy sixteenth-century costumes, but I doubt that.

I don't think it is a difficult problem to do a full-length work like *The Tempest*, because it is a conventional story ballet. You have segments of exposition, and story, and other segments that are just dance. There are certain things you know, like the fact that the corps de ballet is going to be dressed alike, suggesting God knows what! They're doing waves one minute and the next minute they're doing a celebratory dance. And you know the conventions of dance, and you try to work within them.

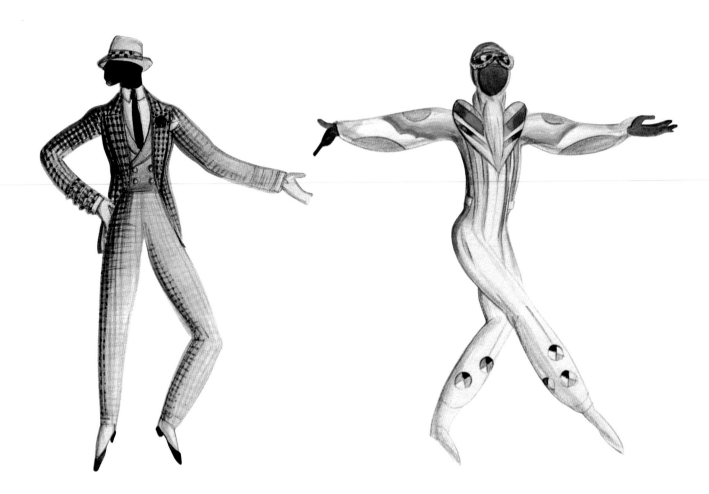

SOPHISTICATED LADIES
Costume designs by Willa Kim
Musical staging and choreography by Donald
McKayle and Michael Smuin
Directed by Michael Smuin
Lunt-Fontanne Theatre, New York (1981)

You also did *Sophisticated Ladies* with Michael Smuin. Was there anything different in that production as a musical, as opposed to working with him on a ballet?

No, I don't think so. Once again, we were dealing with song and/or dance. It was really a revue form. And you do each number as it comes along. You worry about fast changes a bit here and there, but those things are usually figured out in advance.

If young people wished to pursue costume design in all phases of theatre, ballet and opera, what would you tell them to study?

I only know about my own background. I would tell them they should take some art classes, so that they are able to draw and paint well enough to be able to put on paper what the costume is going to look like. That is necessary anyway, because you're working with directors and choreographers who tend to be untrusting and suspicious. What you're doing is persuading them visually to your point of view, to what you want to do,

and the more skillful you are at this, the better. If you have a lovely drawing, you'll have a better reception.

Then I would say they ought to get some experience working in a costume shop and see what the techniques and the procedures are in making a costume. I'm sure designers start off by working as shoppers, so they get to know the territory and they get to wander around the shops in between running out on chores, and get to see how designers work and how costumes are put together. I think they should apprentice themselves to good designers and find out how different designers solve different problems.

What do you like least about working in the theatre?

The accounting you have to do. You're constantly dealing with the business part of it, especially on a big musical. You have this budget and you have to stay within it. How do you allocate your money? How do you spend it? There is the constant need to keep the computer up to date on what you're spending, and where. My assistants spend all their time

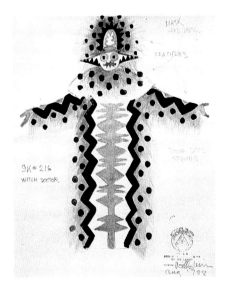

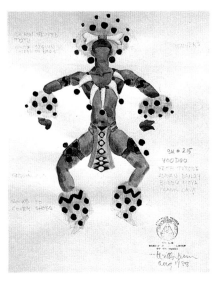

trying to feed that kind of information to the office. The office demands that. "Alright now, how are we spending the $55.27, and where is the receipt for it? And have you fed that into the computer?" It just goes on and on. My assistants are spending as much time with that as they are doing the work I want them to do.

What do you like most about working in the theatre?

I think the change. It's not something that goes on and on tediously. I get bored easily, so I guess it's probably just as well I ended up a designer instead of a painter. I like working on new projects, new challenges, new people and new ideas. It's the only studying I do. I research and study and find out about things that I would never have thought about, and that is exciting. You know, the form is imposed on you—you have a beginning, a middle, and an end, and it's very satisfying.

LEGS DIAMOND
Costume designs by Willa Kim, for (clockwise from top left) the Witch Doctor, the Voodoo Man, and Christmas Reindeer Dance
Musical numbers choreographed by Alan Johnson
Directed by Robert Allan Ackerman
Mark Hellinger Theatre, New York (1988)

SAM KIRKPATRICK
Costume designs for Undiscovered Country
Mark Taper Forum, Los Angeles (1985)

TONI-LESLIE JAMES
Costume designs for Jelly's Last Jam

ROBERT PERDZIOLA
Costume designs for La Calisto
Santa Fe Opera (1989)

SAM KIRKPATRICK
Costume design for Michael Learned as Elizabeth
in Mary Stuart—*Act II*
Ahmanson Theatre, Los Angeles (1981)

SAM KIRKPATRICK
Costume design for Michael Learned as Elizabeth
in Mary Stuart—*Act I*
Ahmanson Theatre, Los Angeles (1981)

A Conversation with
WILLIAM IVEY LONG

William Ivey Long lives in an elegant townhouse in downtown New York. Born in 1947 in Williamsport, Pennsylvania, he was educated at William and Mary, the University of North Carolina, and the Yale Drama School. His first Broadway play was 1979's *The Inspector General,* at the Circle in the Square, with Liviu Ciulei directing.

Since then, Long has designed costumes for a wide variety of productions in the entertainment world. For opera, he has done Leonard Bernstein's *A Quiet Place* and *Trouble in Tahiti* for La Scala, Vienna Staatsoper, the Houston Grand Opera, and the Kennedy Center; Liviu Ciulei's production of *Wozzeck* for the Welsh National Opera; and *Postcard from Morocco* for the Washington Opera. His dance credits include work for Twyla Tharp, Paul Taylor, David Parsons, Dan Wagoner, and Peter Martins. For television, he has done *Ask Me Again* for American

Playhouse, several CBS specials, James Lapine's *Table Settings* for HBO, and Leonard Bernstein's *Mass* for PBS. He has also worked on the film *The Cutting Edge* and on such projects as the Pointer Sisters' national tours, *Siegfried & Roy* at the Mirage Hotel in Las Vegas, Robert Wilson's *Hamletmachine* European tour, Patti LaBelle in *Tommy*, Mick Jagger for the Rolling Stones' *Steel Wheels* tour, and *The Lost Colony.* In addition, he has designed costumes for Arena Stage, Long Wharf Theatre, American Repertory Theatre, Cleveland Play House, PAF Playhouse, Goodspeed Opera House and Alaska Repertory Theatre.

Long is head of design at Playwrights Horizons Theatre School, Tisch School of the Arts, New York University. Among his honors are two Tonys, three Drama Desk Awards, two Outer Critics Circle Awards, a Maharam Award, and an Obie.

THE ABDUCTION FROM THE SERAGLIO
Costume designs by William Ivey Long,
for Belmonte (above) and Constanze (right)
Directed by Stephen Wadsworth
San Francisco Opera (1990)

How did you become interested in designing costumes for the theatre?

My parents are in the theatre and I'm a second-generation theatre person. They did and do theatre in South Carolina and North Carolina, and they were with the Carolina Playmakers at the University of North Carolina. All my family worked at *The Lost Colony*. My father was director, my mother played Queen Elizabeth, my brother worked there, and my sister is in the choir. So I sort of followed in my parents' footsteps. At home, the front hall was always the scene shop and the dining room table was always the costume shop. In fact, we had to clear away the costumes in order to eat.

I just finished my twenty-second season with *The Lost Colony*, and I designed the costumes. It's been a total of 22 years.

Were you involved with *The Lost Colony* before you went away to study?

Yes. I was the prop master there and then the technical director. This was under Joe Layton and Fred Voelpel, and I was still a teenager. But I didn't take this "theatre stuff" seriously. I went to William and Mary and received a degree in history.

Then I studied art history for three years at Chapel Hill. Next I went to the Yale School of Drama for three years. So I was in college for 10 years.

I was encouraged to go to Yale by Betty Smith, who was at Chapel Hill, and I was her companion for the last three years of her life. She wrote *A Tree Grows in Brooklyn*. I have a pretty strong idea that her influence was the extra thing that made me leave art history and go into set design, which is what I wanted to do. My teacher, of course, was the great, ultimate teacher of all time, Ming Cho Lee, and I consider my training at Yale [to have been] in set design.

Did you also study costume design at Yale?

Yes, I studied costume design there, but I still didn't know I was going to do costumes.

Where did the change occur?

I really can't tell you. I think I need madness and madcap personalities. I feel I need psychodrama in my life. I found out that there's more interaction with people in costume design than in set design. I think it's a people need. I'm sure

it's psychologically deeply rooted in my makeup that I need to work out these things. I mean, this is really what I believe. Who knows whether this is an art form or not? This is just what we do and it's what we do with people, and I need the people and the personalities. I think it's how I work out my own insecurities, by helping people discover and solve theirs. And there's nothing more basic and more right on the line than the fitting room. There's the mirror and there's the actor and there you are.

What happened after you left the drama school?

I came to New York and didn't know how to get started. I'm not a good interview. I don't do a good portfolio sell. I don't inspire confidence when I interview and I have never gotten a job from an interview. I have only gotten jobs from people I have already worked with. My entire career has been working with people with whom I've worked and whom I've supported before. You work with one and then you work with another, and then you work back with that one.

I moved to the Chelsea Hotel, where

William Ivey Long's costume design credits include:

BROADWAY

Crazy for You (1992)

Guys and Dolls (1992)

Private Lives (1992)

The Homecoming (1991)

Six Degrees of Separation (1990), Beaumont Theatre

Eastern Standard (1989)

Lend Me a Tenor (1989)

Welcome to the Club (1989)

Mail (1988)

Sleight of Hand (1987)

Smile (1986)

End of the World (1984)

Play Memory (1984)

The Tap Dance Kid (1983)

Nine (1982)

Mass Appeal (1981)

Passione (1980)

The Inspector General (1979)

The 1940's Radio Hour (1979)

OFF-BROADWAY

Assassins (1991)

Eleemosynary (1989)

Together Again for the First Time (1989)

Italian American Reconciliation (1988)

Laughing Wild (1987)

Principia Scriptoriae (1986)

One Man Band (1985)

After the Fall (1984)

Hey Ma…Kaye Ballard (1984)

The Lady and the Clarinet (1983)

Poor Little Lambs (1982)

Twelve Dreams (1981)

Hunting Scenes from Lower Bavaria (1981)

Sister Mary Ignatius Explains It All for You (1981)

Johnny on a Spot (1980)

Altar Boys (1979)

The Impossible H.L. Mencken (1979)

The Vienna Notes (1979)

Conjuring an Event (1978)

Two Small Bodies (1977)

NEW YORK SHAKESPEARE FESTIVAL

Wenceslas Square (1988)

Hamlet (1986)

The Marriage of Bette and Boo (1985)

True West (1980)

MICK JAGGER, FROM THE ROLLING
STONES' STEEL WHEELS TOUR
Outfits designed by William Ivey Long (1989)

I lived for five years. I went there to work with Charles James, the great Anglo-American couturier, I wanted to give up theatre and make clothes. So I worked with him and I made a whole collection of historical dolls.

What size were the dolls?
About three feet tall. I cast my shows and then costumed them. I made about a dozen. I still have many of them; some I sold. I did them from historical paintings and things.

How did you get back to designing for the stage after that?
Friends of mine said, "William, you've got to snap out of this." One of my friends, the director Peter Schifter, asked me to do *Gemini* out at the PAF Play-house. But I wasn't ready. And I said, "No, I can't do anything, I just can't work." Later I did Richard Nelson's East

Coast premiere, called *The Killing of Yoblanski*, at the PAF Playhouse. That was my first show. Richard Nelson had a show at the American Place Theatre in Manhattan. I interviewed with the artistic director, who didn't want to hire me. He said I was too flip. It was because Richard Nelson insisted I do it that I got the job.

The next big step was doing *The 1940's Radio Hour* at Arena Stage. People in my class at Yale, Walt Jones and Carol Lees, put together this revue. We did it at the summer cabaret that my class found-ed at Yale. We converted a space and I designed the stage and the scenery and the costumes. We did a lot of wonderful, crazy things. One of the most successful things was *The 1940's Radio Hour*, and we did it again the next year and then we graduated. Walt Jones took the thing around and the Arena Stage agreed to do it with the possibility of moving it to Broadway. And we did it and then it came to Broadway and that was my Broadway musical debut. And suddenly, right before that, I had done *The Inspec-tor General* at Circle in the Square.

That was your first Broadway play. How did that come about?
It was Liviu Ciulei's first Broadway show and he asked Ming Cho Lee, with whom he had worked at the Arena Stage, to rec-ommend some designers, and Ming rec-ommended Karen Schulz to do the set. She was a great friend of mine. We had been at Yale together. Liviu was going to do the costumes himself, but then he realized that he needed a costume design-er and he said, "Karen, who should I hire?" And she said, "You have to hire my friend, William!" And so that's how I was hired. Just like that. By Liviu Ciulei not knowing anybody in the country, that's how I got my first Broadway play.

And I've done two subsequent pro-ductions with Liviu. I did Liviu's *Hamlet*, with Kevin Kline, at the Public Theatre, and then I did *Wozzeck*, the opera Liviu directed and did the scenery for at the Welsh National Opera. So I worked with him three times.

Did *The Inspector General* lead to another Broadway show?

No, a newspaper strike was on and I got no reviews whatsoever except in the *Christian Science Monitor*. And I've been an avid fan of that publication ever since. So one did not lead to the next production.

Would you say the musical *Nine* was the turning point or the high point in your career?

Well, it was the complete turning point of the career. I finally started wearing long breeches after that. I had to cover the scars. The choreographer on *The 1940's Radio Hour* in Washington, D.C., was Thommie Walsh, who had been in the original *A Chorus Line* and subsequently went on to win two Tony Awards as the co-choreographer with Tommy Tune. They were putting *Nine* together and Thommie Walsh worked with Tommy Tune and he kept saying, "You should ask William to come and do this." And they kept saying, "No." And they asked my great heroes, Ann Roth and Willa Kim to do *Nine*. Thank you, Willa, thank you, Ann. Thommie and Michel Stuart, the producer, wanted the people to be there all the time, for like six weeks.

And so then, in order to convince Tommy Tune about hiring me, Thommie Walsh said, "There's a show down at the Public that William did." It was James Lapine's *Twelve Dreams*. They came in previews and they came to the first act. Heidi Landesman had done the scenery and it was not ready. This was the second preview and it was still base-coated white. It was like luan and plywood. It was a white set, but it was not supposed to be. And the first-act dress of Carole Shelley was a black 1930s velvet gown. Now there was a black velvet gown on a white set, and Tommy Tune only stayed for the first act, but she changed to another color later. So that image convinced him to give me a chance to do it, because they were already planning black on white.

Then I was asked to co-design the project with Michel Stuart, the producer. I was so wanting to do this. But I knew myself so well, fortunately, that I had to turn down the assignment. Can you imagine? I said, "I cannot co-design. I'm

just too insane, and of an ego. And I don't know how to do it, because I don't know what it is until I'm in the middle of doing it."

You mean co-designing *Nine* with Michel Stuart?

Exactly. And it's just that I didn't think I could do it. And so I left and I thought, "Oh, well, I blew another interview." The next morning I woke up and called

NINE
*Costume design by William Ivey Long,
for Anita Morris
Directed by Tommy Tune
Forty-sixth Street Theatre, New York (1982)*

the general manager's office and I said, "Could you call and see if I've been offered this job?" And they had to get back to me. And then I found out that, yes, I had been offered the job. It changed my life, the chance to do that scale and that project, and to work with these incredible people.

You won many awards for that.

I was very lucky. Black and white always is a winner. It was a complete setup too, because it was very glamorous, beautiful women in various black outfits on a white set.

How many costumes did you design for *Nine*?

There were about 250. You didn't see that many—you saw about 200, hence the slashing and the beadings on the legs and the body. It was tough putting together.

In other words, you and Tommy decided to cut certain sketches?

Yes, after they were seen onstage. We had to make it shorter and we had to tell the story more clearly.

You mean actual costumes were made?

Actual creative, finished costumes. Then we were able to use many of those costumes in the national tour. So we had put them away in storage. They became doubles and understudy clothes. They weren't thrown out. And Anita Morris's costume was sort of another piece of complete luck. It's the one people think about when they think of me.

How did that happen?

Tommy had worked with Anita and Grover Dale, Anita's husband, who is also a choreographer. They'd worked up this wonderful number that Anita did stationary on this box. It was complete choreography, but she didn't move off the box! She stood on her head. She stood on everything. It was a wonderful number, an absolutely showstopping number. And it was showstopping in rehearsal clothes. They all wanted her to wear what she'd worn in rehearsal, which was black trousers and a long-sleeved turtleneck. Somehow, I felt the backer's audition, or the gypsy run-through, was the most exciting for *Nine*, because one's imagination kicks in, and you imagine what it's going to be like. The rehearsals all took place in Billy Rose's Golden Horseshoe atop the New Amsterdam Theatre.

On Forty-second Street?

Yes. And dust and the rain and the snow would come in and it was just wonderful. You had the ghosts of the past and the stars of the present and the future, and it was just very exciting. After I saw the run-through, I said, "Gosh, we don't need any costumes, this is divine the way it is." And everyone agreed with me, unfortunately. They all felt that Anita looked great. "And what is this lace thing you're trying to do?"

In fact, we were then put on hold because we lost our funding. We just fell apart. For a month we weren't doing the show. Everyone's heart sort of slowed down to normal and I did another show,

The Germans as Courtesans - Nine - [signature] 11 1981

NINE
*Costume designs by
William Ivey Long
Directed by Tommy Tune
Forty-sixth Street Theatre,
New York (1982)*

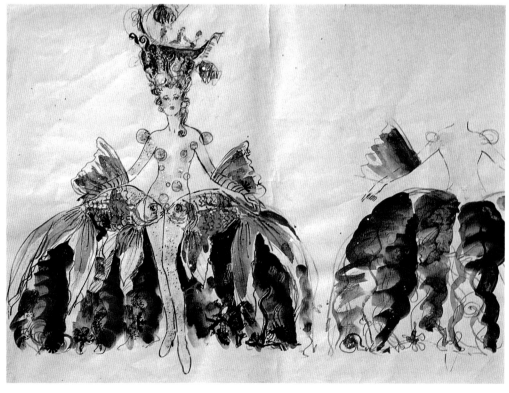

Poor Little Lambs, Paul Rudnick's first show, directed by Jack Hofsiss. David Jenkins did the set, and Beverly Emmons the lighting, with a wonderful cast. I remember Tommy came to the opening night and said, "Well, get out your scissors, I think we're starting up." We had very little time to make the first set of black costumes, because we had two weeks to execute all of these costumes. They had to be photographed and blown up to be put on the front of the house. They took all those vertical doors of the theatre and put one woman on each door. I mean, I was the show-off. It was really slightly embarrassing. Throw me in the briar patch, right?

And the first costume I made for Anita was all out of lace. It just didn't work. We photographed her in it. You could tell this was not a happy creature. But I knew I wanted lace. And she was just ill about it and hated it and everyone hated it. I heard again that they wanted her to wear the trousers and turtleneck, the second time I had been told. And I went to Tommy and begged him to give me a second chance. I said, "Please, I see lace. I see skin through the lace. I just don't know how to do it. It's the only thing I'm asking you to help me with." So Anita was asked reluctantly and she reluctantly came to another fitting. We tried on a plain, net body stocking, all the way from the chin to the ankles, all long sleeves. Everything was totally new. We tried doing appliqués of lace. And it just wasn't working. And then she said, "Well, if you gave me a little expandable elastic right underneath my belt here, then I can move like this," and she started kicking. And the draper, Werner Kulovits, and I went to work. I ran to the wastebin in the cutting room and I took this fabric that I had made for this flocked lace. We had an overlay, black swirls on this lace over green to look sort of like waters, and I brought it in and put it over her and stretched it over her knees and the three of us were electrified. We spent the next four hours literally sewing a costume on her and figuring out the stretch, because it was not stretch. The three of us created that costume right on her body.

The first lace costume you made was ugly?
It was a dog. Oh, yeah, I failed to mention that it was a dog! We'd already missed the first photo call and we had like one week until the first dress, and she said, "Don't tell Tommy. Let's surprise him." So we agreed, okay, we won't tell Tommy. When she came out in the new lace one in dress rehearsal, there it was! A big surprise to us all.

When you did *Six Degrees of Separation*, you worked with Jerry Zaks. How did that come about?
That's one of my most successful and rewarding collaborations. Jerry actually replaced Joseph Grifasi in the Broadway production of *The 1940's Radio Hour*. That's where I first met Jerry Zaks. I went to school with Christopher Durang, Albert Innaurato, Wendy Wasserstein, Ted Talley, and all those wonderful playwrights at Yale. And, of course, I met them working at Playwrights Horizons. Chris had a show that he was doing there called *Sister Mary Ignatius Explains It All for You*, and a little curtain-raiser called *The Actor's Nightmare*, and guess who's directing? Jerry Zaks. It was Jerry's first directing experience. So it was through my friend Christopher and my agent, Helen Merrill, who is also Christopher's agent and Jerry's agent. She put the package together. Karen Schulz did the scenery and Paul Gallo did the lighting. Paul Gallo is now doing the lighting for all of Jerry's shows, and has been the lighting designer of choice. He's wonderful. Right now I'm doing *Crazy for You* and *Guys and Dolls* with him.

How did you approach *Six Degrees*? Was there anything unusual?
I called *Six Degrees* "invisible work," because the assignment is that these people are supposed to be totally believable, and we are not supposed to notice they're wearing anything, just that these are real people. In fact, as Jerry discovered the play with John Guare, they were literally in the audience and got out of the audience and stood onstage. I have done many shows with Jerry that have been invisible costumes, but this was the most

invisible. We started out looking at the play and I didn't know what the play was, because it had never been done before. And it was sort of a dream play—it goes backwards and forwards, and it's real, and it's telling a story, and it's living a story. I didn't know how to read this play. So I asked my friend Paul Rudnick, who wrote *I Hate Hamlet*, to help me read it. He said, "Oh, this is a fabulous play." I said, "I know it's a fabulous play, but what is it?" And he said, "Jerry will tell you." I said, "Help me through the beginning, so I can go to the production meeting and look like I know what it is." It's one of the hardest plays to read that I've ever worked on. I didn't know where to focus. Then, when Jerry started telling us that he wanted it to be storytelling, people telling the stories, that didn't even help too much, because then all I knew was, "Okay, I guess these are just real people telling this story."

So I did collages. I assembled all these collages because I knew these people. I mean, this is the WASP establishment. And I made collages of each person, indicating what they might be wearing in the show, and also I did other clothes that they might wear if they went out, or went here, just to get a character feel, because I'd never worked with John Guare before. I wanted John to be able to see something, since I didn't think sketches were appropriate. I thought real pictures were appropriate.

You used real pictures.
I did collages of real people with some photographs and some catalogs. I used L.L. Bean and Orbus, one of those preppie things, and whatever was appropriate. And also Neiman-Marcus, Bergdorf Goodman and Saks catalogs, and *Vogue* magazine for Ouisa. Then I took pictures of people on the street when it was appropriate, street people.

You cut the actual people out of the catalogs?
I cut the people out and put them on these things. It's the method when stylists do commercials. I've never done one. But I've seen them and they do them like this. But then people can look at real, finished clothes, and it's reassuring,

LEND ME A TENOR
Costume designs by William Ivey Long
Directed by Jerry Zaks
Royale Theatre, New York (1989)

because it doesn't look cartoon-like. Also, the artistic director didn't want me to work at Lincoln Center. He said I did cartoon clothes and that everything I did was cartoon. He said this in production meetings to the people involved, and it made John Guare very nervous. But I had recently done *Lend Me a Tenor* with Jerry Zaks, Tony Walton, and Paul Gallo. And Tony Walton stuck up for me and said, "No, William doesn't do cartoon work, these are real people." You can see them. They are real, living, breathing people. And Jerry Zaks said that, too.

When you say you did collage, did you do actual fabric on the people or did you do swatches?
No, I just did collages of different photographs, like a worksheet. It was to show that these were real people. Of course, I was totally intimidated and scared to death about sketching, worrying that I would produce a cartoon. And of course we had no money to do this show, because it was downstairs.

It had not moved upstairs.
No. Nobody had ever seen it before. We didn't know what it was. Right? Jerry was still trying to work it out. "Well, when do these people really sit in the audience?" You know, it was like it had never been done. And so we all brought clothes from home and I borrowed things from

people, and I went to NBO and BFO and Moe Ginsberg for most of the suits, and I put all my money on Ouisa and on the husband. And I even got a navy blazer for $60 at NBO and cut the gold buttons off one of my blazers and sewed them onto it, and did things like that.

You shopped the show and did not have clothes built?
No, it was totally shopped. And real things. I had worn-out clothes. In fact, the pants that one of the sons wore were mine, and he had shoes that he'd worn. There were lots of Brooks Brothers things, and I used my charge card a lot. And subsequently I remade things, especially for Ouisa. We bought things and they were altered. Then it started coming together and the dress rehearsals happened. Jerry would say, "Oh, well, maybe da, da, da." And I would do a little more like that. Then the shading and the developing began, but I'm a real student of body language and I'd go to rehearsals and I'd watch how people are, how they move, how they sit and drink coffee. The breaks are my favorite times, because you can really watch actors being themselves and not the way they think they should be in the reading, and that's where you get to see body language the best.

It's very interesting in *Six Degrees* when the first boy comes out, the one who pretends to be Sidney Poitier's son. I dressed him in a totally Brooks Brothers uniform, you know, a stripped shirt, a repp tie, and khaki pants, and loafers without socks, and this famous navy blazer with my gold buttons on it. And everyone in the audience goes, "Ah, yes, that's right." Because he comes into this cocktail party and everyone believes him, and they buy him everything, and he goes out. And the show progresses, and then the parents call up their children, after craziness happens and the children arrive back from school. My favorite part of the whole show, costume-wise, is when the children come out onstage. There is a "two-beat gasp," because of recognition, they're wearing what real WASP college students wear. And it's not the navy blazer and the ironed khaki pants and the repp tie. The daughter, I based her on a friend of mine, Alexandra

Styron, who is always epitomized. That was the character—I just thought of Al. She was always in black, and she had a man's tuxedo jacket and black miniskirt, and wore yin/yang earrings. And I remember when Alexandra was in school—she was much younger than I—she was always in black, very severe. This is what WASP princesses really wear when they're in college, because they're very serious and into poetry and all. I went through that all down the line, all the other kids, thinking, "Okay, who do I know? What is that like? Who is that?" And I must say, it was "real cool" when they came out. And the people in the audience, who were—at least for the first six months—mostly New York WASPs, were looking at themselves. There was that beat of, "Oh," and then you'd wait like two or three more, and they'd go, "Oh," like that, because those were the real kids. We'd all been set up by the costuming of the first guy. He had fooled even the audience, and the audience could see. "Oh, that's how he fooled the parents." He was wearing what the parents wanted to believe their children wore at school. So I must say, in a play about people wearing invisible non-costumes, that was very rewarding to me. And that was not in the script. That was just me figuring it out. I was able to add that.

It's interesting how all that came about.

Yes. You don't just do good work, you have to still keep proving yourself on every single project. There's a story that Ann Roth told us. I saw her the day that she was taking her portfolio to show the producers of *Singin' in the Rain*. She said, "Now I put on my little black dress, and my pearls, and my heels, I picked up my portfolio, and I went in there. I said, 'Well, I'm sorry you don't know who I am. Let me show you.'" And I'll tell you, that has been the key to every single action I've taken ever since then. When anyone asks for a portfolio or résumé, I do it instantly, and each time I think of Ann Roth. It tells you everything about how big you are.

On *Lend Me a Tenor* you worked with

Tony Walton, Jerry Zaks, and Paul Gallo again. Comment on that production.

It was actually my welcome back to the fold. I had not been allowed to work with Jerry at Lincoln Center, because the artistic director didn't like me. And so, I had not been considered for anything. On *Lend Me a Tenor* I was working with Tony Walton, who is one of our greatest visionaries. I mean, he's not just a designer, he's human! And I went to the meeting where they were trying to decide whether it should be an ornate 1890s hotel, or whether it should be a sleek-sleek Art Deco, sort of a Fred-Astaire-and-Ginger-Rogers-movie hotel. You know what won out, the movie hotel. So Tony created this incredible cutaway set and he presented it to me. This set had white walls, red surroundings, with a black-and-red rug and with white furniture. Now, you try to find people on this set with Art Deco detailing, right? Well, I didn't know what to do. It was this very difficult assignment, because the set was a beautiful piece of living sculpture. It could have existed as a piece of art without anything else.

And I thought, "What are they going to wear?" I started from what they *can't* wear: They can't wear brown. I started limiting myself and figuring out what they *could* wear. And I said, "Well, they're wearing gray. They can wear black and white and gray and gold and sliver, because it's these strong colors. What do you do for black, white, and red? Well, you wear black and white and gold and silver and gray and red. Someone can wear red, the bellman. And then you have to be careful, because then you're interjecting colors." Tony and I picked a purple for Otello, and then he put a little purple in the carpet. And we picked the perfect color blue. I went back and forth to his studio, from his studio to my studio. We picked a blue that looked good with that red, and he put that blue in the carpet. Then we picked a yellow for one costume, and he put the yellow in the carpet. So there were all the colors of the show in the carpet.

All the colors of the costumes.

Yes, the colors of the costumes were in

the carpet, and so we coordinated completely. It's a play about mistaken identities, and two people dress up in two different outfits and people confuse them for each other. It's sort of a Marx Brothers type of thing, except they didn't quite do it as brilliantly as in this Ken Ludwig production. I thought, how can I keep up with Tony Walton? We had Otello, who is the Moor of Venice, right? And, of course, this play takes place in the early 1930s and the room is Art Deco. I thought, what I should find is Moorish Deco. So, lo and behold, I was doing a dance piece at City Center, and I looked up at the facade and I said, "Oh, my God, this is Moorish Deco." The next day I came with my camera and my telephoto lens and I photographed the Moorish tiles on the inside, and the outside. The pattern on the back of the cape is the courtyard from the Alhambra Palace, which is very Deco-looking. And the doublet and hose that Otello is wearing is all based on the Moorish Deco tiles on the front of City Center.

The other funny thing was that there's a line in the play that the dowager was supposed to look like a wedding cake. But I just didn't want to do a white dress on this white set. So I did a dress that was silver and gray and mauve, and I did silver beading. I thought I was doing a wedding cake. Well, the dress appeared in Baltimore, and everyone was just screaming and yelling and laughing. I thought it was fine, and Ken changed the line to, "You look like the Chrysler Building." I had done the Chrysler Building when I was trying to do the "wedding cake." So the joke's on me.

How did your association with the Pointer Sisters come about?

I was working on a dance piece for Ballet Metropolitan in Columbus, Ohio for David Parsons, who is a choreographer and has his own company, the Parsons Dance Company. It was one of those free projects that I did, and this phone call came from Kenny Ortega. He is a choreographer and director, and he has done some Broadway shows, a lot of film, a lot of rock and roll, and Cher and everybody. And Kenny said, "You have to come and do the Pointers. They need a

THE POINTER SISTERS
Costume designs by William Ivey Long
Choreography by Kenny Ortega (1989)

new look and it has to be you!" So I did the Pointer Sisters the first time. That was six years ago. I've done two other projects with them. And doing the Pointer Sisters has led to Patti LaBelle and ultimately to doing Mick Jagger on the Rolling Stones' *Steel Wheels* tour. Then I think it influenced my getting *Siegfried & Roy*, which is also in Las Vegas, and is the largest production I've ever done.

Are you given a specific budget when you do the Pointer Sisters?
Actually, I set the budget. We have a specific budget and I have to design for that, down to the bead. I'm very fiscally responsible. You have to be in this world. I think it's one of the reasons I work. You have to be responsible to that budget, because it's a very tricky time. And it always has been. You have to be able to know that what you are designing will cost this amount and how to have it done.

What is it like to work with the Pointer Sisters?

The Pointer Sisters are fascinating. They are the most trusting, confident, gloriously serene performers I've ever worked with. They trust you—they trusted me the first time. Can you imagine? I went to rehearsal and I saw them do this one number and I did all these Russian Constructivist things with magic markers on napkins. And they came over and said, "Oh, that looks like the Sidney Opera House." So it was love at first sight. And they will try anything. They're six feet tall and ravishingly beautiful. And they can carry anything. So I consider them my playground. And I just love them and they're wonderful musicians. Michael Peters choreographed the last project.

Do they let you pick the style, the idea, and the colors?
No. Michael sort of has an idea. There are three sections each time and he sort of thinks of something, and I do sketches and then we redo them again, and then we pick the fabrics. And I know them so

well by now. I know what personality traits they have and how that transforms itself onstage. For instance, I know who doesn't like anything around her neck, and who likes no fingers in her gloves, but who likes gloves. It's designing three, so it's a palette. You have to balance it out so that they're all different, but all in a picture. So it's a fascinating design assignment. I love my relationships with them.

Do you work the same way with Patti LaBelle?

I did only one thing with Patti LaBelle, *Tommy* by the Who. She was absolutely amazing. I met her on the phone on Tuesday night. I did sketches on Wednesday. I sent them to Fed Ex Thursday. She picked one Thursday night. We put it in the shop Friday, and we worked on it Friday and Monday. And Tuesday she came by and had a fitting.

Describe what you did for her.

She was playing the Acid Queen in a benefit performance by the Who, doing *Tommy.* It was a benefit for AIDS, in Los Angeles at the Hollywood Bowl, and it was a big deal. Billy Idol and Phil Collins were in it. And Patti LaBelle was the only woman, so it had to be something special. We all did this for free. This was all a gift. It had to be done instantly.

I've always been impressed with her hair. Her childhood friend, Norma, does her hair. And Patti in real life does not wear this hair—you know, it's only in her performances.

Are they wigs?

No, they're not wigs. They're hair paper. They're woven hair things that then she cuts and puts up, and shoots around it. It's pure futurism. But I just played cutting up her body with futuristic shapes that we boned out, and it had a fish tail she could swing around. One leg showed, and she had big, angular, swinging sleeves, and a swinging pendulum.

Who made the costume?

Barbara Matera. Patti took a limo from Philadelphia, where she lives, right to Barbara Matera's fitting room, and then took the limo back with Norma. And I

took tissue paper and masking tape and built out all these jutting-out shapes from this sheath. So Patti LaBelle stood there giggling and laughing at me with this paper dress.

You said she had a fish tail?

I just gave her a twisty sort of dragon tail, which moved when she moved. It sashayed, and I had it wired so that it moved with the hips. It was very insane. And there was a big cape that went with it. So she came out and took off the cape and it was revealed. It was black and magenta. She was really quite exciting. And so we made that in a week.

Now if this was a benefit, who paid for it?

I'm not sure who paid for the gown, but everyone else gave their time. And I flew out, I think on my own. Bob Mackie let us have the fitting in his offices. And Bob and Ret Turner came to the fitting.

Do you feel that actors expect you to tell them, "Oh, you look good in this," or do they expect you to tell them how to wear something more than the average person would?

I find that most actors are incredibly intelligent. I don't think actors believe one word we say to them. I feel you just present. I try not to say, "Now look at this. Here it is, you look great." And they look and see it. If you tell them one thing, they will not believe it, actually. So you have to show them. And it's through the fitting and showing, where you cut on the hip line or where you cut on the shoulder, all the lines that you draw on the body with the fabric. You have to convince them that this enhances their look. Also, you make them feel good. I mean, you are doing things like building understructure or not, and making fabric choices. And of course, you're telling the story. But the main thing is, it's not about looking good. It's "Is this the character? Will this help them portray the character?" So looking good does come into it. But it's necessary for you to intellectually capture their imagination and talk to them, and explain, and work through this process of making a costume and help them become a character. If you include them, and talk them

THE POINTER SISTERS
Costume designs by William Ivey Long, for Ruth (top) and Anita Choreography by Michael Peters (1991)

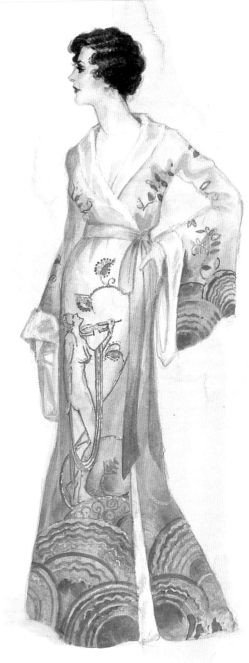

PRIVATE LIVES
Costume designs by William Ivey Long, for Joan Collins
Directed by Arvin Brown
Broadhurst Theatre, New York (1992)

through it and then show them, step by step, I think that's what makes them come to me and enjoy the process of developing the character. And all the while, we're doing psychological, in-depth charges, which hopefully they can build on. The fitting is a very important part.

Do you go to all of your fittings?

Absolutely. I go to every fitting. Recently I did fittings in the south of France with Joan Collins for *Private Lives*, and of course, we did toiles over there. "Toile" means thin cotton. That's what the English call it.

Are the fittings similar to those you have here?

Yes, but with super-duper care. We were halfway around the world and so we took second and third choices of toiles. We were so far away—we had to make this fitting work.

Why were you so far away?

Because she was writing a book over there, in between doing the television series, and appearing in *Private Lives*. I think Nolan Miller, who is an excellent designer, and who has done her clothes on *Dynasty* for years and years, has a shorthand when he works with her. They have a dummy, a mannequin, which has been shaped to her actual, complete figure. And it's a hard mannequin. So

you can really pull in on it. I think he does a lot of the fittings on the mannequin. And then she comes in for the final fittings. But here we were starting from absolute scratch. We had never seen her before.

Do you prefer a particular medium to work in?

What I pride myself on is doing every medium. Also, I am not a snob—I don't think there is any project that is unworthy of doing. I think you can inject your vision and your perception into anybody's dream—anybody's being the director's, the performer's—and enhance it. And I think that's what our job is. We are a support unit and we are employed and included in order to help other people perceive their dreams. We are not just doing costumes, of course—we are doing the visual embodiment of the personality you see up there on the stage.

Comment on the *Siegfried & Roy* production.

Well, it wasn't like a play, it wasn't like a musical, it wasn't like an opera, but it was like all of the above. It's a spectacle, a fantasy, and a mind trip. John Napier conceived of the project and was hired by Siegfried and Roy.

Because of his Broadway and London work?

They saw *Time* in London, for instance,

and they were particularly influenced by that. They said, "We want something mind-boggling and mind-enhancing." They were building a brand-new hotel out there, and they were building a theatre just to house this. So John Napier was in on the ground floor. He designed the auditorium, the permanent theatre design, the scenery, and the lighting setup. So he was our leader, and he co-directed and co-wrote it. So it's really *The John Napier Show.*

I didn't realize that he did the writing.

He did the whole thing. The rest of us who came in on it were John Caird, the Tony Award–winning *Les Mis* director, he co-directed it; Anthony Van Laast, the London choreographer; Andrew Bridge, who did *Phantom*, he did the lighting; Jonathan Deans, the English sound guy, did the sound; the only two Americans were Tom Bähler, who did the music, and me. And Michael Jackson wrote the finale song. He's a friend of theirs. He came up and was wandering around when we were doing the rehearsal.

During the first 10 or 15 minutes of the show, it's the most exciting spectacle. People arrive and they float down on these big extraterrestrial things and you don't know how they do it. It's just amazing. There's music, and the creatures come out, and it's really quite wonderful.

SIEGFRIED & ROY
Costume designs by William Ivey Long
Directed by John Caird
The Mirage, Las Vegas (1989)

Did you co-design the clothes, or did you design them?

No. I designed the clothes. Thank you, *Miss Saigon:* John was busy doing *Miss Saigon* in London and could not do the clothes. Otherwise, he would have designed them. He set the overall plan for the lights, the sound, the choreography, and everything. There are like 450 costumes. And it's 40 chorus girls, for instance, and 12 male dancers and various animal handlers and the leading lady, Lynette—and it was the largest production and the most money I've ever spent.

Was the show done in a shop out there?

No. All of it was executed in New York and then flown out. And some of it was done in Los Angeles, some of the boots and shoes and things. We were in six shops here.

Where were your fittings?

Out there. There are no shops in Las Vegas. There's nothing—it's just desert. The show plays six days a week, two shows a day. That's twelve shows. And this stuff takes a beating—all these 450 costumes get beaten up. So over the last year and a half, we have been adding doubles. The maintenance is so incredibly important. And one of my favorite assistants is still out there looking after things as the wardrobe master. It's a very complicated ongoing project.

Did you have to have dupes as far as the chorus people?

At the very beginning? No. Now, as it has been running, we've been doing duplications.

Do you have understudies?

Yes, we have understudies and swings, absolutely.

But in New York you don't usually do that until the show is a hit.

Right. But you see it has a guaranteed five-year run, with an option for 11.

You mean Siegfried and Roy would play in it that long and they don't mind?

Well, it's their show. They've created it. That's what they do. These are major professionals.

Their acts are incredible.

It's amazing. And talk about requirements—I not only had to design these things, but I had to guarantee that they would hold up, and be made correctly. So it's not just drawing a picture. The show is about good and evil. I have a whole Amazon army and an Amazon puppet army and the pieces are sculpted individually for the body, all out of Kydex. Kydex is what American Express cards are made out of. It's that plastic, and then we laminate it. The pieces were sculpted by Nino Novellino, this great sculptor at Costume Armour. And they've got this armor that's all affixed onto body stockings, and it's the only Las Vegas act ever to have no sequins, no plumes, and no fur. We don't have animal products on us, because we feature animal acts. And so everything's done with plastic, and it is sort of the Samurai Shōgun, Japanese influence. We have a big headdress, the headdresses are all Shōgun headdresses, and are imaginary and futuristic.

But you do have wear and tear, and you have to replace things.

Well, the responsibility of spending that amount of the producer's money is that you have to make sure that you get your money's worth. The art part, hopefully, is what you see, and the excitement of all that. But the producer wants to have stuff that lasts, and it's also my job to have done enough tests in the shop to guarantee that it's going to last. So you have to become a chemist and an engineer.

Did you have to change things because their act said, "We can't quite work this," or "This is too slippery," or what have you?

No. I'll tell you why: Siegfried and Roy are such consummate professionals. They can perceive any problem before it happens. And they will tell you. I was steered toward what they needed. In the beginning, and then in the fittings, they would say, "The grip needs to be stronger here," or something like this. There are specific needs. John Napier had to know how everything worked in order for him to provide the support. Actually, they pre-ferred that I not know how everything worked. So it was a slight disadvantage. I didn't want to know. I wanted both to support it and to be an audience member at the same time. I wanted to believe, and that's the only way I think you can do it.

You're doing a new production of *Guys and Dolls* with Jerry Zaks, Tony Walton, and Paul Gallo. Are you sticking to the original script?

We are indeed sticking to the original script. We are pleased as punch. What we are doing, though, is a fresh, innocent, and energetic approach. We're just diving in and doing it. We're doing it as if we'd never known it happened before. And that's the only way I think that you *can* do it, because one of the greatest designers in the history of the world designed the original—Jo Mielziner did the sets and lighting.

But we're not going to try to do *Guys and Dolls* different just because they did it one way. As Jerry Zaks said, "If we happen to have a red dress when there was a red dress before, and it seems right, then we'll just do it." But we can't pussyfoot around the original production, nor do we want to copy the original production.

What would be two of your favorite productions that you have done in your career?

I know exactly and I live with them every day—I compare my work every day with the two projects. One is *Nine*, directed by Tommy Tune—the Maury Yeston, Arthur Kopit production of *Nine*, for the aforementioned reasons, and because it made me realize that there was a lot of pure design in it. So that was very thrilling. And the second one, which I think about all the time, is *The Marriage of Bette and Boo*, which is Christopher Durang, and he is a very dear friend of mine. I did it at the Public Theatre, and Jerry Zaks directed. Loren Sherman did the scenery and Paul Gallo did the lighting. And it was a very special production to me—I felt it was the most perfect production I've ever worked on. I thought it achieved what it set out to do. It was thought-provoking, it was unsettling, it was a thrilling performance and production, and we were all working together. And I just thought it was why we do theatre.

Christopher was in it, playing himself, actually. And it was very personal. He brought the wedding photographs of his parents' wedding to me and let me have them for the run of the production period. It was a story about his parents, and we made them come alive, plus some. And it had a terrific cast: Joan Allen and Kathryn Grody and Mercedes Ruehl and Olympia Dukakis.

So there's one of each—one's a musical and one's a play. One of them was a show-off piece and the other was a non-show-off, an invisible design project. You didn't notice that it was designed. It's very tricky.

What do you like most about the theatre?

The people! I think it's the best group of people to spend your life with. I think the intelligence, the commitment, the humanness of the people in the theatre is of the highest order, and it is a constant delight. You can't drop the ball with this crowd. You've got to stay in there. I've never known such a group of people who read the paper so much. Everyone knows what is happening, and there's just a wonderful commitment to life. And I'm privileged to be among those people. I think it's the best group of people in the world. I love the people I work with, and that's why I enjoy doing theatre.

GUYS AND DOLLS
*Costume designs by William Ivey Long,
for "A Bushel and a Peck" (above) and
"Take Back Your Mink" (right)
Choreography by Christopher Chadman
Directed by Jerry Zaks
Martin Beck Theatre, New York (1992)*

PETER HARVEY
Costume design for Unto Thee a Garden
Brooklyn Museum (1968)

DOROTHY JEAKINS
Costume design for Dorothy McGuire in the film
The Friendly Persuasion
Allied Artists (1955)
(Collection of Lewis Brown)

JOHN SCHEFFLER
Costume design for the Krewe of Selena
Mardi Gras, New Orleans (1986)

LEWIS BROWN
Costume designs for Stephano in The Tempest
Old Globe Theatre, San Diego (1991)

TONY STRAIGES
Costume design for Ross
A project for the Yale Drama School (1974)

SAM KIRKPATRICK
Costume design for Lisette in La Rondine—*Act II*
New York City Opera (1983)

LINDSAY W. DAVIS
Costume design for A Little Night Music
New York City Opera (1990)

ALLEN CHARLES KLEIN
Costume design for Suzuki in Madama Butterfly
Miami Opera (1984)

SANTO LOQUASTO

Santo Loquasto resides in a large apartment in a pre-War building on Manhattan's Riverside Drive. Born in 1944 in Wilkes-Barre, Pennsylvania, he graduated from King's College and the Yale School of Drama. His first Broadway show was *Sticks and Bones,* in 1972.

Loquasto has designed sets and costumes for a great many companies, including the Guthrie Theatre, the Hartford Stage Company, the Long Wharf Theatre, the Williamstown Theatre Festival, the Yale Repertory Theatre, the New York Shakespeare Festival, Arena Stage, New York Pro Musica, the Mark Taper Forum, the San Francisco Spring Opera, the Michigan Opera

Company, the Brooklyn Academy of Music, the Manhattan Theatre Club, La Mama E. T. C., and Playwrights Horizons.

Among Loquasto's production and costume credits for film are *A Midsummer Night's Sex Comedy, Falling in Love, Stardust Memories, Desperately Seeking Susan, Zelig, Radio Days, Another Woman, September, Alice, Big, Crimes and Misdemeanors, Shadows and Fog, Husbands and Wives,* and *Bright Lights, Big City*. He has received the Tony, Drama Desk, Joseph Maharam, Obie, and Outer Critics Circle awards, as well as the British Academy Award.

AS YOU LIKE IT
Costume design by Santo Loquasto
Directed by Liviu Ciulei
Guthrie Theatre, Minneapolis (1982)

How did you become involved in designing costumes for the theatre?

As I've said to people working with me, as well as just in conversation, I think of myself as a set designer who designs costumes. And I discovered early on as a college student in the '60s that I felt compelled to create the entire picture. Even though I had none of the technical skills, it didn't seem foreign to me to think about designing what the actors were wearing. It was integral to the visual concept.

In working with John Conklin for many years at Williamstown, I found him to be very much of the same mind, having studied in Europe where it was common for one designer to do both sets and costumes. But my concern was not so much control—an unfortunate word—but to bring a consistency to the visual picture. The costumes became an instrumental way to punctuate the set. For example, years later, when I designed *The Cherry Orchard,* which was rather minimal and spare, I wanted to know exactly what the stage looked like at all times. Now, I could make a phone call and ask the costume designer. But as much as I believe in the healthiness and the excitement of real collaboration, it's just often simpler when one person is thinking and doing. And directors love it, because it's one less person they have to talk to.

You know, for many years I was among the faithful pilgrims to go to Stratford, Ontario, where there was very little scenery on the festival stage, and I became aware of the importance of costumes as the most potent visual element—the single source of period, class, and style. I think the work at Stratford really taught me as much about the history and theatricality of costume design as any place or class I ever attended. Between Tanya Moiseiwitsch, Desmond Heeley, Brian Jackson, Leslie Hurry, and Robert Prevost, the experience was so rich in every way, in its detail and selectivity, and in its approach to the text. Seeing all those elements so successfully

Santo Loquasto's scenery and costume design credits include the following:

BROADWAY SETTINGS

Jake's Women (1992), and C

Lost in Yonkers (1991), and C

Grand Hotel (1989), C only

Cafe Crown (1989), and C

Sweet Sue (1987)

Singin' in the Rain (1985)

The Wake of Jamey Foster (1982)

The Suicide (1980), and C

Bent (1979)

The Goodbye People (1979)

The King of Hearts (1978)

Sarava (1978), and C

American Buffalo (1977)

Sticks and Bones (1972)

The Secret Affairs of Mildred Wild (1972)

That Championship Season (1972)

BEAUMONT THEATRE SETTINGS

The Tenth Man (1989)

The Floating Light Bulb (1981), and C

The Cherry Orchard (1977), and C

The Dance of Death (1974)

NEWHOUSE THEATRE SETTINGS AND COSTUMES

The Tempest (1973)

DANCE COMPANIES

Twyla Tharp Dance

American Ballet Theatre

Joffrey Ballet

New York City Ballet

Paul Taylor Dance Company

The Royal Ballet

Les Grands Ballets Canadiens

National Ballet of Canada

San Francisco Ballet

PUBLIC THEATRE SETTINGS AND COSTUMES

Virginia (1985)

DELACORTE THEATRE SETTINGS

Richard III (1983), and C

Hamlet (1975)

Measure for Measure (1975), and C

The Comedy of Errors (1975), and C

Pericles (1974)

King Lear (1973)

As You Like It (1973)

AS YOU LIKE IT
Costume design by Santo Loquasto
Directed by Liviu Ciulei
Guthrie Theatre, Minneapolis (1982)

synthesized excited me so much that I realized I wanted to design this way, which meant designing the costumes as well as the setting.

Meanwhile, I found myself involved with dance projects where there were only costumes. In fact, when I first worked with Jerry Robbins, he didn't know I designed scenery. He just assumed I was a costume designer exclusively.

What about when you designed costumes for *Grand Hotel?*

Grand Hotel was a very special situation with many irresistible features. It meant working not only with Tommy Tune, but also with Tony Walton and Jules Fisher. I had worked with Jules Fisher, but not with Tony, whose work I have always admired, and he was a friend. I thought this truly was an offer I could not refuse. I would happily do it again, I must say. Tony and I worked rather closely on that show. By the time I became involved with *Grand Hotel,* certain questions about the look of the production had already been resolved, which actually allowed me to proceed more swiftly. Now, *Grand Hotel* is not really a big splashy musical; in many ways, it's more like doing a play. The set is rather elemental and suggestive, and in certain ways impressionistic of an era and time and architecture. It serves as a catalyst for the fluid unfolding of the story.

The costumes needed to punctuate or clarify, as well as bring a more complete sense of complexity to the hotel lobby setting. Using the line of bellhops and telephone operators, the staff of the hotel, and the guests in the introductory number, Tommy Tune created the provocative and atmospheric world of the piece.

Tony and I had to meet in a rather concentrated way to make sure that we were saying the same thing or that what we were saying would complement each other. It was about knowing, on a rather pragmatic level, what we had to do and how little time there was to do it—that is to say, for the audience to comprehend or perceive it. We could not confuse or blur or stumble in relating the crucial bits of information.

The way *Grand Hotel* is constructed, everyone is introduced in the opening number, and it is almost like a costume parade of characters and people, and it

GRAND HOTEL
Costume designs by Santo Loquasto
Directed and choreographed by Tommy Tune
Martin Beck Theatre, New York (1989)

says a lot about the evening, and the period, and the world, and the decadence of it. And then you have these overlaid dramas that are about to unfold. And you have to help the audience keep track of who's who.

Did Tommy Tune tell you what he wanted, or did you and Tommy get together and say what you wanted, or did you do both?

I'd seen the workshop and then I met with Tommy. At the time there was not really a script. There was the book and notes and a tape of the workshop. I had a cast of characters, and I asked questions as I went through it. Tommy had notes and he just said what he thought. When he drew a blank or was vague, he always said, "This is my impression, and take it from here and we'll see what you come up with," which of course was fun. And that's how we proceeded. I would see him almost every day during rehearsals, and I did sketches well into the rehearsal period.

You did rough sketches and thumbnails and then went on to finished sketches?

Right. And then there was research and photographs and all that. I kind of do that the way everyone does. I suppose now I work with more and more primary sources. For one thing, it gives people a true sense of the reality of the time, and also, because *Grand Hotel* is very theatrical, it needed to be grounded by period authenticity. We wanted it really to feel that it had its own credibility. I think that directors, no matter how experienced they are, become nervous about sketches and distrust their ability to read them. They're just more secure with photos. I find this to be particularly the case in my film experiences. Directors won't fully commit to the information in a sketch form as readily as they will to photos.

You mean photos you had found for research?

Right. They really want to see them. I do a sketch and then I flank it with photographs so that they can see where I'm going and what's fed me, and then I can see what excites them. And this in turn

might lead them even further or encourage me to be bolder in my ideas.

Were the costumes made for most of them?

Largely. Overcoats and accessories were found, but almost everything else was made.

Did you make muslin patterns?

Yes, except for suits. Tailors just make them, although mock-ups were made of overcoats. Barbara Matera did mock-ups of all the women's clothes.

How long did you have to design the show?

I was working in London and I came back around July 4th and started. We opened out of town in September, in Boston at the Colonial. Then we opened in New York in October.

Have you also done road companies?

Yes. There is a national tour, which is out now. And soon there will be a London company.

Are you keeping both of those the same?

Yes. Tommy wants it essentially the same. I have little things I want to change. Also, when I see the actors I make certain accommodations.

You mean in cut and style, as opposed to color and texture?

Right, exactly. It has more to do with character in this case, too. You know, it's easy to feel it has to be like the original New York production. But if someone looks better or worse depending on what is appropriate, you respond to the physical attributes and hopefully do the right thing.

***Lost in Yonkers.* How did that come about?**

I got a call last summer from Manny Azenberg's office asking me if I wanted to read this new play by Neil Simon. And having done that, if I were interested, and if so, would I care to meet with Gene Saks, the director. I did those things and I met with Gene. We had a terrific meeting and started working. It never occurred to me that I would do the costumes—I had assumed Joe Aulisi would design them, but he was doing

Billy Bathgate, the film, and was not available.

At that point, the play had not been cast. It turned out that Irene Worth was in it. She was an old chum from *The Cherry Orchard* and even earlier days. And Mercedes Ruehl and I had worked together on a film, although I didn't know her well. I thought all this will be great! And it turned out to be wonderful to work on. I talked to Gene and to Neil about just general character things, and I said, "This is how I want to do this, if it makes sense to you." I brought them pictures—again, research. I said, "Just so you know the period that we're talking about. We're all clear on how much money these people make, where they live, what the seasons are," which, of course, changed during out-of-town try-outs. They just hated all those overcoats, as much as I loved them. So just get rid of the cold months!

Did you have an assistant?

Claudia Stephens was my assistant. She really did a fantastic job. We hadn't worked together before. So we went out shopping together at vintage clothing dealers so she could become familiar with my preferences, and eventually she collected most of the garments herself. We found a lot of real stuff, more than I ever expected. I find dealers will let you take things out on consignment, so you can try them and return them. It's important to maintain good relationships with clothing dealers. Their services are indispensable. We now have contacts all over the country.

There were specific garments I knew I wanted, which I'd found in old Sears catalogs from the late '30s and '40s. I would say, "We should find something like this. If we can't find this, then we'll make it."

The kids' things, for the little boys, we had to make, because children's clothes are just hard to find. We found a few things, but kids wore their clothes to death, or they were never kept, or they were held onto by the family—no one ever felt they were of any interest to people. Naturally, there was a problem finding day dresses too. You find evening dresses and good clothing. We discovered a woman who bought in triplicate from some mail service and she had the same dress in about four colors, because she would find a style she liked. Many of them had never been worn. It was amazing.

Anyway, I had a palette I wanted to work out that was harmonious with the scenery. I knew that I wanted it to be in warm tones and to look uncalculated. I didn't want it to be exactly like a *Post* magazine or to be too Norman Rockwell. But nonetheless, you cannot be a designer and resist coordinating so that the sofa sets off the bathrobe and the house dresses. You are just too conscious of what's happening onstage. You want to feature the actors sufficiently and yet you want them to belong in the same kind of nostalgic feel of the whole picture.

But I didn't want it to seem sentimental. I wanted it to have a little more punch to it. So there's actually a good bit of color. They are not necessarily bright, but there is real activity, a real kind of color—not in conflict, but not necessarily obviously harmonious. That was my effort, to make it seem credible, as opposed to designed.

Did you have to make any changes once it got onstage?

I'm happy to say very little. Neil came up to me and actually was extremely complimentary. I think both Gene and Neil were delighted with the kind of energy of the clothes. But Neil did give me one note. It was that thing that often happens when a director or playwright says someone looks too nice and maybe you should beat up this or that. In fact, it is not the solution. What was needed was specific detail to reinforce the offstage action of the scene. This nerdy little kid was working in the soda fountain, and he needed an apron with smudges on it and some touches like that, so Neil could really feel that he was working, and not look at all like he was in a Brooks Brothers sweater, which he was. Later, the seasons were changed, and the winter coats and jackets were cut. It starts in the summer, in August of 1942, and ends almost nine months later. Originally it ended in the winter.

So you went through a period of many months?

THE CHERRY ORCHARD
*Costume designs by
Santo Loquasto
Directed by Andrei Serban
New York Shakespeare Festival
Beaumont Theatre, New York
(1977)*

THE CHERRY ORCHARD
DUNYASHA - ACT I - MERYL STREEP

#18

REAR
VIEW

THE CHERRY ORCHARD
MME. RANEVSKAYA - ACT I - IRENE WORTH

#1

THE CHERRY ORCHARD
DUNYASHA - ACT II - MERYL STREEP

#19

THE CHERRY ORCHARD
VARYA - ACT II PRISCILLA SMITH

#15

Yes. And they actually wear what they arrived in, with a change of shirts. These are very fast costume changes and you have to cheat on things. The poor kids do a lot of underdressing of pajamas under their knickers. But we don't change the knee socks within the act. I spared them the agony of underdressing socks. The audience doesn't notice those things as much as you'd like to think they do. I'd rather concentrate on changing the rest of the wardrobe. Also, this family doesn't have an extensive wardrobe. It was important for them to repeat clothing.

Are there wigs in the show?
Grandma Kurnitz wears a wig. She wears an entire body suit to make her look much heavier and "grandmotherly." And then she wears a fierce armadillo corset over it. Paul Huntley made a beautiful wig for her. It was fine, frizzy hair with broken ends, hardly glamorous. I was hoping to avoid wigs on the rest of the cast, and did. Someone was brought in to style their hair and work with them. But then they were on their own, and they became rather experts. It was very impressive. I worried that after a few months they would be bored dealing with this. But they never seemed to be.

Do you go back and check?
Oh, yes, police it, make a sneak attack!

When you go back, do you talk to the stage manager?
First I go to the wardrobe supervisor, Penny Davis, and then to the actor. Often I visit the actors anyway, because they're chums.

How frequently do you police the costumes in a long run?
It varies. In the beginning of *Grand Hotel,* I was there often. The thing about *Grand Hotel* is that if you see the first number, you almost see everybody in about 10 minutes, so it's great! You try to do it monthly; in reality, it winds up being not so often, but I keep in touch through my assistant, Mitchell Bloom, who polices regularly. If someone new is going in, Mitch will alert me if it is a whole new physical type, so that I can attend the fitting.

Do you have to change the designs?

You want to make sure that it's being changed to make sense on each man. It's the same design, essentially.

Since *Grand Hotel* and *Lost in Yonkers* are hits, do you have to do understudy costumes for both?
Of course. But I have all that set up with the wardrobe supervisors, especially on *Lost in Yonkers.* By the time it opened, we were covered, and even as we were first accumulating things, Penny Davis kept saying, "Well, we should keep this, this is good to have for someone else who comes along." And now we have another young man who starts tonight. We had enough things in our stock that we had accumulated, except for one knicker suit and one of the shirts, a period shirt that we can no longer find.

Grand Hotel is a different situation. Many costumes need to be exact duplicates for the cover or understudy, and others need to be flexible, so that one person can cover several characters and wear the same suit. It's rather tricky.

Your association with Woody Allen on films—how did that come about?
I was asked to do the costumes for a film called *Simon,* which Marshall Brickman had written and was directing, his first film as a director. He had been a long-time collaborator of Woody's. They wrote *Annie Hall, Sleeper,* and *Manhattan.* Anyway, I thought costumes are costumes, why not?

I can't help but believe that Woody called me based on my work with Marshall. I actually remember that my heart raced. He asked me about doing the costumes for a film, *Stardust Memories,* which I did. And subsequently I did the costumes for *A Midsummer Night's Sex Comedy* and *Zelig.* Not only were they interesting films to work on, but they allowed me to be around and to watch what a camera sees or doesn't see, and what a cinematographer needs or doesn't need, or doesn't want, or takes away. During that time, Woody was working with Gordon Willis, who is a truly great cinematographer. And I just learned so much from what his demands were in terms of color, pattern, and in general the role that wardrobe played in the graphic composition of the shot.

Now you may ask, "Where was Woody in all this?" Woody was there as well, but Gordon was often more articulate. It was a wonderful collaboration, which they had for many years. Gordon was authoritative but was not domineering. Woody's instinct and impulse were always being realized. And even now, what is regarded as Woody's style is clearly the result of those many years of work with Gordon Willis.

You would chat about costumes for the production in contrast to doing it for the stage. Would you also bring in photographs and research to talk about?
Oh, I would bring in garments. With Woody I did sketches or I had photographs or paste-ups—the entire gamut. But for Woody's movies you do endless wardrobe tests.

How do you decide on what materials you'll take to him?
First of all, I read the script and then talk to him. And we meet regularly, actually maybe twice a week, every other day or so. It depends on the scale of the movie. When we did *A Midsummer Night's Sex Comedy,* we decided on the period, which was 1906, and I remember I tried to entice him with Lartigue photographs. But he found them rather bewildering. He thought they were wonderful photographs, but didn't know why I was showing them to him. He found them reflective of too special and sophisticated a world.

Someone once said to me, "You never did any costumes for Woody in color?" I said, "*A Midsummer Night's Sex Comedy* was in color. It was beige and green. The costumes were hardly reflective of any real color, just diffused warm tones set off by the grass and trees everywhere." But it was beautiful, the way Gordon captured the period and romance of the story. It was sepia-toned, but had a glow reminiscent of European summer films that I love to watch. Those films have a different texture to them, quite honestly, and this is as close as I'll get to them.

To return to your question, I did do sketches for the film *A Midsummer Night's Sex Comedy,* because we were making the costumes. And that is when I

really learned how no one wanted to look at sketches. They made him nervous. Woody thought the costume sketches were pretty and fun. But he preferred the Xeroxes of the research of the blouse or hat. He just wanted the security of knowing it wouldn't look like a musical. It was fascinating. We were dealing with real paranoia about sketches.

Would you take an assistant and go shopping for things to bring in and show them the next day?
Sometimes. There's enough hysteria involved in movies when you are really doing them. I try not to cater to that atmosphere. Jeff Kurland was my assistant on these films. Since *Zelig,* the last film for which I did costumes with Woody, Jeff has done all of the subsequent films.

I can't help but think about this, especially on *Stardust Memories,* where I was so nervous about Woody and the whole situation, and did race around and try to come up with new ideas overnight for Charlotte Rampling or Jessica Harper or whomever we were trying to costume.

An interesting thing happens in films often, and I've talked to Ann Roth and other designers about this: There is a tendency for this frenzy of choices to erupt. It is like racing to Robert De Niro's camper with 33 ties so that he can find the perfect one. Well, I feel after six, unless they're all wrong or all the same, it's ridiculous. The designer is actually creating a pressured situation for the actor. You're not doing your job, in a way. It's not even a matter of ego, but there's a reason as to why you've been hired. And anyone can just go out and acquire racks of clothing and then ask the director or actor to rifle through them until he sees something he likes. Yes, options are helpful and choices are not something to be afraid of. But designers need to at least narrow down the range to a point where everyone involved is talking about the same thing.

A MIDSUMMER NIGHT'S SEX COMEDY, THE FILM
Costume designs by Santo Loquasto, for Mia Farrow (left) and Julie Hagerty (right) Directed by Woody Allen (1982)

HAFFNER SYMPHONY
Costume designs by Santo Loquasto
Choreographed by Helgi Tomasson
San Francisco Ballet (1991)

Do you ever worry about liking the actress's dress with the actor's suit in a scene, if the director may have an opinion? Or a group of clothes not really looking like you had envisioned them in a particular scene?

That is sort of the day-in/day-out fear of it all. One hopes that the results are serendipitous. It's very interesting with Woody—since he is usually concerned with style or even a lack of style, we come to terms on the rules and after that it becomes routine. When you work in black and white, you are immediately spared all that by the elimination of color. When we were doing *A Midsummer Night's Sex Comedy,* it was a limited palette. It was a similar situation when Jeff did the costumes for *Another Woman.* In both films, the final result was that of desaturated color as a conscious design decision, as opposed to a technical manipulation by the lab.

Is that common?

No. But it is done. Style is an issue and must always be acknowledged.

But to get back to your question about the kind of harmony on the screen and the randomness of bringing in other elements, you have to try to be prepared for that. When we were doing *A Midsummer Night's Sex Comedy,* we had scenes up at Columbia University, and there were many students, and you just knew that there was this kind of sea of the same values, that you could mix people together indiscriminately and it would be alright. If anything, you worried it would appear too calculated. It should generate a kind of beauty that avoids being precious. It can't be as perfect as an all-white stage picture, but somehow you want the same effect. Essentially you want that sense of heat and summer and light.

In working with Woody Allen on a number of projects, a vocabulary has developed. He may have a specific style in mind or want to discover a style in preproduction, and while I have past experiences to build on, I try to explore other avenues, not simply to rely on what has worked in the past. What I try to avoid is what is too familiar, unless of course that's what is requested.

He's one of the few directors who are conscious of all the elements that make a movie. The way in which he photographs the story is as important to him as the story. It's interesting that he's that concerned, since he's really a writer and an actor more than anything else. And you would think the words would be more important to him. But he's really involved with the whole process in a rather sophisticated, refined way.

Are you expected to be on the set every day of the shooting when costumes are involved?

Well, when I'm doing costumes, once they've been established I don't necessarily have to be there. And often I can't be. When I was doing *Zelig,* which was mammoth, I would make sure everybody was dressed, especially all the new people. It was new groups of people practically every day, or often several different groups a day, and I was always there when Woody was viewing them for the first time.

Then I returned to the shop, or wardrobe loft or whatever, and dressed the people scheduled to work in several days. And I would leave Jeff to deal with anything that would come up on the set. So, yes, I was there, but I didn't necessarily hang out. If I had the time and the inclination, then I could easily spend the day there. And often I was there because there was so much to be done. And there was a lot to supervise.

Would you have extras on hand in case something didn't work or if the director wanted something a little more flashy or if something's too bright?

Yes, that can happen. When I'm doing principals I often put together a wardrobe for them with certain variables that may not be accounted for specifically in the scene breakdown. This is dependent very much on the situation—that is, the actors, director, cinematographer, and, of course, the budget.

But this approach is somewhat problematic on a period project. It's possible that's the way directors like it to be, but it can be expensive and nerve-racking.

Does someone make calls for extra costumes?

There's a wardrobe truck around the corner. You know, the assembled masses that it takes to make a movie is quite awesome.

It's much different than doing a stage production, isn't it?

Yes, and I remember always how impressed I was ultimately by what the wardrobe people did and could do instantly on a film. It is really hard, hard work, difficult personalities, horrible pressures, and a deadly pace.

If you're shooting a scene in the rain, do you have three copies of the same thing?

Definitely. If the scene is written to be in the rain, yes. If it turns out to be raining that day, it's different. It depends on the situation—if it's somebody caught in the rain, I'm ready. Because invariably it's necessary to see the person dry and then wet. But if it's a cut to someone in the park in the rain, then I have backups largely for actor comfort or as a precautionary measure.

What is the most challenging show for which you have designed costumes?

I suppose the most challenging has invariably been my work in dance, for various reasons. If there is a narrative, it can be rather oblique—clear only to the choreographer. He or she may choose to keep it that way, or may ask you to help clarify it. Or they may ask you to design it in a way that ultimately conceptualizes it. Deciding on the attack can well be the challenge.

Comment on what you enjoy when designing for dance.

What I love about designing for dance is working within such rigorous limitations. It is necessary to accommodate the needs of the dancer, to allow for the visibility of the movement, and to reinforce or augment the movement in a way that complements it. This is to say you may actually dress someone in something that obscures the body, which is not consistent with the notion of designing for dancers, but which in fact might be very appropriate for the piece, and perhaps allow it to be more distinctive-looking or referential in a way that's surprising.

Usually I begin designing during the choreographic process. By attending rehearsals I can engage in a certain amount of give and take with the choreographer, depending on the person involved, and depending on whether he or she is a giver or a taker.

When I worked with Twyla Tharp on *The Catherine Wheel,* we worked not only on that particular piece for months and months, but actually on seminal works that led to it. It wasn't necessarily clearly discursive, but you can't help but refer to previous efforts, even though they do not currently relate to what we are doing. We take the ideas and build on them, or edit them, or change them. It's always been fascinating, even with projects that have failed or are unsuccessful or are not well received, or whatever you want to call them. With Twyla I always feel the gratification of the exercise. It's because she doesn't ask of anyone more than she asks of herself. So you can't help but feel that you've got to meet that challenge.

I've worked with Paul Taylor now for about four or five years. He's a fantastically interesting person to work with. His visual sense is entirely different from Twyla's, even though she danced with his company. It's interesting for me to now work with Paul, having worked with Twyla.

Twyla was a member of his company.
Right. It was his company and she was a dancer in it. And his influence on her is very apparent to me, although his sensibility is entirely different from hers and actually more traditional. One particular piece I did with Paul, *Of Bright and Blue Birds and the Gala Sun,* I went full-circle on that during the year I worked on it.

What do you mean "full-circle"?
Talking about how I thought people would be dressed and going from Walker Evans/Depression to contemporary Gap-ad clothing and winding up being a combination of medieval and Japanese dance clothes. The movement in them was beautiful. Again, Barbara Matera made them.

How many people, roughly?
There were 16 to 18 people. It wasn't huge, but big enough.

In designing for the dance, do you find there is a tendency for the choreographer to want to get the dancers onstage in costume and try them out as soon as possible?
With Paul there is often a dress rehearsal in his studio, because of economics and because the company is often going out of town and we will want to be able to fix the costumes in the shop, rather than in the basement of a theatre. But also, Paul doesn't want to be surprised. Some people want to get them onstage instantly—you know, they can only look at things in the real space. I often work with Jennifer Tipton on these dance pieces, and she doesn't even want to light if she doesn't have the people in the costume, or at least a comparable color.

You mean there's no point in starting until she sees them together?
If it's an all-white ballet and the dancers come on and they're in their warm-up clothes in black and green, she says, "You know, there's no point to it." Her work is too refined and her eye too subtle to waste time on a picture that is misleading.

The piece you did in Washington was *Company B.* That was for the Houston Ballet?
Paul Taylor choreographed it on his company, but it was commissioned by the Houston Ballet as part of a program that's being sponsored by the Kennedy Center. It's part of a program of pieces being made by choreographers for regional ballet companies.

Was this a typical way of working with him, this ballet?
No. What was sort of quirky about it was that it was a piece that was done with a score of Andrews Sisters songs, and what he said to me was that they really had no money to do it. Paul said, "You know, we have this piece and you have to do it for Houston and you have to do it for my company. I want to see what you are going to do for my company first, and I want them to be essentially the same." He said when the ballet companies do his work, he maintains they always look better because they have more money to execute the cos-

tumes, which is sometimes true, but not always the case.

Mitchell Bloom has been assisting me on costume projects for the last few years. I explained what I wanted to him and he and I went out and started shopping together and separately.

As opposed to the costumes being built?
Yes. We just couldn't afford to do it that way. For Houston we made things, because it was efficient and preferable for them, rather than altering purchased garments to accommodate the dancers' needs.

Such as?
We rig them. Even though it all looks like casual clothing, the shirts are rigged to leotards or briefs. The trousers have inner elastic in the waistbands so that they don't drop down and split. And the trousers are lined so that they will slip on their legs and drop properly.

And also for wear?
Yes, also for wear, as well as the look. But we found trousers that were lined. This is really so that they don't stick to their sweaty legs. Actually, in Houston we wound up with guys wearing footless tights as well as shoes and socks. The tights help the trousers to maintain their movement.

I watched a rehearsal of this piece and I said to Paul, "Now you don't really want to have this be a nostalgic piece with shoulder pads in the dresses." And I said, "We can't really do anything like that anyway, because there's no money." He said, "No, no, you're right. I'm not quite sure what it should be. You just think about it." So I went to another rehearsal a month later. He works on these things over a period of time. When the company goes out on tour and then gets back, there is a rehearsal period. He told me that Jennifer Tipton was coming to a rehearsal and that if I could attend it would be great and then we would all talk.

I sat next to Jennifer, and Paul was on the other side of her. So I would say things during the run-throughs, of which there were two. And we talked about our impressions of the piece—that there was

THE OTHER
Costume designs by Santo Loquasto
Choreographed by Agnes de Mille
American Ballet Theatre, New York (1992)

a sort of pathos underlying its movement at times, and there was counterpuntal action in this movement across the back of the stage, whether they were to evoke the sense of dying soldiers or the sadness of the 1940s, along with the kind of romance of the music. He wanted it to have a little more happening rather than just a suite of dances reminiscent of a period.

Then I said, "It would be nice if there were a way to desaturate the picture." If you think of the 1940s—and I cited *New York, New York*—and if you thought of De Niro in that wonderful Hawaiian shirt and his khakis, that gives you a sense of the period.

But we took all of the color out of it. So that if we wanted to, it could be quite bleak as well as being lush at times—not so much colorful lush, but just sort of buoyant in the general atmosphere. So without sounding trite, they were almost like ghost figures at times. I said it would be wonderful to find a way to do that. And Jennifer said that if we did a white floor, which we had in the repertory at the Taylor Company, and if we had a white backdrop of filled scrim, then she could really light this in a particular way to give that effect. Now all I had to do was find the clothing to support that idea!

Mitch and I were amazed at how much we found. Of course, the first thing we did was walk into the stores, and everything was black and chartreuse and orange. I said, "Oh, great! Obviously it's the perfect spring to do this." When the piece opened and was this remarkable success, both in the *New York Times* and the *Washington Post,* I was in San Francisco doing another ballet, and I called Mitch and said, "Start buying shirts. In two years this piece is going to be done the way other pieces of Paul's have been done and we're going to go crazy trying to find shirts." Today a package arrived with more shirts from Saks.

Company B was perceived exactly as we hoped it would be. It actually does have color in it. We had a sketchy rehearsal, just so we could see everyone wearing their shirts, and how the partnering worked. I wanted to make sure there wasn't some awful mistake that happened, where all of a sudden a girl and a guy were dancing together and the patterns that had looked fine when they were on the opposite sides of the stage were terrible when they were in each other's arms.

During "Rum and Coke" Paul said to me, "Oh, don't you think Mary should have some color for this scene?" So I wound up just lining her skirt in bright orange to feature her. Some of the girls wore slacks so they look like Rosie the Riveter. I said, "If I line the skirt in bright orange, I'll have to use orange in other places. So we'll give everybody an orange belt, and then the girls can have orange earrings and orange ties in their hair." So again, it just gave everyone a little punch.

If I ask you to include two productions you've designed costumes for in a time capsule, what would they be?

I suppose *Push Comes to Shove,* which is a Twyla Tharp piece, and I don't know what the other one would be, but I bet it would be something like *The Caucasian Chalk Circle* or *Peer Gynt* or one of those epic plays I've done in regional theatres, because they were bigger than life. *Peer Gynt* at the Guthrie was quite a marvelous project.

The Caucasian Chalk Circle at the Arena Stage was, of course, more flamboyant. Both of these plays have a kind of romantic exuberance, visually. You're really trying to tell stories in both of them very differently, but not lose the actors in the telling. It is important to keep in contact with the primitive imagination that the audience can recognize and relate to.

You've worked on *Push Comes to Shove* again. Comment on that.

I've recently redone it in Paris. I have clarified ever so slightly the color schemes, so there is a little more distinction.

Describe the color schemes.

It is what I call smokey colors. There's a group of corps de ballet girls in beige and in gray, in simple silk chiffon dresses with vaguely oriental-inspired sashes. Two principal women are keyed off the corps de ballet, in cream and pale gray. This is more clearly done than in the original production at ABT.

I kept the men pretty much the same. Patrick Dupond, who did Baryshnikov's role, is very much the same. And the men in his group I call the "Imperials." They are a courtly assortment, in a version of dancer's rehearsal clothes. These are made of velvet and satin and brocade and all sorts of luminous fabrics in smokey shades of olive, Payne's gray, teal blue, and aubergine.

There is also a group of four women in long jersey gowns and turbans, who were pretty much the same as in the originals, except that I lined their dresses in red and I added little metallic cords to accentuate their heads and wrists, so you'd see all their movements a little more clearly. The changes I did on the one principal woman had more to do with her body and skin color. The original dress was for Martine van Hamel, and this woman was just entirely different and needed something to make her feel and look better.

What production did you do in Nashville?

Nashville was *Speaking in Tongues,* for Dance in America, the Paul Taylor piece that I had done originally onstage.

That was filmed for television?

Yes. The scenery was entirely redesigned, but the costumes remained the same. We wanted it to be more narrative and not as abstract as it was onstage, and not so much a staged television piece. Matthew Diamond was the television director, and he was wonderful. He and I really worked on designing and blocking out where and how things would be shot and what kinds of spaces could be created. Matthew really understands television and the use of the camera. I had never worked in television.

We often confined the dancers. And it turned out that cramping the dancers makes it look better. The dancers were always complaining, "We can't do it in this little space." But they were great at adjusting to what the limitations were. And we moved around and changed the space sculpturally to make corridors and passageways or large open spaces or a big ramp or whatever.

You said you used the same costumes. Did the same dancers perform?

Yes. And they had rehearsed on the new ground plans in the studio. Paul Taylor had to restage some things and they had to make certain adjustments.

If you had the choice of designing the costumes for any production, what would it be?

You know, I don't know. For many years I designed Shakespeare for Joe Papp, both indoors and out. And I find designing for Shakespeare not so much always satisfying as much as always a challenge. I suppose I could limit it to almost any Shakespearean play, because I think there's room to really design. Even if the production were disciplined and limited to a period, as implied by the text, and uncluttered by concepts, it would still be gratifying. Actually, I would love to design sets and costumes for the ballet *Romeo and Juliet,* assuming that the situation is desirable—that is to say, a wonderful choreographer, good company, excellent shops, and sufficient funding.

If I'm a new student and I want to go into costume design, what would you suggest for me?

It depends. The people who have assisted me I have invariably met working in costume shops more than by reviewing their portfolios. This is New York, and there are only a handful of shops, but they're all quite good—the ones that have survived. And the young people who work there as shoppers often serve as a kind of liaison between the designer and the shop, and the drapers. These people become very informed, and you can see how they think, and you can see if they catch on to how you're thinking. You can often find interesting people in that job, and you try to steal them away.

Frequently you meet designers who come in and show you their portfolio and you just want to shoot them, they're so good. The negative side of all that is they have little practical experience, or they have a remarkable ego and aren't really interested in the schlepping that the job demands. There are great assistants out there who actually get the show on for people. So the competition is ruthless. But it's hard to know what to do with people who have enormous talent and no experience. It's frustrating for everyone involved.

You rely on assistants who know about where to get everything, what

works well, what's needed, and can have ideas about your work and how to translate it. It's the give and take of these collaborations that often make the work more interesting. It's not that you're exploiting someone any more than we're being exploited by directors or anyone else—it's healthy studio life.

Do you also find costume designers need to be good hand-holders or psychiatrists to actors, to make them feel secure?

It depends. You can do some of that.

There's all sorts of ways. You know who's wonderful at that? Theoni Aldredge and Ann Roth and Jane Greenwood—they're charmers.

And it does take a certain amount of effort.

Oh it takes incredible effort. You can be tired of shopping and you still have to be able to have coffee and be amusing in the green room. Sometimes you're amazed that you can really go in there and rally. And it's fun for you too, no matter how you protest.

JEANNE BUTTON
Costume design for Raven in The Robber Bridegroom
Biltmore Theatre, New York (1976)

JEANNE BUTTON
Costume design for Rosamund in The Robber Bridegroom
Biltmore Theatre, New York (1976)

ROBERT O'HEARN
Costume design for Samson et Dalila
Metropolitan Opera, New York (1975)

JEANNE BUTTON
Costume design for Cecco in Peter Pan
Alabama Shakespeare Festival, Montgomery (1991)

JOSÉ VARONA
Costume design for Queen of the Gypsies in Don Quixote
Teatro Municipal, Rio de Janeiro (1982)

JOSÉ VARONA
Costume design for King of the Gypsies in Don Quixote
Teatro Municipal, Rio de Janeiro (1982)

JEANNE BUTTON
Costume design for the Indian in Peter Pan
Alabama Shakespeare Festival, Montgomery (1991)

JEANNE BUTTON
Costume design for Dead Eye Diego in Peter Pan
Alabama Shakespeare Festival, Montgomery (1991)

BOB MACKIE

I spoke with internationally renowned costume and fashion designer Bob Mackie in his studio at Bob Mackie Associates, located high above Seventh Avenue in the heart of Manhattan's Times Square. Mackie, a native of California, was born in 1939. After studying at Pasadena City College and earning a degree in costume design at Chouinard Art Institute, he worked with legendary designers Jean Louis and Edith Head. He made his Broadway debut, with Ray Aghayan, designing the costumes for the revival of *On the Town* at the Imperial Theatre in 1971.

Other Broadway productions that followed were *Lorelei* (1974) at the Palace (with costumes for Carol Channing), *The Debbie Reynolds Show* (1976) at the Minskoff, and *Platinum* (1978), with Alexis Smith, at the Mark Hellinger. Mackie has also created a great variety of spectacular costumes for Elton John's many stage and concert appearances. His first operatic assignment was designing the costumes for Alban Berg's *Lulu* for the San Francisco Opera in 1989.

Mackie began a long list of television credits when Ray Aghayan chose him as his assistant for *The Judy Garland Show* in 1963, and he designed for *The Carol Burnett Show* through-

out its 11-year run, as well as for the *Sonny & Cher Comedy Hour*. His designs for Cher were displayed at New York's Metropolitan Museum of Art in 1975.

With countless credits for film, television and stage productions, Mackie has earned numerous honors and awards, including three Academy Award nominations, nine Emmy nominations, and six Emmy Awards, including the first award in the history of television to be presented for costume design in 1967. In addition to working on his show business projects, Mackie keeps busy creating fragrances and designing an array of high fashions, furs, jewelry, scarves, and knitwear, with plans to expand into the fields of lingerie, swimwear, and shoes. He still designs special-occasion dresses for longtime friends: Cher, Diana Ross, Carol Burnett, Diahann Carroll, Brooke Shields, and Bernadette Peters. Today he is president, partner, and designer for a New York–based ready-to-wear company bearing his name, and his clothes are sold across the country at the finest department and specialty stores, such as Martha's, Bergdorf Goodman, Saks Fifth Avenue, and Elizabeth Arden. Mackie has also written a successful "how-to" book, *Dressing for Glamour*.

PENNIES FROM HEAVEN, THE FILM
Costume designs by Bob Mackie, for (from left)
Christopher Walken, Steve Martin, and Bernadette Peters
Directed by Robert Ross
Released by Metro-Goldwyn-Mayer (1981)

How did you first become interested in designing costumes for the theatre?

While growing up in California, I became interested in designing costumes for the theatre by going to movies. When I was a kid all the movies were about getting to Broadway and playing the Palace and having a hit show. So those were the ones I liked best. They were usually musicals, and it was always the idea, "We'll have our name in lights on Broadway" and all that, and I thought that was quite wonderful.

Even though I lived near the film studio, I might as well have been in Kansas City, because if you live in the suburbs in Los Angeles, you have nothing to do with the film community. So it was strictly a fantasy thing on my part. I was a little shocked the first time I walked in the stage door at the Palace Theatre in New York and a rat went right in front of

my feet! And I said, "Well, I guess it's not quite as glamorous as in the movies."

Did you go on and study costume design?

Yes, I did. During my whole childhood I was studying costume design on my own, one way or the other. But then I went to the Chouinard Art Institute in Los Angeles, which is no longer there. The school had been around since the 1920s, so it developed a lot of very fine costume designers for film. There was Edith Head and Howard Shoup and Rene. It was a fun school to go to, because these people would come back and give classes and speak.

What was the costume design course like?

It was sort of a combination of ready-to-wear, film design, and stage design. It was a little bit of everything, including

research, cutting, draping, pattern-making, and sewing, which I didn't like too much. But I eventually found how to do it. It was the only way I could get through the class. And when I was working in small theatres, I was sewing the costumes on an old Singer of my grandmother's in my bedroom.

You say theatres—where did you go? Did you get jobs while you were in school?

This was in Los Angeles after I got out of school. When you're in school you don't particularly have time to do "little theatre," but the minute I got out I started doing small plays and original plays around Los Angeles and Hollywood, where they have a lot of little funny theatres. I worked cheap and usually it cost me money to do a show, because I was always wanting it better. I put my own money into it and bought better fabrics. It's a big ego problem if your name is on it. You want it to look wonderful. That's been a problem all my life.

What happened after that? Did you come to New York?

No. My ambition was to come to New York and conquer the theatre, but it was already late fall. I didn't have a coat and I didn't have any money. I was out of school and I was working in a restaurant, washing dishes at night, so I could be sure to get my calls during the day, in case somebody was just clamoring to find me. The thought of an answering machine was just out of the question. People had them, but that wasn't for me. Anyway, it didn't take that long, but it seemed like it took forever. I got a couple of jobs in the studios, working for Jean Louis and Edith Head. They used to trade off on me because I was not the regular kid. I was the new one and I was a sketch artist. This means that in Hollywood, when they are doing several films, they will have somebody draw the designs on a big board, like a regular costume sketch, to show to the producers and the stars and whoever. I guess certain designers don't draw that well, but in this case, it was something that they had to have, since they were doing lots of work at the same time. So I was a sketch artist for a couple of years in Hollywood.

CAROL BURNETT
Costume designs by Bob Mackie, "Before and After"

That must have been wonderful training.

I learned a great deal. Usually you were sitting right in the designer's lap, and the stars and actors would come in and you'd hear opinions and you'd find out what didn't work. Occasionally they would let you do a costume if they ever had a blank. They'd say, "Well, you try something." And then if your dress got passed, it was like, "I knew I was right. I knew I was right." You're still anonymous, but it's fine.

Your first Broadway musical was the revival of *On the Town*, with Ray Aghayan in 1971. Did director Ron Field know you two from California?

Yes. We worked together on the Academy Award show, and Ray had done

Applause with him. When we did *On the Town*, I must say I realized that Broadway was not as instant as some of the things on the west coast, where you are doing weekly television or you are doing a film where the set is ready, the costumes are ready, we're ready to shoot, and this is it—you do it right now! You don't go out of town and massage it for weeks and weeks. I hated that. In fact, I think sometimes good things were thrown out because people got sick of looking at them then. I think that often happens in the theatre, and I don't mean just costumes. I mean scenes and moments, and it's kind of funny. I always think that the big fault on Broadway is the fact that they're not ready to go. And they put it up on that stage when they start, and sometimes you can develop it into some-

thing, but other times it just goes nowhere fast.

The Carol Burnett Show—how long were you involved with that series?

I did it the whole 11 years, 1967 through 1978, and I've done many things with her since then. And I'm still doing her current show, for her only.

Did you design costumes for the complete show in those 11 years?

The complete show, yes. I designed costumes for the dancers and everybody, and all her funny clothes. Many people think I just did her opening dress.

The show played once a week?

We taped a show every week. We'd have a week off once in a while, but basically it was once a week and it was done very live. Even though it was pretaped, it would take an hour and a half to tape an hour-long show, just to allow for scene and costume changes. That extra half hour was all it was. So it was really like working live. Carol prefers to work in front of an audience; I think that's why she's never been really happy in films. It's because you don't have that instant response.

So Carol Burnett knew of your talent before the show began?

Well, I guess I was relatively unknown in 1967. I'd done a lot of television specials and other things. I had just finished a nightclub act for Mitzi Gaynor, who had a lot of comedy, as well as glamour, in her act, and Ernie Flatt choreographed it. Ernie was very close to Carol, and was going to do her show after she had her second baby. She was pregnant at the time we did Mitzi's act. Then the next fall we started in on her show.

Ernie was a big fan of mine. I'd worked with him in television on *The Judy Garland Show* when I was an assistant. This was in Los Angeles in 1963. *The Judy Garland Show* was an incredible thing for me. I met many influential people that would help me in the next 20 to 30 years.

And you were just an assistant?

I was an assistant to Ray Aghayan. I'd been working in films, and that's when the film studios were kind of closing down and the independents were starting, and everybody was very frightened. I had some time off, because I still was that extra boy they brought in to do the flashier movies. It's true. Every time they had showgirls and models and extravagant-looking films, they would hire me to do the drawings, because I suppose for some reason they thought I had a feeling for it.

When you worked on *The Carol Burnett Show*, how many costumes did you have made and how many did you pull and put together? How did that work?
You mean how much stock did we use and how much did we make to order? We did a lot of made-to-order in the beginning. After about five or six years, you start having sets of this and sets of that. You have all your men's tuxedos and all your dancers' jump suits in different colors and full, fluffy petticoats, a set of antebellum dresses, and so forth. So things would sometimes be retrimmed and get used again. But I always made new things every week. Carol's clothes were always new, except those for running characters—we would use those over again.

But you did mix and rework?
Oh, I did rework and mix, quite often. What happened was at the beginning of the season we would always start making new things, and I had so much money per show. If I had $10,000—which isn't very much money today, but in those days that was a nice budget for a weekly show—for each show and I used $15,000 on one show, well, naturally, along down the line I'd have to save somewhere in the 21 or 22 shows.

This is in the span of a year?
Yes. So you could kind of balance it that way, and some weeks were heavier than the others, depending on the subject and what we were doing.

How many people did you have helping you back then?
I had two direct assistants, a man and a woman. The woman helped me with shopping and pulling everything together, and she would dress Carol as well. Then I had a man who would help me

DANNY THOMAS'
WONDERFUL WORLD OF BURLESQUE
*Costume design by Bob Mackie,
for Lucille Ball (1965)*

with the men's clothes. And anytime we had to pull stock, pull cowboy things or whatever, he would do that and put it all together for me. If I were designing and making a group, of course, then he would work with me on that. But there were only two assistants, really. Then we had sewing people, of course, and workrooms full of people.

We're talking about 10 or 12 people in the workroom?
It varied, depending on the show, because those are people that worked at costume houses, and if you had a big show, they'd bring in more people—milliners and cutters and fitters and dressmakers. It got pretty elaborate at times. We did so much work in such a short amount of time. But when you have to, you just do. You get it done. You have no choice. Or you get out of that business. I never had a free weekend. We'd shoot it on Friday, and I'd receive a new script on Friday afternoon for the next week. And on Saturday I would be trying to figure out what I was going to do, and shopping for fabric. Sometimes I'd also be working on Sunday. By the following Tuesday I would be fitting dancers, and on Wednesday I'd fit Carol. And Friday we'd shoot again. Then, of course, guest stars would come in on

Thursday, the day before the show, and I'd do their fittings and finish it all up. It was crazy, it was really wild!

And then I started doing *The Sonny & Cher* show on top of it at the same time. I did Cher's clothes.

Carol Burnett obviously loved your work. How much input did she have on costumes that you did for her in those 11 years?
She really gave me a very free reign. If she had rehearsed a sketch for a couple of days and she was going in one direction and maybe I was going in another, then she would say to me, "Let's do this or that." But sometimes she had no idea. Sometimes the script would just say, "Woman walks into room and da-da-da." You don't know where she came from, or who she was. I would come up with a theory of who that woman was, and what she looked like, and I would call Carol and say, "What do you think if we do such and such, instead of this and this?" And she would usually comment, "Oh, great, now I know where I'm going." Or she'd put the clothes on and she'd say, "Oh, now I know, now I've got a voice for this!" When you have maybe 20 segments in a show, not every character is always clearly defined. So it helps if the costume designer gives the actor a little help.

We worked together very well. Sometimes I would say, "You've done this kind of character so much lately, why don't we make this woman into something slightly different?" Similar types for Carol would often reappear in the script, and by changing something a little bit or giving it a different point of view visually, it could change her whole performance.

Even though the show is over, do you also design her offstage clothes as well?
I do her party dresses, her things that she goes to events in. Most women who work in Los Angeles, or in the theatre, for that matter, have dress-up dresses and jeans and sweatshirts, but there's usually nothing in between, because they rarely go to lunch and do all that lady nonsense.

You mentioned doing *The Sonny & Cher Show* after that.
Well, no, it overlapped. *Sonny & Cher*

started in 1971, and Carol began in 1967. They started and finished during Carol's 11-year run. First it was *Sonny & Cher*, then it was *The Cher Show* with Sonny. I mean, it was just kind of all over the place for several years.

Did that come about as a result of your popularity on *The Carol Burnett Show*? Did Cher ask for you?
Actually, she was a guest on Carol's show the first year and she said, "One day, I want you to do some of this stuff for me." And then it turned out that we did a couple of TV specials that she was on, just different shows that I was hired to do, and she happened to be on them, and we became friends. So when she and Sonny did the summer show, she called and asked if I would do it. I didn't want to. I wanted to go on vacation. But she's very persuasive. She can make a person do anything.

Are Cher's costumes the most glamorous and wildest as far as theatricality is concerned?
They were at the time. They're probably the most theatrical. Some people think of them as clothes, but they're not really clothes—they're costumes. She's a distinct personality and it's my job to design for that personality. It's like dressing a character in a play. She has an image, and she works very hard to keep it alive. And she likes dressing up. She loves to kind of shock, and she was always like that. The look has changed slightly over the years, but basically designing for Cher is like dressing this wild gorgeous goddess.

Does she tell you what she likes or does she leave it up to you?
Well, she used to leave it more up to me. But now she'll come in with enough ideas for 20 outfits to go on one. And I'll say, "You can't have this all on one thing, let's work it out." So I'll sit with her and we get it down to a wearable situation.

If you're doing a television special or the opening for a nightclub act, how many fittings would you have?
On Cher it could be a lot of fittings. There might be as many as 15 different costume changes. Her clothes are really engineered to stay in place and not slip around. There's not much there, so you

CHER
Costume design by Bob Mackie
Las Vegas nightclub act (1974)

have to be very careful. I don't know how many fittings, but plenty. Of course, it is always at the last minute. I don't get as many fittings as I wish I could, whereas when I'm doing a normal woman's dress, it only takes a couple of fittings. But on the crazy ones, you have to fit a pattern first to make sure everything is just right and doesn't slip and slide, and stays in place. Then we make it. And we fit it again and probably again and again, and then it's done.

I would assume you have forms with the measurements of various women personalities.
I have a form for most of the women. Over the years those forms have taken on lots of different shapes through pregnancies and weight loss and weight gain. And so it's very interesting to watch the figures change.

Do actresses ever say, "Could you do this in another color?" Or "Could you do a gown like you did for so and so, except make it a little more flashy?"
Sometimes they have ideas, sure. They'd be kind of dull if they didn't have any ideas at all. I'd much rather have actresses come in with an idea, some input, because they've been thinking about what they're using that dress for, especially if it's in an act or a show. If I don't agree, I'll tell them. But I'll try to make

them happy and please myself as well. So I just think that it's very important that everything be appropriate for what it's being used for.

In the old days, when I first started getting a lot of attention from doing Cher's clothes, many women would come in and want me to do a dress like hers. I knew they couldn't pull it off and I would do a version in such a way that it looked good on them. But very often people think that the dress makes the woman, but the woman has to have the glamour and the charisma to make it really special. I found that out very early. We'd have little charity fashion shows and things, and I would show Cher's clothes on models. And the models were perfectly beautiful with great bodies. They were gorgeous. But they didn't have the same excitement about them when they wore it as when she wore it. So you knew something special was going on there.

Did you do the costumes for Sonny too?
I didn't do his. Ret Turner did. He's doing the costumes for *The Carol Burnett Show* and I'm doing her costumes. So we're still old friends and we still work together. Thank God he's there, because I'm here in New York a good deal.

You designed the costumes and gowns for *The Debbie Reynolds Show* at the Minskoff.
I think we did it as a nightclub act, which came here and played. I don't think I ever saw the show at the Minskoff itself, but I did it. It was in 1976. And I was doing lots of that kind of work, probably more than anybody, during that period of time, when they were all playing Vegas, and everybody had an act and everybody was out tromping around. I did most of it, actually.

Again, this was because Debbie Reynolds knew of your work?
She knew of my work. I worked with her in 1965 on a film called *Divorce American Style*, and of course it wasn't particularly my cup of tea. She played a housewife and it had wonderful dream sequences, but they were all cut before we shot them. So all the fun stuff was never even shot. Those clothes probably

are still just hanging there at Columbia somewhere. We became friends. I've known Debbie for a long time.

Would someone such as Debbie Reynolds say, "What about my hair?" Do you suggest hairstyles? Do you get into that?

I do sometimes. Some women are not responsive to that kind of suggestion and others are completely. Debbie was always pretty much Debbie, and she always had her look. I didn't have much to say about her hair. It depends on the act. Juliet Prowse will have 20 different hairstyles in one act.

Does she wear lots of wigs?

She wears lots of wigs. She's theatre-trained completely, because she was in *Kismet* in London when she was like 18, so she's used to that. She can go offstage in the middle of a number, change her wig, her hairstyle and everything, and be carried back on, and bang, bang, bang! And she does this all herself. I mean, she's there, she puts the wig on, and she pins it, whereas most actresses just kind of do their hair at the beginning, and whatever is left at the end of the act is that.

When you did *Platinum* with Alexis Smith, did director Joe Layton ask you to do the show?

Joe Layton asked me to do it. I'd known Joe from *Lorelei* on Broadway and television shows and specials. I met a lot of these people because they would bring them out to Hollywood to work and to do specials. Joe wasn't on *The Judy Garland Show*, but almost everybody in the world was. It was amazing the people I met on that show, because they changed producers, choreographers, and directors every other week during that whole season, and I'd get to know all these people. As far as choreographers go, we had

CHER
Costume designs by Bob Mackie

Peter Gennaro, Marc Breaux and Deedee Wood, Ernie Flatt, Danny Daniels, and Nick Castle. Every choreographer working in the business at that time probably worked on that show, one way or the other, for a few weeks. Ray Aghayan stayed the whole time, which meant I stayed the whole time, because I was his assistant. It was interesting, because Ray had his hands full with Judy, so I got to design a lot of the guest stars' and the dancers' clothes and work with the choreographer, and so it was wonderful for me. It was like having my own show but not having to worry about the star. And it was terrific.

What was Judy Garland like as far as dressing? Was she fussy about her clothes?

Not really. She loved dressing up. She enjoyed putting on a new dress and feeling she looked good. She was quite slim at that time, and she got a lot of comments for her clothes on the show. So that was nice. She hadn't for a long time—she'd been a bit frumpy, just wearing little black dresses and jackets to cover up the middle—and she was back to her old self and was enjoying that. She got new dresses every week, which was fun. Every time she'd go out anywhere, she'd have a new dress to wear because she'd always take it from the show.

When you did *Platinum*, did you do sketches and have the show put into a shop and go to fittings and follow the usual routine?

Well, when I worked on that particular show there were no number numbers. I mean, there were numbers, but everybody played themselves every time that they were on. Everybody had a character. It was a small cast, and each person in the cast had his own character. So whatever they were doing, they were always dressed as that character. They didn't do a musical number where you had something else in that number and something else in another number. It was always that same thing. We had a lot of discussions about what a character would look like and what she would wear. Unfortunately, it wasn't a hit, but of course working with Alexis is a dream. I mean, she's five-foot-eight, has a great figure, and

CHER
*Costume design by Bob Mackie,
for Cher as Laverne*

wears clothes well. And when she walks onstage, you know somebody has walked onstage. It's a shame she doesn't do more theatre. Theatre is very hard. My friend Bernadette Peters loves doing it.

Did she know you from the revival of *On the Town*?

No. I first met her on *The Carol Burnett Show* in 1968. A friend of Carol's called his friend, Tom Hammond, who had just started managing Bernadette, and he said, "You've got to see this girl. She's just incredible. So when you come to New York, you have to see her." Of course, you hear this all the time. Carol went to see Bernadette and immediately booked her for the show. So over the years Bernadette must have been on *The Carol Burnett Show* 20 times, and we're all still good friends. That's a long time ago, 1968.

One doesn't think Bernadette Peters is that old.

This chubby little girl with a dog in her

purse came to the fitting with funny, old, secondhand clothes on. And I thought, "Well, she's adorable. She's like a Kewpie doll." And now she really is first-class. I think she is one of our best Broadway performers, and I'm wishing that she'd do it again. But I know how hard it is and how you really have no life when you're in a Broadway show. That's all you do.

It's very demanding.

Especially if you sing the kind of things that she's been doing. You can't get a cold, you can't get a sore throat. You can't do anything except work.

Elton John. How did you come to do his concert and club date clothes?

Elton was doing some specials and things with Cher. He had noticed Cher's clothes and he said, "Do you think you could do some things for me?" And I said, "Yes, what would you like?" He said, "Oh, some things like Cher's." So I did some costumes for him. And he had lost lots of weight. He was very slim, and we did several wild jumpsuits and capes. It was that sort of early- to middle-1970s period, and I did all kinds of wild things. They just couldn't have been crazier. I did a Statue of Liberty and, of course, his Donald Duck and Minnie Mouse costumes. It was just fun with him. He's a nice man and enjoys the clothes. They were like toys for him, really, because people come to hear him sing. It was the music that counted. It was fun to give him that extra little jolt when he came out.

Does Elton John keep these costumes in his repertoire, in case he wants to use them again?

No. Actually, a few years ago he decided to get rid of things, and he had this huge auction and made a lot of money. He had so much stuff, because he had been collecting antiques and jewelry and costumes, and he had all these things in his house, and they were just moving him out the back door. So he sold a lot of stuff and who knows where it will turn up.

Did Elton John leave the design of the costumes completely up to you?

Absolutely. The first time, I gave Elton six choices of costumes and he had me make all six. If I gave him a choice, he'd have them all made. He'd never choose just one.

That's very flattering.

Well, it *is* flattering. But you only have a week to do them.

But you would put on extra people and get them done.

Oh, sure. And he was so lovely and sweet. I mean, he still is. I just supplied some gowns for a commercial he was doing here in New York. I was in Los Angeles, and he called me. He said, "Get Bob Mackie, call him! See if he can get some clothes for these girls..." And we did, and they were there the next day. I haven't seen the commercial yet.

Comment on how Elizabeth Courtney Costumes came about.

It was 1968. I was doing *The Carol Burnett Show* and a lot of specials. Ray [Aghayan] was doing a lot of stuff and Ret Turner was doing a lot of stuff. We were all kind of unhappy with the facilities that we had on the west coast. So we opened our own business in California with a wonderful lady named Elizabeth Courtney. She was from Columbia Pictures and was the head lady in the workroom during the 1940s, when they were doing pictures with Rita Hayworth and Marlene Dietrich and all those glamorous stars under designer Jean Louis. It was at the time when the studios were closing down the extra kind of stuff that they'd always had—the workrooms and the hair salons and the sewing places.

She left Columbia and was doing *The Ice Capades*. It was not what she really wanted to do. So we said, "We'll open a place and you can work with the different stars that come in there." And we opened a place called Elizabeth Courtney Costumes, and she did our work for all those years. She's gone now, but the place is still there, and we still do the same kind of clothes.

This is in Los Angeles?

Yes. Very often we made things for Broadway shows there. We'd make them in that place and then take them to New York. We did Carol Channing's clothes for *Lorelei*, and all of Alexis Smith's clothes were made there for *Platinum*.

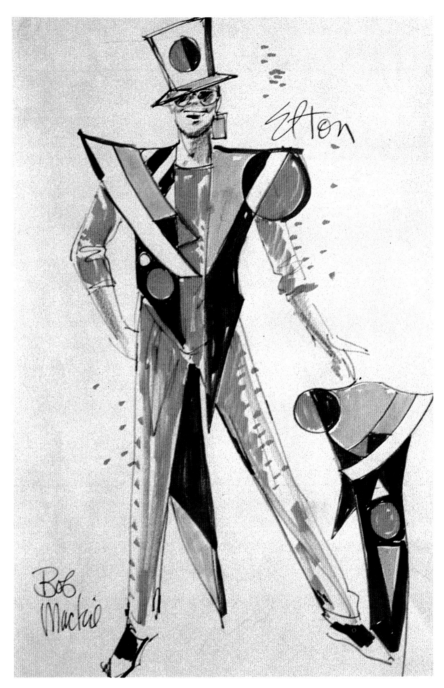

ELTON JOHN
Costume design by Bob Mackie

Do you do evening clothes or special event clothes for Alexis Smith?

I don't do her clothes at all anymore. She lives right there in West Hollywood. But I haven't seen her for a while. She's a good friend. If I have a project or have anything opening, I send her an invitation and she's there. She's wonderful.

How did your business venture here in New York evolve?

This was my sort of midlife-crisis kind of decision. I tell you, the 1970s were nonstop. I never had days off. I did those huge Vegas shows; I did nightclub acts; I did TV specials; I did Broadway. It just got to be so much work that I really was tired. And also, I turned 40 and I thought, "What happened?"

How long have you had the business here?

LORELEI
Costume design by Bob Mackie,
for Carol Channing
Choreographed by Ernest O. Flatt
Directed by Robert Moore
Palace Theatre, New York (1974)

PLATINUM
Costume design by Bob Mackie, for Alexis Smith
Directed and choreographed by Joe Layton
Mark Hellinger Theatre, New York (1978)

Exactly nine years. I still feel like I'm a newcomer to Seventh Avenue, but I guess I'm not. I'm actually the first costume designer ever to come from Hollywood and stay. A lot of them have come, and they'd stay about a season and then they'd go back, saying, "I don't want any of this, because it's hard."

Obviously you're doing something right, or it wouldn't be going so well.

Well, it's very difficult. We all thought it was hard out there, but this is hard. This is tough. The other's more fun.

How so?

It just is. You have a small group of people to please. You stay in budget or you don't.

You mean on a production?

Yes. For any given production, you just do it, then it's over and you go on to the next one. In this business, you do a collection and you live with it for six months. You sell it, and you know, it's just harder!

Do you find this a 24-hour job? Do you have it down so that you don't take stuff home with you?

I always take stuff home with me. I'm always working all the time. Last night, in the middle of the night, I was dreaming about my collection that I'll show next April. And I've just finally had a kind of inspiration about what I was going to do. The minute that happens, then your mind starts clicking like crazy, and I was having trouble sleeping last night.

You did your fashion show here and had great luck with it. How long did you work on that?

We have about six weeks of concentrated work, but I started buying fabrics and planning it last April, after my fall collection. The minute it's over, I have to start buying fabrics and things for the next one. It's not like in the theatre, where you just draw a picture and then go find the fabric to make it. Here we have to make sure that we can get it in quantity when we need it.

Because of the orders?

Yes. And then we put in orders early and we have to estimate. "We think we'll sell more of this dress or more of that." And

you put in an order for that, and hopefully you come out even. It's tricky.

You don't want to underdo it or overdo it.

If you underdo it, then you can't fill the orders. And if you overdo it, you are stuck with rather expensive fabric. Some things are basic fabrics, but when anything's a novelty or a print or something that you wouldn't use every season, then you're in trouble.

How many fashion shows do you have during the year?

They're twice a year—spring and fall. I started out doing them straight, like fashion shows. And then the minute I started putting a theme to them, people started liking them more and more, and I realized that I got a better reaction. So now I always have a theme. Last fall it was the music of Cole Porter, which is kind of an odd theme, because it's not terribly visual, but yet it is. And my whole collection was based on Cole Porter. This last season, the spring season, I did a tribute to twentieth-century legends, women that had made a difference, and it had a lot of style and charisma. I started with Lucille Ball and I went to Mary Martin, Martha Graham, Grace Kelly, Rita Hayworth, Billie Holiday, Betty Boop, and Diana Vreeland. It was inspired by those women, and I had little sections in the show. It was a big hit. People loved it. So now I'm sort of stuck into always having to have a theme. It's like being a producer, really.

You got great notices in the press.

Sometimes I think they are so enthralled with the show that they don't see the clothes. But I don't have dancers, I don't have singers, or anything like that. I still keep it a fashion show. But we have nice lighting, and this time we did it at the Hudson Theatre over at the Hotel Macklowe. It's a lovely little theatre, and there's something nice about raising the curtain, which nobody does in a fashion show, because they never have a curtain to raise on a whole stage.

It's usually a runway, isn't it?

Yes, we had the stage and a little runway coming off the stage. But in the beginning of the show the curtain raised and the music was going and the girls were revolving on the stage and all of the legends were dressed in the clothes. It set up beautifully from the beginning. I won't be able to do that when I take it out on the road, because we do shows in different cities.

How many times, and where will you be doing the fashion show?

I bring this show just three times this season. I do a big, full-blown production. I'll be doing it in Beverly Hills, in San Antonio, and in Miami. Now sometimes we do as many as six in a season, and sometimes we don't do any. It just depends on the situations. You have to work with the department stores and the charities—it's an expensive situation, and they pay for all the extra costs, and so it depends.

The evening bag you designed to go with the fragrance is great.

It's really a gift with purchase. It's something that they often do at Christmastime. They'll have something like that with the fragrance in it. And that all comes through the fragrance company.

Did you design the bag that goes with the fragrance?

We just did some sketches. It's made in the Orient, and for $80 you get a bottle of perfume and the bag, so it's a pretty good deal. All the saleswomen that work in the stores are buying them. There's never any left for the customers. But it's a nice little handbag.

I have other lines of things. We have the body and beauty products, and we're having even more coming after the first of the year [1992]. There's more coming out of that, and a wonderful men's fragrance soon.

If you were asked to put a group of costumes in a time capsule to be exhibited later on in the future, what would they be? Do you have one or two special groups that are your favorites?

Well, that's hard to say. I always think that old costumes are like old clothes: They don't mean much. Unfortunately, on the stage, you have to look at photographs or look at the old clothes. There's nothing left, except now every-

thing is videotaped. But I think old movie costumes are real boring, because they're just old clothes. But you see them on film, and all of a sudden they're magical. I would rather leave some videotape or some film for people to see my work than leave the dirty, smelly, old clothes. But seeing old rags that Helen Hayes wore in 1910, I don't care unless they're beautiful and have been kept up. But even then, Helen Hayes isn't in them. And that's part of the magic, especially on film. The magic happened on the screen, on the star, and the clothes just happened to be there. And then maybe they put a filter on the lens and it all sparkled magically, and then when you see it in person, it's always kind of a letdown.

Although I must say that I have saved a lot of the Cher clothes of the 1970s. I thought I'd better save the wild ones, because I'll never be doing those kind of clothes again, and there will never be anybody who can wear them quite like she did. So I have saved some of those— I don't know what for. But they'll probably go into a museum one day as a curiosity.

Would you do duplicates for Cher's acts, in case one got damaged or dirty?

No, not usually. Things were cleaned and kept up very well. Sometimes we would have a couple of different things that could work in the same spot that she could trade off, but never the same dress twice. That's boring, you don't want to do that if you don't have to. You always have to in film, though. You always have to make doubles and triples because an actress could wear the same dress for the whole film. That means she'd be wearing the same product for a couple of months straight, so she's got to have more than one, and also for safety's sake, or if it gets dirty or ripped or whatever.

If you are doing a nightclub act for Cher, does she call up and say, "We have a budget of so and so"? Or does cost enter into it?

Well, no, cost comes into it eventually. But in the beginning I don't think about cost. I just draw it. Whatever it should be, I put it on paper, and then we worry about cost. And usually it's not a problem.

MAME
Costume design by Bob Mackie,
for Juliet Prowse

ANYTHING GOES
Costume design by Bob Mackie,
for Mitzi Gaynor
Touring company

BARYSHNIKOV IN HOLLYWOOD
Costume designs by Bob Mackie
Produced and directed by Don Mischer
CBS television special (1982)

Do you make all your sketches in roughs and work up to the finished product?

Yes, sure. That's how I think. I think with a pencil in my hand.

How do you like to work as far as renderings?

I used to do them all with paint and make them very wonderful. But then, with all my bad habits in television, I started using markers. Of course, if you give somebody a "marker sketch" now and they put it on the wall, in a year it's faded away to nothing. So I try not to give away marker sketches. I try to do a painted sketch, or pen-and-ink sketch, so they won't fade.

If I'm a producer and I ask you to do a big musical today, would you have time to do it with all your other interests?

It depends on when it comes. I always have two or three extra weeks during most seasons, although this year has been hard, due to the fragrance and everything. I've been out on the road with it. But a couple of years ago I did an opera for the San Francisco Opera Company, and I enjoyed that.

What was the production?

Lulu, which was not a huge opera, but it was time-consuming, and I did suffer a little over on the other side, because I was taking time away from the collection. It worked out fine. I just worked harder.

Who directed *Lulu?*

Lotfi Mansouri.

And you designed complete costumes for the opera?

Yes, complete costumes for everybody.

How long did you work on that?

It's hard to say, because I did sketches early in the year just to prove to some of the opera people that Bob Mackie could do an opera. He wasn't nervous, but a lot of them were. And then I left it alone for

LULU
Costume designs by Bob Mackie
Directed by Lotfi Mansouri
San Francisco Opera (1989)

a few months. I did a collection and then I went back and did the actual costumes.

But people are funny. They want to peg you and put you in a little niche and say, "Well, he doesn't do opera." I mean, if you've ever seen *Lulu*, it's just sexy clothes and period costumes. We set it in the 1930s and it looked great. It got good reviews.

Were the costumes executed in San Francisco?
Yes, at the opera costume house there.

Did you have to be there a great deal?
Yes, quite a lot. I was back and forth. I was in Los Angeles at the time, so it wasn't too hard. But it's still time-consuming.

You're saying you would like to design operas and musicals if you could work them in with your business?
I would love to, yes. Or ballets now and then, if I could work them in. Or a star's clothes, if it's some play where the woman had to be very glamorous, I'd love to do that. But right now I don't have to make a living doing that, so I can pick what I want to do. I don't have to say yes to everything. In the old days as a costume designer, if I had the time I just did it. I did all kinds of things that nobody knew about, because it was a job. I never did soap opera, and I'm just as glad.

Is there anything in particular that you would like to do as a project in a new production?
I don't know. I haven't thought about that. Everybody thinks the obvious thing for me to do is something with this female star that's very glamorous, like in a Noël Coward play. That wouldn't be as

time-consuming as something that has chorus lines of people tromping in and out in different clothes every five minutes. I love doing that. I've done huge shows. But I would enjoy doing that very much.

What do you like least about working in theatre?
What I like least is, "Oh, we'll fix it when we get to New York." I hate that. For me, it's the wrong attitude. You should go into the theatre having everything complete. I don't want to open a show with half the costumes not there. I hate that attitude that exists in the theatre, "By the time we open, it will be ready." Open? There are people sitting out there—we're open. I really think that it should be as complete as possible. Sometimes that's what's wrong with plays. There are things that people are waiting to fix later. What are we waiting for? Do it now. I think if something isn't working and you've done your best, then we fix it. But don't go in with that

in mind. "Oh, well, these are just previews." Anytime anyone is sitting out front, I want it to be as good as it can be.

When you design shows for Cher, Carol Burnett, and Carol Channing, do you also do their shoes?

Oh, yes. Unfortunately, sometimes they have to be in some sort of dance shoes, which hopefully don't look too orthopedic. I mean, I hate that nasty Capezio shoe with a strap across the instep. All the chorus have to wear that, but the star will say, "I'm not going to wear that ugly shoe." And she'll go out there in a beautiful shoe and do the whole number. So you have to think, "Well, I guess that's why she is a star."

When you started out was there any particular thing or designer that influenced you?

During my whole childhood I was looking at pictures of Broadway shows in *Life* magazine. And then when *Show* magazine came out, I could read it and absorb everything about the theatre and show business. But the first time I ever stopped to read the credits to find out the designer was on *An American in Paris*, when I was about 10 years old. I saw that ballet and I just thought, "This is like something special." I watched the credits, which I really never paid any attention to before, and I saw the name Irene Sharaff. I started watching for her name. And, of course, I realized that I'd seen her things before, and I liked them.

Do you have a comment on what a designer should do when creating a costume in the theatre?

I think when you're working in the theatre, if you can make it look like it's all out of butterfly wings and yet it'll last forever, that is the secret. If you can make something look fragile and mystical and magic and incredible, and yet make it last more than opening night, then you've made it happen. You have to be practical about what you use on the stage—you have to make clothes last, or at least be repairable. And I'm always quite disdainful of people who make clothes for that one moment in time. That doesn't work in the movies, because they'll wear them solid for days on end.

If I'm a young person starting out to study costume design, what would your advice be?

Know the history of costume inside and out, because that's what you're going to be dealing with. Get experience. Work in the theatre, even if it has nothing to do with costumes. Understand what an

MADONNA
Gown design by Bob Mackie
Academy Awards (1991)

ANGELA LANSBURY
Gown design by Bob Mackie
Tony Awards

STAYING ALIVE, THE FILM
Costume design by Bob Mackie,
for John Travolta
Directed by Sylvester Stallone
Released by Paramount Pictures (1983)

audience is about and how to get reactions. Sometimes people want to be costume designers and have no feeling for the theatre at all. They have no feeling for how to get a reaction from an audience. It isn't just designing cute clothes. And also, having a strong personal style does not make you a good costume designer. Every character that you design for has their own style, and you have to take that into consideration. And then if you are designing for celebrities or personalities, they'll have very strong personal styles, and all you're doing is enhancing and making them stronger. I always say, "Design anything anyone will let you design." If some rock group is going out and they haven't got any money, but you can somehow get it together and you want to do the clothes, fine, do it! But so many kids these days will say, "Well, how much am I getting paid?" And then they will comment, "But that's not enough. I can't live on that." You don't do it for that. If you don't love it, don't do it, because you never come out even.

Is there one star performer you haven't designed costumes for who you'd love to design for?

Well, that's hard to say. I haven't done much ballet and, of course, I would love to do more of that. I think that's exciting, but I have no particular star. There are some of these young, gorgeous new stars, like Michelle Pfeiffer and Julia Roberts. They are great-looking girls, and sometime I would love to do clothes for them. But there's not really a costume thing in my head. I'm sorry I never really designed for Mary Martin, although she did wear clothes of mine that she bought off the rack. She knew who I was, which I found very flattering. I liked her.

You mean Mary Martin never came on *The Carol Burnett Show*?

No. But Ethel Merman did, and Pearl Bailey was on it. And even if you didn't do that much for them, it was kind of fun to work with them. And speaking of stars, Betty Grable was my childhood goddess when I was a little kid, and I thought she was the most beautiful thing, with all that yellow hair and pink marabou. And between Betty Grable and Carmen Miranda and Rita Hayworth, I

was in Technicolor heaven all the time. That's probably why I'm doing what I do now.

Would you enjoy doing men's costumes, as well as women's?

I've done lots and lots of men's costumes. I mean, I'm not interested in doing a double-breasted suit for three acts. But a great period show or a show with a lot of characters and things, that would interest me. Like in *Lulu*, I did all the men's clothes as well as the women's. They were sort of wishing I wouldn't, because I was too much trouble. But it's a time-consuming thing. They're big and you have to design them way ahead and then go and be there. It's hard when you have the kind of schedule I have.

What do you like most about working in the theatre?

What do I like most? I love it when performers walk out and the audience reacts before they open their mouths. They react to the way they look, the fact that they're there. That is so thrilling to me, just that audience reaction, which you don't get when you're making a film. In television you get it if you have an audience. But you lose a lot of it by the time it gets home. You don't feel it as much as you do when you're really there. Performing for that audience at that moment and making and keeping the timing going, I think that's the most exciting thing. That goes for the clothes too. You can whip an audience into a frenzy just by the way you've dressed a star. Get somebody who really performs in a great costume with a great audience and terrific music—then you've got magic. That's what it is all about.

THE SUPREMES AND THE TEMPTATIONS GETTING IT TOGETHER ON BROADWAY
Costume designs by Bob Mackie, for the Supremes (1968)

JOHN SCHEFFLER
Costume design for Krewe of Aphrodite
Mardi Gras, New Orleans (1988)

JOSÉ VARONA
Costume design for Margot Fonteyn in Grand Finale
Ballet do Rio de Janeiro
Teatro Municipal, Rio de Janeiro (1975)

JOSÉ VARONA
Costume designs for Cinderella
Zurich Opera Ballet (1982)

JEANNE BUTTON
Costume design for Fricka in Die Walküre
Produced by Art Park (1986)

ROBERT PERDZIOLA
Costume design for La Calisto
Santa Fe Opera (1989)

CHARLES E. MCCARRY
Costume design for Desdemona in Othello
A project for the Yale Drama School (1986)

JOSÉ VARONA
Costume design for Cinderella
Berlin Deutsche Oper Ballet (1976)

ROBERT O'HEARN
Costume design for the Witch in Hansel and Gretel
Metropolitan Opera, New York (1967)

A Conversation with
CARRIE ROBBINS

Carrie Robbins lives and maintains a studio in a top-floor loft in lower Manhattan. She was born in Baltimore, and graduated with a double-major in art and theatre from Penn State University, where she was a member of Phi Beta Kappa. She received her MFA from the Yale Drama School.

Robbins's first Broadway show was *Leda Had a Little Swan*, at the Cort Theatre in 1968, with Andre Gregory directing. Her costume designs have been seen in a diverse range of companies and theatres, including the Guthrie Theatre, the Mark Taper Forum, the Ahmanson Theatre, the American Conservatory Theatre, the Chelsea Theatre Center, the New York Shakespeare Festival, the Long Wharf Theatre, the Alaska Repertory Theatre, the McCarter Theatre Company, Baltimore's Center Stage, Buffalo's Studio Arena, Sarah Caldwell's Opera Company of Boston, Germany's Hamburg Staatsoper, John Houseman's The Acting Company of Juilliard, and the Candlewood Playhouse. For the San Francisco Opera she did *Samson et Dalila*,

starring Plácido Domingo and Shirley Verrett, which was televised on PBS. Her drawings are in the Time-Life series *The Collectibles* and in many galleries, and her designs and articles have appeared in numerous publications.

For over 20 years Robbins has taught costume design at New York University's Tisch School of the Arts, and several of her graduates have work appearing in this book. She has been costume designer for the film *In the Spirit*, as well as for television's *Saturday Night Live*, *The Rita Show*, with Rita Moreno, and the *Theatre in America* series. In addition, Robbins has collaborated on 11 musical projects with choreographer Patricia Birch, and has designed all the staff uniforms for the Rainbow Room and the Aurora Grill in New York City and for the Empress Court in Caesar's Palace, Las Vegas. She has received two Tony nominations, and her awards include the Drama Desk (four times), the Maharam, the L.A. Drama-Logue, the Diplome d'Honneur, and the Silver Medal at the Triennial of International Theatre Design.

THE TEMPEST
Costume designs by Carrie Robbins,
for Stephano (right) and Anthony Hopkins
as Prospero (above)
Directed by John Hirsch
Mark Taper Forum, Los Angeles (1979)

How did you first get involved designing for the theatre?

I went to Penn State, where I had a double major in art and in theatre, because I loved them both. I think 16 credits was the standard load for a term or a semester, and in order to do the double major I had to run 23 to 25 credits. I was like the living dead for four years. And a professor said, "Look, why don't you make it easier for yourself? You could design for the theatre. That way you'd have art and you'd have the theatre and it would all be so much easier than taking an art major and a theatre major and doing 25 credits a term."

I had no idea theatre design was a field of endeavor. I was not a terribly rich kid, so I hadn't seen much theatre, and the thought of this as a profession simply didn't enter my mind.

Did you start out studying costume design, as opposed to stage design?

Actually, this professor, whose name was Bill Allison, had graduated from Yale as a scenic designer many years before. He came to Penn State and ran the department, and there weren't many courses. He designed all the shows and I worked as his assistant as much as I could. He taught me about drafting and a little bit about modelmaking, and how to make and paint scenery. And since he had been to Yale, he suggested that I apply there as a set design major, and I did, and Oenslager accepted me.

Then you went to the Yale Drama School?

Yes. The funny thing was that I had been awarded a McKnight Fellowship to the Guthrie Theatre to study acting with an emphasis on musical theatre. But I turned it down. I thought at the time that performing was a crazy and unreliable field, and that design for the theatre was a steady and reliable field. I had been in art school since the age of three, and I always loved to draw. My parents told me that I drew on the walls when I was still in the crib, and they thought this was rather destructive of me. So they took me to a shrink. The shrink said, "No, she's really fine. She's not destructive, she simply wants to go to art school. Give her some crayons and find a school that takes toddlers." So at three years old I was enrolled in the Maryland Institute of Fine Art, and I've been in art school every year of my life until relatively recently. When I got out of Yale and I came to New York, I continued art classes. I've been to almost every school here including, FIT, Parsons, the School of Visual Arts, the National Academy, Art Students League, Pratt, Traphagen, and Cooper-Hewitt, and any other place that offered courses with a good teacher. To draw for a living was something my parents never thought was conceivable. If you were a girl back when I was a kid, you were supposed to be a teacher. My folks were not happy with my choice, so I mostly survived those years on scholarships, loans, chicken wings, and Jello.

Did you graduate from the Yale Drama School?

Yes. I think at the end of the first year, we had one of those odd but inevitable cuts the way Oenslager worked the program, and he was probably right. He felt that girls were not meant to be set designers.

Carrie Robbins' costume design credits include the following:

BROADWAY

Anna Karenina (1992)

Raggedy Ann (1986)

Sweet Bird of Youth (1986), pre-Broadway tour

The Boys of Winter (1985)

The Octette Bridge Club (1985)

Agnes of God (1982)

The First (1981)

Frankenstein (1981)

Yentl (1975)

Over Here! (1974)

Molly (1973)

Grease (1972)

The Secret Affairs of Mildred Wild (1972)

Look to the Lillies (1970)

NEW YORK SHAKESPEARE FESTIVAL

The Misanthrope (1977)

The Stronger and Creditors (1977)

Rebel Woman (1976)

The Merry Wives of Windsor (1974)

MARK TAPER FORUM

A Flea in Her Ear (1982)

The Lady and the Clarinet (1981)

The Tempest (1979)

OFF-BROADWAY

El Bravo (1981)

Sisters of Mercy (1973)

GUTHRIE THEATRE

The Threepenny Opera (1984)

Hamlet (1978)

Julius Caesar (1969)

REPERTORY THEATRE OF LINCOLN CENTER

An Enemy of the People (1973)

The Plough and the Stars (1973)

Narrow Road to the Deep North (1972)

The Good Woman of Setzuan (1970)

The Time of Your Life (1969)

CHELSEA THEATRE CENTER

Polly (1975)

The Beggar's Opera (1972)

OPERA COMPANY OF BOSTON

Mass (1990)

Taverner (1986)

Rigoletto (1977)

Russlan and Ludmilla (1971)

HAMBURG STAATSOPER

West Side Story (1978)

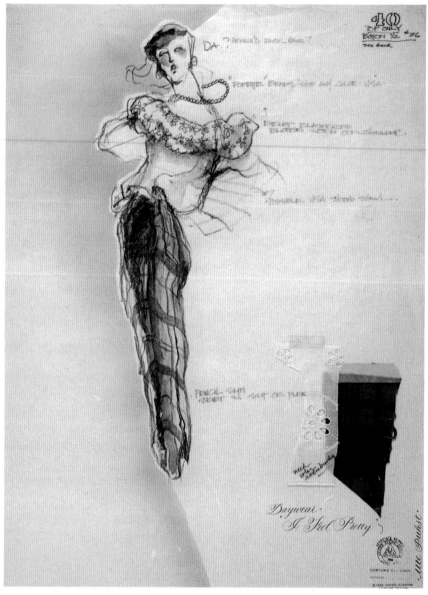

WEST SIDE STORY
Costume design by Carrie Robbins
Directed and choreographed by John Neumeier
Hamburg Staatsoper, Hamburg (1978)

He could think that way.
He did think that way. And my final project that we turned in got "lost" or misplaced by the graduate student who was supposed to collect all our work and take it down to New York, where the "O" was living, for grading. My work was not in that packet. It turned out the work had fallen behind some drawer or somewhere. The "O" said, "Well, you know she's not even turning her work in. For God's sake, let's cut her, get rid of her. Who needs these girls anyway, they'll never work!"

Look at how many women set designers are able to actually practice their work in any major sense. I don't mean regional theatre, where you get now a maximum of maybe $3,000 for killing yourself for 10 weeks; I mean something more substantive. Now it's getting a little better. But certainly the Broadway market is not terribly open. Marge Kellogg is one set designer, and Heidi Landesman is another. But the list is very short.

Oenslager was probably right after all! I had, of course, taken Mr. Bevan's costume class, and I simply asked if it was possible to switch my major at that point and do a major in costume. He looked at my work and said, "Absolutely." And then my emphasis was switched to costumes. I didn't care, actually—to me, design is design—though walls don't talk back like people do.

What did you do after you finished at Yale Drama School?
I was very lucky to get a job out in Los Angeles as a resident costume designer to a theatre Gregory Peck had somehow gotten involved in, called the Inner City Cultural Center. This was immediately after those horrible Watts riots in the '60s. I guess it was an attempt to bring theatre to the Watts community and some of the other really restricted communities. And the artistic director was Andre Gregory. You might remember him from the movie *My Dinner with Andre.* He had run a very successful theatre in Philadelphia. Eugene Lee had gone down and done a lot of work with him.

Anyway, that job opened up and I interviewed for it and became the resident costume designer. Stephen Hendrickson, also from Yale, was the resident set designer. And so the two of us went out to L.A. and worked on that. It was just luck that I got the job. We had a good time. Our first show was *Tartuffe,* with Louis Gossett. He was sensational.

Then you stayed out there for a season?
I left before the end of the season because Andre had been offered a Broadway show. And he said, "Come, let's do this show. You have to move back to New York. You have to give up your contract." I was completely impractical. I must say I sure like the East Coast and New York more than I like L.A. You know, in L.A. if you worked past six o'clock and didn't go out with your suntan lotion at lunchtime, they thought you were really nuts and highly neurotic.

This was your first Broadway show?
Yes. It was called *Leda Had a Little Swan,* with Michael J. Pollard of *Bonnie and Clyde* fame. I did that Broadway show and it closed the day before it was to open. I had no idea that such a thing

could even happen. This was in 1968. I had moved everything back to New York, and I didn't know what the hell to do. I'm not one of those aggressive job-seeking people, and I didn't have a clue.

I somehow got some vague connections with illustrations, since I drew fairly proficiently. I got the worst job in illustration I ever had in my life: I had to draw dental equipment, and I have to tell you that the client hated it and kept turning it back with a note that said DOES NOT HAVE STYLE. And I couldn't figure out how to draw stylish dental equipment. It's the only drawing assignment in my life that I just couldn't do. I did pickup stuff. I did the lettering inside Marvel comic books, because my printing was proficient. I had drafted for George Izenour at Yale to make money, because I had learned fairly solid drafting from Bill Allison. So again, that helped me get some money.

Did you look for more theatre work in New York?

In retrospect I can't imagine how I even managed to live, because I was very passive about pursuing work. I had virtually no connections and I didn't have a clue where to go. And luckily for me within a few months I got a call from a guy out of the clear blue. I didn't know him. He had somehow heard of me. It was Doug Schmidt, and he had been asked to do something by Jules Irving, who at the time was running the Vivian Beaumont. We did a little piece over in the basement of the theatre. It was called the Forum then, but now it's the Mitzi Newhouse. The play was *The Inner Journey*, and it starred Michael Dunn. He was a wonderful actor. Anyway, that was a tremendously lucky break.

Then I did a whole bunch of things upstairs at the Vivian Beaumont and more things down in the Mitzi Newhouse, and I guess my name started to get around. And you know, once you get on a roll it becomes a little easier.

How do you approach a show once you get a script?

I read it, obviously, and I think about what it says. And then I try to put myself in a visual framework. I will sur-

HAMLET
Costume designs by Carrie Robbins
Directed by Stephen Kanee
Tyrone Guthrie Theatre, Minneapolis (1978)

round myself with as many images as I can find that make some sense or seem relevant. Of course, if it's something you have to research specifically, some period you might not know anything about, you're going to have to find that out. When I did Martin Charnin's musical *The First*, for example, I knew very little about baseball. It was about Jackie Robinson. One of the first things I did was fly up to the Baseball Hall of Fame in Cooperstown, pen in hand. It really depends on the demands of the script, but I try to move to visual input real fast.

How do you go about doing your sketches?

I draw large if I've got the time. I might do lots. But I do them on the same page, starting light, and getting darker as I become more sure that what I'm doing for the character makes sense. But I don't sit down and draw until I've talked to the director; if there's music, I've got to talk to the choreographer and listen to the music many times. And if there's any casting, I want to know who it is, and I want a full-body picture. I want to feel like I know what the piece is about and what it sounds like and maybe how it moves. And I want the director's viewpoint toward the piece. And I'd like to see what the set designer is working on, if he's already at work. Then I talk to the director about how he feels in a very specific sense per character. Then I sit down and draw—lightly. And I stay on the same page until I kind of feel I know what I've drawn is relevant for the scene and right for the character. Then I add details, the specifics, the minutiae. Sometimes I will know right away what color it is, and sometimes not. I think about the psychological "weight" color carries. I try not to just make pretty frocks, unless that's what's called for.

Do you like to do a great deal of research, depending on what it is?

It really does depend on what it is. In the case of *The Boys of Winter*, which took place in South Vietnam, I had to do a lot of research. There is no way that you are going to get a show like this right by making it up. You simply must go and do the research, and those Army manuals are very complex to read! Even the same uniform varies from year to year in its details. In the Marines, uniform pockets went on differently from one year to the next. It's too current. There are too many people who wore it and I worry about getting it wrong. I have to admit I'm obsessed with detail. It's very time-consuming.

But you enjoy it.

I do enjoy it, and actually for me that quiet time—it's you and the drawing

TAVERNER
Costume designs by Carrie Robbins
Directed by Sarah Caldwell
Opera Company of Boston (1986)

board—lets me think and learn about the play and the character. I'm slow. A drawing could take me from three to eight hours, easily. But when I finish, I feel I know that character.

After drawing, which paints do you like to use?

The medium doesn't matter that much. It varies a lot. But I try to capture what the final costume will look like. I usually know what the fabric is and almost always how I want it to move. I don't like going into the costume shops, wasting their time not knowing what the fabrics are or what detailing I'll require. I feel if you can't explain what you want, the shop can't make an intelligent bid. After all, the costume sketch is our drafting; costume designers don't do technical information like the set designer's drafting. And on the basis of my sketch they've got to say it will cost $2,500, or whatever. I don't want them to get screwed. I don't want them to forget to figure all the details I'm going to have them custom-make.

You're saying that when you do a sketch, not only do you know the fabric you want but also its color, its texture and the way it hangs?

Absolutely. And its shine or lack of shine. That all becomes clear to me in this long-ish drawing/painting stage. As I sit and draw, I hire assistants and start them swatching and feed them information by phone. So they can be out on the streets and I can say, "Okay, it's a sharkskin, it's a pale sharkskin, it's probably lighter cream or beige or oyster. And it's the most fluid one we can get."

And I will begin to know these things only because I have drawn them. There have been many times where I'm sitting at the drawing board painting, and the swatchers who work for me, the assistants who I've used, bring back the exact right fabric, even down to a specific print. I will start painting it and I will say on the phone to my assistant, "It's kind of watery, like a moiré, and it's sort of greenish-bluish-tealish, those '50s green-blue colors," and they show up with the very fabric I've just finished painting. And sometimes I'll know which store the

fabric "lives" in, probably because I've been to the stores myself.

You designed the costumes for the big musical hit *Grease*. How did that come about?

Grease was produced by Ken Waissman and Maxine Fox. And believe it or not, they had gone to my high school in Baltimore. And by the time they got that

FRANKENSTEIN
*Costume design by Carrie Robbins,
for Dianne Wiest
Directed by Tom Moore
Palace Theatre, New York (1981)*

project together—they brought it from Chicago—I suppose they had heard that I was working as a costume designer. I had not seen them since high school.

They just called you out of the blue?

Yes. And I agreed to do it. It was done first at the old Eden Theatre on Second Avenue. Doug Schmidt did the scenery. I don't know how they knew Doug. But they called me out of the blue. I worked out the original poster graphics for them. We had very little money, but it was successful enough, and they moved it uptown to Broadway.

Do you remember what the original budget was on the show?

I don't. I remember it being pathetic. And I remember needing a watch to put on a character at the last minute. There wasn't one cent left! I recall taking my husband's watch off his wrist, saying, "I

have to have a watch." There we were, doing a show, and we didn't have five bucks for a Timex. It was that bad. There was a point where I think they ran completely out of money. The scenery was dropped off at the door and the stage-hands wouldn't bring it in. It was one of these union things. Doug nearly had a heart attack, and Ken and Maxine said, "Oh, my God, we're going to have to ask for some kind of overcall or additional investors. Do you have $5,000 more?" Nobody had $5,000. But Doug managed to scrape some bucks together, I think a unit of $5,000—I'm not sure— and put it into the production. That's how we actually got the scenery off Second Avenue and into the theatre at the Eden and got the show on, and from that investment, I hope, Doug made a pretty penny. However, he and I had a pathetic royalty. Who would think this show would run?

How long did *Grease* finally run?

About eight years. I think it beat out *Fiddler on the Roof*, and then *A Chorus Line* overtook us. Each week of those years we received $67.50 apiece. At the time I had an agent—which I no longer bother with—and the agent forgot to renegotiate this royalty when the show moved to Broadway. *Grease* was the one hit phenomenon that I've been associated with, and that's what I got. It really was very funny in retrospect—and ironic.

The same two people did *Over Here!* Did you do that as a result of knowing them?

Yes, I did. And so did Doug. We did *Over Here!* with the two Andrews Sisters and Janie Sell. We were supposed to do a road company, but one of the Andrews Sisters was a little difficult in negotiations and there was a lot of backstage craziness, and I think Ken and Maxine finally said, "Forget it, we're not doing it, it's too much trouble."

As a theatrical costume designer do you find that your work also involves making the star feel comfortable and secure in the costumes?

I think it's our job. I think that's part and parcel of our job, unlike Seventh Avenue, where you design on a perfect

MASS
Costume designs by Carrie Robbins
Directed by Sarah Caldwell
Opera Company of Boston (1990)

easy. And sometimes it's a bit of a pain in the ass, but I think it is part of our job.

I try to separate out the neurotic components, you know, like very thin people who still think they look fat. I try to separate that out from the reality. You can't always do it. And I do try to accommodate when I can. But I think there's other things that you do for the performers with the costume so that they know that you are on their side. I spend a lot of time on that sketch and I'm thinking about the play and the character. I usually have very good conversations with the actors about the part and I think they know that I have an understanding of what the character is supposed to look like, which is connected with what the character is supposed to get out there and do. I don't do something because I think it looks "fabulous." I don't consider it my ego. It really comes from the play and the piece and the character and the director and a certain point of view. But I will do things that some people think are crazy —not because the audience sees them, but because they show to the actor.

For example, I was doing an Irish play, *The Plough and the Stars*, at the old Lincoln Center, with Dan Sullivan directing. That wonderful actor, Jack MacGowran, was in it. He was the guy who had done so much of the original Beckett work. Many of the cast were Irish. The play needed real Irish uniforms, and we didn't have enough money to get authentic uniforms. We had to take existing generic rental uniforms and turn them into Irish uniforms. The Irish uniform is green, and I had read that an Irishman can distinguish 20 different shades of green. And I thought, "Oh my God, if I pick the dye swatch I will get the wrong shade of green, and I will have a bunch of genuine Irish actors trying to play the military section in phony green uniforms, and they'll go nuts."

I went and bugged the Irish Consulate. I took my PANTONE book, the little book of color chips that we use, and I said, "Do you have a good enough photo of the green uniform that I can match to a color chip, or can you with your Irish eyes help me to pick the shade, because I really don't want to get

size 6 or 8, then it's sent to some factory, where it's turned out in all the different sizes and you never see the people who really buy it. We're right in there at the fitting. We get two or three fittings. So we get very close to the actors. And they, I believe, do a tough thing. They're out there with 100 or 1,000 people watching them, and they must be comfort-able. There might be some neurotic component to it. But it's a difficult business, and anyone whose name is above the title, for example, who's carrying the show on his or her back, deserves a certain amount of support! That person deserves to feel that he or she looks good and he or she looks right for the character. And that doesn't mean it's it wrong for the actors." They were very wonderful and they helped me pick the green. We dyed the uniforms to that color chip.

Then it came to putting on the buttons. Irish uniforms have Irish buttons with harps on them, like American Naval uniforms have eagles on the buttons. You've probably seen this harp on signs outside Irish pubs. So I said, "I'm in New York City. I can get these Irish buttons. What's the problem?" I went to every button vendor in the city. Nobody had these Irish military buttons. Then I thought, well now, we're in the Vivian Beaumont. It's a huge theatre. Probably nobody will see these damn buttons! Maybe American eagles on the buttons won't matter. But I couldn't live with that. These particular actors would know.

Finally, I called the Consulate back and I said, "Is there any way I could possibly buy from Ireland some of those military buttons with harps on them? I'll pay anything for them." And they said, "Don't worry, we have this diplomatic pouch and it comes every other day, and we'll throw some buttons in there," and they did. I forgot how many uniforms there were, but they gave me a bunch of buttons, and I divided them up into how many uniforms I had. Then, for however many I ran short, I either took an American eagle button and smashed the eagle and painted it down so you couldn't see it—figuring they were at war, so it could easily be a damaged button—or I made a little matte, sprayed around it with a little dark shadow, and then pulled it away, so that you could see the light spot where the button had fallen off, and I made some threads hanging. This is wartime, right?

I guess this is all crazy, but I felt I couldn't give those genuine Irish people less than the real buttons. They probably had a brother or father who wore the uniform in Ireland and had seen them. I did that for this specific group of actors because I thought it would help them.

Did you ever change a costume design because the leading actor or actress insisted on it, more so than the director?

Well, I try not to have that happen. I talk to the star and I listen, which is the other important half of that component. I think if you do your work up front, you are better off. I guess I have this reputation of working fairly well with some very difficult people. I did a show with Lauren Bacall, and she's a very important woman. Her name is above the title.

You are talking about _Sweet Bird of Youth?_

Yes. It was to come to Broadway, but the reviews were such that it did not. Anyway, she's very particular, especially about clothes, hair, and makeup. I did quite a few drawings about the ways that I saw her character. She played the princess. And I went to her house with all these sketches. I tried to have a conversation on what I thought the character was about and what Tennessee Williams prescribed. For example, he says, "the color blue for her character's dress," and I am uncomfortable dismissing that. And from a certain amount of conversation, I realized that she already had in mind a specific gown. It was black, not blue.

SWEET BIRD OF YOUTH
_Costume design by Carrie Robbins,
for Lauren Bacall as the princess
Directed by Michael Blakemore
Denver Center for the Performing Arts (1986)_

Blue was out of the question. She had just stopped smoking. She was nervous about being a little heavier than she had been. Black to her was the most "thinning" color; even navy was unacceptable. She described the dress and I listened to that. I had researched a lot of clothes that she had worn previously, in other shows and for various public appearances. I had heard the stories of expensive clothes being made, and then thrown out. I didn't think that was right. And she even told me a very good gown was made for her in England where she previously had done the show. She wanted to send for it. You might say the implication is, if Robbins screws up, she's got a backup dress. Well, she is the star here, and she has the weight of the show on her back, and she doesn't know me or my work. I said, "Fine! It's simply not a problem, let's get it here! It's nice to have a backup dress. You'll try the new gown and if you don't like it, you've got something you know works for you." And I'm actually proud to tell you she never looked at that backup dress. She wore the one I designed for her, as designed, every day! And after the show opened, she actually thanked me.

You know, Bacall has worn some beautiful clothes throughout her career. There are photos of her being fit by Norman Norell. She had donated some beautiful pieces to FIT and the Met, and I researched them. And I listened to what she wanted. I designed a dress that accommodated that. I don't think that dress is right for the play, and I told Michael Blakemore, the director. And we both agreed that our options here were somewhat limited—and very much shaped by the woman playing the part. This dress was designed to accommodate this particular woman. And sometimes that's what a designer does. This is a collaborative art, not Seventh Avenue.

Do you attend all your own fittings and allow enough time for that?

Absolutely. I'm too compulsive not to. The truth is, I like talking to the actor or actress. And I think ultimately if there is a problem and I'm in the fitting, I'll catch it. That's the point. I know a lot of people have their assistants do the "unimportant" people; I don't believe in that.

What do you find students want to know most about design?

They like to know what "The" answer is, with a capital T. What is "The" answer or "The" rules? And I don't have any rules. So I can't give them that. But I do try to establish some guidelines and ways to think about a piece. I believe that if they put their time in thinking it through, they will get a good product in terms of the conceptual part of it. I ask them not just to do a drawing, but to think while drawing about moving it into three dimensions and to decide what fabric it's going to be made of, how they want it to move—stiffly, flowingly, with a rustle, and so on. To me, it's meaningless to just make a pretty drawing; the two-dimensional picture is only the beginning. It may or may not come out as intended, depending on how thorough the designer's follow-through is.

And I insist that students look at the tools that the costume designer has—the fabric that you choose, its flow or its lack of flow, the choice of color, and the power of color, the incredible range of detail we have at our fingertips. If we know enough about these things to use these details in our designs—embroidery, pleating, tucking, ruching, appliqué, cutwork, God, it's endless—those choices will impact on the final project.

I know some teachers don't take the sketch beyond the 2-D. But this just doesn't make sense to me. If the designer doesn't have a clue what the 3-D version will be, who decides? So who's really the designer? I don't always care if it's not drawn well—though for beginning designers, the "look" of the portfolio is very important. But I do care if it's a secure idea, and if they've really thought

THE THREEPENNY OPERA
*Costume designs by Carrie Robbins,
for Polly (top) and Jenny Diver (right)
Directed by Liviu Ciulei
Tyrone Guthrie Theatre, Minneapolis (1984)*

about the design, thought about the play, thought about the character, thought about what they want to do with it or what the director wants to do with it. Usually I have the costume majors for two years, and we move through many different projects. I start with simple exercises in color and scale. We build up to very complex design problems—Chekhov, Shakespeare.

Recently we did soap opera, and one of my graduates is the designer for *Another World*. He has won two Emmys for his work! He works with a girl who was not a student of mine, but she was my assistant on a number of shows. I am delighted that they won those Emmys, and I believe they bring a great design credibility to their work. I know they don't just go shopping at Bloomingdale's and spend a lot of money; they are thinking about the characters—if they are in a coma or they've married their twelfth husband or whatever it is. It may sound silly to you, but I know they consider the situation seriously, and make responsible, good choices and bring dignity to the soap.

We also do kind of crazy, "way-out" projects. My other class just did *Alice in Wonderland*, and we have some extraordinary designs—each one its own personal take on a masterpiece of inventive writing.

Comment on your design work at the Rainbow Room.

I have a wonderful time at the Rainbow Room. They are the hospitality industry, as they call themselves, and they truly are hospitable. Quite frankly, there's less of the neurotic, chaotic component than there is in the theatre world, although there's some pretty last-minute things. I designed all the uniforms for the Rainbow Room's recent over–$20 million renovation—waiters, busboys, captains, maître d's, several orchestras, including a Latin band, a cigarette girl who doesn't sell cigarettes, and lots of special holiday clothes. I guess there are 400 on the staff. It goes up and down, depending on the economic times. I found it very challenging! But I learned a lot about conveying levels of status quickly and effectively, and a lot about wear and tear. Everything was custom-made, and because of the

longer lead time, I actually got to design and have made my own Rainbow buttons and Rainbow woven trim. I loved that. And I got to design a silk muffler and have several thousand screened abroad, six months lead time. I never get that in the theatre.

Do you really prefer the theatre over television or other mediums?

No, not necessarily. I've done most of my work in the theatre, and some opera and some degree of dance. I did do a year of *Saturday Night Live*.

Was that enjoyable?

It was kind of fun. Part of it is the challenge: "Can I prepare 70 costumes and have them look like anything in three days?" It's not easy. There are a lot of things you just give up on if you are into detail like me. When I got there they said, "Oh, we don't bother with fittings. We don't make anything custom because it can't be done in three days." They didn't even have a full-length mirror in the very small room that served as the costume shop. We did manage to get a three-way full-length mirror, but I know they thought I was a lunatic.

I've done a few PBS specials and a series pilot that wasn't picked up. I've only done one feature film, which again was interesting. I don't like the hours. I hated getting up so early and being on call so constantly. In my dotage, I admit I don't like 16-hour days, six days a week for six months. But the money is good. And I tell all my students that the money is better in both television and movies than in the theatre, and that there's no shame in wanting to make a reasonable living, and that they have a right to want to pay their bills without panicking.

Also, now I find I like a certain amount of flexibility and variety in what I do. I do not like being on the same project for half a year, unless it continues to challenge me. Perhaps if you do a lot of movies, after a while you can have your assistants do the tough parts, and you go home when you want. I was not in that position on the movie I did. But again, I feel that I ought to be there "in the trenches," and that I ought not leave my assistants to sort out the inevitable chaos.

What do you like most about working in the theatre?

I like the collaboration when it works well. I find it's stimulating when the collaboration is with people with whom you really enjoy working. That's the fun. And I love this process of starting with words in a script and words that a director or choreographer will say to you and music, and this becomes a drawing and then this becomes a fully realized three-dimensional thing, that whole process of moving from the verbal through the sketch to the three-dimensional final product. This is very exciting to me. It's never boring. I don't think I could do a nine-to-five job that remained the same, day after day. I don't have the personality to take it well. I'm fairly disciplined, but I don't like the same thing over and over. I like new challenges, and different ones.

You know the most design fun I've had recently? I got the chance to design some huge wrought-iron gates and window grills—very New Orleans. And believe me, there's no bias in wrought iron, so curves are very tricky.

And I've gotten to do a lot of graphics and package and display design through the Rainbow Room. It's also great fun, and the actor component is not involved, just pure design.

And, most secretly, I've been performing and actually getting paid! My tap-dancing, three-part harmony trio—like the '40s-style girl groups—has been very warmly received in the downtown club circuit. Of course, I'm not giving up my day job!

THE RAINBOW ROOM
Apparel designed by Carrie Robbins, for the staff Rockefeller Center, New York (1987)

GREGG BARNES
Costume designs for The Merry Widow
Paper Mill Playhouse, Millburn, New Jersey (1991)

EDUARDO SICANGCO
Costume designs for The Rocky Horror Show
Cincinnati Playhouse in the Park (1989)

EDUARDO SICANGCO
Costume design for On the Verge
Cincinnati Playhouse in the Park (1988)

EDUARDO SICANGCO
Costume designs for Candide
Cincinnati Playhouse in the Park (1988)

ANDREW B. MARLAY
Costume designs for Die Fledermaus
Santa Fe Opera (1986)

A Conversation with
ANN ROTH

I spoke with Ann Roth at The Costume Depot in lower Manhattan. Roth, who was born in 1931 in Hanover, Pennsylvania, was educated at Carnegie-Mellon University in Pittsburgh. Her first Broadway show was *Maybe Tuesday* in 1958 at the Playhouse, which was followed that same year by Budd Shulberg's *The Disenchanted*.

Since then, Roth, who lives in Bangor, Pennsylvania, with her husband, Harry Green, has created costumes for numerous plays and films. She has designed costumes for the American Shakespeare Theatre in Connecticut, the Repertory Theatre of Lincoln Center, the American Conservatory Theatre, the McCarter Theatre, the Long Wharf Theatre, the Old Globe Theatre, the Hartman Theatre Company, the Goodman Theatre, the Cleveland Play House, the Huntington Theatre Company, the Ahmanson Theatre, and the A.P.A. Repertory Company.

Among the many movies for which Roth has designed costumes are *Midnight Cowboy, The World of Henry Orient, The Day of the Locust, Klute, Hair, Coming Home, The Unbearable Lightness of Being, They're Playing Our Song, Slugger's Wife, The Goodbye Girl, The World According to Garp, Up the Down Staircase, Murder by Death, Silkwood, Mandingo, Places in the Heart, Working Girl, Biloxi Blues, California Suite* (a section), *Sweet Dreams, The Owl and the Pussycat, Only When I Laugh, Dressed to Kill, Regarding Henry,* and *Postcards from the Edge.* She has also created costumes for television and for Off-Broadway.

WAITING FOR GODOT
Costume design by Ann Roth, for Lucky
Directed by Mike Nichols
Newhouse Theatre, New York (1988)

THE MISANTHROPE
Costume design by Ann Roth
Directed by Stephen Porter
Circle in the Square Theatre,
New York (1983)

How did you first become interested in designing for the theatre?

I really began with scenery when I was at Carnegie Tech in Pittsburgh. Then I haphazardly started to paint scenery at the opera house to make some money, and I loved doing that. I thought, "Boy, this is for me." And I enjoyed doing drafting as well. I painted for four years, and I actually traveled in an old car to places and painted drops, and I also used to hang drops. I painted at the Bucks County Playhouse and the Shavian Festival at Martha's Vineyard, but mostly I worked for the Pittsburgh Opera. This was in the early 1950s. There was a group of brothers who provided and painted the scenery for the Pittsburgh Opera, and then what changes had to be made were done there. In my early days I was the glue pot girl, because they used pigment paint then.

When you were at Carnegie Tech, you did painting and drafting. Did you also study costume design there?

Yes, certainly. One time, I remember, Irene Sharaff said to me that she wanted to be a scenic designer, but that she thought it was really impossible for women to do that. I just can't believe now that I heard her say those words, because it's so unlike her. Of course, she did the scenery for the "Born in a Trunk" sequence for the film *A Star Is Born*. And then she did a fabulous job. But I recall that she had wanted to do scenery, but felt it was just too tough for women to break in at that time. I found that so odd that she of all people would say that. You know, she is a strong, talented woman.

But there were women like Peggy Clark and Jean Rosenthal who were well-known in the theatre, even though Jean was primarily a lighting designer.

Absolutely. They were great friends of Irene's as well. Aline Bernstein did scenery and Irene worked for her.

What happened to you next?

I went to California to see what it was about. And I got a job painting Irene Sharaff's costumes for the movie *Brigadoon*, and that's how I started. It was very interesting. I mean, I was not a participant on the set or anything like

that, although I did go a few times, and I worked for Irene for a long time after that. Ironically, Bridget Kelly, whose father, Gene Kelly, was the leading man of *Brigadoon*, is currently working for us here at The Costume Depot. Isn't that amazing? It's a very small world.

Later, when I came east with Irene, I remember riding to Philadelphia on a train, and we were talking about the moment when you were supposed to decide whether you wanted to be a designer, and which of these two made a better assistant. And that is still a big question. But we had this plan. We were talking about untying the apron strings and actually going out and saying, "Okay, I'm going to do this myself." And at that moment it is much more difficult than standing behind the designer and letting her take the blame for it all.

So we decided that I would do so many plays and so many movies and that would be it. And that's exactly what happened. I got a Broadway show to design, called *Maybe Tuesday*. It was produced by Ethel Linder Reiner, who had also produced *Candide*, which Irene Sharaff had designed. I had been Irene's assistant on that, and a year or so later Ethel produced a very tiny, young career-girl show on Broadway and she gave me that one to do. That was my first Broadway show, in 1958.

You designed the costumes for *The Disenchanted* after doing that production?

Yes. When Irene and I weren't working together, I went to Florida on a famous movie. I mean, it is not a cult movie, but it is famous among New York moviemakers—it was called *Wind Across the*

Ann Roth's costume design credits include:

Death and the Maiden (1992)

A Small Family Business (1992)

Born Yesterday (1989)

The House of Blue Leaves (1986), Beaumont Theatre

Social Security (1986)

The Odd Couple (1985)

Biloxi Blues (1985)

Arms and the Man (1985)

Singin' in the Rain (1985)

Hurlyburly (1984)

Design for Living (1984)

The Misanthrope (1983)

The Best Little Whorehouse in Texas (1982)

Lunch Hour (1980)

They're Playing Our Song (1979)

Strangers (1979)

The Crucifer of Blood (1978)

Do You Turn Somersaults? (1978)

First Monday in October (1978)

The Importance of Being Earnest (1977)

The Heiress (1976)

The Royal Family (1975)

Seesaw (1973)

The Women (1973)

The Merchant of Venice (1973)

6 Rms Riv Vu (1972)

Father's Day (1971)

Purlie (1970)

Play it Again, Sam (1969)

Something Different (1967)

The Odd Couple (1966)

The Star-Spangled Girl (1966)

The Impossible Years (1965)

Mrs. Daly (1965)

The Last Analysis (1964)

Slow Dance on the Killing Ground (1964)

A Case of Libel (1963)

Natural Affection (1963)

A Far Country (1963)

Purlie Victorious (1961)

Face of a Hero (1960)

HAIR, THE FILM
Costume designs by Ann Roth
Choreographed by Twyla Tharp
Directed by Milos Forman
Produced by Lester Persky and Michael Butler
(1979)

Everglades, and supposedly at one point in the film the birds flew backwards. It was a wild and woolly crowd in the Everglades of Florida. There was a lot of gin flowing. It was Nicholas Ray, Gypsy Rose Lee, Christopher Plummer, and Burl Ives. And this core of New York moviemakers all went down to the Everglades of Florida. About then, Budd Shulberg had written this script, a really interesting script. At any rate, I survived that experience, and then I got asked to do *The Disenchanted.*

That was a period play with quite a number of costumes.

Yes, it was right up my alley. It was a good period show, and it was the kind of period I loved to do. It took place from about 1913 to 1939. Ben Edwards did the scenery for that. And out of that play

I met Rosemary Harris, and in my life Ellis Rabb had been a very good friend of mine, and he then married Rosemary.

It's funny, because in my career I've worked with the same people over and over again. I very rarely get a chance to work with new people. I've done just loads of shows with Ellis Rabb and also a great many with Rosemary. So that was my beginning on Broadway. I did a lot of Broadway and then I went to Princeton with Ellis and did A.P.A. productions. I had worked with Bill Ball in San Francisco at the American Conservatory Theatre. And I had started doing some Chekhov with Bill Ball at the Westport Playhouse.

What was the first film you did on your own?

I was asked to do *The World of Henry Orient.* George Roy Hill directed it and

Jerry Hellman produced it. Since then, I've been asked to do every Jerry Hellman film and have done most of them, including *Midnight Cowboy, The Day of the Locust,* and *Coming Home.* I loved that one.

When you did the film *The Day of the Locust,* did you have an assistant on costumes?

Yes. When I got there at Paramount, I brought Bob De Mora out from New York. He is one of the great costume designers and he is extremely talented. I asked him to come to California, because if you have 500 people to dress or 300 or 30 in a day, I knew that he and I had the same sense of humor about how to dress these people. But I had one assistant and probably five or six wardrobe people. And sometimes we did 600 people, which is what we had at the end. It was huge.

The California system at that time was still in heavy observance. There was such a system of how to get on a movie, and what designers do, and what the wardrobe people do, and so on. And it was not sympathetic with me in any way. What the studios foster is that each studio had its contract designers and those people were especially involved with the actors and actresses on the roster of that studio. There could be Grace Kelly, Bing Crosby or whoever on one studio, or Lana Turner and Esther Williams at MGM. For instance, at MGM, there are Walter Plunkett and Helen Rose. Walter would do the period pieces and Helen would do the glamour pieces. And so certainly it was indicative that when these people did big musicals, like *An American in Paris,* or whatever, they would have Irene Sharaff go out and design those.

But in the old system it was unlikely that the designer would do not just the background, but even the second leads; the wardrobe people would do those. And they would pull stock and they would dress them. But these designers generally did the stars. For example, let's say they were doing *Robin Hood.* Robin Hood would be dressed perhaps by Walter Plunkett, along with three or four of his merry men, and Maid Marian. But for the background people, they would pull stock from what they then called "the Middle Ages aisle." And then they would dress them.

So when I got to California there was a lot of pressure for me to hire certain wardrobe people. I must have had a lapse—I allowed them to tell me who to hire. Eventually I found a compatible and talented staff.

The Day of the Locust was a big event movie. People were not doing many period movies. And if they did do period movies, they were making them more palatable for the 1970s eye. I don't think it was easy to get an actress in a real girdle of the period, because this was the high period of thrift shop or vintage clothing. I was a vintage clothing person myself, and I remember that I could go to the Upper East Side and find a wonderful vicuna coat in one of those thrift shops. And everybody from Woodstock on was dressing up in his mother's or his granny's clothes.

The Day of the Locust was difficult, and I didn't want it to become a "costume piece." At the same time, I had sort of vaudeville people. It was a lot of fun, and John Schlesinger is one of the great directors of my life. He loves the atmosphere of the people. And in *The Day of the Locust*, all those people are very integral to the atmosphere of Hollywood in the 1930s.

Did you do sketches for the principals?
Yes, all these drawings were done.

How many sketches would you say you did in total?
Oh, around 200.

Were the costumes built for these?
Yes. They were all built from scratch. And I had the child's clothes, and his mother's, made at Paramount for no other reason except that Paramount had the most phenomenal stash of fabrics in the world.

How long did you spend preparing for the movie?
I think that I prepared maybe nine or ten weeks for it, something like that.

How would you compare doing the film *Working Girl* with *The Day of the Locust*?

SILKWOOD, THE FILM
Costume design by Ann Roth,
for Meryl Streep as Karen Silkwood
Directed by Mike Nichols
Produced by Mike Nichols and
Michael Hausman
Released by Fox Pictures (1983)

DESIGN FOR LIVING
Costume design by Ann Roth
Directed by George C. Scott
Circle in the Square Theatre, New York (1984)

The Day of the Locust was a period picture; *Working Girl* is the kind of picture that Mike Nichols does. It's a whole different thing. Mike rarely does period pictures—what he likes to do is some sort of his own comedy. And what I love to do are character clothes. I enjoy doing them. It just really depends on the production. In *Midnight Cowboy*, those were character clothes, and they were not period clothes, except for the flashbacks. But they were costumes in that they were comments in a sense, on the characters in the literature. They were clothes of those characters. I do not do movie stars' clothes—I don't dress movie stars. I don't know how to do that and I don't like doing that. And I'm not good at it.

But when you did *Working Girl*, you still designed the principal's clothes.
I don't do clothes for Melanie Griffith; I do Melanie Griffith playing Tess McGill.

You just don't do movie stars' clothes.
That's what I'm saying. For instance, Kim Basinger is a movie star—she's actually a friend of mine. But people don't dress Kim Basinger to be other than Kim Basinger. She is going to play Kim Basinger. I don't do those clothes. And I don't think that's what costumes are.

Of course, you had worked many times with Mike Nichols on stage productions prior to doing the film *Working Girl*.
Yes, we have been working together for 26 years. *The Odd Couple* was the first thing we did, and there have been millions of things in between.

So you knew the way he liked to work, and you liked to work with him?
Well, it takes about three times. If you sort of get the sense of humor of someone, and you key into one another, then it's a mutual liking of working together. I have trailed Mike Nichols around for so long, and will always trail him around, because he is the most interesting director. He's fascinating and you want to be there. He is sensational.

That makes a big difference on how you prepare a film and go at it. Would you change your way of working for another director?

No, I don't think I would change my way of doing it for another director. I mean, obviously if a director calls me up and asks me to do a project, he would have looked at something that I had done in the past.

A new director, you mean?
Yes, anybody.

Mike Nichols knows you and he would call you and say, "I've got a picture I want you to do"?
Yes.

How much of a challenge was *Working Girl*?
It was a big challenge. The director who

I'm working with now [Robert Mandel] has said to me, "Miss Roth, how do you justify the fact that Sigourney Weaver's clothes were two or three sizes larger than Melanie's?"

What did you say? Is that true?
Well, they were fudged.

***The Best Little Whorehouse in Texas*, with Tommy Tune. Comment on that production.**
The Best Little Whorehouse in Texas was Off-Broadway, and we had $7,000. That was our budget for costumes. A young lady named Sue Gandy had come in from Kansas to take singing lessons in New York, and we asked her to shop for

us. There was a new set of costumes put into the show, and they were referred to as the "siege dresses," because the sheriff was coming in to siege them. These dresses were just a terrible problem with us. We literally begged, borrowed, and did everything for this show—we just didn't have the money for it. So we got down to where we had less than nine dollars apiece for each girl for the siege. And we sent Sue Gandy out on the streets to find these dresses. About every 24 hours she'd say, "I found one," and she'd bring in this piece of garbage, and eventually we had these very good character dresses. They were just wonderful.

Another funny thing happened on

THE GOODBYE GIRL, THE FILM
Costume designs by Ann Roth
Directed by Herbert Ross
Produced by Ray Stark
Released by MGM (1977)

that show, when we did the football half-time thing. Tommy Tune wanted the girls to come on, run out the other side, and come back in, so it looked like we had a lot of the Texas A & M cheerleaders. I figured out these dolls that were mounted on a board, so that a girl dancer could have this board across her back, and then there was a cardboard doll on either side of her. So one dancer became three dancers. We made those boards with cardboard dolls and balloons on them. And each doll had legs that went up and down and tap-danced, and I had two balloons for her boobs and two balloons for her heinie. The dolls had Styrofoam faces, cowgirl hats, and gloves, and they worked like a charm. Then we had mirrors, and so when the girls danced on we suddenly had a whole stage full of them. Tommy was surprised, and they were absolutely terrific!

Had you worked with Tommy Tune previous to this?

Yes. I had made him balloon dresses for another show, *Seesaw.* One director left. Michael Bennett came in, and in order for Michael to get it on in time, he hired Tommy to help him with a certain section. And again the money was gone—it had already been spent. So I made more balloon dresses for *Seesaw,* the musical. Anyway, we had a very good time.

Then *Whorehouse* moved uptown and we had more money to do the costumes, but by this time we were in love with the sleaze of the cheapness of it, and we got hooked on it. When we did the Houston Company, we retained the same cheap quality of the show. And I remember the audience was dressed beautifully, and they all came in expecting this glamorous thing, but basically it was pretty sleazy. It was fun, though.

When you design a production and you do sketches, what medium do you work in?

I use watercolor and Dr. Martin's dyes, and I use inexpensive paper, so that I don't fall in love with the sketch and I can tear it up when I want to. But when I'm cooking, I can do nine drawings a day. These are what I call real drawings. But I can actually do more than that. It takes me a while—it takes me about four

SINGIN' IN THE RAIN
Costume design by Ann Roth
Directed and choreographed by Twyla Tharp
Gershwin Theatre, New York (1985)

days to get into it. When I did *Singin' in the Rain,* I made almost 300 drawings, maybe more. I did them for every single person.

When you make sketches with hair and wig styles, do you chat with someone, such as hair designer Paul Huntley?

Yes, I do. And Paul Huntley might very well say, "It's a divine sketch, but the actress cannot wear that color." Or he might say, "She cannot wear her hair in this manner here," or "She needs this." And of course, I certainly listen to that. I listen to everything he says. The director, designer, hairdresser, and actor should all want the same thing. And in our business it has nothing to do with ego; it has to do with getting the piece on.

You worked with Jerry Zaks when you designed the costumes for *The House of Blue Leaves* at Lincoln Center.

Yes. He was the director and Tony Walton was the scenic designer. I remember that for some reason or other it was just one of those very easy shows. John Guare was around. And Jerry Zaks was the easiest person in the world to work with. We talked about each character. We used to sit down at the loft and chat, and I did a very, very realistic approach to it. The big key to it was getting Swoozie Kurtz's degree of "off-the-wall, mentally imbalanced costume" right—that was such a fine line. Swoozie played Bananas Shaughnessy. I was working with Roy Helland, a very fine hairdresser who did her wigs. And when the reality of her clothes fell into place, then everybody else's did.

Why was it an easy show to do?

If I remember correctly, it wasn't very hard. I had this feeling I had to worry about the budget, but I think it was okay. I loved working with the actors and they were all wonderful. So yes, it was a nice show to do.

Would you talk about doing initial preparation on a movie?

Because I am Broadway-oriented or theatre-oriented, I tend to deliver a movie up front. I am not a stylist, I don't wing it. The movie I'm doing now is a 1955 piece. It is about a New England prep school that buys itself a Pennsylvania coal miner's kid, who is a football star. They need a football player, and he turns out to be Jewish, and that's indeed the crux of it, but there we are in preppieland. And we are going to film this in Chelmsford, Massachusetts, in its entirety. It is 40-some miles outside of Boston in very heavy traffic. So I can't rely on running into Boston and getting something for the next day or for that afternoon. So I am preparing this picture here and now. And as I drove in this morning from Pennsylvania, I thought, "Oh, my God! I need some brown knee socks with some little designs around the top of them for the faculty's children. I also need some Buster Brown shoes for those children as they would appear in 1955. I need some boxer shorts with a yoke for the scene where you see guys wandering around in the hall. I need jockey shorts that come to a diamond in the front, rather than a

SINGIN' IN THE RAIN
Costume designs by Ann Roth
Directed and choreographed by Twyla Tharp
Gershwin Theatre, New York (1985)

straight-form jock/Calvin Klein thing. I need garter belts for 125 girls at a little tea dance. I don't have 125 nice tea dance dresses to start with." But that preparation I do up front is what I'm saying.

When you started on the movie *Silkwood*, did you do a lot of research?

I started with research on *Silkwood*. No matter how many times I've done it, research is the biggest thing for me. The script had been done by Nora Ephron and Alice Arlen, two divine women and good friends. The script was awfully good. And I kept seeing Silkwood's name in graffiti on buildings in New York. But where she came from in Oklahoma, I didn't know anything about it. So I started by delving into her life. And it's funny, because I trust my immediate impression, no matter how much studying I do. On *Silkwood*, it was Meryl Streep and Cher, and it was like rose red and snow white, and Mike Nichols was definitely fascinated by these two tearing beauties, a blonde and a brunette.

I thought these girls came out of this Oklahoma cowgirl atmosphere, but that wasn't true, because they came from Oklahoma City, and they were urban girls in real life. And so I did not see them in cute jeans and neckerchiefs and that kind of thing at all. I saw them dressed like I dressed them, and that was in a rather tough, urban, suburban mall–oriented way. These were mall girls in mall clothes with Pentecostal hair.

Cher was going to play a lesbian. What we decided to do with Cher was to give her a rather androgynous, sexless, "lack of self-esteem" quality of dressing. And consequently, the pants fit, maybe at the waist, but they didn't have any real feeling. It was like so many young girls who don't feel very good about themselves, and who have no real eye to making themselves dress to appeal to anyone in particular. Consequently, they generally look uniformed, like a child. And that was what we tried to get, and I think we did.

Meryl was great. When I met with her for the first time over this thing, I said, "I have to tell you that I see Karen Silkwood in black T-shirts, and her black jeans, and the clothes of the period, the 1970s, because if you are buying cheap clothes, you know that you get a truly trendy outfit, as opposed to quality timeliness, right? And so we zeroed in on that. She [Silkwood] didn't know who the designers were in the early 1970s. That was not part of her vocabulary. She went out and bought something that was going to be cute for Saturday night. And you know, that disease of buying a new pair of pants to get you through the weekend—when you are a laborer or a worker in a factory, small compensation makes you feel good.

Did you go on location?

Yes, I was on location. It was roughly 10 weeks. So it's long. I took an assistant, but mostly to shop.

You also did *Postcards from the Edge*, with Mike Nichols and Shirley MacLaine and Meryl Streep. Was there

anything different or unusual about that as compared to other Nichols films?

Every film with Mike is different. What we decided to do, since we were shooting in southern California in a sort of secret way, was to use the color of Technicolor as southern California in the costumes. That was for the healthy people. Then there were those who were not unfamiliar with drugs, and they were going to wear black. That's encapsulating it, but that's basically the way we thought about that piece.

Did you carry that through in the film?

Yes. And at times Mike just went crazy and said, "Why am I looking at all these M & M's and all those terrible colors?" I said, "Do you remember?" He said, "Oh, I'm sorry I did that."

But you had discussed it prior and agreed to that?

Oh, we had discussed it a thousand times. But I pretty much like the way the movie looks. And I also like the way *Regarding Henry* looks, I really do. Tony Walton and I worked very closely on that. I think that's successful.

Comment on what you did for *Regarding Henry*.

I just decided the script demanded a nonevent costume situation. I suppressed everything. I did a whole new kind of thing for me. I think if you went to see it, you would not see one iota of clothing. It all mushed together.

And you say you suppressed the costumes, you suppressed color, texture, form, and shape?

Everything, totally.

You felt it needed that?

Yeah, I did. And I enjoyed doing it very much. It was a challenge to me, actually.

If you were to put two of your favorite stage productions in a time capsule, what would they be?

One would be *The Merchant of Venice* at Lincoln Center, with Ellis Rabb directing. I loved doing Shakespeare, I loved Ellis Rabb, and I loved the costumes. They were very successful, and I got

good notices. I liked doing *They're Playing Our Song* for Neil Simon, with Bob Moore directing. I thought I did a good job on that. I enjoyed designing costumes for the original *The Odd Couple*, where I had six men who changed their clothes three times each, and they each sort of retained their own personality. That was with Mike Nichols in 1965. But that's not time-capsule material. Then I did a piece with George C. Scott where I liked the costumes, and that was *Design for Living* at Circle in the Square.

What do you like least about working in the theatre?

I don't like staying up late at night. That's a problem with me. I'm really geared for daytime. I can't sit in the theatre over and over at night because I just go to sleep. Put it on in the daytime!

Do you feel listening to actors is part of the costume designer's job?

That's part of it, and I can do that part. I can stand and listen to actors tell me about their right hip being higher than their left hip, and all that nonsense.

But is it your job to tell actors they look wonderful?

Well, it's not a matter of telling them they look wonderful; it is telling them

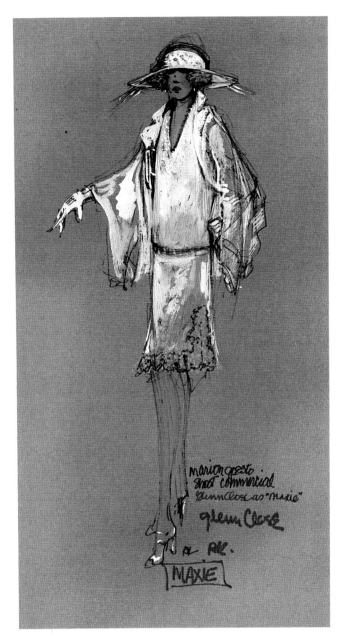

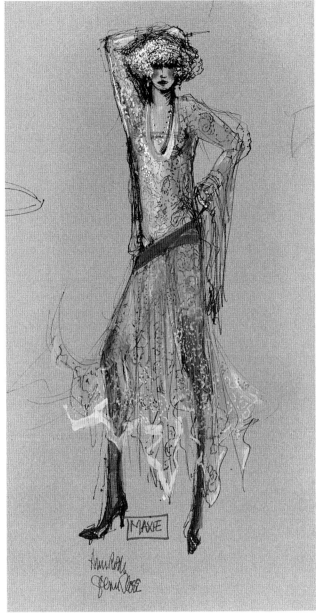

MAXIE, THE FILM
Costume designs by Ann Roth, for Glenn Close
Directed by Paul Aaron
Produced by Carter De Haven
Released through Orion Pictures (1985)

that you trust him or her to create a character. You're not interested in hearing about that person's personal likes and dislikes—you don't expect to hear that. You expect to hear that person dealing with the problems of creating a character. And in that case, I'll do anything for that actor. But when the actor says, "I don't like yellow" or "I can't wear a girdle," then you don't want to listen to that. It's just not part of it.

I'm sure you know how to cope with that and tell them they must.
Well, I say, "Wait a minute, we're not talking about you. We're talking about this character. And you're going to create it better than anybody! Now let's start thinking whether that character likes yellow. If that character hates yellow, I'll listen. But prove it to me!"

What do you like most about working in the theatre?
I wanted to be in the theatre when I was a little girl, and it has never disappointed me. You work on plays and fall in love with directors, and you figure that you are going to know each other for a lifetime. You have the same ideas and it's a thrilling little marriage, and it's a good ride along the way!

HAL GEORGE
Costume design for Samuel Ramey as Odabella in Attila
Chicago Lyric Opera (1981)

LEWIS BROWN
Costume design for Roubillon in There's One in Every Marriage
Old Globe Theatre, San Diego (1987)

GREGG BARNES
Costume design for
The Roar of the Greasepaint—The Smell of the Crowd
Paper Mill Playhouse, Millburn, New Jersey (1990)

LINDSAY W. DAVIS
Costume design for John Jasper in The Mystery of Edwin Drood
Imperial Theatre, New York (1985)

GREGG BARNES
Costume design for Papageno in The Magic Flute
June Opera Festival of New Jersey, Princeton (1985)

MARTIN PAKLEDINAZ
Costume design for Sir Andrew Aguecheek in Twelfth Night
Shakespeare Theatre at the Folger, Washington, D.C. (1989)

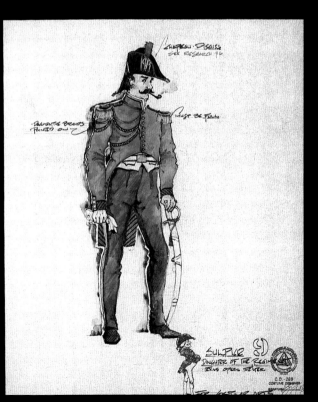

EDUARDO SICANGCO
Costume design for Daughter of the Regiment
Texas Opera Theatre, Houston (1982)

HAL GEORGE
Costume design for Anthony Quinn in Zorba
Broadway Theatre, New York (1983)

A Conversation with
JOSÉ VARONA

José Varona resides in an attractive apartment on New York City's Upper West Side. A native of Argentina, he studied varied subjects in Buenos Aires and Paris. Varona, an international designer, has created sets and costumes on four continents, and has also done occasional work in films and television. He has collaborated with Joseph Papp and Alan Jay Lerner, with choreographers Frederick Ashton, George Balanchine, Natalia Makarova, and George Skibine, and with dancers Margot Fonteyn, Rudolf Nureyev, and Alicia Alonso. In the field of opera, he has designed for Beverly Sills, Joan Sutherland, and Plácido Domingo, as well as for directors Günther Rennert, August Everding, and Marguerite Wallmann, and conductors Karl Böhm, Riccardo Muti, and Claudio Abbado.

Varona's renderings have been exhibited at the Cooper-Hewitt Museum of Design in New York, and also at the Library of the Performing Arts at Lincoln Center and various other galleries. In Europe, his work can be seen in the permanent collection of the Museum of the Paris Opera. In addition, he has exhibited at the Museum of the Stage in Amsterdam, and also in Berlin, Buenos Aires, Montevideo, and Lima.

Varona has taught at Lester Polakov's Studio and Forum of Stage Design, and has lectured and given master classes at Boston University and the University of Connecticut.

José Varona has designed sets and costumes for the following companies and theatres:

BALLET COMPANIES

New York City Ballet
American Ballet Theatre
Dallas Ballet
Pacific Northwest Ballet
Milwaukee Ballet
San Francisco Ballet
Paris Opera Ballet
Berlin Opera Ballet
Ballet do Rio de Janeiro
Pennsylvania Ballet
Geneva Grand Theatre

National Ballet of Canada
Universal Ballet—Korea
Zurich Opera Ballet
Chicago Tribune Ballet
Miami City Ballet

OPERA COMPANIES

Hamburg Opera
Berlin Deutsche Oper
New York City Opera
Paris Opera
San Francisco Opera
Washington Opera Society
Baltimore Civic Opera
Dallas Civic Opera

Netherlands Opera
Holland Festival
Australian Opera Company
Vancouver Opera
American Opera Center

**OTHER COMPANIES
AND THEATRES**

Teatro Colón—Buenos Aires
Kennedy Center—Washington, D.C.
Spoleto Festival—Spoleto, Italy
Teatro Municipal—Rio de Janeiro
Teatro Municipal—Caracas
Caramoor Festival—New York
Teatro Teresa Carreño—Caracas

THE MAGIC FLUTE
Costume designs by José Varona
Directed by Marguerite Wallman
Teatro Colón, Buenos Aires (1983)

THE MERRY WIDOW
Costume designs by José Varona
Directed by Lotfi Mansouri, Vancouver Opera (1979)
Directed by August Everding, Berlin Deutsche Oper (1979)

How did you first become interested in designing for the theatre?

I think that attraction, in a way, was born with me. I was interested in the theatre, in painting, and in music as far back as I can remember. I don't recall a time when I was not fascinated by the arts, and especially by the theatre.

Did your parents take you to the theatre?

Yes. In my home town—Mendoza—we had a couple of theatres, used mainly by visiting companies. I saw everything when I was a child, good and bad. Opera, ballet, and legitimate theatre. I saw some incredible things, like the original production of *The House of Bernarda Alba*, by Federico Garcia Lorca. The world premiere took place in 1944, in Buenos Aires. Lorca's favorite actress, the great Margarita Xirgu, in exile from the Franco regime, played the lead and directed. It ran for a long time in the capital. Then she went on a tour all over Latin America, and she came to my home town and caused a sensation. I was 13 years old. My parents thought that since I was artistically oriented, it would be a tremendous experience for me to be able to say that I had seen that production. So they smuggled me inside the theatre. They knew the owner of the theatre and they took me to a box where I could go in undetected, because it was forbidden for children, of course. What happened onstage was magical, so I decided that the theatre was for me, although I wasn't sure in what capacity. I also loved the acting part, the directing, and above all the music. It was a tough thing for me to make up my mind. I ended up doing sets and costumes, as you well know, but how I miss the other disciplines!

Did you actually study drawing and painting?

No, I didn't. Basically I am self-taught, I only took a year of set and costume design, but I was never trained in design or painting. I studied commerce. Wrong as it was, my father suggested that I become an economist, although he was aware of my artistic inclination. He wanted me to have something practical, in order to be protected. However, he was on my side, and very encouraging, when I finally decided to go ahead and plunge into the theatre.

What made you leave your hometown?

I left because I couldn't become a professional in the provinces. I had to go to the capital. I went there to study set and costume design at the Fine Arts Institute in Buenos Aires. I really needed my other degrees from the other fine arts schools—something like the grammar and high school of the art career—but I didn't have those degrees. In those days, in Buenos Aires, set and costume design was taught as a specialization at a very high level, so you needed a lot of preparation to reach that point. Fortunately, they were impressed with my work and they accepted me on the condition that I took an exam. It was quite complex. The course was four years, but I took only one, and I was on my way! It was too soon.

How old were you?

I was 21. Before that, I had tried to study architecture, but it was not what I expected. I wanted to design beautiful buildings without having to bother with the technical preparation. I still hate to draft.

When did you decide to come to New York?

I came to New York from Buenos Aires in the early 1960s. The situation in Argentina was getting worse politically, economically, and artistically. Buenos Aires had always been the cultural capital of Latin America. An interesting city, with a tremendous artistic life. But with the years, that was going downwards, and my own career with it. In my mid-20s I was rather busy designing opera,

ballet, legitimate theatre, movies, TV, and even music hall! But I noticed that I was taking shortcuts and trying to get away with a number of things the easy way, not really doing interesting creative work. It was just one job after another. Artistically, things came easy for me, so I didn't bother to improve. I was becoming a bad artist. Aware of my potential, I decided to change places and go where nobody knew me and where I had to start from scratch, in order to reevaluate my merits. I arrived in New York at the end of 1962, when I was 31. New challenges, new language. New fears also: I was alone.

How did you get your first production in New York?
It was Joe Papp who gave me my first chance. I have a wonderful memory of him. Exciting times! An Argentine director with whom I had worked in Buenos Aires heard that I was in town, and he contacted me. He had been hired by Joe Papp to direct plays in Spanish. Osvaldo Riofrancos was his name. He told me he was going to direct Lorca's *The Shoemaker's Prodigious Wife* for the new mobile

theatre, designed to tour the different neighborhoods, especially the Latin American neighborhoods. He introduced me to Papp and the American designers. Ming Cho Lee was the head artist for the Shakespeare Festival then.

Is that where you met Ming Cho Lee?
Exactly. That's where I met everybody. Theoni Aldredge and Ming's assistants: David Mitchell, Doug Schmidt, and Marjorie Kellogg. Imagine!

For Joe Papp I designed sets and costumes for *Romeo and Juliet,* also for the mobile theatre, and costumes for *Volpone* and *Macbeth*, this time in a bilingual version. My English *Macbeth* was James Earl Jones.

How did you first start designing for the New York City Opera?
They saw my sketches and pictures of my work and they were interested. Also, an opera director whom I had worked with in Buenos Aires had been hired by the New York City Opera. He highly recommended me. His name is Tito Capobianco.

So the beginning of your American

career was made possible by two Latin American directors.
Absolutely. The Argentine connection—one for opera and one for legitimate theatre. And that's the way I started with the City Opera.

You designed the costumes for Handel's *Julius Caesar*.
Yes. It was the first opera I ever designed in America. It was such a success! Ming Cho Lee did the sets. Actually, I recommended Ming to the City Opera, and he was so ecstatic, because he loves opera. So we started working together. *Julius Caesar* was the first of many, and it opened the doors of the professional operatic stage for Ming and me, and also for the director of the opera and even for Beverly Sills and Norman Treigle. That was like their second debut, really, but it was the production that made them stars. After that, I designed about 15 operas for the New York City Opera.

If I were to ask you how you go about designing costumes for an opera, what would you tell me?
Every designer has a different way of

accomplishing this task, and every designer changes his or her approach according to different directors, theatres, and even audiences. The production budget is important. The singers for whom one is designing are worth considering too. Let us imagine that all these elements are ideal, that the designer can do whatever his knowledge, versatility, taste, and imagination can afford. I think it is still impossible to give a precise answer, because the approach can be so varied.

Do you approach your design by the style of the music?

Yes, I do, definitely. But an opera can be approached also by the school of its composer or by the historical situation, by the period of the actual story. It can be approached even as an abstraction. All these methods have proved successful or incorrect at some time or other. It could be a combination of elements that happens to be the right one. The same thing applies for the sets, also. If you ask, for instance, which is the perfect *Marriage of Figaro*—a Viennese baroque Figaro, or a Spanish baroque one, or a French rococo

one, considering that its original writer, Beaumarchais, was French—I would say that whichever is better designed, because Mozart can blend beautifully with any of these frames, as long as it's a good one.

Comment on research books, and on how you go about doing research with reference books.

Of course, we designers have to do a lot of research. You reach a point when you just don't do as much research as you're supposed to because you know your periods well. And after many years of acting in a field like the opera or the ballet, you know what you have to do. There are numerous books that help, and they started many, many years ago. One of the first was done by Cesareo Vecellio. He was Titian's nephew, who in 1590 published the first history of costume. And then you have all sorts of books— Racinet, Max von Boehn, François Boucher, Millia Davenport, and dozens of practical volumes. A designer should not neglect history books either.

Books help point you in the right direction, but the imagination of the

artist is indispensable. He or she should be able to devise or invent a costume that will situate the audience in the right atmosphere. More than imitating or copying period costumes, it is a matter of recreating a period for the stage, its drama. The stage has its own laws, and generally the fake element is far more effective than the real one. Whoever has seen an authentic costume taken right out of the museum and put onstage next to a well-designed theatrical garment will understand what I'm talking about. After all, theatre is make-believe, and opera even more so. Extreme realism in opera is somewhat illogical, although it is right for films. But that is something else.

How about verismo opera?

Verismo is a style of opera that depicts reality. It started at the turn of the century with Mascagni's *Cavalleria Rusticana,* which is very real in most of its scenes. Some scenes are just plain old-fashioned operatic. But that is all right, because Italian reality is very operatic in itself. Believe me, Italian reality, like Spanish reality, is not like English reality! There are not that many verismo operas. They are very few, really. There are many operas that are performed under the label "verismo," but they are not. They are fictional, they have historical subjects. What happens is that they all came about in the same period and were absorbed by the new movement. But let's be honest: An opera cannot be completely true to life, due to the fact that real people talk rather than sing. Opera is a grander than life expression; you cannot project total realism.

Grand opera implies a grand spectacle; often it uses classical or historical plots, poetry, heroic gestures, and, above all, the sublime language of music. Not many modern composers understand the eloquent artificiality of opera. They minimize certain things and they go into a kind of neutral territory that is simply boring. Why don't they talk, instead of apologizing musically? But you have also the realm of chamber opera. You can do wonderful things in a smaller format, without losing the flair of the sound.

Ginastera, Penderecki, Glass, Corigliano are modern composers who understood opera. Opera design is, with exceptions, better when it is grander than life, dealing as it does with bigger theatres, bigger stages and all that fantastic sound.

You're talking about both sets and costumes?
Yes, and voices that are grander than life, so the costume has to serve that type of expression. Also, at times, you have to dress people who are larger than life in physical terms. No offense, Luciano.

How important is it for a designer to refer to the painting masters?
Extremely important. For example, who can design a good *Romeo and Juliet* without going to the late-medieval and early-Renaissance painters and taking a good look at Piero Della Francesca, Lippi, De Roberti, Carpaccio, all those wonderful painters! Who can design Gounod's *Faust* or Boito's *Mefistofele* without visually devouring the work of Dürer, Lucas Cranach or Lucas van Leyden? There it is, the period, the people. You have to look at them. And when you say *Der Rosenkavalier*, you are talking about Bellotto and Hogarth, because it was the picture of the levée by Hogarth that inspired Richard Strauss to compose *Der Rosenkavalier*. If you are familiar with Daumier, you can design a better *La Bohème*. And if you design *Manon,* you have to look up Watteau, Lancret, Boucher, Fragonard, all those exquisite French painters who will give you the right feeling, the right atmosphere, the right color, and blend your palette with that score that is quintessentially French. It sounds very, very eighteenth century, especially in the ballet music. So those are Manon's best friends.

And how can you design *Rigoletto* and the Duke of Mantua without looking at those old Titian paintings, Lorenzo Lotto, Bronzino, or Tintoretto? Then if you do Mozart's *Cosi Fan Tutte*, you have to study Pietro Longhi. Those paintings put you in the right mood. This is if you are doing a traditional version. And if the theatre you are working for requires a traditional approach, with a grand, historical style, you have to be familiar with those painters.

How about working for directors like Peter Sellars?
When you work for a director like Peter Sellars, nothing of the above makes any sense. Stay away from museums and follow his wishes. I recommend tabloids! If he wants to use the Trump Tower or the Bronx for your setting, you have to reproduce that. It's a different view, but I think it speaks well of the possibilities of opera, that it can be done, and that it can attract people to that type of modern expression. I'm personally not interested in that anarchic approach, as I hear a different sound when I think in those visual terms. Rap? MTV? Maybe those directors don't know it, but they are being patronizing with the material they serve. But if it works, that's fine. It is not a matter of what I like. It is important that the public is attracted to the theatre, and to music in particular.

What about specific historical operas, like *Don Carlo* or *Un Ballo in Maschera*?
Some of them deal with real characters, like Don Carlo, the son of Charles V, Spanish King and German Emperor. *Don Carlo* is based on a tragedy by Schiller, and Verdi set it to music. But we are talking about history seen through the romantic eyes. So everything is changed and beautified.

You can approach it from a more historical point of view visually. If you look at the portraits of the period, like those of Sanchez Coello, for instance, there you have them—stiff, powerful aristocrats. That majesty of late-sixteenth-century Spanish fashion suits the mood of the Schiller characters. Verdi's music blends with them in a grandiose way. But it is only the surface of history; the real courtiers in this story were miles away from Schiller. Eboli, for instance, had a black patch over her blind right eye. How could she sing "I curse you, my beauty!"? I should say that her beauty was already cursed.

If some designers indulge in these touches of authenticity, then they should have to draw a Don Carlo somewhat deformed, obviously retarded, cruel, and neurotic to the core, as the real one certainly was. You cannot go halfway! But I don't think Plácido Domingo would agree.

CINDERELLA (PROKOFIEV)
Costume designs by José Varona
Choreographed by Valery Panov
Berlin Deutsche Oper (1976)

The other Verdi opera you mentioned, *Un Ballo in Maschera,* is presented in two different versions. One takes place in Sweden, which is the real historical setting for the assassination of Gustavus III during a masked ball at the end of the eighteenth century. But as Verdi was not allowed to depict historical characters under the light of truth, as he had to submit his work to tremendous censorship, he used a fictional governor of Boston, in America, in the seventeenth century, for his story. So you have the Swedish version, which is the one that is usually performed today, and occasionally you have the Boston version. Dealing with the second one, would you approach it as if you were designing *The Crucible?* Listen to the score! Let yourself be engulfed in the sweeping wave of that sumptuous music that Verdi wrote. You cannot really bring it to the dry, puritanical view of the early American period. It just doesn't go with it. If you design a Boston version of *Un Ballo in Maschera,* you have to go to the Italian painters of the period like Neri, Dolci, Ceresa, or the Flemish Van Dyck and also the late Rubens, but not the early American painters, with their constricted look at life, which contradicts the music. And what music!

Is elegance or grandeur expected in the design of opera?
Yes, in a way it is taken for granted. It is expected on the operatic stage. I have an anecdote: Some years ago I designed for the Teatro Colón, the opera in Buenos Aires, a modern opera that took place in the slums of a contemporary city. Its characters were very picturesque indeed. During an intermission on opening night, I overheard part of a conversation led by an elderly lady, who expressed her annoyance: "They make me dress like a queen to come to the opera, and all I see is hoodlums and prostitutes!"

Do you think that fashion influences operatic design?
It used to, a great deal. Today we tend to be more loyal to the different historical periods, which is much more wholesome and believable. Old nineteenth-century illustrations give away the fashions of the

LA SYLPHIDE
Costume design by José Varona
Choreographed by Flemming Flindt
Dallas Ballet (1987)

time. But with great romantic charm, I must say. All through the turn of the century, the historical look is subjected to the use of the corset, with hilarious results. The '20s, '30s, and '40s are not less comic, I must say. No offense, cara Rosa.

The thing about the period in which you're living and the influence it has in the way you design is interesting if you consider that the ideal beauty is always in constant metamorphosis. Centuries ago, it even changed from country to country.

Not so much today. Every country used to have an ideal of beauty, although they suffered influences from abroad. Rabelais, the French writer, talking about the headdresses of the French ladies of his time, said that it was French only in the winter; in spring it was Spanish, and in summer it was Tuscan, whatever that means.

Then you have a nation dictating "the look" of a century. Example: The first half of the sixteenth century in Europe was decidedly German in its fashion,

L'INCORONAZIONE DI POPPEA
Costume design by José Varona
Directed by Günther Rennert
Paris Opera (1978)

while the second half was overwhelmingly Spanish. Spain was not only a leader of fashion at the time, but was also an arbiter of manners and court etiquette in the Western world. All those periods are great for operatic music!

How about Wagner?
What about him?

Have you designed any of his operas?
In three different circumstances I have turned him down. With no regrets.

Any particular reason?
Not comfortable enough. I chickened out. Mind you, I love his music, although I dislike the character. I used as an excuse the poor quality of my German. The director, August Everding, wouldn't buy my reasoning. He thought that I should design Wagner precisely *because* I didn't have a German mind. He was sick of the German approach of the postwar Bayreuth.

Was Wagner ahead of his time?
Only musically. Visually, he belonged in the nineteenth century. Some people who saw pictures of the first American Tristan, Albert Neimann, are still laugh-

ing! I am too. There is a funny story related to Wagner's world. The saga called *Nibelungenlied,* on which the Ring Cycle is based, was once performed as a play, with this German actress impersonating one of these mythological ladies wearing a crinoline. When the time came for the lady to die—she had not rehearsed the death scene—down goes the lady and up goes the crinoline, giving the delighted audience a chance to wallow in the Prussian indecencies of Krimhilde.

But there are tragic things also, like the case of Emma Livry, who was burned alive onstage. She had refused to have her costume fireproofed! Her crinoline caught fire from the footlights!

Are there any difficult operas to dress?
To me, one of the most difficult operas to dress is *Aïda.* In terms of the sets, you are in wonderful territory—the Egyptian world is exquisite, so there's no excuse if you don't come up with something right. But in terms of costumes, if you want to be true to historical facts, you should send your singers onstage practically naked. That is, if you are the "historically accurate" nut. There you have it: tons of liberated operatic flesh. Cheap, too. On the other hand, if you overdress them, they look ridiculous in the heat of the Egyptian summer. If you go in between, the balance of the design and the music is somewhat upset. I designed it once in Berlin. No more. The boos were so powerful that I wondered why I needed an airfare to return to New York! And what an Aïda I had—a young, relatively unknown singer named Jessye Norman. Let me tell you, it was a privilege to be there. It was worth all the boos in the world.

How about *Carmen*?
Carmen is another difficult opera, almost invariably converted into what the French call an *espagnolade*, which is something kind of Spanish, but tongue-in-cheek. So what an endless wardrobe of wrong Manila shawls, red ruffled dresses, modern toreador outfits, and polka-dotted nonsense this fascinating opera has been forced to wear! That proposal has nothing to do with the true Spanish

character of Bizet's music nor with the authenticity of Merimée's story.

A Goya-like manner is better, but not completely so, as Goya's popular types have more to do with Madrid than with Andalusia. The southern Spanish smuggler was, during the first half of the last century, a character of a certain refined, natural elegance, even in poverty. This world and its type are beautifully described in Washington Irving's prologue to *Tales of the Alhambra.* Spain is one of the least known, most misunderstood countries in Europe. It is mostly, and sadly, known through its caricature.

What do you think is the real goal of the costume designer?
To me, the real goal of the costume designer is to be able to design characters, rather than costumes. If you are very aware of what the character is, in any particular opera or play or whatever you are doing, the costume will come to your imagination very naturally. It is very difficult, for me at least, to think in terms of costumes alone. I have to see the character in order to design it, get to know its motivations. A frustrated director? You bet.

By the way, the clarity with which the costume designer sees the character helps him sell his ideas to the director. Designers who portray faceless characters in rigid positions often go through frustrating processes of trial and error with the director, to end up with a mistaken choice of the garment.

Then the posture and body language of the character should be rendered with the costume?
Oh, yes. If possible, absolutely. It enriches, it justifies the costume, don't you think? But it should be perfectly balanced, it shouldn't be too extreme, otherwise the sketch might look too contrived. It used to happen to some of my students, when rendering ballet designs. Sometimes they would depict the most extreme dancing positions, like a tremendous arabesque, distracting from the costume itself. A graceful attitude is sufficient, without designing the choreography also.

And how do you feel about ballet design?

ROMEO ET JULIETTE (GOUNOD)
Costume designs by José Varona
Directed by Cecilio Madanes
Teatro Colón, Buenos Aires (1981)

Well, all of what I've said about opera applies to ballet to a certain extent, in terms of style and research. When you are designing for the ballet stage you have to be very careful to make things much lighter than when you're designing an opera. You do not need the tremendous statement that you need sometimes in opera. Everything is more limited.

In terms of sets, you have to leave plenty of space to dance, unless the story or the ballet requires a specific type of set or prop or whatever. But usually ballet forces you to use much more imagination in a way, because what you can do is so limited.

If you're doing classical versions of *Swan Lake* or *Coppélia*, you have to follow the style of the period or the style of the music. It applies to what I said about opera, but in a lighter way. You don't have as many problems with the physique of the dancers. They are usually very good-looking people and you don't find surprises when you go to the costume shop and meet the prima donna for the first time. But, of course, in opera now all of that has changed. You have spectacular singers, superbly trained, with great physiques and glorious voices. Excellent musicians, too! These artists are extraordinary professionals.

If you are designing costumes for the Paris Opera, how does it differ in the shops and execution as opposed to New York?
There are some differences. But even here, you find contrasts between the shops. You are going to see differences of approach and differences of judgment, and they can all be very good. Or not. When you change countries, you'll see differences stemming from their roots. Whether you go to France, Germany, Australia, or Brazil, you are going to appreciate qualities and face limitations, and not necessarily in the same places, so you'd better adapt to their possibilities and be flexible, in order to get the best from them. If you are unbending, or too severe, you might miss a chance to learn some wonderful things yourself.

Does the Paris Opera have its own shops?
Yes. For sets and for costumes.

How long in advance would the Paris Opera want you to give them sketches to work on an opera?
Months and months in advance. It depends on the particular case. Sometimes some productions are planned in a more rushed way, due to a replacement or something.

How long is it from the time when you get the commission until opening night?
A year, two years, eight months, six weeks—it depends.

LOLITA, MY LOVE
Costume design by José Varona
Directed by Tito Capobianco
Shubert Theatre, Philadelphia (1971)

When you design a production for a foreign country, how long a time do you spend there?
It varies with the complexity of the assignment. Whatever is necessary to keep your personal control. Without it, you will get a result that may be very good, but it's not yours. If you are being hired by the theatre, it is your eye they hire. It is your control that they want.

Do you attend all fittings?
Yes, principals and others. Occasionally, when you have a group of women or a group of men that are all using the same design, I see one or two, that's all. But it is not a bad idea to be able to control all of them, as proportions change so much from body to body. But your sketch will

not become your costume until you bring it to life in the fitting room.

Would the Paris Opera still have a muslin fitting?
Definitely. If it is something special or difficult, they have to. But on some costumes, it's not necessary to do so.

How many fittings would you usually have for each principal?
Oh, it depends. Sometimes one fitting is enough. Sometimes you have four fittings and it's still not right.

Do the people in the shop have the patience to keep doing that?
They have to, because it's part of their pride. They are professionals with important positions in those shops. So it's part of their job to do a thing right and to please a designer. And if it's not correct, you have all the right in the world to say, "No, this is not what I want," or "This is not my design." They have to understand that it is not only a drawing, it is your name, it is your reputation as a professional that is going to be judged. If you make a mistake, it should be your own. But you cannot present something with somebody else's mistake or lack of judgment.

I have to be the one who decides about the visual aspects of the show. And if a prima donna or a tenor says, "I don't like this," I answer: "I'm very sorry. If it's a matter of taste, it is my taste that has been hired, not yours. You sing and deal with your own business. I don't make any comments on the way you sing, do I?" On the other hand, if it is something that is not working right or that is uncomfortable, I am the first one to say, "We have to change that." We have to serve the people who carry out the straining job of singing or dancing, just as the composer does. They have to be very comfortable and very secure with it, because what they do is already extremely difficult. Those artists have a lifetime dedicated to a discipline that requires total collaboration on the part of the designers and directors and even composers. I understand that very well. But if it is a matter of personal taste, I pay attention to my own judgment. That is my jurisdiction. It is my name there, not

COPPÉLIA
Costume designs by José Varona
Pennsylvania Ballet (1978)
Rio de Janeiro (1982)
Teatro Colón, Buenos Aires (1983)

theirs. You can accept some suggestions if they don't interfere with your palette or with the look that you are aiming at. Then, by all means, keep them happy.

And you find the director agrees with you?
Of course. The director has okayed the designs. You know that certain designs have to work out. But sometimes you have surprises. There is nothing absolutely sure. You can design a certain costume that looks right on paper, but you put it on a performer and suddenly it's all wrong. Then you have to change it. You have to ask yourself, "Is this the character I was trying to depict?" Frequently, performers want to look their best, whether the character is a good-looking character or not. And that's when you have to serve the author, not the singer. But you have to keep the performer happy and comfortable, when possible.

When you make sketches, what materials do you like to use?
For costume sketches I like gouache and tubes of watercolor of the first quality. And the brushes, especially, should be tops—sable, of course. When I do ren-

derings for sets, very often I use first an acrylic texture, gesso, over the pencil drawing. I then apply my paint over that white texture. If I don't like the color, I can erase it, but I don't lose the design because the texture of the gesso has already defined the drawing. But for costumes, I never do that.

How much time would you spend on an average costume sketch?
It depends on the importance of the sketch. A simple sketch can be done in an hour, in a half-hour, even in five minutes if it's a quick little rough with a little note of color. You can do that very quickly. But if it's a good-looking sketch, you can spend a whole day on it.

Or two days!
I don't favor that any more. I used to when I was younger. I "overlabored" my sketches. The need to say too many things, I guess.

What do you like least about working in the theatre?
One: Dress rehearsals. Everything looks wrong, usually. Two: Opinionated people who were not involved in the creative

part but feel the right to express their opinion, whether they are the wives, boyfriends, parents, sisters, or lovers of performers or directors. That bothers me. Three: It doesn't happen often, but it happens occasionally—working with incompetent professionals. Four: Arrogance in directors or performers or colleagues of any kind. I do not suffer well that kind of foolishness. Cruelty, disrespectful attitudes towards working people, egotism, self-centered manners—no matter how talented the artist, they lose stature in my esteem. Once I know artists, I cannot judge their talents away from their personal behavior in their profession. I am of the opinion that our world is going to the dogs, in terms of values, overpopulation, greed, the failure of the educational system, and so forth. One thing that can help the struggle is some basic manners, don't you think? Egotism is out of the question; we might as well go back to the Ptolemaic system!

What qualities do you admire the most in artists and human beings in general?
Intelligence.

FOREST OF THE AMAZON
Costume designs by José Varona, for Rudolf Nureyev and Margot Fonteyn
Choreographed by Frederick Ashton and Dalal Achcar
Rio de Janeiro (1975)

Over talent, over genius?
Yes. Intelligence is light. True intelligence implies understanding, kindness, and the means to reach the highest goals, at times surpassing the accomplishments of talent. Intelligence opens inner doors and helps us take the shortest road to self-respect. Wow! Did I say that?

What do you like the most about working in the theatre?
The most enjoyable part for me is to design, to think, to imagine, and to paint. To be there at my drawing table with my music, and just concentrating on what I have to do, that is the most satisfying part of my work. And when it goes into the theatre, it's exciting and can be very exhilarating. It gives me happiness.

What I also like immensely is collaborating with gifted people, such as musicians, dancers, singers, directors, and conductors. It is a true privilege. Absorbing their art, learning, laughing, eating and singing along, arguing and interchanging stories, traveling and reencountering old friends, making new ones, visiting new countries, and so on—there is not much money in it, but it is a great life. I feel lucky.

Do you have some favorite productions that you would put in a time capsule?
That's difficult. I have many that bring happy memories, wonderful artists with whom I collaborated, and also personal artistic satisfaction. Let me try to go back in time, to the Mesozoic Era, almost:

1953—My professional debut, at 22, with a flamenco spectacle for Carmen Amaya, in Buenos Aires. I got hooked.

1959—Still in Buenos Aires. My operatic debut with *Love for 3 Oranges* by Prokofiev was a great event in my life.

1967—My American debut at the City Opera: *Julius Caesar*, Beverly, Norman, Ming, et al. A wonderful and special year. Mary and I got married.

1969—My European debut, in Hamburg. *Julius Caesar* again, this time for Joan Sutherland.

1973—My Parisian debut with *Il Trovatore*. Great time with David Mitchell, who did the sets.

1974—Also at the Paris Opera Ballet, *The Sleeping Beauty*, for Alicia Alonso. Sets and costumes. *The Tales of Hoffmann* for the New Opera House in Sydney, Australia, with Joan Sutherland again. Great new experience; difficult stage, though. Fascinating country.

1975—*Forest of the Amazon* at the Municipal, Rio de Janeiro, with that great artist, Margot Fonteyn, and Frederick Ashton. He was an incredible man, spoke perfect Spanish. We had a ball. And Fonteyn—my God, she should have been the Queen of England!

1976—Geneva. My Balanchine *Coppélia*, not one of my best designs, but one of my best memories meeting the great Mr. B. and having dinner with him every night for a week, engulfed in the most fascinating conversation and drinking heavenly wine. Berlin. My production of *Cinderella*—not my debut—for the Panovs. Great experience learning about their Russian experience. Eating and crying a lot.

1977—*The Abduction from the Seraglio*. Paris Opera. My first design for the great German director Günther Rennert. An ogre! But he taught me a lot. Incredible cast, great conductor—Karl Böhm.

1978—My second production for Rennert—*The Coronation of Poppea*, also at the Paris Opera. Another sublime cast: Gwyneth Jones, Christa Ludwig, Nicolai Ghiaurov, Jon Vickers, and so on.

1979—Again, Berlin: *The Merry Widow*, Everding directing. Another superb cast: Gwyneth again, René Kollo, and Siegfried Jerusalem.

1981—I return like the prodigal son to Buenos Aires, after a professional absence of 20 years. Sets and costumes for the opera *Romeo and Juliet*, one of my best productions—superbly built, and so on.

1991—Chicago: My fifth *Nutcracker*.

Tell me about the designers that you admire.

They are many and varied! In Europe, among the old ones: Teo Otto, Lila de Nobili, Christian Bérard. Among the new ones: Jürgen Rose, Andrzej Majewski, Michael Stennett and Maria Björnson. I could drool over their sketches.

In America, I have one of the softest spots in my heart for Donald Oenslager, artist, collector, and gentleman. He was fun to be with. How about that terrific artist, great teacher, and colleague, Lester Polakov? And so many, many more: Boris Aronson, Jo Mielziner, Ming Cho Lee, Oliver Smith, Tony Walton, John Conklin, Santo Loquasto, David Mitchell, Robert D. Mitchell, Frank Thompson, Douglas W. Schmidt, Robin Wagner, Lewis Brown, Rouben Ter-Arutunian, Stanley Simmons, and Desmond Heeley. And the ladies: Patricia Zipprodt, Willa Kim, Theoni Aldredge, Jane Greenwood…

How about my students? These people cannot imagine how much they have taught me over the years. In small or big measure, I have learned from all of them, and I am grateful. I do love all artists, all those people who have faced patronizing attitudes from family and society, just like myself, who have worked hard to achieve an incomprehensible goal in today's practical world.

I believe that it is the artist who defines and honors the upper levels of our Western civilization, don't you think? Not the Napoleons, not the Buchanans, but the Rembrandts, the Shakespeares, the Duses and Bernsteins and Grahams and Astaires—great company! I'm proud of it.

DON QUIXOTE
Costume designs by José Varona
Choreographed by Dalal Achcar
Rio de Janeiro (1982)

LINDSAY W. DAVIS
Costume design for Rosa Bud in
The Mystery of Edwin Drood
Imperial Theatre, New York (1985)

JOHN CONKLIN
Costume design for Sasha von Scherler as a Bawd in Pericles
Delacorte Theatre, New York (1974)
(Collection of Leigh Rand)

GREGG BARNES
Costume designs for Auntie Verna in Twenty Fingers, Twenty Toes
WPA Theatre, New York (1989)

LEWIS BROWN
Costume design for the parlor maid in La Ronde
Guthrie Theatre, Minneapolis (1977)

PETER HARVEY
Costume design for Madame Sin-Sin in Dames at Sea
Bouwerie Lane Theatre, New York (1968)
(Photograph by Linda Alaniz)

DAVID MURIN
Costume design for Kiss Me, Kate
Berkshire Theatre Festival (1991)

EDUARDO SICANGCO
Costume design for Candide
Cincinnati Playhouse in the Park (1988)

A Conversation with
TONY WALTON

Tony Walton talked about theatre and his work in one of Manhattan's historic Upper West Side apartment complexes, where he lives with his wife, Gen, and maintains a studio. Walton was born in 1934 in Walton-on-Thames, Surrey, England, and was educated at Radley College, the City of Oxford School of Technology, Art and Commerce, and the Slade School of Fine Art in London. His first assignment in New York was *Conversation Piece*, in 1957, and during his long career he has created both sets and costumes for a wide variety of productions.

Walton has designed operas and ballets in England, Italy, and the United States, and has created settings and costumes for Britain's National Theatre and many principal West End theatres. Among his ballet designs are *Peter and the Wolf* for the American Ballet Theatre and seven productions for the San Francisco Ballet. His numerous production and costume design credits for film include *Mary Poppins, Murder on the Orient Express, The Wiz, Deathtrap, Star 80, Equus, Petulia, Heartburn, The Boyfriend, The Glass Menagerie, The Sea Gull, Death of a Salesman, Prince of the City,* and *All That Jazz.* In addition, Walton has designed for television. His honors include three Tony Awards, four Drama Desk Awards, an Emmy Award, and an Academy Award.

THE CUNNING LITTLE VIXEN
Moth and Grasshopper costume designs by Tony Walton
Directed by Colin Graham
Santa Fe Opera (1975)

You studied design in London at the Slade School. How did you become involved with designing costumes for the theatre?

If you were a theatre designer in the European tradition, you designed the whole show. It was the same in England. And there were very, very few instances of people who did only sets or only costumes at the time I started out. So it was just traditional. There was one exception for me early on, and it was *The Pleasure of His Company*, which I did for Binkie Beaumont of H. M. Tennant. He was the czar of the London Theatre, and he had a good relationship with Balmain. So for any show that had high-style, contemporary costumes, he would go to Balmain for the clothes. And for *The Pleasure of His Company* he did that. That was the first time and for 15 or more years, the only time that I didn't do the complete production. I found it very strange at the time. And a bit tricky trying to make a good professional marriage, although I sent swatches of every color I was using, scene by scene, over to the house of Balmain. He would not necessarily relate to them, depending on the palette of his current line of clothes

or his mood. So at the time it just seemed much easier to keep visual control over the entire palette and the whole visual style of the production by doing the sets and costumes yourself.

I did start out hoping to do sets, costumes, and lighting. And I did try lighting, too, very briefly, but the wear and tear of doing all three things was just too extreme. And, rightly or wrongly, I felt at the time that it would probably be easier to make a creative marriage with a lighting designer, and to keep doing the sets and costumes myself, than it would have been at that stage in my life to have made a creative marriage with a costume designer. That came much later as I hit the Broadway system, where it's so hard to just be everywhere all at once, and because of the speed at which everything has to happen.

Did you get work right away after you got out of school?

I was actually simultaneously an assistant designer while still at school. It was partly to pay my way for being at the Slade. I was assistant designer at Wimbledon Repertory Theatre. It was like year-round summer stock. I didn't do costumes there, though. They were mostly rentals.

The first production I did in New York was a revival of Noël Coward's *Conversation Piece*, Off-Broadway. And I had originally planned to do the costumes on that, but the thing suddenly moved too fast, and for a variety of reasons I ended up doing the sets and rather naïvely attempting to do the lighting. Although in that instance, Abe Feder came in to help on the lighting, and it was a glorious experience. He was a wonderful Runyon-esque character. He made the rafters ring.

But after that there was a long stretch when I always did costumes, along with the settings. In one instance I did the costumes only, because the set already existed. That was Anouilh's *The Rehearsal*, which Peter Coe directed for David Merrick. It had originally been done in England. I think it started out at the Bristol Rep prior to London. And Merrick realized that he could take advantage of the existing Bristol set. He found a way he could get that set over here inexpensively, and Peter Coe decided to have the set repainted white, which gives the costume designer a pretty wide palette, so on that production I did costumes only. But otherwise, up until *Pippin* in 1972, I always

---

Among Tony Walton's theatre design credits are the following:

BROADWAY SETTINGS

Guys and Dolls (1992)

Conversations with My Father (1992)

Death and the Maiden (1992)

The Will Rogers Follies (1991)

Grand Hotel (1989)

Lend Me a Tenor (1989)

Linda Ronstadt's Canciones de Mi Padre (1988)

Social Security (1986)

I'm Not Rappaport (1985)

Leader of the Pack (1985)

Hurlyburly (1984)

Whoopi Goldberg (1984)

The Real Thing (1981)

Sophisticated Ladies (1981)

Woman of the Year (1981)

A Day in Hollywood/A Night in the Ukraine (1980)

The Act (1977)

Streamers (1977)

Chicago (1975)

Pippin (1972)

LINCOLN CENTER THEATRE SETTINGS

Four Baboons Adoring the Sun (1992)

Six Degrees of Separation (1990)

Waiting for Godot (1988), Newhouse Theatre

Anything Goes (1987), and C

The Front Page (1986)

The House of Blue Leaves (1986)

BROADWAY SETTINGS AND COSTUMES

Jerome Robbins' Broadway: "Comedy Tonight" (1989)

Little Me (1982)

Bette Midler's Clams on the Half Shell Revue (1974)

The Good Doctor (1973)

The Apple Tree (1973)

Shelter (1973)

Uncle Vanya (1973)

Golden Boy (1964)

A Funny Thing Happened on the Way to the Forum (1962)

OFF-BROADWAY SETTINGS

Elliot Loves (1990)

Square One (1990)

Drinks Before Dinner (1978), and C

did both sets and costumes, whether it was theatre or film. Though in the case of *Mary Poppins*, of course, there were many other people involved on the sets as well. Then *Pippin* came along, and Bob Fosse was used to working with separate set and costume designers, and was also known by then to be an amazingly demanding taskmaster.

So at that point it seemed to be the wisest course to concentrate solely on sets. Bob Fosse and I had actually known each other for quite a while.

He had originally asked me to work on the film of *Cabaret*, but it was a clash with *The Boyfriend* film, so I wasn't able to do it. *Pippin* was right after that. And of course, Pat Zipprodt did the costumes for it, and again on Fosse's *Chicago*, and those were thoroughly enjoyable collaborations. The costumes on *Pippin* were by and large white, off-white, pale mushroom, with just the occasional little rush of color for royalty, which meant that the palette for the scenic end of the production was wide open. And in *Chicago* it was the reverse: Pat had a very full palette for the costumes, and I kept the stage pretty much black and chrome, with just occasional explosions of color from the translucent painted images that were behind the black Plexiglas. Also there was a great deal of neon, which initially appeared to be chrome, that could light up with very brilliant colors. Bob Fosse was interested in having harsh imagery for the show, a "non-pretty" imagery, though he had nothing against it being beautiful as long as it looked strong. He just didn't want it to be pretty-pretty.

You did sets and costumes for the film *Mary Poppins*. How did that come about?

Well, it came about because Walt Disney was trying to persuade Julie Andrews, to whom I was then married, to be in it. And though we had once worked together on her BBC television series, we had a general rule not to work together. So we originally thought Disney's invitation to us both, while delightful, was probably a bad idea. *A Funny Thing Happened on the Way to the Forum* had just opened, and he had seen my work for that the same week that he had seen Julie in *Camelot*.

And he said, "If you don't want to do it, I'm going to have to get an English designer anyway, because it's such an outrageously English subject, so you might as well make up your mind to do it." And for a while we thought, let's not, and then rather belatedly it dawned on us that since Julie was pregnant, our baby

A FUNNY THING HAPPENED
ON THE WAY TO THE FORUM
*Costume design by Tony Walton,
for David Burns as Senex
Choreography and musical staging by Jack Cole
Directed by George Abbott
Alvin Theatre, New York (1962)*

would be arriving only moments before Julie would be due to start on the film. So we thought it would be a dumb time to be apart. And we ended up deciding, oh, well, what the hell, let's do it together. I was so extremely ignorant of the processes of filmmaking that I hadn't really considered that my end of it would involve many months of work before Julie was even needed.

Also, I was still very much a theatre snob. Oddly enough, I was doing three productions set in ancient Rome in England while I was also doing the preproduction work on *Mary Poppins*. One was the English edition of *A Funny Thing Happened on the Way to the Forum*. The others were Benjamin Britten's *The Rape*

of Lucretia, for Colin Graham, and again, for Peter Coe, a production of *Caligula*.

You were doing sets and costumes for all of those?

Yes, and though they were all Roman, they were all totally different. So that was very interesting. It was also interesting to be plunging into the semi-fantastic early-twentieth-century *Mary Poppins* at the same time I was doing all these Roman variations.

While I was starting out on the design work for *Mary Poppins* in California, I would get up at 3:00 or 4:00 in the morning and do my costume sketches for these operas. *Forum* was steaming along, because I had already done the designs for that in New York, but for *The Rape of Lucretia* and *Caligula*, I'd go to the studio post office at about 6:30 to 7:00 in the morning and mail my just-completed costume sketches off to England and say, "Well, that's my work done for today. Now I can have a great time in this splendid candy factory." I regret that I had such a good time that I didn't pay more attention to all the processes that were available for study there. It was such an extraordinary place at that time. Disney, of course, was still very much alive and very much involved in every aspect of that film, as he had been with most of his films up to that time. After *Mary Poppins*, he was less so, because of his intense involvement in the birth of Disneyland and all the sophisticated technology of W. D. Enterprises, which even contributed to space technology. But before *Mary Poppins*, with the *Flubber* movies and *The Absent-Minded Professor* and so on, he would make little drawings of how the car could be made to seem to fly without giving away the trick of it, and things like that. They were fascinating doodles. He was deeply involved with the creative people there in every aspect of production. I was just enjoying all this instead of really taking advantage of the opportunity to study it. So I would knock off my sketches and just revel in the fact that no sooner had I done a sketch for a park gate or something than it would be whisked away and a model made of it and brought back almost instantly for approval.

MARY POPPINS, THE FILM
Costume design and costume by Tony Walton,
for Jane Darwell as the Bird Lady
Directed by Robert Stephenson (1964)

Did you do sketches for every costume in *Mary Poppins*?
Yes, even though there were some for the street extras that came from Western's rental department. But I did sketches for all of those as well, so that we would know what to look for from their stock.

They didn't build every costume?
Pretty much everything was built, but there were a few, as I say, just for the background and street people that we adapted from the stock at Western Costume, but always working from a color sketch, because there was a very controlled palette in the movie. And this was something that Disney was also interested in at that time. In some of his films—certainly not the early animated ones, but in some of his features—there had been a fairly loose palette. But *Mary Poppins* had been so exquisitely storyboarded that everything was very controlled and

the palette was very specific and you just couldn't go and get any old rental item and hope it would fit in. You had to establish the color exactly first.

It was all rather high color, because of the nature of the fantasy somewhat. And it needed to look fairly buoyant. But obviously you couldn't just throw in colors randomly. I very much regret that at one point I had to go back briefly for one of the productions I was doing in England and was missing when the "fly a kite" sequence was shot. It suddenly looks a bit random there. The kites are rather drastically colored. But by and large, given how brazen the color palette was throughout, it was all reasonably well-controlled. It's very hard to maintain that in films.

There are so many people with so much input and so many things that happen on the spur of the moment, and people are trying to be helpful and offer

up things. The on-the-set prop man is seeing the way the scene is going and would suddenly like to offer up a couple of ideas and bring in a couple of unplanned hand props that might end up right in the foreground, and they might be completely the wrong color. These improvised additions suddenly become the most prominent thing and may be completely at odds with everything that everybody has been carefully controlling up until that point.

Does it happen with costumes too?
Yes. Sometimes an actor might bring in something of his own and might think a scarf or something would be helpful in a certain scene, and it might be completely off.

It doesn't usually work like that, does it?
No. though it occasionally happens that a costume may not work out. In films,

THE TRAVAILS OF SANCHO PANZA
Costume designs by Tony Walton, for (left to right) Don Quixote, the Inn Girl, and Sancho
Directed by Joan Plowright and Donald McKechnie
National Theatre, London (1969)

generally speaking, the costume may not even be seen by the director until it appears on the actor or actress on the set.

How does that happen? Do you have fittings in films, like you do for a theatre production?

You do, but it's spread over a long time span. For the theatre, you need everything for the dress rehearsal or, if you're lucky, the dress parade; with films, it's nothing like that at all. Much of it trickles in as needed and as the first day of shooting may be for a scene that's three-quarters of the way through the story. You can't work out a plot in the same way as you do for the stage. You work it out as far as possible according to the shooting schedule, which invariably changes, of course, so that all the things needed during the early part of shooting are the things you work on first. If something isn't going to be needed for two or three months, you don't need to work much on it until you're halfway into the movie.

When you designed the costumes for the film *Murder on the Orient Express*, you met with the director. How did you start and what did he say?

It started out with Sidney Lumet saying,

"This is all just delicious dessert. The only reason to do this movie is to remind people how delightful a certain kind of movie used to be." And he said, "I'm not interested in its even being believable. I'd just like to have people be reminded of movies they used to love." He said, "I don't even want you to break down the costumes and make them look as realistic as clothes normally do in movies. They can look like costumes in movies." I was very nervous at this whole approach, because one gets used to making things look at least somewhat believable in movies, unless it's a musical or a flat-out fantasy. One needs to do a fair amount of breaking down—hanging costumes up soaking wet, with rocks in the pockets and so on, and working in a little imperceptible wear and tear here and there, just things to make it all look lived-in. A brand-new costume always looks like a brand-new costume. So it was a little unnerving to not do any of the usual aging or misshaping or whatever.

I started it in the way one would normally do for a stage show, just sketches and swatching for everything.

What about swatching? Did you do that or did you have an assistant?

Yes, I had an assistant. She was actually the nanny to our daughters, but she was very helpful. She and I were going to all the flea markets in London, shopping for '30s scarfs, rings, buttons and bows, moustache tweezers, and so on.

Did you design more than one costume for a scene? Did you have that luxury?

No, I don't think so. You mean alternates?

Well, in case something didn't work. Or we want to try his costume with her costume. Or will this costume look better with him?

No, because that's part of the design process, always, from the word go, to try and place them all together in your head or on paper or wherever you can.

But there were a couple of awkward moments on that film. One was when the nightgown for Jacqueline Bisset didn't work out as we had hoped. It wasn't as flattering as it should have been. It was a particularly hard time in London then. For some reason, fabric of many sorts was very hard to come by, and there were tremendous shortages, and the Japanese had been consuming all the

SEAGULL

Arkadina IV

SEAGULL

THE SEA GULL, THE FILM
*Costume designs by Tony Walton, for Simone
Signoret as Arkadina (left) and Vanessa
Redgrave as Nina (above)
Directed by Sidney Lumet (1968)*

wool, and so on. We were very dependent on French fabrics and silks, and sometimes, despite something being on order for weeks or months, it just wouldn't turn up. In one instance, we had been banking on a very beautiful embossed silk from Paris, which didn't arrive. We sent hysterical telegrams and made impassioned phone calls and it was always promised for the next day, and yet still didn't arrive. It was for a gown for Jacqueline Bisset. We had made a pretty exact version of the dress in muslin while waiting for the silk. We didn't for a minute think that the real material wouldn't eventually turn up, and yet, surprise-surprise, it didn't!

So on the morning of the shooting, which had suddenly been rescheduled earlier, we realized that we were stuck with nothing. There we were with just the muslin version, which was in a kind of ice-blue. It was nicely cut and draped, but it was far from the sophisticated silk version we'd intended. One of the seamstresses who had been working on it saw me in complete despair and said, "I do potato cuts—maybe I could duplicate the motif from the swatch, and stamp the little Deco design all over the muslin." So that's what we did, and that's what Jacqui wears in the finished film. And it just about gets by.

In a similar instance, there was a beautiful French striped fabric for a jacket that Lauren Bacall was to wear. This fabric also never turned up, so we had to create the striping by bugle beading in variegated coloring on black silk charmeuse. That one ended up looking more exciting than the original material would have.

The Wiz—how did that come about?
Well, it was a rather surprise success on Broadway, and Motown had acquired the rights to it and had approached Sidney Lumet. We had already worked together on four or five films by then, maybe more, and he called up about it. I remember we had just done the film of *Equus*, and I had ended up with a health problem and was feeling pretty wiped out, and was actually in California going through some medical stuff. And he called up and said he was going to do *The Wiz* on film, and that Motown

owned it, and that Diana Ross was going to be playing Dorothy.

And I had the extremely bad taste to say, "Sidney, I think this comes very, very low on your list of terrific ideas." And he said, "No, wait until I tell you about it. I want to do this Valentine to New York, and I see my children being told to believe in themselves, in song, by their grandmother." Well, his children's grandmother just happens to be Lena Horne, and suddenly that was a very touching image! He also said, "Don't think about it until you come back and then I'll get you excited about it." And of course he did. We kept having this fear though that it would be hard to get to the fantasy through the eyes of an adult, an adult Dorothy. But Diana Ross is personally so appealing that all those concerns somehow faded.

So we plunged into it. Originally I was only going to do the production design, as it was to be so substantial and all happening so fast. But some problem came up between Sidney and the costume designer, and one day he just said, "Would you do it?" It was just a daunting project by then anyway, given the very tight timetable that we had. I said, "I don't think I can." But he was very pressing. I had done the costumes on all the films we had done together up to that point. So he said, "Just try and figure out a way of doing it." So I thought about it, and I said, "Well, the scenes with the most hair-raising number of costumes are the Emerald City scenes, and to some extent the Poppy Field scene." By that time, Joel Schumacher, who is now a very successful film director, was writing the screenplay, and he had come from the fashion world. I said, "Joel, would you be interested in getting back into your old line of work?" So he agreed to do the costumes for the Poppy girls, the sort of druggie scene on Eighth Avenue by the porno movie theatres.

I asked Sidney if he would mind if we approached all the high fashion designers in New York to see if they would be interested in doing the Emerald City sequence if we provided them with the fabric. And that's what happened. We went to Oscar de la Renta and Norma

Kamali and all the other stars of New York fashion, and in most instances used the outrageous things from their current line, but in our colors and our inexpensive fabric. In the case of Norma Kamali, she actually designed a whole range of brilliant new things for the Emerald City sequence.

I did all the fantasy characters, the principals, the crows and the Munchkins, and the graffiti kids who were found in Graffiti City, where Dorothy originally arrived. For those costumes, I had the most wonderful associate designer, Dona Granata. I did both the Good Witch and the Wicked Witch and 20 or so Graffiti City kids, then Dona did a very creative follow-through on all the big numbers of those, because every single Graffiti City kid's costume was quite different. Each was based on a different piece of graffiti. The Munchkins were the creatures who were the Wicked Witch's little slavies in the sweat shop, who, as they were released from the spell of the Wicked Witch, after she gets melted, gradually unpeeled themselves from their husks and became these beautiful freed creatures in "A Brand New Day." In the Emerald City sequence, in addition to the fashion clothes, there were guards and robots, the giant TV cameras and giant microphones, and so on. These were all great fun to do.

Did you draw on your imagination more than you did on costume research for that?
Yes, very much so. The principal characters were made by Barbara Matera or, in the case of the Tin Man, Barbara Matera with Eoin Sprott. The costumes were so unrelated to any research that Barbara said, "I'm only seeing the front of this in your sketch. What does this really look like?" And so I made three-dimensional figurines for all the principal characters and for the crows.

How large were the figurines?
About 15 inches high. And that seemed to be quite helpful. It was also very enjoyable and very good therapy.

You must have had a lot of help. You didn't attend all the fittings by yourself, did you?

THE WIZ, THE FILM
Costume designs by Tony Walton,
for (clockwise from left) Nipsey Russell as
the Tin Man, Richard Pryor as The Wiz,
and Diana Ross as Dorothy
Directed by Sidney Lumet (1978)

No. In fact, I had wonderful help from Anna Hill Johnstone, amongst others. She had done many films for Sidney before I came on board. Without her I would never have attempted it. She was really the bones of the whole thing. I was just wildly fantasizing and painting and drawing up a story. But she is the one who made it happen! Another extraordinary contributor to the costumes in *The Wiz* was Stan Winston who did the makeup for the Tin Man, the Scarecrow, the Wicked Witch, the Lion, the motorcycle gang of Flying Monkeys, and so on. The makeup became a crucial, integral part of the costume.

As a costume designer, naturally you are involved with hair, wigs, and makeup. Did you have more concern on a production like this?

Well, to the extent that everything was invented and was a fantasy creation. It involves you very much more than things that are rooted in research or the present day, in that you have to think about every square inch of every portion of the body, or every part of every prop, no matter what it is. You can't just put a contemporary thing into the scene. It all has to be filtered through the same fantasy alphabet. So it does require very strict visual attention on every aspect of it. In many theatre productions and many films, if you have a wonderful makeup team or hair stylist or whatever, you can learn to be absolutely trusting about

THE WIZ, THE FILM

Costume designs by Tony Walton, for (counterclockwise from top left) Michael Jackson as the Scarecrow, Ted Ross as the Lion, and Mabel King as Evillene the Wicked Witch Directed by Sidney Lumet (1978)

RIGHT: In this production still from the film the Scarecrow (Michael Jackson) and Tin Man (Nipsey Russell) find Dorothy "collapsed" after having passed through the Poppy Perfume Sign.

them, even though their work may ultimately come within your area of responsibility.

For example, I've worked often with Roy Helland, who always works with Meryl Streep; Linda Ronstadt, amongst others, always asks for him. He's been on most of the productions that I've done with Mike Nichols, and his work on *The Real Thing* was extremely helpful to Glenn Close and Christine Baranski. And if you have somebody like that, you keep your lip buttoned and enjoy their work. Although you may, of course, offer an occasional discreet opinion. But otherwise, it is very much a part of the costume designer's job to be responsible for every aspect of the overall appearance of every character.

You particularly watch for their shoes, because as they're frequently out of the shot, the actors quite often get into whatever is comfortable for them instead of the shoes that you may have chosen for a given scene. And then the way the scene is shot may abruptly change and suddenly this actor's inappropriate footwear may become visible.

And posture can change depending on what kind of shoes the actress is wearing.

Yes, and what kind of underwear, corsetry, or whatever. That, of course, is a big factor in theatre, but it can be in films too. And many actresses, luckily, are very aware of how their underpinnings affect their posture. That has always been a very intriguing part of research.

When you're designing both sets and costumes on a production, does one come before the other?

Generally speaking, if I'm doing both I like to approach both at the same time rather than establish one first. I know some costume designers wait for the stylistic attack of the set to be established and then move into an allied visual alphabet. But if you're doing both, you don't think of them as separate.

One of the great frustrations for me about the way theatre is visually recorded now is that, because of the union problems and the necessities of newspaper imagery and so on, it's very much the exception to have production photos that show the set and costumes scene by scene. Whereas in the Friedman-Abeles era, photographers did exactly that. In the picture collection of the Library of Performing Arts you can find out exactly what the original production of *Guys and Dolls* looked like, or what any show of that era that Friedman-Abeles or their associates covered looked like. For me, from *Pippin* on there's almost no way you can find that sort of photographic coverage. There are some exceptions, though: Boris Aronson wisely insisted on fuller coverage and fought for it, and quite often used to bring his own photographer in to get it covered properly.

I've moaned about this to poor Martha Swope, and once in a while—on *Lend Me a Tenor*, for example—she or her assistant actually took a shot of the bare set. I'm touched that she did it, though it has virtually no interest for me, because the set without the characters in it is nothing. I mean it's the whole point of theatre. The set isn't a separate artwork or a display object; it's only the complete and animated thing when the characters and costumes and so on are part of the overall picture, which is why it is so nice if you can control both. I don't mean to imply that I don't love the collaborations with costume designers that I've had lately—I do. But whether I'm designing the costumes or somebody else is, I do try to think of everything simultaneously and not as in any way separate. Whatever the final composition or illusion will be is the collision of all of the design elements, especially including lighting. It's all equally crucial.

Of course, the thing that separates theatre from the movies is that as a stage designer you are, in a way, selecting the frame that the audience is looking at, and you are creating the visual funnel through which the audience will receive the experience of the play, musical, opera, or whatever it is. Whereas in film, you hand over an environment in which many things are hopefully possible for the director and cinematographer to choose and select the framed image from. For that reason, you have, as a designer, a very great deal less control over the way the film looks. Though if you are lucky and have a visually oriented director, and have a good relationship with him, you can get somewhat "closer" to the experience you have in theatre, but you can never get anything really like it.

For costume designers, the starting point is quite similar for theatre and film, though everything in film is obviously inspected much more minutely. In theatre, so much of your initial design impulse, I think, is to create a sort of silhouette of the character. You recognize exactly what kind of person this is by the full image of the overall silhouette. Whereas in film, that's something you can't bank on seeing very much of—you may see mostly from the waist up, or even closer. So it has more to do with the face and upper torso of the character than with the silhouette.

Usually they establish a long shot, don't they?

Yes, but certainly not always. And much less so nowadays, as the way that people see things through television affects the way that people shoot movies.

The same way they don't get set pictures of the whole thing when they're taking photographs...

Yes. Because of all this, you may pay much more microscopic attention to the details from the waist up on a movie costume, because that's going to be seen very, very magnified.

Something I like to do, if I can, is to include details that might help the actor prepare, because of the way actors have to work in the movies, which is usually with much less rehearsal than in theatre, and often none. Anything you can do for them, to help them toward being in character, can be quite constructive. For example, on *Murder on the Orient Express,* there are a lot of things that have no visual importance for the audience, but that were, I hope, helpful for the actors. For example, Albert Finney, who played Poirot, greatly enjoyed the fact that we made a pinkie ring for him from a bullet, a shell casing, which was something that people used to do after World War I. In our way of thinking, this was the bullet that had caused the leg wound that made Poirot limp. It was something he could play with, and it would even be a little reminder to limp. And we had monogrammed cufflinks, as a reminder of his fastidiousness. But I doubt that they were noticed by anybody in the audience.

Comment on designing the costumes and sets for *Anything Goes* at Lincoln Center.

With the exception of the tiny scene in the bar, that is the prologue for the piece, everything else happens on the boat. So, basically, you are talking about cruisewear, and it's 1930s cruisewear. It's very inviting and very romantic. It's a period that I love. I was very much drawn to doing just a kind of blue-and-white wash throughout the whole production. Then you think, well, what's going to define each character? And you start to make variations and changes within that. But that overriding blue-and-white imagery—the smokestack, of course, was going to be red, white and blue—was the first impulse. I'd come over on the *Queen Mary* when I first came to live in New York, and I had extraordinarily romantic memories of it. I knew it was now out in Long Beach, California, so I went to visit it again and spent some time there and photographed a lot of things. In addition to a lot of other visual research, many of the visual impulses for the set came from that visit. But, as any Deco structure is apt to be very geometrical and symmetrical, and not freely flowing, my simultaneous impulse was that, whenever possible, a good vibration could be created by getting as many of the costumes as possible to be free-form and flowing to counter the strict lines of the set. So I tried to do the two things simultaneously, so as to keep this kind of tightrope act going, to get a little energy flying back and forth between the nature of the costumes and the more rigid nature of the set. Most of the set was going to be very sculptural, so again I thought it would be nice if the costumes tried to recall a more illustrational quality. I love all the high-fashion advertisements from that era. They have a really graceful quality. The French illus-

trators drew those clothes so beautifully. They were a big turn-on for me.

If there's a star or an actor of importance in the piece, you know that you need to make that performer feel good. In this case, we had Patti LuPone as Reno Sweeney, and I knew she was a powerful personality and might have strong feelings of her own, so I met her very early on. To my surprise, she said that she didn't really want to have any input at all. She just loved costumes and she loved using them. She said not to be afraid of anything, and she didn't have

any particular ideas that she wanted to impart. So that was generous and very freeing.

Did you keep the clothes for the tour of *Anything Goes* pretty much the same?

Yes. On the national tour they were the same. Just slight changes for Leslie Uggams, who was playing Reno Sweeney, things that would better suit her particular build and style. And then in the bus-and-truck version, Reno was played by Mitzi Gaynor, who for many years has had all her costumes made by

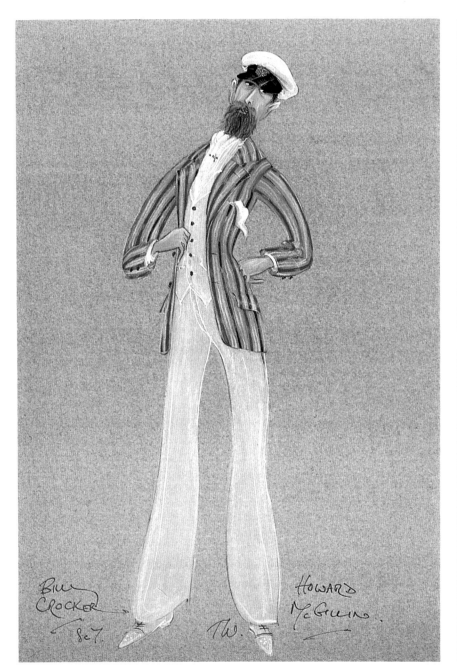

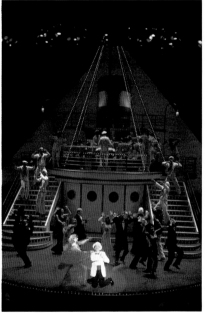

Bob Mackie. So in that case he came in and did all her clothes.

You designed the scenery and Willa Kim designed the costumes for *The Will Rogers Follies*. How did that production go?

We really didn't get a go-ahead until around Christmas, and the scenic part of the show had to be in the theatre within about six weeks, so there was no chance of going through the normal process of doing all the designs and making models and drafting them, and then going for bids and the whole procedure, which can

normally take anywhere from three to six months or more on a big musical.

This was built by Showtech?

Yes. And when you're working this fast, you often don't have the opportunity to double-check everything properly during the shop process. There were many bloodcurdling instances on *Will* when things had to be loaded out of the shop, although, due to the fact that I was still designing around the clock, I hadn't had a chance to approve the finished version. It wasn't until they were in the theatre and sometimes into the second week of

ANYTHING GOES
Costume designs by Tony Walton, for Patti LuPone as Reno Sweeney (opposite page), Howard McGillin as Billy Crocker in disguise (above left), and Rex Everhart as Elisha Whitney (top right)

BOTTOM RIGHT: A view of the settings
Settings and costumes by Tony Walton
Lighting by Paul Gallo
Choreographed by Michael Smuin
Directed by Jerry Zaks
Beaumont Theatre, New York (1987)

tech that a drop might finally appear from the flies, so that I could really see whether it was correctly finished or not. But that was the premise from the word go. Everybody was very clear about what a lunatic schedule we were working under, so it was agreed that there would be some fairly substantial paint calls to pull everything into shape, once we were up and running in previews.

When you were working on *The Will Rogers Follies*, did the scenery come first, the costumes first, or did they both come together?

Together. Well, we'd been dimly meeting about the show on and off for three years or so. But it was a very different animal in those days. What happened was that Tommy Tune left the production at one point, because it just looked as if it was never going to happen, and he needed to earn some money. So he signed on to star in the *Bye Bye Birdie* tour with Ann Reinking. He wrote a letter to the *Will* producers saying he had to depart from the project. That threw everybody into a great swivet because they realized he was the one director/choreographer ideally suited to this particular kind of show.

So the producers and writers gathered together with tremendous speed and energy, and got Japanese money involved, and so on. And they came back to Tommy and said, "If we could get it on before you go into rehearsals for *Bye Bye Birdie*, could you still somehow manage to do it?" He called me up and said, "What do you think?" And I said, "It's completely impossible. It's much too fast. I would collapse in a heap and die." I was still in the process of designing Mike Nichols's film *Regarding Henry* out in California. Tommy said, "Well, I understand, so I don't think I'll do it either." Then the creative team all came down on me like a ton of bricks. So we tried to figure out a way to do it at breakneck speed and that's why we were able to establish an immediate relationship with Showtech, the scenic shop. It was a very unusual arrangement, because normally management doesn't like to make a marriage with a shop without going to bids with a variety of shops and getting some fairly locked-off prices. But luckily, in

this situation, everybody knew each other well and an atmosphere of trust was established, so it went very well.

So it all came together very fast.

Yes. Tommy actually started a kind of showcase version of rehearsals and we started designing at the same time. When we had all had our initial meetings on the show, it was conceived as a very sophisticated Ziegfeld production. But you know, as sometimes happens when you take leave of something, or when you get a little distance from it, a revealing flash happens. Well, the minute Tommy had said goodbye to it, he had had one of those flashes. He said, "Oh, if I had done it, what I could have done is Will's own Cowboy and Indian version instead of the more sophisticated 'Ziegfeld version,'" because that was what tied his own background to Will's. Tommy has that Texan and Indian mix. Will's was Oklahoman and Indian, but that Western/Indian mix was what they had in common, plus the obvious show-biz flair.

So the motivating image that he started again from was this Cowboy and Indian Follies, and that was wonderfully helpful for Willa Kim and myself. Once we decided to make a stab at it, he and Willa, Jules Fisher, and Tommy's choreographic associate, Jeff Calhoun, flew out to California to join me, and we all met at Tommy's early Hollywood hotel and just kind of schmoozed the show—just tried to shake it up and reinvent it. Tommy was extraordinary. He had just been on a cruise on which he was performing his club act, and there had apparently been some sort of watercolor class being given on the cruise, and he'd taken this class. So he was now able to do wonderful, very simple line sketches, very clear and very imaginative, kind of storyboard sketches.

He kept feeding those to us all throughout this early process. There was a moment, for example, when he went to a big, old St. Louis Theatre to do his act and, as was his habit, went out front to see what it felt like to be in the auditorium of that house. He phoned from the mezzanine and said, "There's an arrangement of central steps between the seats

here that I think would work for us. I've just been pacing them and I can imagine staging the show on stairs of these dimensions." And so he faxed through to me his little drawing showing the dimensions of the steps and how they alternated from a short one to a long one and so on. And that's where the *Will Rogers* staircase originated.

For the scale of the steps and risers?

He liked this idea of having a short, regular step and then a long step twice as deep that would be easier to perform or tap dance on. From the orchestra you can't tell that there's any difference from step to step—it just looks like a regular staircase. But from upstairs, if you're observant, you can see every alternate step is an actual playing area.

So Willa and I plunged in. She has this uncanny knack of really being able to plug into what everybody's doing. We've worked together a lot, and she doesn't often give the illusion that she's absolutely clear about what's going on. But somehow, empathetically, she wanders around the studio and picks up bits and pieces, and later you find she's used these things as starting points for her glorious designs. For example, we have a "ponyskin" split traveler curtain—it's a silly western desertscape, and the clouds are kind of ponyskin blotches, and Willa's costumes for the opening number echo this and anticipate the ponyskin traveler in a charming way. It's a wonderful tie-in. She's a most extraordinary collaborator. And as I say, in some bizarre and empathetic way, she just gets it! And on *Grand Hotel*, this was true with Santo [Loquasto], too.

How did you approach that? You and Santo Loquasto both do costumes and sets.

Yes, and it was a wonderful collaboration. We've known each other forever, and I love him dearly. But it was the first time we'd ever had a chance to work together. Santo used to come by and I would just start to say, "I think the seats on the chairs are going to be…" And he'd say, "Got it." He would always be just a step ahead. He'd know exactly what the impulse was. And he'd plug right into it.

And of course in lighting design, Jules Fisher is another example of that. He's somebody who's so eager to work within the overall visual alphabet that the designers create for the show, and then of course he heightens and heightens it. It's not as if he's coming in just to do his thing. *Grand Hotel* was almost a shock in that way. It was such a comfortable and exhilarating collaboration. Willa does very occasionally design sets, particularly in ballet, And maybe there's something helpful in that. Some schools do teach their costume design students something about set design. It's certainly a valuable thing to be fully aware of the entire design process.

When you did *Lend Me a Tenor*, you did the scenery and William Ivey Long designed the costumes.

Yes. That was a lovely collaboration, too. I think William teaches design at Playwrights Horizons, so there again, he's a designer with a fascination for the complete process. He's very plugged into the whole thing. *Lend Me a Tenor* was pretty brazen in some of its color approaches. There was this very powerful color mix from the carpet. Much of the set was white and chrome, but the carpet has this brilliant coloring. The surround of the set was bright red, but the carpet had not only red but bright yellow, bright blue, and bright purple. And it was quite a fascinating juggling routine to try and

make all this jibe. William gutsily went along with and took advantage of every one of those colors for the costumes and never made it seem too much of a clamor. And he did that even more courageously for *Guys and Dolls*.

Do you have a favorite production you would like to put in a time capsule?

I'm not sure what leaps to mind most powerfully, but a special favorite was the Mike Nichols production of *Uncle Vanya*, with George C. Scott, Julie Christie, Lillian Gish, Nicol Williamson, Barnard Hughes, Cathleen Nesbitt, Elizabeth Wilson, and all. It was such a treat to work with them and to work with Nichols on this particular play. He doesn't allow himself to work with the classics as much as he should. It's clear to everybody that he can be our best director. And that was one of those rare instances where he went head to head with a masterpiece, and it was just a beautiful production. Given this cast, we thought it would be wonderful if the jewels of the production were the faces of this extraordinary group of actors. So we very consciously kept a very restrained palette for the set and costumes.

What do you mean when you say "restrained"?

Avoiding any kind of flamboyancy of color or detail, and in a way trying to make all the details disappear and meld into each other. So it would seem to be

almost like a sepia photograph, perhaps. Jules Fisher lit this production at Circle in the Square Theatre. In the grid he had little follow spots with operators lying on their bellies and following these extraordinary faces around, and nobody ever knew. The faces of these magic people would just keep glowing all the time. And I was really thrilled with how we got them to look and how all the physical production came together. But because we were working with a very long-thrust theatre in three-quarter round, once the audience got in there with their red gum boots and Bloomingdale's bags, there was suddenly this riot of color surrounding our restrained gem. So I wanted to spray the audience down.

Of course, there are much more flamboyant productions that also stick in the mind, because they were such fun to do. *Guys and Dolls*, of course, but the very first one that I really had a chance to go hog-wild on was the Sandy Wilson musical called *Valmouth*, based on the Ronald Firbank novel. It was a turn-of-the-century piece with an opportunity for an extraordinarily heightened approach. It called for a witty design attack, almost like high-style caricature, and I loved that. It was a wonderful launching pad for me and I reveled in it.

I do hope I get another opportunity to work on something as far-out as that before I get too old and silly to handle it effectively.

UNCLE VANYA
Costume designs by Tony Walton, for (left to right) Julie Christie as Helena, George C. Scott as Astrov, and Lillian Gish as Marina Directed by Mike Nichols Circle in the Square Theatre, New York (1973)

BORIS ARONSON
Costume designs for The Snow Maiden
Metropolitan Opera House, New York (1942)
(Photographs by Tony Holmes)

BEN EDWARDS
Costume design for a slave in Coriolanus
A project (1937)

BEN EDWARDS
Costume design for Tomazo in The Changeling
Repertory Theatre of Lincoln Center, New York (1966)

BORIS ARONSON
Costume designs for Cabin in the Sky
Martin Beck Theatre, New York (1940)
(Photographs by Tony Holmes)

LESTER POLAKOV
Costume design for Subtle in The Alchemist
Columbia University, New York (1939)

BEN EDWARDS
Costume design for Antonio in The Changeling
Repertory Theatre of Lincoln Center, New York (1966)

A Conversation with
MILES WHITE

I talked with Miles White at his charming home on New York's East Side. Born in 1914 in Oakland, California, in the San Francisco Bay Area, he was educated at the University of California. One of Broadway's most gifted and prolific designers, he is well-known for the beauty of his costumes in every phase of the entertainment world.

For the Broadway theatre, White first made his mark with the George Abbott musical *Best Foot Forward,* and his reputation was further enhanced with the Lunts' production of *The Pirate* and the first Rodgers and Hammerstein successes— *Oklahoma!* and *Carousel.* Since then he has made distinctive contributions to numerous memorable productions. Samuel Goldwyn brought White to California to work on two Danny Kaye films—*Up in Arms* and *The Kid from Brooklyn.* His other screen assignments were *There's No Business Like Show Business,* with Marilyn Monroe and Ethel Merman, Cecil B. De Mille's *The Greatest Show on Earth,* and Michael Todd's *Around the World in 80 Days.*

For the American Ballet Theatre, White designed the costumes for Agnes de Mille's *Fall River Legend,* Herbert Ross's

Tristan and Jerry Robbins's *Fancy Free.* He has also worked with the Martha Graham and Todd Bolender companies. For television, he did *Pinocchio,* for the Hallmark Hall of Fame and *The Fabulous Fifties,* starring Ethel Merman.

One of White's most demanding assignments was Ringling Bros., Barnum & Bailey Circus. For 10 years he designed all costumes, decor, and floats. For many seasons he also did Sonja Henie's *It Happened on Ice* and *Ice Capades.*

In the heyday of nightclubs, White designed revues for the Copacabana and Billy Rose's Diamond Horseshoe. His work was on view at World's Fairs in Tokyo, Seattle, and New York. As a high fashion couturier designer, he has created collections for Lord & Taylor and Marston's in San Diego. His original costume sketches are in the permanent collections at the Smithsonian Institute, the Museum of the City of New York, the Metropolitan Museum of Art, the Museum of Modern Art, Yale University, Williams College, and the Ringling Museum in Sarasota, Florida. He has been honored with two Tony Awards, four Donaldson Awards, three Academy Award nominations and a Tony nomination for *Tricks.*

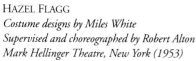

HAZEL FLAGG
Costume designs by Miles White
Supervised and choreographed by Robert Alton
Mark Hellinger Theatre, New York (1953)

How did you first become interested in designing for the theatre?

I wanted to be a couturier. I was brought up on *Vogue* and *Harper's Bazaar* and *Vanity Fair* and all that, and I wanted to be a designer in Hollywood, but I couldn't get a job there. I didn't finish college but I had just gotten out of the University of California at Berkeley. I was of age, so I could leave home. I think I was 21 at the time, and I thought perhaps London would be a good place to go.

Where did you get all these wonderful ideas at such an early age?

The crowd I ran around with at the university was always interested in Noël Coward and the theatre. We read a lot. And in the theatre, people would come by, like Mickey Rooney, who as a child was in *A Midsummer Night's Dream*, which was done at the University of California. That was a great tour at the time. It was produced by Max Reinhardt. And we had a lot of interesting theatre, and naturally movies, being in California.

Did you study sketching and painting in school?

Yes, I majored in art in school. I had great teachers at the University of California. And then I studied some dressmaking on the side. I was interested in clothes and fashion and styles.

What made you decide to come to New York?

I knew a Spanish dancer who was a sister of friends I went to school with. We ran into each other in Hollywood and she suggested that I go to New York, and I thought that was a good idea. So I arranged and came to New York. I didn't know anybody here. But I was peddling sketches to couturiers on Fifty-seventh Street and around.

And you had your own portfolio before you came?

No, I just thought I'd take it up. But Herman Patrick Tappé had an elegant couturier shop on Fifty-seventh Street. He bought a couple of the sketches, but he said I was much too theatrical for a couturier and he sent me to an agent he knew on Broadway. And the agent asked me to do sketches for a nightclub show

on speculation. So I did these sketches and the lady choreographer who saw them thought they were marvelous. It was exactly what she wanted.

Who was the choreographer?

It was Marjery Fielding. She had been married to Bob Alton, also a choreographer. He was one of the biggest choreographers in New York and Hollywood. He did *Pal Joey* and the top shows in films. And so that was my introduction on getting into show business.

How did your first Broadway show come about?

Before that time I became ill with pneumonia and returned to California to recuperate at home with my family. And I spent almost a year there. Then I returned to Hollywood and nothing was any better, so I came back to New York and looked up Marjery Fielding. She was about to do the choreography for a big Broadway musical and she suggested that I be the costume designer. So I designed a show called *Right This Way*, and that's how I got the first show. I think that was sheer good fortune to have something like that happen. I had never designed a complete show before. But I learned a great deal by just being thrown into the whole situation. I didn't know Broadway. As a matter of fact, I didn't know which was Times Square.

You were still in your early 20s?

Right. That show opened in 1938. It didn't last very long.

What happened after that? Did that lead to another show?

Well, not immediately. I went on to design for clubs. Marjery Fielding was superb at staging very lavish nightclub shows. Versailles was very grand then, and the productions included showgirls and dancers. The Paradise was another club on Broadway. That was a very well-known club at the time. The shows were quite elaborate. I was very fortunate. So I designed a number of clubs after that. There was one in Philadelphia and one in Florida. They were all very stylish in that period. Of course, they haven't done those things for years. We opened the Copacabana and I did the first show

Miles White's Broadway costume design credits include:

Jerome Robbins' Broadway: High Button Shoes (1989)

Toller Cranston's The Ice Show (1977)

Best Friend (1976)

Tricks (1973)

Candida (1970)

Milk and Honey (1961)

Show Girl (1961)

Bye Bye Birdie (1960)

The Unsinkable Molly Brown (1960)

Take Me Along (1959)

Oh Captain! (1958)

Eugenia (1957)

Cheri (1957)

Jamaica (1957)

Time Remembered (1957)

Ankles Aweigh (1955)

The Girl in Pink Tights (1954)

Hazel Flagg (1953)

Pal Joey (1952)

Three Wishes for Jamie (1952)

Two's Company (1952)

Bless You All (1950)

Gentlemen Prefer Blondes (1949)

High Button Shoes (1947)

Duchess of Malfi (1946)

Gypsy Lady (1946)

Carousel (1945)

The Day Before Spring (1945)

Allah Be Praised! (1944)

Bloomer Girl (1944)

Dream with Music (1944)

Early to Bed (1943)

Oklahoma! (1943)

Ziegfeld Follies (1943)

The Pirate (1942)

Best Foot Forward (1941)

Right This Way (1938)

THREE WISHES FOR JAMIE
Costume designs by Miles White
Choreographed by Ted Cappy
Directed by Abe Burrows
Mark Hellinger Theatre, New York (1952)

EUGENIA
Costume design by Miles White
Directed by Herbert Machiz
Ambassador Theatre, New York (1957)

there. That was very glamorous. We had stars built around the shows. There were about three or four production numbers and showgirls and dancers in each show.

Did you still take the nightclub show costumes to a costume house and have them made? And you knew the costume shops and where to go?
Yes. I learned from the first show. I used Brooks then.

When you designed club shows, did you have suggestions of your own that you mentioned to the director and choreographer?
I don't know whether I suggested so much as I drew. I did that alone. So my suggestions were my drawings. And we talked everything over. And then I would discuss color schemes.

How much time did you have to do a show?
We were in rehearsals for a few weeks. I guess we had a couple of months.

Did you go to the rehearsals to see the action, the dancing, and the choreography to see what was needed?
Often I couldn't get to the rehearsals, because I was usually in the workrooms supervising the making of the costumes by the time rehearsals started. However, I usually went by the rehearsals to check up on everything.

Comment on how *Oklahoma!* came about.
I designed *The Pirate* for the Lunts, and that was connected with the Theatre Guild. I was very pleased with the job and I got good notices, and everybody at the Theatre Guild was very impressed. But before that I had designed *Best Foot Forward*. This was the original. George Abbott had seen my work at the Copacabana because he was a big dancer and he was always taking his lady friends there.

Was this the same George Abbott who's now 100-and-something?
Yes. I'm a bit younger than he is! So I'd done that. I did *Best Foot Forward* in 1941 and *The Pirate* in 1942, and that led to the assignment of *Oklahoma!* in 1943. Before that I had started designing the Ringling Bros. Circus for Norman Bel Geddes.

Before you designed *Oklahoma!*?
Oh, yes. That's why I think I got *The Pirate*, because as you know it was about a sort of traveling circus in Santa Domingo. Nightclub work was sparse at times. So I got a job with Norman Bel Geddes to design an ice show, *It Happened on Ice*. It was one of the productions that Sonja Henie did. She wasn't in it—she produced it with her then-husband.

When you designed for the circus, how many costumes did you do? About 500?
Oh, there were thousands. In that situation I was part of Bel Geddes's staff. He wasn't interested in costumes as such.

He was mainly involved in doing sets, wasn't he?
Yes, but mostly industrial design. And for John Ringling North he was interested in designing a tent that had no poles in it. It was a superb job he was doing, but his interest wasn't in the production of the show, so it was laid at my drawing table in his office. And I designed all the costumes and floats for Ringling Bros. and he okayed them. That was the first year I did it. Then the second year I got that assignment again, and it was very good money to do it in that period. But I wasn't particularly thrilled working under the name Norman Bel Geddes.

You didn't get your own credit?
I did eventually. I think it was the second year. The first year we had Albertina Rasch choreographing the thing. She was well-known in the late 1920s and 1930s, that time period. But we didn't have very much of a show quality of any fantasy. So the second year they were trying to think who to get to stage it and I suggested John Murray Anderson, because he was closely associated with Marjery Fielding, and her ex-husband, Bob Alton. That's where my connection with John Murray Anderson comes about.

He was a grand director. He was quite imaginative and he changed the whole format of the circus around into a great, marvelous fantasy. Certain numbers in certain areas following the animal acts were very involved.

Did you go on location to learn what the trapeze artists needed to wear and what the people who stood on the

elephants needed? How did you learn all that?

By discussing it with them. I discussed things with the elephant trainers and other people. Then after that I did the acts under my own name for about eight or ten years while I was doing Broadway shows. I was extremely busy then. And I never ever found out how many sketches I did. I wouldn't let anyone tell me how much I had to do because I never would have done it.

But you made sketches for all of the circus people?

I was the first one. That was because of the power I had, by knowing Bel Geddes—I could change the idea of doing the circus, doing everybody's costume design and props, I could control the color scheme, because before that they wore their own costumes in their acts. So I changed the whole thing. I don't know whether it's still done like that. I doubt it, because I don't think people can afford that anymore.

Was there anything unusual costume-wise that you had to watch out for?

Practically everything. I couldn't possibly go through it all. For instance, if someone didn't like sequins, that sort of thing.

And you had to cope with substituting things sometimes?

Oh, yes. There were very complicated details. The elephant girls had to have very, very short pants but the bottoms had to be covered in leather, because sometimes the elephants weren't shaved and they had hairs like wire. So the girls' pants were backed with leather. That's just one bit of detail. There were a lot of funny, peculiar things like that.

What about doubles when things wore out?

If you have good wardrobe people, you don't really make doubles for the shows. It's rather expensive to make copies of things. My stuff is expensive enough.

Were there lots of feathers and plumes?

Yes, and I ended up by having most of the feathers made in Paris, France.

And you went there?

Yes. I had a lot of the sequin work done in

THE PIRATE
Costume designs by Miles White
Directed by Alfred Lunt and John C. Wilson
Martin Beck Theatre, New York (1942)

Paris, too, because I could get many more sequins on in the Paris price than here.

How did you find out about that in Paris?

Well, Johnny North wanted more sequins, so we were all having a difficult time financially with getting more sequins. They complained about the cost, so we found that going to Paris made a difference.

When you designed the costumes for *Oklahoma!*, was that an exciting time in your life?

Yes. Well, *The Pirate* had been just a marvelous experience with the Lunts. And it was John C. Wilson, who had come to see the circus rehearsals, who had discovered me in Florida when we were there. He'd arranged for me to meet the Lunts, and the Lunts had given me the job of designing the costumes for *The Pirate*, which was one of Lemuel Ayers's first jobs, too. So between us we'd done a rather excellent job for the Theatre Guild, and after that I suppose they were interested in both of us.

He also designed costumes, didn't he?

Eventually, yes. But not when I was there. So when the Theatre Guild offered us separately the job of doing *Oklahoma!*, it was then called *Away We Go!*. But when I designed *Oklahoma!* I thought of it rather as a challenge, because I don't really like westerns, and I thought of it as a western with cowboys and farm folk. I thought, "Oh, good God! That's been done to death. I don't know what I'll do to make it unusual." So Lem and I had a long chat about it.

He was doing the scenery for *Oklahoma!*?

Right. And at the time Grandma Moses was very popular and I thought that that as a marvelous "flat look" would be a good idea.

The "flat look"?

Yes—the American primitive. Then we discussed it and we both thought that rather than doing it in any other way, that this would be a good approach. I felt that approach just made it much more interesting. So I could do big flat pattern-on-patterns and things like that.

For the women in particular?

THERE'S NO BUSINESS LIKE SHOW BUSINESS
Costume designs by Miles White, for Ethel Merman
Choreographed by Robert Alton
Directed by Walter Lang
Twentieth Century-Fox (1954)

Yes, very well. It had body and I could make my own patterns on the skirts, shirts, and so on, because I couldn't get large patterns. There was just no selection of large patterns to be had. I'd have them appliquéd instead of trying to buy material and pattern. So it gave it a marvelous sort of stiff, primitive look, a very formal design.

The *Ziegfeld Follies*—how did that show come about?
I had worked with John Murray Anderson on the circus and he wanted me to design the *Ziegfeld Follies* for him, so I did that. That was the *Ziegfeld Follies of 1943*, with Milton Berle, the beautiful Ilona Massey, and Arthur Treacher. Jack Cole, the dancer, was in that, too. He choreographed his own act. Robert Alton choreographed the rest of the show.

Couldn't you be counted on for glamorous and lavish show girl costumes in your day?
If that's what they needed. There were no lavish showgirls in *Oklahoma!* I changed attitudes for every show. You've got to be versatile. That's what makes it very interesting. Actually, I also always change the kind of paper I draw on for each show.

What kind of medium do you like to work in?
I like to work in watercolor, because it's fast. I do hundreds of rough sketches, but I leave the final sketches to the very last. I have dress dummies that I drape on. And I drape muslin on them to see how everything will look. I have a feeling for that, and I don't know where it comes from.

In other words, you drape a form like you want it and try it and then you sketch that form?
Yes. Then I know what happens in the back of the costume as well as in the front. Today I'm always amused to see people's sweaters beautifully designed right up to the shoulder and then they're absolutely nothing in the back. But on the stage everybody turns around so much that the backs have to be as detailed as the fronts.

Was it a pleasant experience to design the costumes for *Gentlemen Prefer Blondes?*

Yes, the whole attitudes in that area being the American primitive painting. And of course Agnes de Mille's work was fascinating.

Was this the first time you'd worked with her?
Yes, I'd seen some of the productions she's done at the Metropolitan Opera House, like *Three Virgins and a Devil* and things like that, which were very witty and wonderful. So that, I suppose, was exciting. I don't know what is exciting when you start working on something. I think it's after you've done it, maybe it's exciting in retrospect.

When you did that show years later in a revival, did you keep it pretty much the same?
In a way, yes. Maybe not strictly. I don't really remember my attitude about redoing it.

You also did road companies of the original company, didn't you?
Yes. Then you had to copy them. It was during the war and I couldn't get fabric. So I did most of it in linen—I could always get linen. The dye colors were good.

And the linen worked well on the stage?

Oh, that was great fun to do. Anita Loos I met for the first time. She was charming and became one of my best friends. And of course I also met Carol Channing, this being the show that made her a star. She was terrific and I still see her now and then.

That was the nice thing, going from one set of people to another. In the theatre, when you do one show you get to know a lot of people and you travel with them for a while before the New York opening. So you end up with one or two good friends from that show. And then the next show is a whole new set of people to meet. You get some new friends there.

When you did the musical *Jamaica* with Lena Horne, did she have any suggestions about costumes?
There was another person who became a friend, Lena Horne. No, very few people ask what they want. To begin with, I think you are trusted. And I always got along well with the leading ladies, because I would first discuss what they particularly liked in the way of colors. Every woman, especially in the theatre, seems to have something they don't like about their bodies. It's either a shoulder or a hip or an ear. There's something everybody dislikes about themselves, and in my business I can ask those kind of questions quite freely and I get some very honest answers. That's why I am very careful when I design for them to take that into consideration. And by this time the star knows I'm interested in making her look marvelous, and so we're usually quite friendly by now because I'm the keeper of the secrets.

Did you do your own fittings and have muslin fittings then?
Oh, always. We used to have muslin fittings then—they're very important! We would have two or three fittings for each thing.

Would you stay in the costume shop all day?
Yes. That's also an important thing, to be there all day. It is exhausting, and people don't realize that. But it is unlike sets, which you can leave for a few days and go back to where they're making the sets.

TWO'S COMPANY
Bette Davis Revue
Costume designs by Miles White
Choreographed by Jerome Robbins
Supervised by John Murray Anderson
Alvin Theatre, New York (1952)

You have to be in the workrooms practically all the time. And with costumes being made, there are so many peculiar details and people's bodies are so different when they're in for fittings—you can't ignore them, especially if you're interested in detail, which I like. I like perfection.

Would you have assistants to help you?
I have different types of assistants. For *Bloomer Girl* and *Carousel*, I brought in an assistant, a friend of mine, who knows more about period costumes than practically anybody in the world could. He knew the cut of them, the fit of them. We were great friends when we were young in California. His name is Jack Birchenall, and actually he's my dear, old friend. He still lives in Alameda, California.

And he knows details of the period?
Of course he does. He has a feeling for

that sort of thing. He has a fantastic mind for detail and research. And particularly in a show like *Bloomer Girl*, it's very important to do the hoops of that period where they are very difficult to make because they balance mathematically. It's sort of like music. He's a great musician, too, incidentally, and he has a mathematical mind, which I don't have. But you have to have a certain number of hoops and they have to work right.

They have to be just right when you dance and they can't go up too high or they have to stay down. Do they have to be weighted?

No. If they are made correctly of simulated whalebone, very narrow and on tapes very close together, they move beautifully when you go through a narrow door without touching them. To teach a costume house how to make them is very difficult. But my assistant was great with those things. I brought him back for *Carousel* in 1945, when we were doing bustles. He was with me quite a while.

Tallulah Bankhead: You did her clothes for her appearance at the Café

JAMAICA
Costume designs by Miles White
Choreographed by Jack Cole
Directed by Robert Lewis
Imperial Theatre, New York (1957)

de Paris in London and her costumes for the play *Eugenia*. How did you get along with her?**

Oh, I was terrified of her at first. She was peculiar, flamboyant, talked a lot, and had enormous self-confidence. But I did nice sketches for her and I had time to do research and work on those. When she was wearing a costume, she wanted nothing to fit her too closely. She liked loose things, having come from the 1920s and 1930s. They didn't wear corseted, fitted things then, and I had to have these costumes corseted for *Eugenia*, because it was the 1870s.

In the end was it a pleasant experience working with her?

Yes, I got along famously with her and we became very good friends. But I used to have a setup when she came for fittings: I'd have the costume all put together on a dress dummy positioned on stage with the lights on it. And I'd have the jewels and hat placed by it and I'd have everything looking absolutely wonderful on it as though it were in an elegant shop window. And she'd come in and she'd see this lovely-looking thing put together and she'd say, "Is that me?" And I'd reply, "Yes, that is you." And we'd start the fitting and she'd complain about the corset being too tight. So we'd let it out a little bit. Then I'd have it taken back in when we'd take it back to the workrooms. But I basically did everything to please her.

You really were into psychology and all of that with the performers when you worked with them. You knew what to do to make them happy.

Well, I tried to. I felt that was very important to the show. *Eugenia* didn't run too long. Unfortunately, Tallulah was drinking a good deal at the time and she didn't make one matinée, which just threw the whole thing off, and it closed. But out-of-town, she was grand. But because of that, she then got a job at the Café de Paris in London and she asked me to design and make some of her costumes, some modern things.

When you say modern, you mean…

Modern clothes, not costumes. So that's how I got into that situation.

Did she sing and do talk acts in her club appearances?

Yes, similar to what she did on television, I suppose, but a bit more lengthy.

Did she want to know your opinions about how she wore her hair and makeup?

No. She had her own opinions. She knew what it was like to look like Tallulah. So I had no suggestions.

You were very fortunate to work with so many great performers. Bette Davis in *Two's Company*—what was she like?

Well, I'd met Bette Davis in Hollywood before I came east, and I'd done some caricatures of celebrities for a magazine and she was one of them. So I'd met her. And then I met her again in Florida when her third husband was a painter. He had an exhibition in Sarasota when I was down designing the circus. So we became friendly then. And when this job came up with her starring in this musical revue, I had an advantage of knowing her before. She wasn't difficult with me, but she gave everybody else a hard time. She was not suspicious of me. She was suspicious of Jerry Robbins, who did the choreography. Nora Kaye, the dancer, was in it too. As she was a great star, and because Jerry kept her after everybody else practically half the night rehearsing, Bette Davis thought that was taking terrible advantage of a star like Nora Kaye.

But he'd worked with her in ballet?

They were very good friends, but he was tough on her. He's a hard taskmaster on everybody. And I don't think Bette Davis and Jerry ever got along. That kept things boiling. And her secretaries were always quitting and having a difficult time. But I got along beautifully and enjoyed it. Then, of course, she had to stop the show. The show was not wildly received, but she had something that was similar to cancer of the bone marrow of her jaw and had to go to the hospital. So she had to close the show. She *was* the show of course.

Did you keep your costumes the same as in the original for *High Button Shoes* when they were in *Jerome Robbins' Broadway*?

ZIEGFELD FOLLIES
Costume designs by Miles White
Choreographed by Robert Alton
Directed by John Murray Anderson
Winter Garden Theatre, New York (1943)

Yes, they were copied religiously by Joe Aulisi, who was the supervising costume designer. And we found some old colored photographs and copied them perfectly. I suppose here and there a few things were changed, but not much.

Did you go to the fittings?
I was down at Barbara Matera's, where they were made. But I never went to rehearsals, because I avoided Jerry Robbins. At rehearsals he's not easy to work with during that period. Socially, he's sweet. But in work, as I said, he's a very hard master.

When you designed the costumes for *Fall River Legend*, wasn't that considered a very prominent piece in the dance world?
Yes. Well, Agnes de Mille had been prominent for many years, and even then. Yes, it was a prominent thing of Agnes's. It was a distinguished piece of work.

Would she tell you what she wanted for *Fall River Legend*, or, again, did you do sketches for her?
I did sketches. I'm much better doing

sketches than talking things over. Oliver Smith does the talking.

Did she ask for changes along the way?
No. She changes them after they're made. She always changes something.

How did you cope with that? Did you expect that?
Yes. I learned to expect it after *Oklahoma!*.

Were there a lot of changes in *Oklahoma!*?
No, not many, but I got the general drift. So I used to add in the sketches a little more than I'd planned. Basically, I could do a simple thing with the trimmings and such. I always knew something would have to come off and to be simplified. So I always did things a little flossier than I expected them to be.

Little Velcro things that could pull off?
No. She'd yank them off. Velcro wasn't invented then. Things like a jabot and some trimmings. She always pulled things off, so I always planned on little bits. If I had basically a good design, I was safe. You can't ruin it if something is

basically good. Jerry rips things off, too. He's the worst, though, he's terrible. He enjoys it and he likes to do it onstage. Agnes at least would do it when it was in the basement. It would offend the wardrobe people.

You also designed the costumes for *Billy Rose's Diamond Horseshoe*. How did that come about?
Through John Murray Anderson. He directed those productions. And Murray and I were working, naturally, on the circus. I was with him a lot.

You were with him when you did the circus?
Well, when he came in the second year and brought the new format. And he did that for a number of years, and I designed it with him for John Ringling North.

BLOOMER GIRL
Costume designs by Miles White
Choreographed by Agnes de Mille
Directed by E. Y. Harburg
Shubert Theatre, New York (1944)

CAROUSEL
Costume designs by Miles White
Choreographed by Agnes de Mille
Directed by Rouben Mamoulian
Majestic Theatre, New York (1945)

What was that experience like?
Oh, that was quite marvelous and wild. Big showgirls. Billy Rose's long-stemmed American beauties, they were called. And we had beautiful showgirl stars and, of course, magnificent costumes. They were very elaborate with feathers and jewels and silks and laces and all that jazz.

After doing all these different productions in New York, how did you get invited to Hollywood?
Musicals become so successful in New York that Hollywood sort of had a run on getting New York talent at that time. Well, like MGM had Lem Ayers and a number of the New York talents. And Sam Goldwyn wanted one, so he picked me. He sent for me in New York, and he offered me that job for the Danny Kaye musicals he was going to do. So we came to an agreement and I went out to do Danny Kaye's. I only did two of them. I did one one year and one the next year.

When you worked on movies, did you still make sketches?
Yes, and of course Sam Goldwyn okayed the sketches himself.

No matter who the director was?
Yes, because I don't remember seeing the director very much. Sam Goldwyn was a one-man show, you know.

Did he tell you what was needed?
No. I had to think it out. I got a script and we broke it down.

I would think you had a great deal of freedom.
I've always had a great deal of freedom, it seems to me. You break down a script and you discuss some things but you don't really discuss them until the sketches are presented. It's like Rouben Mamoulian in *Oklahoma!*—Rouben Mamoulian was very interested in the color that I'd used. And so we had big discussions with him and the color sketches and samples and everything. But he was one of the few that I remember that had that much interest in it.

Did they have a costume shop in Hollywood like they have in New York?
We had our own workroom. I brought out one of the head women from the workrooms here, from New York, and she ran the costume business shop in the studio. We opened it up. Chanel had been there before me, and the whole costume suite was done with a stage and dressing rooms. So it was all set up with the sewing machines and everything for costumes. The whole costume setup was there to work, to do all the work there rather than going out to a costume house. So, yes, it was great fun. Stewart Chaney, the set designer, came with me. We went together.

What kind of control did you have on hair and makeup when you did the Hollywood films?
It's the same general thing that any designer has. You had good people who were working there. The Sam Goldwyn studio had superb hairdressers and makeup people. So you simply discuss things. They do their own job.

Were there any surprises in doing films?
Oh, yes: the boredom of hanging around while they do and redo so many times. That was a surprise to me. I didn't know it was so dull.

You also did the film *There's No Business Like Show Business*, with Marilyn Monroe and Ethel Merman. How was that?
That was extraordinary. I got to know Ethel very well. She also became my closest pal.

You had not done a stage play with her?

No. I knew her through a friend. We had mutual friends. But it was she who had sent for me. They'd started the film and she didn't like what was being designed. How these things work, I'll never know, but she sent for me, so I designed the whole show, except for a couple of odds and ends that had already been started.

The whole show, meaning costumes for the whole cast, including principals and chorus?

Yes, production numbers. Yes, every detail. Bob Alton was the choreographer. See there, I have an old friend. And of course it was great fun working with him again. And everything just seemed to work out. Ethel Merman was just terrific and we had a good time together.

Did Merman have any input, or did she leave it all up to you?

She left it all up to me. I had no time. I made sketches, but the film had started and I had to do everything over from the very beginning. So I didn't have any time to sit around and think about it for too long.

What about Marilyn Monroe?

I didn't do Marilyn Monroe's things. That was part of the stipulation. She had her things made by the studio designer.

You did everybody else's, though. Wasn't that an unusual way of working?

Yes, but it was certainly easier for me. She was comfortable with her designer.

But you must have had some communication in order to be sure that the gowns were different.

I never met her, except later, when I designed the costume for her elephant in the circus escapade. Ethel was the control. She was the whole story, really, and so it didn't make much difference what anybody else wore. She was just the biggest star that had ever been in musicals. And she was the loudest too. So you didn't notice anybody else except Ethel.

You also did _The Greatest Show on Earth_. That must have been a natural

for you because you had so much experience designing for the circus. Was that helpful?

Yes. I was designing the Ringling Bros. Circus at the same time.

Then you knew it was going to be in that movie?

Yes. So I designed it with that in mind. What I designed had to go on for that whole year. And I was designing it anyway, so I simply copied things I was designing for the stars. I went out to see Cecil B. De Mille and I had many discussions with him. For anybody who was

TWO'S COMPANY
Bette Davis Revue
Costume designs by Miles White
Choreographed by Jerome Robbins
Supervised by John Murray Anderson
Alvin Theatre, New York (1952)

That was with Betty Hutton, James Stewart, Gloria Grahame, Charlton Heston, and Dorothy Lamour?
And the divine Dorothy Lamour. She was superb, and is still a good friend.

Did you elaborate a bit more on the star costumes, or keep them exactly the same as the actual circus?
No, they were exactly the same. That's when I made two of each, one for the Cecil B. De Mille stars and one for my stars, my showgirl stars in the circus, and the stars of the high trapeze and so on.

When they were shooting the film, were you on location in case something happened or had to be changed?
Yes. Some things were changed. In the story there was the train wreck and then the parade, and that's the end of the film. And for those costumes from the wreck, you had to make them for the parade. So for Dorothy Lamour I took a towel and did the usual wrap of a towel to make her headdress. Then on top of that I put some feathers, which were taken from the headdresses of the Liberty horses. These would have been left over in the wreck. I took some marvelous ostrich and pheasant feathers and put them in her headdress.

I had it all sewn together on her and we were sitting in her trailer, and it turned out in the course of things that the horses were going on first in the shot. So I had to take the headdress apart. And Dorothy pretended to be upset that the horse had star precedence. When the horses finished being shot in the film, I had to go get the headdress from the horses and have it sewn back on Dorothy Lamour's headdress. She is a very funny lady with a pithy sense of humor.

Were you able to do any plays or musicals at the time you were doing *The Greatest Show on Earth*? Did you do any other work?
I don't know what. I forgot what year it was, probably.

That was a full-time assignment, wasn't it?
Oh, no. Not particularly.

In other words, the circus was playing with those costumes?

TOP: THE DAY BEFORE SPRING
Costume designs by Miles White
Choreographed by Antony Tudor
Directed by John C. Wilson
National Theatre, New York (1945)

BOTTOM: BLESS YOU ALL
Costume designs by Miles White
Choreographed by Helen Tamiris
Directed by John C. Wilson
Mark Hellinger Theatre, New York (1950)

producing, he was interested in everything about costumes.

Was he like Sam Goldwyn in his own way?
He was more interested and more knowledgeable.

In terms of actual costume design? The splashiness, the color, the line, the cut and all that?
Yes, he was involved in all that. He had a very fine organization of his own at the Paramount Studio.

So when they were shooting *The Greatest Show on Earth*, you had designed the circus costumes?
I designed the whole circus and the props and the floats.

No, the circus hadn't started. I was just starting on it for the next year. I'd worked out the whole layout with Murray Anderson. We knew what production numbers we were doing, so I designed the whole thing. But then the motion picture deal came through in the middle of all this. They had to use the existing production numbers, they had no say. So Cecil B. De Mille couldn't exactly tell me what to do. He had to ask me. He couldn't say, "I want this in a different color." He could only say, "Could you make this a little something-or-other?" My color schemes and everything had already been laid out. I'd already started the work at the costume houses. He could ask me to change things. If I could, then I would.

Did you have a good budget for the movie of the circus?
Oh, yes. We had a marvelous budget.

Did they ever say, "You can't go over this, or you can't do anymore, because you've spent enough already"?
No, they didn't say that. I did spend money. But as you know, you have bids. Different costume houses bid on it.

It was usual on regular shows to get at least three bids for costumes, wasn't it?
Yes. But then, as I say, I'd often overdesign. Then I could take off things. I'd cut down certain sequins here and certain embroideries there.

Did you think of that always when you were designing?
Yes. I had to go through arguments. You had to do it. The general business managers would always say, "You have to cut a certain amount of money off. This bid is too high."

So after you showed the sketch, did you say, "We can take the bows off here."
No, not the bows. We'd cut down on the embroidery here and there.

And appliqués?
Some, yes.

Beading?
Yes, some. We'd cut down, also.

What about feathers?

Feathers? Never! But then, I could ease back, you see. In the workrooms I had more control, and I could get things back. It was all part of a strange game.

Wouldn't your colleagues in the shop say, "We know you want these and we'll stick them in at the same price"?
After the bids were done and had already been cut down and okayed, yes. In reality, they would slip things back for me. I had great people in the workrooms. They loved their work so much. They were very proud. And the milliners were particularly proud. They would all stick another feather in for me. Or they would paste a few more sequins on, if I wanted more glitter.

When you did *Time Remembered*,

THE UNSINKABLE MOLLY BROWN
Costume design by Miles White,
for Tammy Grimes
Choreographed by Peter Gennaro
Directed by Dore Schary
Winter Garden Theatre, New York (1960)

with Helen Hayes and Richard Burton and Susan Strasberg, was that a rewarding experience?
That was very nice. I'd known Helen before that, through Anita Loos. Helen Hayes has a big rose garden at her home up in Nyack. And she had beautiful roses. I went up and took a lot of materials—chiffons and furs and things. I threw them all on her porch and they all had the same colors as her roses.

BYE BYE BIRDIE
Costume designs by Miles White
Directed and choreographed by Gower Champion
Martin Beck Theatre, New York (1960)

Did you know that or was that planned?

Oh, I knew that. I'd been there prior and I'd seen her rose garden. So I did her in shades of her roses. And she did me a great favor: She had light chestnut hair then, and I wanted her hair pure white. Now, that's a hard thing to do. And in curls, like a sort of marvelous halo look, very fuzz, in pure white. And that's a very difficult dye job to do. So she had it stripped and had it done the way I asked her to. She has white hair now. But this was dyed, stripped white.

You could do it that way to get it done?

Oh, it's very difficult. Very few people can do it. Joan Diener used to have her hair done by someone and I used that person. But I thought Helen Hayes was great to do that instead of wearing a wig, because I think a wig always looks like a wig.

When you designed the costumes for Michael Todd's *Around the World in 80 Days*, did that take a long time? That must have been incredibly lengthy.

Yes, it was lengthy. I stayed in two places in California then. I moved out there for a while. Yes, that was quite a production.

Was Michael Todd as attentive to costume design detail as Sam Goldwyn or Cecil B. De Mille?

He was a different type. But he was interested in everything. He was an enchanting man, absolutely enchanting. He was one of a kind. Unusual, a great man, I thought.

What do you like least about working in the theatre?

The business end of it. The complications of trying to do the budgets, which get worse every year. It's hard to get perfection in the theatre if you're trying in

that area. But generally, it's very interesting. It certainly is much better than Seventh Avenue. I tried a bit of that.

You did a collection for Lord & Taylor. Tell me about that.

I did one for my good friend Sara Lee. She was an executive there at the time. And I did a collection sort of based on

The Unsinkable Molly Brown. She liked a lot of things I'd done for that and for Tammy Grimes. That was a big show. It was fun to do and Tammy was fascinating.

I had Jack Birchenall come back again to work for me on that show. It was very expensive, because he's so good on details, but I couldn't get him for every show. I mean, he wasn't expensive himself, but his work is done in such beautiful detail. He knows so many things, how to cut period things, and when you do that there's much more labor involved in the workrooms with the cutting, especially in this particular way, and doing the hems and the underskirts perfectly for that period. They're very elaborate. The underwear is more elaborate than some of the outerwear.

When you did *Bye Bye Birdie*, was that a new departure for you?
No, no, it was modern. It was contemporary. I design a lot of period pieces. I create contemporary things, that was what I first started out to do, because I don't find anything contemporary that's that interesting. But then yes, that was an unusual performance, and it was fun to work with Gower Champion, who had a lot of style. I'd never worked with him before.

What do you like most about working in the theatre?
I think it is always a new challenge. Don't you think everybody enjoys a new experience? It's a challenge to think out how we're going to have all the *Fall River Legend* redone. That's sort of fascinating. It's the working out of a whole new set of ideas, how many colors, what the materials are, what you can do that might astound the audience. And you never find out until you have an audience, until you've got it onstage with the lighting and the scenery and the music and have everything together. Then you find out if you've done it right. And if you have done it right, it's a thrill, and if you've done it wrong, it's terrible.

I think it's worse in the movies, because once something you've done is in the movie, if you don't like it, you can't change it. I can change things before they get to Broadway—at least I used to be able to. But I prefer designing for the theatre because of all of that.

HAZEL FLAGG
Costume designs by Miles White
Supervised and choreographed by Robert Alton
Mark Hellinger Theatre, New York (1953)

LUCINDA BALLARD
Costume design for Ethel Merman in Annie Get Your Gun
Imperial Theatre, New York (1946)
(Collection of Paul Stiga)

ROBERT EDMOND JONES
Costume design for a Court Lady in The Buccaneer—*Act III*
Plymouth Theatre, New York (1925)
(Collection of Paul Stiga)

FREDDY WITTOP
Costume design for Chita Rivera as Anyanka in Bajour
Shubert Theatre, New York (1964)
(Collection of Paul Stiga)

WILLIAM AND JEAN ECKART
Costume design for a stepsister in Cinderella,
by Rodgers and Hammerstein
CBS Television, New York (1957)

RAOUL PÈNE DU BOIS
Costume design for a member of the ensemble in Ziegfeld Follies of 1936
Winter Garden Theatre, New York (1936)
(Collection of Paul Stiga)

IRENE SHARAFF
Costume designs for a group of dancers in The Age of Anxiety
New York City Ballet (1950)
(Collection of Paul Stiga)

MILES WHITE
Costume designs for The Girl in Pink Tights
Mark Hellinger Theatre, New York (1954)

OLIVER MESSEL
Costume design for Regina Resnik as Marcellina Le Nozze di Figaro
Metropolitan Opera House, New York (1959)
(Collection of Paul Stiga)

A Conversation with PATRICIA ZIPPRODT

Patricia Zipprodt lives in a large penthouse apartment atop an old Victorian school building in downtown New York. A native of Chicago, she graduated from Wellesley College and studied at the Art Institute of Chicago. Her first work on Broadway came in 1957, supervising the costumes for *The Potting Shed* at the Bijou and for *A Visit to a Small Planet* at the Booth.

Over the years, Zipprodt has designed costumes for an impressive roster of prominent Broadway and Off-Broadway productions. Her work is represented at the Metropolitan Opera by *Tannhäuser* and *The Barber of Seville;* in dance by the New York City Ballet (Peter Martins's *The Sleeping Beauty*), the American Ballet Theatre (*Coppélia*, Antony Tudor's *The Leaves Are Falling*, and Jerome Robbins's *Les Noces*), and Ballet Hispanico; and in film by *The Graduate* and *1776.*

Zipprodt's designs have been seen at the Guthrie Theatre, Playwrights Horizons, the Repertory Theatre of Lincoln Center, the Phoenix Theatre, the Boston Opera, and the New York City Opera. In television, her credits include the costumes for Katharine Hepburn's *The Glass Menagerie* and Anne Bancroft's Emmy Award–winning special, *The Women in the Life of a Man.* For the National Theatre of the Deaf, of which she was a founding member, she has designed both sets and costumes.

Zipprodt has received a Distinguished Alumni Award from Wellesley and the Fashion Institute of Technology, and was inducted into the Theatre Hall of Fame in 1992. She teaches at Brandeis University and has spoken and taught at numerous universities around the country. She has garnered three Tony Awards (for *Fiddler on the Roof, Cabaret,* and *Sweet Charity*), 11 Tony nominations, three Maharam Awards, and nine Drama Desk Awards (for *Sunday in the Park with George, Pippin, Chicago, Sweet Charity, Alice in Wonderland, King of Hearts, Mack and Mabel, 1776,* and *Zorba*).

PIPPIN
Costume designs by Patricia Zipprodt
Directed and choreographed by Bob Fosse
Imperial Theatre, New York (1972)

How did you first become involved in designing costumes for the theatre?

I think if I look back, I became unknowingly "involved" when I was growing up. I grew up in Kenilworth, one of the Chicago suburbs, and my mother started taking me to the Goodman Children's Theatre. Every winter, every Christmastime, we went into the Chicago Lyric Opera House to see the Humperdinck opera, *Hansel and Gretel*. I could hardly wait for the angels to stand on the steps to make them light up! I came out with awestruck eyes, and I think that experience was the "beginning."

What I didn't realize until well into my design work years later was the importance of the fact that I had designed paper dolls as a child. I made my own paper dolls. I didn't cut them out of a book—I drew them myself and I mounted them. I had a little group: the brunette lady, the blonde lady, and the red-haired lady, the men in their lives, and servants and what have you, depending on the adventure they were on. I would clip out, from my mother's magazines, exciting places for them to go—like a trip on the wonderful Cunard line, a hunt, or a ball, and I would design their wardrobes for these events and march them around from piece of paper to piece of paper as the various adventurous plots I'd invent for them required.

Then you started out designing at an early age.

Yes. I really started early, like seven. It only belatedly dawned on me that I was storytelling with clothing then. My paper dolls didn't just have clothes, they had clothes designed to be worn in a very specific environment in which they were to do very specific things that I had plotted for them. And when they changed their outfits, the shoes changed and the parasols changed and even the hairstyles changed! Years later, when my mother closed down our house, she sent them all to me. Suddenly, my past popped out of those envelopes—these funny little people with their yellow shoes and their matching yellow parasols. Early on, I knew I was an artist—that I liked to draw and paint—so I started going to art school.

Where did you go to art school?

To an annex of the Chicago Art Institute in Evanston. I could get there by myself, so I started there when I was nine or 10, going to Saturday classes drawing from "life" and learning to paint with watercolors and chalks. I kept on going that way for really quite a while. Later on I went to the Art Institute Summer School. And I took all the art classes I could at New Trier High School in Winnetka. Then I had some strange idea about going into surgical art, because I drew a very fine line. I would draw things under the microscope—you know, the amoeba, and what was in the hay water solution after one, two, or three weeks. And I would just get into all these little drawings and people said, "You should illustrate medical books." This was when I was around 17 or 18. I thought, "I could do that." I was advised to take a premedical major. So instead of going two years to college and then back to the Art Institute, which had been my plan, I stayed four years at Wellesley College and found I loved the academic life.

But I found their premed was a total bore. It had nothing to do with eloquent lines. So I ended up with the social sciences, and I began making studies of the group, and the family, and this and that, all of which saved me when I came into real life. You know, with a few courses in

---

Among Patricia Zipprodt's costume design credits are the following:

BROADWAY

A Little Hotel on the Side (1992)

The Master Builder (1992)

The Crucible (1991)

Cat on a Hot Tin Roof (1990)

Shōgun: The Musical (1990)

Dangerous Games (1989)

Jerome Robbins' Broadway: Fiddler on the Roof (1989)

Macbeth (1988)

Big Deal (1986)

Sweet Charity (1986)

Accidental Death of an Anarchist (1984)

Sunday in the Park with George (1984)

Brighton Beach Memoirs (1983)

The Glass Menagerie (1983)

Alice in Wonderland (1982)

Whodunnit (1982)

Fools (1981)

King of Hearts (1978)

Poor Murderer (1976)

All God's Chillun Got Wings (1975)

Chicago (1975)

Mack and Mabel (1974)

Pippin (1972)

1776 (1969)

Plaza Suite (1968)

Zorba (1968)

The Little Foxes (1967), Beaumont Theatre

Cabaret (1966)

Fiddler on the Roof (1964)

She Loves Me (1963)

Oh, Dad, Poor Dad (1963)

Sunday in New York (1961)

Period of Adjustment (1960)

The Gang's All Here (1959)

The Rope Dancers (1957)

OFF-BROADWAY

Sunset (1983)

Dear Nobody (1974)

A Man's a Man (1962)

The Blacks (1961)

The Balcony (1960)

Camino Real (1960)

Our Town (1959)

The Crucible (1958)

COPPÉLIA
Costume design by Patricia Zipprodt
Choreographed by Enrique Martinez
American Ballet Theatre, New York (1990)

abnormal psych under my belt, I was very comfortable in the theatre.

Did you work in the theatre at Wellesley?

No, I didn't. I performed in modern dance, the class musical, and so forth.

You didn't design costumes?

None, except the ones I wore and patched together myself. I wasn't thinking about costume. I was thinking about painting and drawing. After graduating from Wellesley, I came to New York in search of some kind of life-dream.

I was very dear friends with a man named Gjon Mili, a very noted photographer, who at the time, the early '50s, was doing a *Life* essay on the New York

City Ballet. We went to the ballet frequently. One night there was a performance of Ravel's *La Waltz*. By this time I was painting—I had a scholarship at the New School in the Art department, I was ushering at Carnegie Hall, and I was living in a cold-water flat and trying to paint, just doing all the traditional things you did if you were young and slightly "beat" in the '50s. My family had just thrown up their hands. You know, "She's lost."

Who designed *La Waltz*?

Karinska, and the costumes she created were just so extraordinary. She always designed for Balanchine. She eventually set up a costume studio into which the designers of the day would go to have their designs built. But Karinska was also very much a designer in her own right. The colors that she put in those silk tulle skirts were like my colors. I gazed in wonder and thought, "I can paint with fabric!" So very soon thereafter—I mean, it may well have been the next day—I began groping around in my head, wondering how to refocus myself and get trained for this newly revealed field. I would need financial aid, because having become "lost," I didn't have any access to family funds. A painter friend told me about Fashion Institute of Technology, which ran a scholarship program, and I think they realized they would have a pest on their hands if they didn't take me, that I would keep bothering them until they let me in, so they said, "Well, alright, come in as an experiment." At that time, everyone going there came out of the high school system right into the freshman-year level of the four-year state university system. So there were all these freshmen and there was this college graduate—me, the "experiment." And they couldn't understand why anyone from Wellesley would even need a scholarship. I mean, weren't we all rich and riding around in Cadillacs? Well, maybe some were, but I was living without heat, and *with* peanut butter.

So you studied at the Fashion Institute?

Yes. They gave me a scholarship! So now I could start putting the two together—

the art training and the craft training that FIT gave me. Their fourth term was an apprentice period, but I got a small job with Charles James, so I took that instead. He was one of the great couturiers of the '30s, '40s, '50s, and a little bit into the '60s. I worked with Charles for a year, helping with the making of enormous ball gowns, making pattern charts, picking up pens, anything useful.

But what was I going to do about my tutu dreams, painting with fabric and all that? I found out that I needed a union card from the United Scenic Artists, which required a full-day exam for costume designers. I quit my tiny job in Trigere's workroom on Seventh Avenue, borrowed some money to live on, and jammed myself full of the entire *History*

of Costume. By late at night before the exam, I'd gotten up to 1928, stopped there, threw up, slept, got up, took the hideous exam, and passed!

So now I had the union card, but I'd never worked in the theatre. So I began working for any designer I admired who would hire me—Rouben Ter-Arutunian, Irene Sharaff, Robert Fletcher, the Eckarts.

Did you just call these people?
Wrote and called. And I also went around to all the set designers. I went to see Jo Mielziner, Boris Aronson, Oliver Smith, David Hays, and showed them my portfolio. It was a time in the theatre when small, modern shows were very common on the Broadway scene. And

because of the attitude toward costume design, most people never even thought that modern clothes were "costumes." But according to the League of New York Producers's contract with the union, producers had to hire someone to do the costumes, and frequently one of these three or four major set designers who were always hired well in advance would be asked by the producer, "Who can go to the store on this show?" Well, I got to go to the store a lot.

How did your own first show come about?
Somewhat the way I got into FIT and the way I got my job with Charles James: I just sort of sat at the door for a long time. I had this way of packing up my

lunch and taking my portfolio and a book and just sitting.

There was a play called *The Potting Shed,* which Carmen Capalbo was directing. And a friend of mine knew about it—he was a friend of Carmen's. He knew that they didn't have a costume designer, and he said, "Get over there." So I did. I sat and I waited and I waited. And finally they said, "Oh, come on in." It was five o'clock. They had given me some kind of idea that I would see them in the morning. And for want of anything else better to do, they hired me.

Did *The Potting Shed* lead to another show?

No. At the same time, there was a show around called *A Visit to a Small Planet,* by Gore Vidal. At the time, Florence Klotz was assisting Lucinda Ballard as well as doing her own shows. She was asked to do *Visit,* but she couldn't, she was booked. But she said, "There's someone who's been doing a great deal of assisting who might be good for this show and her name is…" So Florence Klotz helped me get my other first show. I'll never forget that show. It was directed by a man named George Axelrod, who couldn't remember "Zipprodt," so he called me "the girl": "Tell the girl we need…"

That was your second Broadway show?

Well, they overlapped, so they are both first or both second, it doesn't matter.

What happened next?

After doing *The Potting Shed* and *A Visit to a Small Planet* and a couple other Broadway shows, I saw that all of my assisting experience had been in great, huge shows and all the jobs I was getting were these teeny, "go to Macy's" jobs, while the producer's wife went to Bergdorf's and let's see who gets the best white dress. I realized I really didn't know what I was doing. It was learning on the job like you've never seen. So I began working Off-Broadway through friends. I started out down at Circle in the Square with José Quintero. David Hays brought me in. He was doing a Brendan Behan play, *The Quare Fellow.* He had done the costumes for all these prison inmates, and with the little budget that

THE GRADUATE, THE FILM
*Costume design by Patricia Zipprodt,
for Anne Bancroft
Directed by Mike Nichols
Produced by Joseph E. Levine (1967)*

Circle had, they really were white cotton waiter's uniforms that he dyed maroon. And so they looked like maroon waiter's uniforms. He got really frantic and called me to help him. I came with my sandpaper and my vegetable grater and bottles of bleach and "broke them down."

The next Circle show was *Our Town,* and José said, "Pat, come and do *Our Town.*" He had seen me slaving away on *Quare Fellow* and saw I was friends with David, who was not really a costume designer. And that's how the work started out there. We worked together for a long time. We did *The Balcony* and *Camino Real.*

You did all those shows with David Hays?

Yes. And I built the costumes for them in the upstairs loft space. You see, this is where I truly started my work. The FIT stuff, and the year with Charles, and starting art school at the age of nine, and drawing—it was all beginning to come together. I could draw, design my sketches, and execute what I drew. I could set up my little workrooms, because I'd had that very concrete, tough training at FIT—you know, you put the zipper in again if you put it in wrong, and so on. And I could literally run a workroom and produce a show like *The Balcony,* right upstairs at the Circle on Bleecker Street, with a few members of the crew. I knew how to shop my fabrics and I knew which fabrics I needed. I learned to dye and age fabrics. I knew how to cut and drape, and design and draw. All I didn't know was when to get any sleep. I stayed up for years.

Then I went on to do *The Blacks.* Gene Frankel had seen *The Balcony* and had asked, "Who was that girl who designed that?" So there was yet another workroom created, and this time we were also making the masks along with building all those clothes. I did a lot of early Off-Broadway like that.

During the time I had worked for Irene Sharaff on *Happy Hunting,* Ming Cho Lee was drafting for Jo Mielziner, who was designing and producing. Paul Libin was coffee boy and errand person, and helped in Jo's producing/designing office. And of course, watching our elders like thieves, we all said, "We can do it better." So we eventually all went off and "did it better" with a revival of Arthur Miller's play *The Crucible.* Ming, who is a theatre designer and a space designer, designed the theatre shape in the old ballroom of the Martinique Hotel. I came along with my sewing machine and all of us little kids from Jo's and Irene's show were like Judy [Garland] and Mickey [Rooney].

So I'm sewing in my cold-water flat on my little Singer sewing machine, and Ming is building and Paul is doing what—selling tickets?—I don't know. Another person in Jo's office at the time was a man named Word Baker, who was a kind of executive secretary/casting combination. He'd recently come up from the University of Texas. He got the rights from Arthur Miller and became the show's director. So there we all were. This whole nexus of the next generation.

In this same period, at the Phoenix Theatre T. Edward Hambleton and Norris Houghton were opening the doors to theatre professionals who wanted to direct, but hadn't. They could be producers or writers or whatever. One of these people was preparing to direct a show, and T. and Norris could not find a costume designer that he could accept. So it goes down to Friday evening, and Monday was rehearsal. And someone said, "Remember that girl who did *The Blacks* and *The Balcony*? What about her?" Well, what about *anybody* at five o'clock on Friday? Then I got this funny call from this man named T. Edward Hambleton: Would I come up and bring my portfolio? So I did, I raced up from the Village to the Phoenix by taxi, with probably my last bit of money, and I walked in and guess what? The director was Jerome Robbins, and the show was *Oh, Dad, Poor Dad*, et cetera.

Is that how your association with Jerome Robbins began?

Yes. The next director to turn up at the Phoenix was Hal Prince. He wanted to start directing. Hal had previously looked at my portfolio and hadn't

responded at all well—it "lacked color." But having become friends with T. and Norris on the *Oh, Dad* project, there I was. We did *The Merchant of Yonkers*, starring Sylvia Sidney. It was umbrellaed by the New York State Council of the Arts, and so it played Binghamton and Schenectady, all those places. Then Hal went to Broadway to do *She Loves Me* and took me with him.

She Loves Me was with William and Jean Eckart?

Yes. And the Eckarts had also done, *Oh, Dad, Poor Dad*. I had been their assistant on costumes in the past, and I think it was Jean who said, "What about Patty? She did *The Blacks* and *The Balcony*. What about seeing her portfolio? We've got to get a costume designer for *Oh, Dad*." See how it all works?

Then Jerry popped up with Hal producing and Jerry directing *Fiddler on the Roof*, so then I did *Fiddler*. And that's what got me out of shopping at Macy's, and out of working all night in the lofts around town. That was my Yale training period. That period, starting with just seeing the costumes for *La Waltz* until, let's say, *Fiddler*, covered about 10 years.

So *Fiddler* became a big hit and you had many productions of it.

Yes, some of which I got paid for. Some I

didn't; some they just copied. But I did the national company and the London company.

Comment on your collaboration with Boris Aronson.

Well, it was wonderful, because Boris was like my mentor. And in a way, Boris was my Yale. I learned so much from him.

Was working with Jo Mielziner on *1776* an interesting collaboration?

Oh, yes, because he was a joy to work with. I had found my way to him when I was working for Irene Sharaff on *Happy Hunting*. I would go to his studio every other morning and check the fabric colors in his light room. That was one of my jobs. Jo's office was open at eight or eight-thirty, and I could go up there then before I started the day at Brooks Costume Company. I'd check through the color swatches under Jo's unique lighting. You really had to check every single thing that went under his gel system to know what your end results were going to be. So he sort of got used to me popping in and out. It was like, "Oh, here I am, Mr. Mielziner." He'd set up the lights for, say, Act Two, and let me go into the darkroom to check out the latest batch of swatches. And when you went in and closed the door, you were in pitch dark

FIDDLER ON THE ROOF
Costume designs by Patricia Zipprodt
Directed and choreographed by Jerome Robbins
Imperial Theatre, New York (1964)

1776
*Costume design by Patricia Zipprodt, for
Howard da Silva as Benjamin Franklin
Musical numbers staged by Onna White
Directed by Peter Hunt
Forty-sixth Street Theatre, New York (1969)*

with Jo's lights. Then you put your fabric colors under them. Can you imagine? That doesn't happen any more.

No. Jo was unique.
I said, "When the show's over, Mr. Mielziner, I'd like very much to show you my portfolio." You see, he'd seen me working long and hard and functioning on a very tough show. So when I came and showed him my portfolio, he knew me as a person and as an artist.

When it came to recommendations, Jo never would suggest just one person. If he were asked, he would suggest two or three costume designers, and then have Josh Logan, or whoever it was, interview them. Sometimes you would get the job and sometimes you wouldn't, but whoever got it had his blessing.

How did your productions with Bob Fosse come about? *Pippin* **was first, then** *Cabaret*?
Well, this gets back to Jo Mielziner again. There was the show *1776*, which Jo was designing, and I think he recommended me to Stuart Ostrow, the producer, and to the director, Peter Hunt. Stuart and I became good friends. He liked the costumes for *1776*. So when he got Bobby to do *Pippin*, he brought me in as costume designer. Bobby's previous show had been *Sweet Charity*, with Irene, and they didn't get along.

This is the original *Sweet Charity* **she did with Robert Randolph?**
Yes, that's right. And so he was really battle-weary. Bobby didn't have a particular costume designer that he wanted to work with, so Stuart suggested that I design the *Pippin* costumes. That's how the relationship started. I did four of Fosse's shows, which were *Pippin, Sweet Charity*—the second one—*Chicago*, and *Big Deal*.

You must have had wonderful patience and control to do that.
You learn it. You have to have it, or you just can't survive. I mean, you won't be invited back to the party. You have to "out-stay" these people. Sometimes I think anyone who has worked with Jerry just sketches himself silly, while Jerry is sketching along with you, at his house

and home, so that you end up competing with the person you are designing for. You show him your sketches and he pulls out his—that has happened. I think I must have done at least 18 different sketches of the Tevye family, just to get going on them and find out who they were.

But didn't you find that a learning process once you got over that initial hurt?
Oh, very much so. Also, it is part of the directorial growth process, too, because until we as designers come along and start to try to physicalize what directors are talking to us about, they can't complete their thinking. Bobby would see it and say, "That's it!"

If you were offered a modern dress show, would you take it? Say, *Plaza Suite*?
Oh, *Plaza Suite* I'd do again, because it's based on clearly defined characters in very sharp situations. So it's not like "modern," where you just go out and put vaguely ambiguous clothes on people. At this point I'm, in a sense, far removed from what people are actually wearing. I'm astounded at what I see at various areas of town, the country, the world. I have to research as if it were period. For example, there's one group of people dressing up for Lincoln Center at the ballet or opera. Last night I was at the Asia Society for a farewell dinner and there's a whole other way the men and women dress. The night before, I was over at St. Marks in the Bowery at the Dance Space. It's a whole other section of people in that part of town. So I don't know what a modern dress show is anymore. I might try to avoid it, because it becomes too arbitrary. Too many people think they know about it. And you end up with just agents and lawyers' wives and producers thinking that's the wrong dress for so and so.

If you're doing a period show, would you do a sketch for every character?
Yes. You have to.

What materials do you like to work with?
I start with pencil and I start on any kind

of paper, but I get on to tracing paper as soon as I can, because I like to reverse it and look at it this way and that way.

Do you use more than one view for a major character?

It depends. Not as a rule, no. Unless it is a very complicated animal costume or something that needs to be dimensionally clear to the director or choreographer.

Do you work in watercolor, tempera, or oil?

I work primarily in watercolors, pencils, pens, and inks.

How tall are your figures?

The figures usually run between 8 and 12 inches.

You have designed costumes for the Metropolitan Opera.

I've done a lot of designing for the Met. The first time I went to the Met was in 1977 or so, when they were planning to stage a new production of *Don Giovanni*. Jo Mielziner designed the sets and I designed the costumes. Then the Met canceled it and stayed with the Eugene Berman sets. That was my first job with the Met.

Your first association at the Met came about through Mielziner.

Yes. Then I turned up there again full-blast when John Dexter became part of the troika that James Levine, Anthony Bliss, and John Dexter made, sometime in the early '80s.

Had you worked with John Dexter before?

Off and on, yes. He'd been a fan of mine, and I was thrilled that he would bring in myself, and also Jane Greenwood—non-European women costume designers—into the Met, our national opera institution, now busily importing the Italian and German design Mafia. Dexter really tried to bring modern spare design onto that stage. I designed a production of *The Queen of Spades*, with Liviu Cuilei, which also got canceled.

You had designed at the Guthrie. Did you work with him?

Yes. But I met Liviu at the Met. And then from there we went on to the Guthrie.

It's usually the other way around. You come from the Guthrie to the Met.

I know. John had actually given me a list of three years' worth of things, because they had canceled so many of "my" operas by that time. I was always designing for the Met and never getting anything on—it was weird! John felt very badly. He gave me a three-year future production list and said, "Pick one opera for each year." And for one I picked *Pique Dame, The Queen of Spades*, with Josef Svoboda designing the sets and Liviu Ciulei staging, and I

CABARET
Costume design by Patricia Zipprodt
Dances and cabaret numbers by Ronald Field
Directed by Harold Prince
Broadhurst Theatre, New York (1966)

SWEET CHARITY
Costume designs by Patricia Zipprodt
Directed and choreographed by Bob Fosse
Minskoff Theatre, New York (1986)

thought, "If I were just hired to empty wastebaskets, I would take that one." So that was designed and then canceled. And finally I costumed *Tannhäuser* with Otto Schenk and Schneider-Siemssen. And then John Cox came over from Glyndebourne to do *The Barber*. Those two operas got on the boards, out of about six.

When you design an opera for the Met, how does your work differ from designing Fiddler on the Roof?
Opera is wonderful to do, especially after you've done a few musicals, because Tannhäuser always goes to Rome, Mimi always dies and always stays dead. All the things that happen in *Tosca* happen every time, every production. The story stays put and they don't try the first-act song in the second act. All that has been done. So you're working with a certain kind of stability that is impossible in the musical theatre.

Is your method of listening to the opera, the score, talking with the director, and making sketches similar to how you work on musicals?
It's the same process.

What about working in the shop and getting the designs executed? How does that vary at the Met as opposed to doing a musical?
Well, at the Met you have to work in their shop. And you have to work within those parameters. They have their way of doing things and you do them that way.

Do you ever have to revamp because of budget at the Met?
I haven't. It doesn't mean it isn't done.

How long a time did you have to spend on it and how long were your designs in the shop there?
I probably worked on it over a period of a year. And I can't remember when they went into the shop, because they do go

in the shop at the Met in a totally different way. The big difference between working for an institutionalized opera company like the Met and working for a Broadway musical is that, first of all, you are likely to be booked three or four years ahead. The schedule stays pretty much on course, unless something unusual happens—a director dies or they run out of money. You can say that three years from now *Tannhäuser* will open on such and such a date and it usually does. You can't say that about a musical—even a month before it opens, you don't really know when or even *if* it's going to open at all!

Take, for example, *The Barber of Seville*. You have a big mass of soldiers and you have a costume shop that is sort of like an orthodox wedding. All the men do the tailoring, and all the ladies do the ladies' work. And there's a line in between and nobody crosses over. Now the women's department may be busy

SUNDAY IN THE PARK WITH GEORGE
Costume designs by Patricia Zipprodt,
for Bernadette Peters
Directed by James Lapine
Booth Theatre, New York (1984)

doing *Tosca* and the men's department may be empty. So they're going to schedule your soldiers in there then. It may be two years before the production is even in rehearsal, or a year and a half. But they know who is in the chorus, because the chorus is very, very permanent. And they've got a 52-week year, unlike a costume shop, which lets people off and brings them back and off and brings them back. They have a 52-week year and upkeep, maintenance, salaries, pensions, and the whole rigmarole. So their whole game is to avoid overtime and keep everybody steadily busy, because they have to pay for them. It doesn't mean that their lower people aren't let go, but their staff, their key people, are hired by the year.

So it's a whole different economics. And therefore, they may want the soldiers' uniforms. There's 30 of those. They can just drop that in a two-month slot that's open in the men's department

schedule before they have to do *Don Carlos.* Or they have such and such a slot where they have a very light amount of men's clothes going through, or they're refurbishing something. So that if you design far ahead, then they can work it in. So you might be there for a while and then stop for a while. It usually ends up with everything being as it always is with anything having to do with the performing arts, and it's called "the last minute." Without "the last minute," we would have nothing.

When you're doing costumes at the Met, do you go to every fitting yourself for the principals?

You try. And I'll tell you why I say "try"—because they don't really make appointments there. People sort of float in during lunch or work breaks. If you happen to be out, the Met shop will just go right on with the fitting, because they want to get it sewn up.

Do they do them in muslin for the principals?

Yes, muslin or an inexpensive version of what the actual fabric will be.

They don't do it for supers or for chorus?

I don't even have the answer to that, because it varies with the intricacy of the costume and who the star is. With some stars, you start right out in the chosen fabric.

Are you given a budget for a star costume at the Met?

No, no.

No one says, "You can only spend $2,000 and that looks like it's going to cost $4,000"?

No. They give the budget to the head of the shop, who then goes over your sketches and sees what the relationship is. Are they overbudgeted or are they shy on money? Well, first of all, you have to

understand that a costume shop like Barbara Matera's or Sally Ann Parsons's has to put the rent, gas, light, phone, pensions, and so on into its price. The Met, again, is an institutionalized, ongoing enterprise, so their budgets don't have to pay for their roof—that's under another budget. So they get two different cost systems. The Met costume shop budgets actual fabrics, labor and potential overtime, how much the boots cost, and do they or do they not have the wigs and so on. There's no overhead involved, no maintenance involved. The head of the shop has an annual budget, and each new opera gets a certain hunk of it. Who decides that? Who knows?

Do you take in swatches with your sketches?
Sometimes.

Do they have anything in stock there?
Yes, but really, mostly, they swatch and start from scratch. As we're going along,

you may say, "Let's look in stock and see if we can find a blouse material." We're always prowling through the fabric stock. They have some good things.

What about jewelry and accessories? Do they have those?
Yes.

Detailed appliqués?
Appliqués are usually made or patched together from smaller elements.

When you do your sketches, do you discuss lining as far as practical purposes?
That's the Met shop's responsibility. It's all in how they build it. That's one reason they have their own shop, so they will have a consistency of construction approach. Their garments must be built for a long life of many years.

Do you get a flat fee for designing at the Met?
Yes.

Are there royalties involved for performances?
Each one has to figure out his or her own. It's not one of the things they're happy to do. I think our union has finally struck some kind of an accord, whereby every season that the opera is redone, you get a certain percentage of your original fee, which reduces itself each time, each season. So by the time it has been running about 10 years, they send you this little check for five dollars, just to drive your accountant nuts.

How long have you been teaching costumes in the master's program at Brandeis?
I started going up there for one of the master's classes in the mid-'80s. Howard Bay, the scenic designer, was still alive and running it. And then I just started going up more and more, and one day I found myself on the faculty.

What do you find students want to

know most about costume design in the master's class?

So many things. That's really impossible to answer. It really depends on what the problems are that are coming up. I can tell you what I think they need to know: They need to know how to draw. They need to know how to construct. They need to know how to read a play and analyze it. They need to think in terms of character. They need to remember that an actor is going to wear that sketch when it gets into 3-D. They need to know that they are part of a triad in terms of design—sets, lights, and costumes—that hopefully works with a director who has some vision, or some sense of what he or she is after. And directors can talk to you in very strange obtuse ways. That can be very valuable, but you have to be able to pick up on the subliminal things to get it. They need to know that they will never make any money. Only the wealthy should undertake this, because there just isn't any money. And I think it is going to get worse. I think the only way anyone has made any money outside of films and TV has been in musicals, in the royalties when the shows ran. Because our fees just barely cover our time.

It's very hard to make it clear to students that, for example, right now I can't think of a worse time to go into the design field. I cannot think of a more difficult, restricting, confusing time to try to carve a career as a theatre designer in the theatre in this country. Just forget it. There's no place to do it, except where they don't pay you.

What do you like least about working in the theatre?

The isolation of it. I mean that in several ways. There's a long period of design where most of us sit there alone with people who may run in and out helping us. It's almost like being a painter or a writer at that phase. We are alone a lot. Most of us only really do the creative work alone. I find that when I'm on a show I'm so busy at the damn phone and appointments and meetings that during the day people ask, "When do you design?" I say, "At nights and on weekends." I mean, that's the only quiet

time. You are not master of your own hours. You are at the beck and call of the production schedule, the stage manager, the fitting schedule, the shop requirements, the director's meetings, of this, of that. So you have to be totally flexible

THE BARBER OF SEVILLE
Costume design by Patricia Zipprodt
Directed by John Cox
Metropolitan Opera, New York (1982)

and able to keep it all together. You keep endlessly rolling through this multifaceted series of pulls and demands and areas and layers of knowledge until each work is done. I think that all theatre designers feel that as professionals we work harder than any other group in the theatre. We feel underpaid and we feel underappreciated.

Comment on when your costumes go to the theatre.

There comes a time when the costumes are no longer yours, when they become "theirs." When I hear the actor saying, "Where's my costume?" I think, "I beg your pardon, it's *my* costume." No, it's *their* costume, and you have to let all of

it go and suddenly—bang!—with a drop of the curtain your job is over, after going up to 20 hours a day with everyone yelling and screaming for you, and calling you to fix this and that. And then all at once the opening-night curtain is up, your work is finally completed, and the show goes on. Suddenly, you have no I.D. with it any more. Many people go into a kind of a depression. I used to go into a terrible depression.

There's nothing to ease off on. You've been on the show so long.

Yes, and haven't seen your friends for months. And if you've been in any kind of relationship, it's all out of shape. It's very difficult, and you're probably broke, unless the show is a hit and running. Where is the next show? It's not good. It's only for really crazy people.

It's very hard, because you've put so much into it.

You've picked the thread color and the buttons, and you've gone through fittings where they say, "I can't sing in yellow," or "I'm choking to death," or "I'm itching." And where the star says, "I won't!" And she brings the director and the producer to the fittings. And when it's all over and the show has closed down, they take it all away. At least they have the grace to take the scenery out to Secaucus and chop it up and burn it. But they try to sell the costumes to Eaves. And do. And then Eaves rents them over and over.

Without giving you any credit.

Or money, that's right. And they make copies of your successful shows. They have two "versions" of *Fiddler* right now, which they rent out constantly.

If you were asked to put two of your favorite productions into a time capsule, which would they be?

The Sleeping Beauty for New York City Ballet. I would definitely time-capsule that. That was like falling in love with Karinska's colors and Balanchine's dancing, a long time ago, and making a circle. It's very rare and very precious, and I worked on it for five years. Another production would be *The Blacks*, and another would be *Pippin*.

You received much praise for your

THE SLEEPING BEAUTY
Costume designs by Patricia Zipprodt
Choreographed by Peter Martins
New York City Ballet (1991)

beautiful costumes in *Shōgun.* **What was it like to do that production?**
Oh, it still hurts. I think it was probably the most total involvement I've ever had with a show. It was like a 24-hour day forever.

Where did you do your main research?
Both here and in Japan. I was in Japan for three weeks, down in Kyoto and in the museums.

The producers were aware that you were going and they agreed to that?
They agreed to that. Half the producers were Japanese. They knew very well. What was I going to do? Sit here and invent? We have shows like that. What I had to do was filter through the

Momoyama period and my theatrical sense to suit the needs of that show. And then, physically, I had to get it actually done.

Was it built in the shops here?
Yes. Sally Ann Parsons was the lead shop—Parsons-Meares, Ltd.—and then we used a lot of the small shops. The show was too big for any one shop.

How many costumes were there in the show?
I think 350, including the horses, which I designed and which we made. The costume shops built the horses. And there were the wigs and hairdos.

Did you have control of the wigs?
Yes, as best as I could. I'd researched the styles in Japan. I had one of my favorite hair designers on the show, so he worked from my sketches and then did what had to be done.

I had done all the research, and we had broken down the whole show and figured out the quick changes, of which there were millions. There were 350 costumes and 30 people in the show, and it was two and a half hours long, so figure out how many changes each person had.

What was your costume budget?
The whole show was budgeted for $6 million. For costumes, it was like $750,000. Every department had to go over the budget to get it done.

What do you like most about working in the theatre?
I love the process. I think we are very privileged people to be able to start something every time and not know what we are going to do, whether it's a ballet that Tudor's just choreographing, or what Peter Martins is doing over at the New York City Ballet's *The Sleeping Beauty*, or a classic play at the Guthrie, or especially a big new Broadway script that comes our way. We put a whole new network of people together and we start again on the process. It is thrilling to work constantly and collaboratively in that kind of newness and fresh discovery, because who else has that opportunity, except those of us in the theatre?

INDEX

Page numbers in *italics* refer to illustrations.